D1326369

한 국 말

박 용 득 지음

For Lucia
John
Anna
and Paul

SPEAKING KOREAN

Revised Edition

Book I

by
Francis Y. T. Park

HOLLYM INTERNATIONAL CORP.
Elizabeth, New Jersey

SPEAKING KOREAN

Revised Edition

Book I

Hollym International Corp.
18 Donald Place
Elizabeth, New Jersey 07208 U.S.A.
Tel : (908) 353-1655
Fax : (908) 353-0255
ISBN : 0-930878-82-5
Library of Congress Catalog Card Number 84-80023

Printed in Korea

For orders write to: Francis Y.T. Park
150-65 Jungkog Dong
Seungdong-ku
SEOUL, KOREA
Tel: (02) 457-6907

RECOMMENDATIONS

Dear Reader,

Mr. Park is co-author of the Korean language textbook, 'Myongdo's Korean '68.' That two-volume book was the product of Mr. Park's experience in helping to set up the Myongdo Korean Language Institute, and his years of experience in teaching Korean to foreigners.

This is a book born of Mr. Park's expert knowledge of the Korean language, the science of linguistics, and his excellent knowledge of spoken and written English; but most of all, his long and profound experience in teaching foreigners Korean, and in his long experience in instructing other teachers. This is a book produced from many years of labor and growth. I recommend it to all who embark on the task of learning the Korean language!

John. J. Corcoran
Past Regional Director
Maryknoll Missions in Korea

I congratulate you on the publication of your new Korean Language Books. They will fill a great need among the increasing numbers of people who wish to learn Korean. I believe your new approach marks a significant landmark in the short history of the development of such texts. I am acquainted with your fine work in the past on the texts for the Myongdo Institute.

In the name of the foreign community in Korea, let me express my gratitude to you for your unceasing efforts at helping us learn your language.

Rev. John. P. Daly, S.J.
Past President
Sogang University

ACKNOWLEDGMENTS

Finally, here is the long-awaited and revised Book I. In particular, I wish to thank Father John Corcoran, the past Regional Director of the Maryknoll Missions in Korea. I greatly appreciate his kindness and encouragement. Without his continued assistance, this book could not have been completed.

I am also indebted to many other persons for their assistance in the revision of this book. I wish to express my sincere and deep gratitude first and foremost to Father Joseph Turowski of the Maryknoll Missions in Korea and Father Peter J. Fleming of Sogang University for their help in proofreading and for offering numerous suggestions. They were instrumental in pointing to areas that needed correction and improvement. It is impossible to express adequately my gratitude to them for their time and efforts. I also owe thanks to Ms. Jeong Soo Lee, Ms. Sun Il Kim and all the faculty members of the FSI Korean Language School for their help in proofreading.

Ms. Sang Heun Kwack, an instructor at the Korean Language Institute, Sogang University, tirelessly and diligently typed the manuscript from beginning to end. I deeply appreciate the capable assistance, enthusiastic cooperation and unceasing efforts which she has given.

To my wife, Lucia, I would like to express my love for all the patience, encouragement and advice that she offered.

Finally, a special word of thanks to Mr. Woo Dong Hong, the president of the Dong Kuk Computer Printing Company, who has been very patient and understanding throughout many revisions.

Francis Y.T. Park

Seoul, Korea

PREFACE

This book is intended primarily for those English speakers who wish to acquire a good knowledge of spoken Korean. This is the first of four volumes in an entirely new type of textbook series for students of Korean.

Since I wrote 'MYONGDO'S KOREAN' in 1968 (PART I and PART II) and the first edition of SPEAKING KOREAN in 1977, and in the process of teaching Korean to foreigners since then (at the Maryknoll Missions and the foreign Service Institute, Department of State), I have acquired additional teaching experience, psychological training and insights, which I hope will make the work of both teacher and student more productive and rewarding. During these years I have constantly revised the lessons of the original text to a point where content and method demand the publication of a new book. This book is the result of personal growth and research. It is designed to impart an active practical skill in the use of the spoken language, without neglecting the development of competence in reading and writing.

This book has several unique characteristics to it, qualifying it as an important development toward a more integrated approach to the study of the Korean language. Very simply, the difference is that this new approach develops a new method of learning, rather than simply a method of teaching. The structural-linguistic approach avoids simply repeating, changing or substituting sentences. Instead, the devices are used by the learner to achieve the goal of self-expression.

The approach has been to grade the frequency of vocabulary and patterns, and then to integrate them in such a way as to allow for continual review and assimilation. This approach has been developed in line with the most recent scientific, linguistic and psychological strides made in the language fields; it avoids a reductionistic, analytical approach, and concentrates on structural patterns of spoken Korean.

On the surface, the significant benefits of this approach may not be obvious. To state some of them: the Korean language is studied as a language; i.e., —as a system of meaningful sounds and sound patterns, which occur in various frequencies, intensities, and situations. To do this, vocabulary and patterns had to be recorded and graded over a number of years, and integrated into basic sentence patterns, short stories, and longer readings. As a result, Korean language students will be more successful in gaining the culture and language more quickly and efficiently, and will be led to master the material with a secure confidence in their ability to use it.

This book consists of 46 units. If four or five hours a day are spent on each unit, it is possible for a student to cover one unit a day. On the third day, after studying two units, the students are asked to review them. However, depending on the intensiveness of the curriculum and the size of the class, it is probably better to devote extra time to more thorough drilling on structural patterns and reviewing earlier material, rather than studying new lessons. Each unit consists of the following items: Basic Sentences, Useful Expressions, Notes On The Basic Sentences, Structure Notes, Drills, Short Stories, Reading and Briefing.

Basic Sentences :

The Basic Sentences are organized with graded patterns and words. They are conversational, natural, and the standard spoken language of the educated Korean speaker. The Basic Sentences should be memorized in one's own preparation work and with the help of the native teacher. While drilling the Basic Sentences, the student must not permit himself to speak more slowly than his teacher. The student must follow the way the teacher himself talks, without watching the book too closely. Language is to be spoken, not to be read. The right-hand side gives the English equivalent, which indicates what is said in English in a similar situation. It is not a literal translation.

Useful Expressions :

This section of useful expressions permits immediate use of the language in class, as well as an early command of the most frequently used everyday-life expressions.

Notes On The Basic Sentences :

This section contains assorted information on specific sentences, as well as idiomatic expressions. The student will find cultural meanings of those sentences, which are not evident from the English equivalent of the Basic Sentences or from the Structure Notes. At the same time, the lexical meanings, synonyms and derivations will be studied. The numbering of the notes corresponds to that of the sentences.

Structure Notes :

Grammatical structures will be explained and described in this section. The student will always find the new patterns introduced in the Basic Sentences. The student must not ask the teacher to explain the structure of the language; rather, he should read the Structure Notes outside of class. Lengthy explanations of the structural patterns must be avoided. Instead, the classroom should be filled with the sounds of the Korean language. Emphasis is always focused on acquiring skill in using the patterns. It is not very important to know the rules into which the patterns fit.

Drills :

There are seven kinds of drills in this section : Substitution Drill, Pattern Drill, Intonation Drill, Integration Drill, Response Drill, Level Drill, and Expansion Drill. The diversified drills are intended to develop fluency, as well as to promote the spontaneity of a new set of speaking habits.

While repeating and drilling the patterns in class with a teacher, and in the laboratory or at home with tapes, the student will not only facilitate the mastery of structural patterns, but also will be able to know how to apply the rules or expand the patterns.

Short Stories :

This section is intended to review grammatical constructions already studied in the Basic Sentences, the Structure Notes and Drills, as well as to increase vocabulary in a related situation. There are usually just three lines. The teacher reads them to the student, and asks the student to answer immediately. After that, the student must ask questions just as the teacher has done, and finally must say them all by himself. If fluency and spontaneity has been achieved to the teacher's satisfaction, the teacher begins the expansion drill, and the student repeats the sentence.

Reading :

This section is intended to reinforce audio-lingual skill, as well as to achieve effective skill in reading and writing. It is also intended to increase useful vocabulary. Even though vocabulary is considered of secondary importance, it is better to increase vocabulary from the beginning while studying the structure of the language. This section has many objectives : comprehension, related stories, interviews, interpreting, role play, and so forth. On the basis of the reading, diversified teaching techniques can be used for variety.

Briefing

This section is intended to achieve a goal of self-expression. The student need not restrict himself/herself to the contents of the outline. Use it rather as a guide. Take notes if you wish and refer to them as needed during your presentation. You do not have to translate words and patterns, but should convey concepts by using your own words and patterns, describing the ideas for which you do not have one word available. When you have prepared your remarks, so indicate to the teacher. Following your presentation, the teacher will give you feedback.

CONTENTS

RECOMMENDATIONS……1
ACKNOWLEDGMENTS……2
PREFACE……3
HAN'GŬL (the Korean Alphabet)……13
PHONOLOGY……18
VOWELS……20
CONSONANTS……30
RHYTHM……47
INTONATION AND FINAL CONTOURS……48

INTRODUCTORY COURSE

Unit 1 인사 Greetings (1)……51
Unit 2 인사 Greetings (2)……55
Unit 3 김치 Kimch'i……59
1. Style of Speech……60
2. The Informal-Polite Style……61
3. Korean Verbs……62
4. The Verb 있다……63
Unit 4 한국말 Korean Language……66
1. The Particle -가/-이……68
2. The Verb 이다……68
3. The Object Particle -를/-을……69
4. The Particle -에서 'at,' 'in'……69
5. The Honorific Infix -(으)시-……70
Unit 5 거리에서 On the Street……73
1. The Formal-Polite Style……75
2. The Particle -에 'at,' 'in'……76
3. The Particle -(으)로 'with,' 'by (means of)'……76
4. The Chinese Derived Numbers……77
Unit 6 물건 사기 Shopping……81
1. The Native Korean Numbers……83
2. Classifiers……84
3. The Particle -에 'for,' 'per'……85

4. The Honorific Verbs ······86
Unit 7 몇 시에 What Time? ······89
1. The Particle -에 'at,' 'on,' 'in' (Time) ······90
2. The Particle -까지 'until,' 'by,' 'to' ······91
3. The Particle -부터 'from' ······91
Unit 8 음식점에서 In the Restaurant ······95
1. The Past Tense -았-(-었-, -였-) ······97
2. The Pattern -ㄹ(을)까요? 'Shall we···?' ······98
3. The Contrast Particle -는/-은 ······99
Unit 9 전화 Telephone ······104
1. The Negative Adverb 안- 'do not' ······106
2. Negative Construction of Verbs ······106
3. The Sentence-Final Ending -ㄹ(을) 거에요 'will probably do' ···108
4. The Future Infix -겠- ······108
Unit 10 시간 Time ······112
1. The Particle -하고 같이 'together with' ······113
2. The Particle -하고 'and' ······114
3. The Exclamatory Ending -(는)군요 ······114
4. The Particle -에 'to' ······115
Unit 11 택시 Taxi ······118
1. The particle -(으)로 'to' ······120
2. The Sentence-Final Ending -지요 ······120
3. The Sentence-Final Ending -고 말고요 'Of course' ······121
4. The Exclamatory Ending -ㄴ(은)데요/-는데요 ······121

BOOK I

Unit 12 시장 Market ······127
1. Answers to Negative Questions ······128
2. The Adverb 못- 'can't,' 'won't' ······129
3. The Suffix -쯤 'about' ······130
Unit 13 얼마에요? How Much Is It? ······135
1. Independent Nouns and Dependent Nouns ······136
2. The Particle -만 'only' ······136
3. The Particle -도 'also,' 'too,' 'even,' 'indeed' ······137
4. Adverbs ······138
Unit 14 누구한테서? From Whom? ······143

1. The Particle -한테서 'from (a person)'······147
2. The Particle -한테 'to (a person)'······147
3. Particles Used in Verb Phrases······147
4. Gender······148
Unit 15 백화점 Department Store······153
1. The Particle -와/-과 같이 'together with'······155
2. The Particle -와/-과 'and'······155
3. The Noun Modifiers: D.V.S. +-ㄴ(은)······156
Unit 16 오원짜리 비행기 A Five Won Plane Ride······161
1. Noun+밖에+없다 (or 모르다) 'there is no one (nothing)'······163
2. The Suffix -짜리 '(a thing) worth'······164
3. The Negative Imperative Form -지 말다 'Don't do'······164
4. The Negative Adverb 그만- 'stop (doing)'······165
Unit 17 바쁘세요? Are You Busy?······170
1. The Humble Verbs······171
2. The Sentence-Final Ending -아(-어, 여) 주다 (or 드리다)······172
Unit 18 누구의 책? Whose Book?······178
1. The Particle -의 '(of)'······179
2. The Potential -ㄹ(을) 수 있다 (없다) 'can (cannot) do'······179
3. The Intentional -ㄹ(을)께요 'will do'······180
Unit 19 코피를 마시면 If I Drink Coffee······185
1. -ㄹ Irregular Verbs······187
2. The Sentence-Final Ending -고 싶다 'want to do'······187
3. The Conditional -(으)면 'if,' 'when'······188
Unit 20 수영 Swimming······194
1. The Ending -(으)러 'in order to'······196
2. Verbal Noun Formation -기 and -ㅁ/-음······196
3. The Causal Ending -기 때문에 'so,' 'therefore,' 'because'······198
4. The Contrastive Ending -지만 'but'······199
Unit 21 날씨 Weather······205
1. The Comparison -보다 '(more) than'······207
2. The Sentence-Final Ending -ㄴ(은) 것 같다 'it seems to be'······208
3. The Particle -만큼 'to the extent of,' 'as much as'······209
4. The Superlative Marker 제일 (or 가장) 'the most'······209
Unit 22 얼마나 멀어요? How Far Is It?······215
1. Noun Modifiers: -ㄴ(은), -는, -ㄹ(을)······217
2. The Particle -마다 'every'······218

3. The Suffix -씩 'apiece,' 'respectively,' 'each' 218

Unit 23 기후 Climate 223

1. V.S. +-았(-었, -였)으면 좋겠다 'I wish it would happen' 225
2. The Intentional -ㄹ(을)래요 'intend to' 225
3. The Ordinal Numbers 226

Unit 24 영화 The Movies 232

1. The Coordinate Ending -고 'and' 233
2. The Non-Final Ending (a) -ㄹ(을) 때 'when' 234
   (b) -ㄹ(을) 때까지 'until' 235
   (c) -ㄹ(을) 때마다 'every time' 235
   (d) -ㄹ(을) 때부터 'from the time' 235

Unit 25 괜찮아요 ? Is It Alright ? 242

1. The Concessive Ending -아(-어, -여)도 'even though' 243
2. The Obligatory Ending -아(-어, -여)야 하다 'must' 245
3. A.V.S.+-ㄴ(은) 다음에 'after doing' 247

Unit 26 담배 Cigarettes 253

1. The Non-Final Ending -아(-어, -여)서 'do and do' 254
2. The Transferentive Ending -다가 256
3. A.V.S.+-기 전에 'before doing' 257

Unit 27 무슨 뜻입니까 ? What Does It Mean ? 263

1. The Causal Non-Final Ending -아(-어, -여)서 'because' 264
2. The Particles -께서 and -께 266
3. A.V.S.+-아(-어, -여) 보다 'tries doing' 266
4. 아무도+Negative 'nobody does…' 267

Unit 28 천천히 갑시다 Let's Go Slowly 272

1. The Causal Non-Final Ending -(으)니까 'because' 274
2. 여간+V.S.+Negative '(it) is uncommon' 275
3. The Pluralizing Suffix -들 276

Unit 29 며칠입니까 ? What Date Is It ? 283

1. Time Classifiers: -초, -분, -일, -주일, -년 285
2. A.V.S.+-ㄴ(-은) 지가+Time Word+되다 '(the time) since' 287
3. The Particie -처럼 '(the same) as,' 'like' 288

Unit 30 방문 A Visit 293

1. The Introductory Non-Final Ending -ㄴ(-은, -는)데 295
2. The Time Non-Final Ending -(으)니까 'when' 296
3. The Sentence-Final Ending -기로 하다 'decide to do' 297

Unit 31 재미있게 노세요 Have Fun 303

1. A.V.S.+ -ㄹ(을) 일이 있다 'have something to do'……305
2. The Intentional -(으)려고 하다 'intend to do' ……305
3. The Ending -(으)려고 'in order to' ……306
Unit 32 복습 Review ……312
1. The Progressive -고 있다 '(someone) is doing' ……314
2. The Pattern -아(-어, -여)서 죽겠다 'because of so-and-so, I could die'……315
3. A.V.S.+-지 말고 'not, (but)' ……316
Unit 33 아이들 Children ……322
1. The Particle -(이)나 ……324
2. The Particle -도(…도) 'both… and'……325
Unit 34 공부 A Study……331
1. -ㄷ Irregular Verbs ……333
2. Noun+-에 대해서 'about,' 'toward' ……333
3. A.V.S. +-ㄴ(은) 후에 'after doing' ……334
4. Interrogative+-(이)라도 'no matter… it is' ……334
Unit 35 한식 Korean Food ……341
1. A.V.S. +-ㄴ(은) 일이 있다 (없다) 'have ever (never) done'……342
2. -ㅎ Irregular Verbs ……343
3. Interrogative+-(이)든지 'no matter… it is' ……344
4. A.V.S.+-는 일이 있다 (없다) '(someone) sometimes does' ……345
Unit 36 반말 A Plain Style Of Speech……351
1. The Plain Style ……352
Unit 37 며칠 How Many Days?……361
1. Time Word+-만에 'after (of time)' ……363
2. 이젠, 아직도, 벌써 ……364
3. -ㅅ Irregular Verbs ……365
Unit 38 문 Door……371
1. -ㅂ Irregular Verbs ……373
2. A.V.S.+-아(-어, -여) 놓다 'do something in advance' ……373
3. The Sentence-Final Ending -아(-어, -여) 있다 ……374
Unit 39 기다려 주세요 Please Wait ……381
1. The Informal Polite Question Ending -ㄴ(-은, -는)가요? ……382
2. The Non-Final Ending -(으)면서 'while doing'……383
Unit 40 감기 A Cold ……390
1. The Sentence-Final Ending -아(어, -여) 지다 'it becomes' ……392
2. The Indirect Discourse -고 하다 '(someone) says that…'……392

3. A.V.S.+-는 것 ……395

Unit 41 교통사고 A Traffic Accident ……401

1. The Sentence-Final Ending -ㄹ(을) 뻔했다, 'almost (did)' ……402
2. The Indirect Question Ending -지/-가 ……403

Unit 42 예습 Preparation ……410

1. A.V.S.+-아(-어, -여) 버리다 'finish up doing' ……412
2. The Non-Final Ending -도록 'so that…' ……412
3. A.V.S.+-ㄹ(을) 줄 알다/모르다 'know how to do' ……413
4. -르 Irregular Verbs ……414

Unit 43 피곤해 보여요 You Look Tired ……421

1. D.V.A+-아(-어, -여) 보이다 'someone looks (appears)' ……422
2. The Retrospective Non-Final Ending -더니 ……423
3. The Causal Non-Final Ending -느라고 'because of doing ……424

Unit 44 친구 A Friend ……431

1. The Sentence-Final Ending -줄 알다/모르다 ……432
2. The Particle -(이)라도 'even if (it be)' ……433
3. The Obligatory Ending -아(-어, -여)야 되다 'must' ……434

Unit 45 연하장 New Year's Card ……440

1. The Retrospective Infix -더- ……442
2. The Non-Final Ending -도록 'until' ……443
3. -으 Irregular Verbs ……443
4. The Non-Final Ending -다가는 'if' ……444

Unit 46 독일어 German ……452

1. The Sentence-Final Ending -게 되다 '(it) turns out so that' ……453
2. The Provisional -아(-어, -여)야 'provided' ……454
3. The Sentence-Final Ending -ㄹ(을) 예정이다 '(one) plans to do' ……455

VOCABULARY ……463

INDEX TO STRUCTURE NOTES ……480

HANGŬL (the Korean Alphabet) :

Language is speech. Language learning involves acquiring a new set of habits, and habits must be automatic. Therefore, after you acquire some basic control of the spoken language, it is best for you to begin reading and writing, because they are a different set of habits. But we begin with the writing system from the very start. First, the Korean writing system is so simple that it does not give the student any heavy burden or multiply the learning problem. Secondly, romanization usually misleads the student to wrong pronunciation. For these reasons, it is recommended that you accustom yourself to the use of HAN'GŬL from the very begining. It is suggested that you learn immediately to associate the sound system with the spelling. From the outset, it is essential for the student to master the association of letters with the sound system in Korean. It is to be desired that you study the Korean alphabet, always keeping in mind that the letters are no more than graphic symbols which are meant to remind you of the actually occurring Korean sounds. If you become familiar with the Korean sound system, you will become accustomed to them immediately.

The Korean alphabet consists of 40 letters, including compounds: 10 pure vowels, 11 compound vowels, 14 basic consonants and 5 double consonants. But the basic Korean alphabet consists of 10 vowels and 14 consonants.

TRANSCRIPTION :

In this book, only for the sound system, a transcription system is used as an aid to better pronunciation. It will take relatively little time to master the transcription and to associate the signs with the sounds. It is not necessary for the student to learn to write the transcription.

PURE VOWELS:

letter	transcription	letter	transcription
ㅣ	/i/	ㅡ	/ŭ/
ㅔ	/e/	ㅓ	/ə/
ㅐ	/ɛ/	ㅏ	/a/
ㅟ	/ü/	ㅜ	/u/
ㅚ	/ö/	ㅗ	/o/

COMPOUND VOWELS:

letter	transcription	letter	transcription
ㅑ	/ya/	ㅘ	/wa/
ㅒ	/yɛ/	ㅙ	/wɛ/
ㅕ	/yə/	ㅝ	/wə/
ㅖ	/ye/	ㅞ	/we/
ㅛ	/yo/	ㅢ	/ŭi/
ㅠ	/yu/		

CONSONANTS:

letter	transcription	letter	transcription
ㄱ	/kiyək/	ㅇ	/iŭng/
ㄴ	/niŭn/	ㅈ	/chiŭt/
ㄷ	/tikŭt/	ㅊ	/ch'iŭt/
ㄹ	/riŭl/	ㅋ	/k'iŭk/
ㅁ	/miŭm/	ㅌ	/t'iŭt/
ㅂ	/piŭp/	ㅍ	/p'iŭp/
ㅅ	/siot/	ㅎ	/hiŭt/

DOUBLE CONSONANTS:

letter	transcription	letter	transcription
ㄲ	/ssang-kiyək/	ㅆ	/ssang-siot/
ㄸ	/ssang-tikŭt/	ㅉ	/ssang-chiŭt/
ㅃ	/ssang-piŭp		

HOW TO WRITE HANGŬL:

As a general rule, Han'gŭl letters are formed with strokes from top to bottom and from left to right. Below, letters are given showing the order in which the strokes are written, so that the student may be initiated into the writing of Han'gŭl.

	1	2	3	4	5
ㅣ	↓				
ㅏ	↓	→			
ㅐ	↓	→	↓		
ㅑ	↓	→	→		
ㅒ	↓	→	→	↓	
ㅓ	→	↓			
ㅔ	→	↓	↓		
ㅕ	→	→	↓		
ㅖ	→	→	↓	↓	
ㅗ	↓	→			

	1	2	3	4	5
ㅚ	↓	→	↓		
ㅘ	↓	→	↓	→	
ㅙ	↓	→	↓	→	↓
ㅡ	→				
ㅢ	→	↓			
ㅜ	→	↓			
ㅟ	→	↓	↓		
ㅝ	→	↓	→	↓	
ㅞ	→	↓	→	↓	↓
ㅛ	↓	↓	→		
ㅠ	→	↓	↓		

	1	2	3	4	5
ㄱ					
ㄴ					
ㄷ					
ㄹ					
ㅁ					
ㅂ					
ㅅ					
ㅇ					
ㅈ					
ㅊ					

	1	2	3	4	5
ㅋ					
ㅌ					
ㅍ					
ㅎ					
ㄲ					
ㄸ					
ㅃ					
ㅆ					
ㅉ					

SYLLABLES :

The Korean syllable is different from English. A Korean consonant by itself cannot form a syllable, because the Korean consonant, if not followed by a vowel, cannot be released. However, a vowel by itself can form a syllable. In English, a syllable is a sound or group of sounds accompanied by one of four stresses ; however, in Korean, it is a sound or group of sounds which take up a certain relative space of time, like metronome beats (See RHYTHM p. 47).

HOW TO FORM SYLLABLES :

The vowel in all combinations (Vowel-Consonant, Consonant-Vowel, or Consonant-Vowel-Consonant, etc.) must be written somewhat bigger than the accompanying consonant or consonants.

1. Vowel :

The pronounced vowels, ㅏ, ㅓ, ㅡ, etc. are not written alone. So, when there is no initial consonant at the beginning of syllables, the ㅇ is always written ; it may be regarded as a sort of orthographic 'Filler,' and is not pronounced. In other words, although the ㅇ is written in the initial position, it has no sound value.

아, 야, 어, 여, 오, 요, 우, 유, 으, 이, 위, 외

2. Consonant-Vowel :

a. There are nine vowels which have the stroke standing in a vertical position : ㅏ, ㅓ, ㅐ, ㅑ, ㅕ, ㅒ, ㅔ, ㅖ, ㅣ. These vowels have the accompanying consonants at their left side.

가, 너, 래, 먀, 벼, 섀, 체, 예, 디

b. There are four vowels which have the stroke lying in a horizontal position : ㅗ, ㅛ, ㅜ, ㅠ. These vowels have their accompanying consonants directly on top.

노, 뵤, 주, 퓨

c. There are seven vowels which have the accompanying consonants on the top of their left side. ㅚ, ㅘ, ㅟ, ㅙ, ㅝ, ㅞ, ㅢ

되, 놔, 뮈, 왜, 워, 웨, 희

3. Consonant-Vowel-Consonant :

The final consonant in a syllable is always written below the main vowel.

덥, 간, 참, 팔, 웬, 앞, 읏. 듣

4. Consonant-Vowel-Consonant-Consonant :

a. When there are two final consonants, and the vowel has a stroke standing in the vertical position, the first final consonant is written below the initial consonant, and the second final consonant is written below the main vowel.

젊, 값, 밝, 닭, 삯

b. When the vowel has the stroke lying in a horizontal position, the final two consonants are written below the main vowel side by side.

늙, 끊, 흙, 굶, 옳

PHONOLOGY

Notes On Terms :

1. In the phonetic description of the vowels, the terms high, mid, low and front, central, back are used to indicate the position of the tongue.
2. Open and close refer to the relative size of the oral passage. Frequently open vowels are also lax and close vowels are tense.
3. The terms rounded and unrounded refer to the lips.
4. In regard to consonants, the place of articulation is indicated by the terms bilabial, (made with the two lips) ; apico-alveolar, (made with the tip of the tongue against the gum ridge behind the upper teeth) ; lamino-alveolar, (made with the blade of the tongue against the gum ridge somewhat back of the usual position for /t/) ; dorso-velar, (made with the back of the tongue against the soft palate) ; glottal, (made in the glottis).
5. The manner of articulating consonants is indicated by the terms stop, (the air passage is closed and then released) ; affricate, (a stop and its immediately following release through the articulatory position with a friction) ; spirant or fricative, (the air passage is restricted, but not closed) ; sibilant, (the air escapes through the nose) ; lateral, (the air escapes around the sides of the tongue) ; flap, (a trill reduced to a single movement).
6. Voiced and voiceless are terms referring to the presence or absence of vibration of the vocal cords.

THE KOREAN SOUND SYSTEM :

Every language has a system of sounds. Speaking a language involves being able to make and distinguish its sounds. Therefore, in learning a new language, the most important step in the beginning is the mastery of the sound system of that language. The Korean sound system is pronounced in somewhat different ways from that of English. Many of the Korean sounds are very similar to those English ; but if you were to use the English pronunciation of these sounds, the slight defferences could be enough to change the meaning of the Korean, thus making your Korean difficult to understand. Therefore, if you are to speak understandable Korean, some of your English pronunciation habits must be avoided. The Korean sound system consists of 10 pure vowels, plus two semivowels ; (with these two semivowels, 11 compound vowels are formed.) In addition, there are 14 basic consonants and 5 double consonants.

VOWELS:

There are many more vowels in English than Korean. Except for a few difficult Korean ones such as /ŭ, /ü/, Vowel chart /ö/, most of them are rather simple. Generally speaking, (1) the positions of the tongue are slightly higher than those for corresponding English ones. (2) The Korean rounded vowels are pronounced with a little less lip-rounding than the American equivalents, and without protruding the lips, as in 'boot.' In the phonetic comments to the vowels, the terms of the three top-to-bottom levels (HIGH, MID, LOW) and three front-to-back positions (FRONT, CENTRAL, BACK) describe the positions of the tongue. The chart of ten pure vowels is as follows:

VOWEL CHART :

	Front	Central	Back
High	ㅣ **i** ㅟ **ü**	ㅡ **ŭ**	ㅜ **u**
Mid	ㅔ **e** ㅚ **ö**	ㅓ ə	ㅗ **o**
Low	ㅐ ɛ	ㅏ **a**	

VOWELS

Ph-l

ㅣ /i/ The Korean /i/ is a high front unrounded vowel. It is a tense and short vowel. You make it with the tip of your tongue resting behind the low teeth. The Korean /i/ is longer and more tense than the /i/ in the English 'fit,' but shorter and less tense than the /i/ in 'see.'

Example :	**Transcription :**	**Meaning :**
기분	/kibun/	feeling
시인	/siin/	poet
미소	/miso/	smile
비밀	/pimil/	secret
인기	/inkki/	popularity
지리	/chiri/	geography
이름	/irŭm/	name
피리	/p'iri/	flute

ㅔ /e/ The tense mid front unrounded vowel /e/ is always short. It is slightly higher than the /e/ in the English 'let.'

에너지	/enəji/	energy
에누리	/enuri/	discount
세상	/sesang/	world
지게	/chige/	A-frame
누에	/nue/	silkworm
형제	/hyəngje/	brothers
헤엄	/heəm/	swimming

ㅐ /ɛ/ The open (lax) low front unrounded vowel /ɛ/ is either short or long. It is slightly higher than the /ɛ/ in the English 'action.' The sound corresponding to the /ɛ/ in the English 'action' does not exist in Korean.

애기	/ɛgi/	baby
새해	/sɛhɛ/	New Year
매화	/mɛhwa/	plum blossom
야채	/yach'ɛ/	vegetable
등대	/tŭngdɛ/	lighthouse
개	/kɛ/	dog
생애	/sɛngɛ/	lifetime
해외	/hɛö/	foreign countries

ㅟ /Ü/ The tense high front rounded vowel /ü/ has no approximation in English. It stands for a sound somewhat like the /ü/ in the German 'fünf.' It has the same tongue position as /i/, but with rounded lips. However, many Korean people habitually pronounce it as /wi/.

위인	/üin/	hero
위험	/ühəm/	danger
추위	/ch'uü/	coldness
사귀다	/sagüda/	to associate with
쥐	/chö/	rat
귀	/kü/	ear
뒤집다	/tüjiptta/	to turn over
뉘우치다	/nüuch'ida/	to regret
취미	/ch'ümi/	hobby
쉬다	/süda/	to rest
튀기다	/t'ügida/	to fry
휘다	/hüda/	to bend

ㅚ /Ö/ The tense mid front rounded vowel /ö/ also has no equivalent in English. It stands for a sound approximately like the /ö/ in the German 'Köslin.' It has the same tongue postition as /e/, but with rounded lips. However, many Korean people habitually pronounce it as /we/.

외출	/öch'ul/	going out
외국	/öguk/	foreign country
해외	/hɛö/	foreign countries
뇌염	/nöyəm/	encephalitis
파괴	/p'agö/	destruction
죄인	/chöin/	criminal
최고	/ch'ögo/	the highest
회사	/hösa/	company
뫼	/mö/	grave

Ph-2

ㅡ /Ŭ/ The tense high central unrounded vowel /ŭ/ is rather difficult for American speakers. You make it by pulling back your tongue from the position for sounding /i/ to the central part on the same level. Your tongue position is placed half-way between the /i/ and /u/ sound. Every effort should be made to master this sound /ŭ/. It is an important step toward acceptable pronunciation.

스승	/sŭsŭng/	teacher
슬프다	/sŭlp'ŭda/	to be sad
등산	/tŭngsan/	mountain-climbing
금	/kŭm/	gold
늦다	/nŭtta/	to be late
그믐	/kŭmŭm/	the last day (of the month)
습기	/sŭpkki/	damp
흐리다	/hŭrida/	to be cloudy
은행	/ŭnhɛng/	bank
음성	/ŭmsəng/	voice

ㅓ/ə/ The mid central unrounded vowel /ə/ in Korean is either short or long. It is pronounced with tense muscles in stressed syllables, and with relaxed muscles in unstressed syllables. It stands for a sound approximately like the /ə/ in the English 'about' as a short sound and the /ə/ in 'church' as a long sound.

먼섬	/mənsəm/	far-off island
어디	/ədi/	where
머리	/məri/	head
넘어지다	/nəməjida/	to fall down
더럽다	/tərəptta/	to be dirty
허리	/həri/	waist
거인	/kəin/	giant
선생	/sənsɛng/	teacher
처음	/chəŭm/	first time
터지다	/t'əjida/	to burst
전쟁	/chənjɛng/	war
버섯	/pəsət/	mushroom

ㅏ/a/ The low central unrounded vowel /a/ is either short or long. It is slightly higher than the /a/ in the English 'arm.' It corresponds to the English sound /a/ in 'ideal.'

밤	/pam/	night
밤	/paːm/	chestnut
아들	/adŭl/	son
마음	/maŭm/	mind
밤낮	/pamnat/	day and night

사고	/sago/	trouble
장난	/changnan/	a play, fun
바지	/paji/	trousers
차	/ch'a/	car
칼	/k'al/	knife
타다	/t'ada/	to get on
강아지	/kangaji/	puppy

Ph-3

ㅜ/u/ The Korean back vowels are all pronounced with rounded lips, but making them with a little less lip-rounding and without protruding the lips, as in 'mood.' The tense high back rounded vowel /u/ is similar to the English 'put' and 'soon.'

우유	/uyu/	milk
누구	/nugu/	who
수영	/suyəng/	swimming
구두	/kudu/	shoes
무우	/muu/	radish
공주	/kongju/	princess
눈물	/nunmul/	tears
국수	/kukssu/	noodle
두부	/tubu/	bean-curd
주문	/chumun/	ordering
투구	/t'ugu/	helmet

ㅗ/o/ The mid back rounded vowel /o/ is close to the vowel sound /o/ in the English 'bone.' It is slightly higher than the /o/ in the English 'taught,'

도토리	/tot'ori/	acorn
모범	/mobəm/	model
국보	/kukppo/	national treasure
복음	/pogŭm/	the Gospel
오늘	/onŭl/	today
독자	/tokcca/	reader
비로소	/piroso/	for the first time
복도	/poktto/	corridor
보초	/poch'o/	sentry
눈동자	/nunttongja/	the pupil of the eye

Practice the difference between the /ŭ/ and /ə/ sound.

그리	/kŭri/	거리	/kəri/
등어리	/tŭngəri/	덩어리	/təngəri/
근사	/kŭnsa/	건사	/kənsa/
근성	/kŭnsəng/	건성	/kənsəng/
들다	/tŭlda/	덜다	/təlda/
승격	/sŭngkkyək/	성격	/səngkkyək/
승인	/sŭngin/	성인	/səngin/
승패	/sŭngp'ε/	성패	/səngp'ε
증세	/chŭngse/	정세	/chəngse/

Practice the difference between the /ə/ and /o/ sound. It is very difficult for foreigners to distinguish these two sounds by hearing.

거리	/kəri/	고리	/kori/
버선	/pəsən/	보선	/posən/
거기	/kəgi/	고기	/kogi/
자선	/chasən/	자손	/chason/
부적	/pujək/	부족	/pujok/
장서	/changsə/	장소	/changso/
널다	/nəlda/	놀다	/nolda/
넣다	/nət'a/	놓다	/not'a/
덜다	/təlda/	돌다	/tolda/
덥다	/təptta/	돕다	/toptta/
걸다	/kəlda/	골다	/kolda/

SEMIVOWELS :

Ph-4

/w/ This semivowel /w/ is a voiced labio-velar sound. It is like the inital /w/ soung in 'worth. ' You make it by raising the back of your tongue toward the soft palate, and then moving it quickly into position for the following vowel. The lips are rounded slightly. This semivowel occurs in the initial position of a syllable, and between consonant and vowel, but never occurs in the final position.

/y/ This semivowel /y/ is the voiced lamino-alveolar sound. It is like the English /y/ in 'yes.' You make it with the front of your tongue close to the palate and back part of the gum ridge, with the tip holding against the lower front teeth. The tongue is then moved quickly down into position for the following vowel. This semivowel occurs in the initial position of a syllable, and between consonant and vowel, but never occurs in the final position.

ㅘ/wa/ It is made of ㅗ and ㅏ. When the first sound ㅗ is immediately followed by the ㅏ, the first sound just like a semivowel /w/, and the following sound is heard with a full retention. This sound ㅘ is similar to the English /wa/ in 'wash.'

과찬	/kwach'an/	overpraise
일과	/ilgwa/	daily work
봤다	/pwatta/	saw
완강히	/wan'ganghi/	stoutly
황제	/hwangje/	emperor
기와	/kiwa/	tile
와전	/wajən/	misinformation
쐈다	/sswatta/	shot
회화	/höhwa/	conversation
성과	/səngkkwa/	result

ㅙ/we/ It is made of ㅗ and ㅐ. This sound is like the English /wɛ/ in 'wax.'

돼지	/twɛji/	pig
유쾌	/yuk'wɛ/	pleasure
쇄국	/wɛguk/	national isolation

횃불	/hwɛtpul/	torch
왜색	/wɛsɛk/	Japanese manners
괘씸하다	/kwɛssimhada/	to be disgusting
왜간장	/wɛganjang/	Japanese soy sauce
괜찮다	/kwɛnch'ant'a/	to be alright
왜소	/wɛso/	small stature
쾌활	/k'wɛhwal/	brightness

ㅝ/wə/ It is made of ㅜ and ㅓ. This sound stands for a sound approximately like the /wə/ in the English 'wonderful.'

수월	/suwəl/	several months
정원	/chəngwən/	garden
원인	/wənin/	cause
월요일	/wəryoil/	Monday
권고	/kwən'go/	advice
궐기	/kwəlgi/	rising
천원	/ch'ənwən/	one thousand won
이월	/iwəl/	February
훨씬	/hwəlssin/	very much
원만	/wənman/	harmony
훤하다	/hwənhada/	to be bright

ㅞ/we/ It is made of ㅜ and ㅔ. This sound is like the English /we/ in 'well.'

궤변	/kwebyən/	sophism
금궤	/kŭmgwe/	money-chest
웬까닭	/wenkkadak/	what reason
웬일	/wenil/	what matter
웬만큼	/wenmank'ŭm/	properly
훼손	/hweson/	damage
궤짝	/kweccak/	box
궤도	/kwedo/	track, line
위궤양	/wigweyang/	stomach ulcer

ㅑ/ya/ It is made of ㅣ and ㅏ. This sound is like the English /ya/ in 'yarn.'

양심	/yangsim/	conscience
야당	/yadang/	Opposition Party
성냥	/səngnyang/	match
야단	/yadan/	scolding

약속	/yakssok/	promise
정양	/chəngyang/	rest, recuperation
얄밉다	/yalmiptta/	to be hateful
얌치	/yamch'i/	shameless fellow
고향	/kohyang/	native place
고양이	/koyangi/	cat
만약	/manyak/	if
얕보다	/yatppoda/	to despise

ㅒ/yɛ/ It is made of ㅣ and ㅐ. This sound is close to the English sound /yɛ/ in 'yank.'

얘기	/yɛgi/	story
얘	/yɛ/	this child
걔	/kyɛ/	that child
쟤	/chyɛ/	that child over there

ㅕ/yə/ It is made of ㅣ and ㅓ. This sound is similar to the English /ye/ in 'yodel.'

명문	/myəngmun/	reputable family
여성	/yəsəng/	female
결석	/kyəlssək/	absence
경영	/kyəngyəng/	management
견본	/kyənbon/	sample
벼르다	/pyərŭda/	to plan
병원	/pyəngwən/	hospital
비명	/pimyəng/	scream
변장	/pyənjang/	disguise
처녀	/ch'ənyə/	maid, virgin
겨우	/kyəu/	barely
별장	/pyəlccang/	villa
평화	/p'yənghwa/	peace

ㅖ/ye/ It is made of ㅣ and ㅔ. This sound is similar to the English /ye/ in 'yellow.'

예수	/yesu/	Jesus Christ
경계	/kyənggye/	boundary
계속	/kyesok/	continuation
옛날	/yetnal/	old times

폐렴	/p'yeryəm/	pneumonia
혜성	/hyesəng/	comet
은폐	/ŭnp'ye/	hiding
폐막	/p'yemak/	the falling of the curtain
예정	/yejəng/	schedule

ㅛ/yo/ It is made of ㅣ and ㅗ. This sound is like the English /yo/ in 'yoke.'

교양	/kyoyang/	culture
요양	/yoyang/	recuperation
교사	/kyosa/	teacher
비료	/piryo/	fertilizer
동요	/tongyo/	child's song
식욕	/sigyok/	appetite
효자	/hyoja/	dutiful son
욕심	/yokssim/	greediness
묘소	/myoso/	grave
발표	/palp'yo/	announcement

ㅠ/yu/ It is made ㅣ and ㅜ. This sound is like the English /yu/ in 'youth.'

석유	/səgyu/	oil
대륙	/tɛryuk/	continent
육지	/yukcci/	land
해류	/hɛryu/	current
규명	/kyumyəng/	searching, examination
규모	/kyumo/	scale
야유	/yayu/	ridicule
자유	/chayu/	freedom
휴일	/hyuil/	holiday
유행	/yuhɛng/	fashion
여유	/yəyu/	time (money) to spare
휴게실	/hyugesil/	rest-room

ㅢ/ŭi/ This orthographic diphthong ㅢ is sometimes pedantically pronounced /ŭi/, but is usually pronounced as if ㅡ/ŭ/ initially, and ㅣ/i/ in the second position. However, when it is used as a particle meaning 'of,' it is ordinarily pronounced ㅔ/e/.

의사	/ŭisa/	doctor
띄우다	/ttiuda/	to float

의논	/ŭnon/	consultation
의상	/ŭsang/	dress
유의	/yui/	attention
내의	/nɛi/	undershirt
의리	/ŭri/	justice
의무	/ŭmu/	duty
의자	/ŭja/	chair
의원	/ŭiwən/	member
학교의	/hakkyoe/	the school's
사람의	/sarame/	the person's

CONSONANTS:

Some of the Korean consonants are so different from those of your native language that they may cause you some difficulty. Many of the Korean consonants, however, are similar to those of English if you just avoid some of your English pronunciation habits. Generally speaking:

1. The Korean double consonants ㅃ, ㄸ, ㄲ, ㅉ, ㅆ seem to cause English speakers the most distress.
2 The Korean aspirated sounds ㅍ, ㅌ, ㅊ, ㅋ, ㅎ are pronounced with a stronger puff of breath than their English counterparts.
3. The Korean flap sound /r/ is a rather tricky one for English speakers, and the lateral sound /l/ is also different from the English /l/.
4. When the Korean consonants occur in the final position, they are unreleased sounds.

KOREAN CONSONANT CHART

Where does it happen? / What happens?		Bilabial		Apico-alveolar		Lamino-alveolar		Dorso-velar		Glottal	
STOPS	vs	p	ㅂ	t	ㄷ			k	ㄱ		
	vd	b	ㅂ	d	ㄷ			g	ㄱ		
Glottalized	vs	pp	ㅃ	tt	ㄸ			kk	ㄲ		
Aspirated	vs	p'	ㅍ	t'	ㅌ			k'	ㅋ		
AFFRICATES	vs					ch	ㅈ				
	vd					j	ㅈ				
Glottalized	vs					cc	ㅉ				
Aspirated	vs					ch'	ㅊ				
SIBILANT	vs			s	ㅅ						
Glottalized	vs			ss	ㅆ						
FRICATIVE Aspirated	vs									h	ㅎ
NASAL	vd	m	ㅁ	n	ㄴ			ng	ㅇ		
LATERAL	vd			l	ㄹ						
FLAP	vd			r	ㄹ						

vs stands for voiceless
vd stands for voiced

CONSONANTS

Ph-5

Following the order of the Korean consonants, in which they usually present the greatest difficulty for most foreigners, we shall start with the glottalized consonants. The glottalized sounds are produced by interrupting the breath stream by closing the glottis. They are pronounced with a special tenseness. You make them by tightening up your throat in order to hold on to and get in that extra syllable represented by the first of the consonants.

ㅃ /pp/ This double consonant /pp/ is a voiceless glottalized bilabial stop. You make it by bringing your lips together as in the production of a single /p/, and hold it in that position for a full syllable beat. Then explode the lips tight and clear without any puff of breath. It does not occur as a final sound.

Example:	Transcription:	Meaning:
빨갛다	/ppalgat'a/	to be red
빨리	/ppalli/	quickly
빼앗다	/ppɛatta/	to snatch (a thing) from
빽빽하다	/ppɛkppɛk'hada/	to be packed
빵	/ppang/	bread
뽐내다	/ppomnɛda/	to be proud (of)
바쁘다	/pappŭda/	to be busy
오빠	/oppa/	older brother
기쁨	/kippŭm/	delight
나쁘다	/nappŭda/	to be bad

ㄸ /tt/ This sound is a voiceless glottalized apico-alveolar stop. You make it by bringing the tip of your tongue against the gum ridge behind the upper teeth, as in the production of a single /t/. Then hold it in that position for a full syllable beat and release it tight and clear without any puff of air. It does not occur as a final sound.

따다	/ttada/	to pick, to pluck
따뜻하다	/ttattŭt'hada/	to be warm
때리다	/ttɛrida/	to strike, to hit
때때로	/ttɛttɛro/	now and then
똑똑하다	/ttokttok'hada/	to be smart

똑딱똑딱	/ttokttakttokttak/	ticking
귀뚜라미	/kwitturami/	cricket
끄떡	/kkŭttək/	nodding
뒤뚱뒤뚱	/twittungtwittung/	staggeringly
까딱까딱	/kkattakkkattak/	nodding and nodding

ㅉ/cc/ This sound is a voiceless glottalized lamino-alveolar affricate. You make it by touching the blade of your tongue to the gum ridge, somewhat in back of the usual position for /t/. Then hold it in that position for a full syllable beat and release it as a friction without any puff of breath. It does not occur as a final sound.

짜다	/ccada/	to be salty
짝짝이	/ccakccagi/	unmatched pair
짭짤하다	/ccapccalhada/	to be nice and salty
째보	/ccɛbo/	harelipped person
찡그리다	/ccinggŭrida/	to frown
쫑알대다	/ccongaldɛda/	to mutter
아찔하다	/accilhada/	to be dizzy
아무쪼록	/amuccorok/	as much as one can
무찌르다	/muccirŭda/	to mow down
가짜	/kacca/	phony
슬쩍	/sŭlccək/	furtively
소쩍새	/soccəksɛ/	cuckoo
대쪽	/tɛccok/	split bamboo
여쭈다	/yəccuda/	to ask, to inquire

ㅆ/ss/ This sound is a voiceless glottalized apico-alveolar sibilant. You make it by bringing the tip of your tongue close to the gum ridge, (but without touching it), as in the production of a single /s/. Then hold it in that position for a full syllable beat and release it without any puff of breath. The air strongly escapes at the lower edge of the apex of your tongue which is grooved.

싸다	/ssada/	to be cheap
쌍방	/ssangbang/	both sides
쌀쌀하다	/ssalssalhada/	to be chilly
썩다	/ssəktta/	to rot
쓰다	/ssŭda/	to write
쏟아지다	/ssodajida/	to gush out

말씀	/malssŭm/	word, speech
말씨	/malssi/	use of words
솜씨	/somssi/	skill
글썽글썽	/kŭlssəngkŭlssəng/	with tearful eyes

When this /ss/ sound occurs in the final position and is followed by a consonant, it is pronounced as an unreleased implosive /t/.

했다	/hɛtta/	did
있다	/itta/	to exist

ㄲ/kk/ This sound is a voiceless glottalized dorso-velar stop. You make it by raising the back of your tongue firmly against the soft palate, as in the production of a single /k/.Then hold it in that position for a full syllable beat and release it tight and clear without any puff of breath.

까불다	/kkabulda/	to behave frivolously
까다	/kkada/	to peel
끄다	/kkŭda/	to turn off
꿩	/kkwəng/	pheasant
깨우다	/kkɛuda/	to wake up
꺼내다	/kkənɛda/	to take out
끝	/kkŭt/	end
사냥꾼	/sanyangkkun/	hunter
아깝다	/akkaptta/	to be regrettable
바꾸다	/pakkuda/	to change

When this sound /kk/ occurs in the final position and is followed by a consonant, it is pronounced like an unreleased implosive /k/.

안팎	/anp'ak/	the inside and outside
밖	/pak/	outside
묶다	/muktta/	to bind
꺾다	/kkəktta/	to break off

Ph-6

ㄹ/r/ The Korean /r/ sound is a voiced apico-alveolar flap. The Korean /r/ is quite different from the English /r/, which is a palatal spirant. The English /r/ is made by retracting the tip of the tongue a bit toward the back of the mouth, while the lips move front semiclosed to open, and the air passes between the front of the tongue and the hard palate. However, the Korean /r/ is made by touching the tip of the tongue against the gum ridge behind the upper teeth with a brief flick, and bringing it down quickly. (1) When the ㄹ occurs between two vowels, it is a flap sound. (2) It does not occur initially, except for words of foreign origin, and the name of the symbol "ㄹ."

가르다	/karŭda/	to divide
사람	/saram/	man
무리	/muri/	group
모르다	/morŭda/	do not know
다르다	/tarŭda/	to be different (from)
보리	/pori/	barley
학교로	/hakkyoro/	to school
바람	/param/	wind
리을	/riŭl/	the letter "ㄹ"
라디오	/radio/	radio
레슬링	/resŭlling/	wrestling
로맨스	/romɛnsŭ/	romance

ㄹ /l/ This sound is a voiced apico-alveolar lateral. You make it by putting the tip of your tongue against the gum ridge behind the upper teeth, so that the air escapes at the left side or both sides of the tongue. The front of the tongue is relatively flat, and the back somewhat lowered. The Korean lateral sound /l/ occurs only as a final sound of a syllable which is not followed by a vowel. It stands for a sound approximately like the /l/ in the English 'light,' 'lion,' 'lace,' and 'along,' etc., which occur before vowels; but it is not like the /l/ sound in the English 'still,' 'hilt,' or 'sold,' etc., occurring before a consonant or final sound.

발	/pal/	foot
길	/kil/	road
말	/mal/	horse
불	/pul/	fire
별	/pyəl/	star
울다	/ulda/	to cry
놀다	/nolda/	to play
갈다	/kalda/	to change
졸다	/cholda/	to doze
멀다	/məlda/	to be far
수술	/susul/	surgical operation

As you have seen in the above-mentioned examples, the "ㄹ," depending on the position, is different. When the "ㄹ" occurs between two vowels or in the initial position, it is a flap sound. However, when it occurs in the final position which is not followed by a vowel, it is a lateral sound. When this lateral sound /l/ is followed by the same consonant /l/, it also seems to cause foreigners trouble. You make it with the tip of your tongue touching firmly against the gum ridge behind the upper teeth, as in the production of a single /l/, then bringing it down with a strong voiced sound. Here are some examples:

몰라요	/mollayo/	I don't know.
달라요	/tallayo/	It's different.
졸라요	/chollayo/	Tighten it.
갈라요	/kallayo/	Divide it.
틀려요	/t'ŭllyəyo/	It's wrong.
길러요	/killəyo/	Raise (a dog).
골라요	/kollayo/	Choose.
찔러요	/ccilləyo/	Pierce.
놀라요	/nollayo/	I'm surprised.
울려요	/ullyəyo/	Ring it.

ㅇ /ng/ This sound is a voiced dorso-velar nasal. It is not difficult for English speakers. It stands for a sound approximately like /ng/ in the English 'song,' even though the Korean /ng/ is pronounced slightly stronger than its English counterpart. This sound, however, seems to cause Italians, and spanish speaking people a lot of distress. You make it by raising the back of your tongue against the soft palate, with air escaping through the nasal passage. (The soft palate is slightly dropped so as to open a passage from the pharynx to the nasal cavity.) If Italian or Spanish speakers want to practice this Korean /ng/ sound, hold the tip of your tongue down with your finger or with a flat tongue depresser used by medical doctors. While keeping the tip of your tongue down, try to make the back part of your tongue rise against the soft palate, as in the production of the /k/ sound. Let the air escape through the nasal passage the way it would for /m/ or /n/. In the beginning, you will feel the tip of your tongue trying to come up, but practice this sound until you don't have to hold it down with a tongue-depresser, and you will achieve the new habit which is necessary for the perfect control of this sound. This sound occurs only as a final sound in a syllable. In Korean, this sound never occurs at the beginning of an utterance. Remember that when there is no initial consonant at the beginning of a syllable in the writing system, the "ㅇ" is written, but has no sound value. It is only an orthographic "Filler."

성당	/səngdang/	church
공부	/kongbu/	study
명동	/myəngdong/	Myong-Dong
성명서	/Səngmyəngsə/	statement
정상	/chəngsang/	the summit
생각	/sɛnggak/	thought
응접실	/ŭngjəpsil/	reception room
사랑방	/sarangppang/	drawing room
장성	/changsəng/	Army general
평화	/p'yənghwa/	peace
청명	/ch'əngmyəng/	fairness
왕명	/wangmyəng/	the King's order
용기	/yonggi/	courage
옹고집	/onggojip/	stubbornness

ㄴ/n/ This sound is a voiced apico-alveolar nasal. It is similar to the English /n/ in 'nine.' It is made with the tip of your tongue touching against the gum ridge with the nasal passage open. You will have little difficulty with this sound.

누나	/nuna/	older sister
나누다	/nanuda/	to divide
누구	/nugu/	who
내내	/nɛnɛ/	from beginning to end
내년	/nɛnyən/	next year
노년	/nonyən/	old age
눈물	/nunmul/	tears

When it occurs in the final position, it is an unreleased sound. See the following examples:

돈	/ton/	money
논	/non/	rice-field
삼천	/samch'ən/	three thousand
손	/son/	hand
문	/mun/	door

However, when this sound /n/ is followed by the same consonant /n/, it seems to cause foreigners trouble. You make it with the tip of your tongue touching firmly against the gum ridge with the nasal passage open, then bringing it down with a strong voiced sound. See the following examples:

만나다	/mannada/	to meet
건너가다	/kənnəgada/	to go across
안내하다	/annɛhada/	to guide
인내	/innɛ/	perseverance
단념	/tannyəm/	abandonment
분노	/punno/	anger
천년	/ch'ənnyən/	one thousand years

When it is preceded or followed by /l/, it becomes a lateral sound /l/. However, there are many exceptions. See the following examples:

인류	/illyu/	human beings
논리	/nolli/	logic
불난리	/pulnalli/	the confusion of the fire
천리	/ch'əlli/	one thousand ri

ㅁ /m/ This sound is a voiced bilabial nasal. It is very similar to the corresponding English sound /m/. You make it by bringing your lips together with the nasal passage open. The velum is lowered and the vocal bands are producing voice through the nasal cavity.

마을	/maŭl/	village
미국	/miguk/	America
매일	/mɛil/	everyday
모자	/moja/	hat
무엇	/muət/	what
무우	/muu/	radish
미치다	/mich'ida/	to go mad
마음	/maŭm/	mind
꿈	/kkum/	dream
좀	/chom/	a little
섬	/səm/	island

ㅂ /p/ This sound is a bilabial stop. It stands for a sound approximately like the /p/ in the English 'episode,' which is usually followed by an unstressed vowel. You make it by bringing your lips together with the air passage closing, and then releasing it. When it occurs in the initial position of a syllable, it is a voiceless sound. It is pronounced with a very slight local aspiration. See the following examples :

배	/pɛ/	boat
바늘	/panŭl/	needle
벼	/pyə/	rice plant
보리	/pori/	barley
비	/pi/	broom
버선	/pəsən/	Korean socks
부채	/puch'ɛ/	fan

When it occurs between two voiced sounds, (such as all vowels and the nasal consonants /m, n, l, ng/, it is a voiced sound. The voiced "ㅂ" sound is transcribed by /b/. See the following examples:

수박	/subak/	watermelon
바보	/pabo/	fool
아버지	/abəji/	father
담배	/tambɛ/	cigarette
장부	/changbu/	account book
지난 밤	/chinanbam/	last night
신부	/sinbu/	bride
일본	/ilbon/	Japan

When it occurs in the final position of a syllable and is not followed by a vowel, it is an unreleased sound. See the following examples:

밥	/pap/	boiled rice
법	/pəp/	law
삽	/sap/	shovel
입	/ip/	mouth
연습	/yənsŭp/	practice
월급	/wəlgŭp/	monthly salary

Practice the difference between the Korean /p/ and /pp/.

비다	/pida/	삐다	/ppida/
바르다	/parŭda/	빠르다	/pparŭda
반하다	/panhada/	빤하다	/ppanhada/
벋다	/pətta/	뻗다	/ppətta/
벼	/pyə/	뼈	/ppyə/
불	/pul/	뿔	/ppul
부리	/puri/	뿌리	/ppuri/

ㅍ/p'/ This sound is a voiceless aspirated bilabial stop. It is very similar to the English /p/ sound, which is followed by a stressed vowel, as in 'powder' or 'peak.' You make it by first closing your lips tightly with the air passage closing, then releasing the lips with a strong puff of breath. The Korean aspirated sounds are pronounced with a stronger puff of breath than their English counterparts. If you hold a lighted match close to your mouth, those consonants with a puff of breath will put the match out, and those without a puff of breath will merely make it flicker.

파도	/p'ado/	wave
포도	/p'odo/	grapes
편도선	/p'yəndosən/	tonsils
판매	/p'anme/	selling
아프다	/ap'ŭda/	to be painful
소포	/sop'o/	parcel
살피다	/salp'ida/	to look about
방패	/pangp'ɛ/	shield

When this sound occurs in the final position and is not followed by a vowel, it is like the unreleased bilabial stop "ㅂ." See the following examples:

앞	/ap/	the front
옆	/yəp/	the side
잎	/ip/	leaves
늪	/nŭp/	swamp
짚	/chip/	straw

Practice the difference between the Korean /p/ and /p'/

반반하다	/panbanhada/	판판하다	/p'anp'anhada/
반도	/pando/	판도	/p'ando/
비다	/pida/	피다	/p'ida/
발	/pal/	팔	/p'al/
배다	/pɛda/	패다	/p'ɛda/
변하다	/pyənhada/	편하다	/p'yənhada/
불	/pul/	풀	/p'ul/
변모	/pyənmo/	편모	/p'yənmo/
병균	/pyənggyun/	평균	/p'ynggyun/

ㄷ/t/ This sound is an apico-alveolar stop. It stands for a sound approximately like the /t/ in the English 'kettle' or 'gratitude,' which usually occurs in the unstressed position of a word. You make it by bringing the tip of your tongue against the gum ridge behind the upper teeth, with the air passage closing, and then releasing it. When it occurs in the initial position, it is a voiceless sound. It is pronounced with a very slight local aspiration. See the following examples:

다시	/tasi/	again
더	/tə/	more
도라지	/traji/	broad bellflower
동물	/tongmul/	animal
대답	/tɛdap/	answer
뒤	/tü/	behind the back
돈	/ton/	money
단비	/tanbi/	timely rain

When it occurs between two voiced sounds, it is a voiced sound. The voiced "ㄷ" is phonetically transcribed by /d/. See the following examples:

도덕	/todək/	morals
기둥	/kidung/	pillar
사다리	/sadari/	ladder
동대문	/tongdɛmun/	East Gate
졸다	/cholda/	to doze

When it occurs in the final position of a syllable and is not followed by a vowel, it is an unreleased sound. See the following examples:

닫다	/tatta/	to close
묻다	/mutta/	to ask
곧	/kot/	soon

Practice the difference between the Korean /t/ and /tt/.

다지다	/tajida/	따지다	/ttajida/
데다	/teda/	떼다	/tteda/
다르다	/tarŭda/	따르다	/ttarŭda/
단것	/tangət/	딴것	/ttangət/
대다	/tɛda/	때다	/ttɛda/
대문	/tɛmun/	때문	/ttɛmun/
덜다	/təlda/	떨다	/ttəlda/
듣다	/tŭtta/	뜯다	/ttŭtta/
들	/tŭl/	뜰	/ttŭl/

ㅌ/t'/ This sound is a voliceless aspirated apico-alveolar stop. It is very similar to the English /t/ sound, which is followed by a stressed vowel, as in 'tape,' or 'tackle.' It is made by bringing the tip of your tongue against the gum ridge, with the air passage closing, then releasing it with a strong puff of breath. This sound /t'/ is never voiced. See the following examples:

태도	/t'ɛdo/	attitude
타다	/t'ada/	to ride
토지	/t'oji/	land
탁구	/t'akku/	ping-pong
특사	/t'ŭksa/	amnesty
턱	/t'ək/	the jaws
터지다	/t'əjida/	to get broken
토목	/t'omok/	engineering work

When it occurs in the final position of a syllable and is not followed by a vowel, it is like an unreleased apico-alveolar "ㄷ" sound. See the following examples:

밭	/pat/	dry field
끝	/kkŭt/	end
팥	/p'at/	red bean
뭍	/mut/	dryland
밑천	/mitch'ən/	capital (financial)

Practice the difference between the Korean /t/ and /t'/.

도끼	/tokki/	토끼	/t'okki/
덜다	/təlda/	털다	/t'əlda/
단식	/tansik/	탄식	/t'ansik/
다락	/tarak/	타락	/t'arak/
다작	/tajak/	타작	/t'ajak/
덕	/tək/	턱	/t'ək/
도굴	/togul/	토굴	/t'ogul/
덜덜	/təldəl/	털털	/t'əltəl/

ㄱ/k/ This sound is a dorso-velar stop. It stands for a sound approximately like the /k/ in the English word 'baker,' which usually occurs with an unstressed vowel. You make it by raising the back of your tongue against the soft palate, with the air passage closing, and then releasing it. When it occurs in the initial position of a word, it is a voiceless sound. It is pronounced with a very slight local aspiration. See the following examples:

개	/kɛ/	dog
고기	/kogi/	meat
구두	/kudu/	shoes
고적	/kojək/	historic remains
개인	/kɛin/	individual
가지다	/kajida/	to possess
기도	/kido/	prayer
거기	/kəgi/	there
고치다	/koch'ida/	to repair
그만두다	/kŭmanduda/	to stop (doing)

When it occurs between two voiced sounds, it is a voiced sound. The voiced "ㄱ" is transcribed by /g/. See the following examples:

사고	/sago/	accident
누구	/nugu/	who
가구	/kagu/	furniture
고구마	/koguma/	sweet potato
소개	/sogɛ/	introduction
지게	/chige/	A-frame
저기압	/chəgiap/	low pressure

When it occurs in the final position of a syllable and is not followed by a vowel, it is an unreleased sound. See the following examples:

서독	/sədok/	West Germany
미국	/miguk/	America
약국	/yakkuk/	pharmacy
목각	/mokkak/	engraving on wood
한국	/hanguk/	Korea

Practice the difference between the Korean /k/ and /kk/.

가지	/kaji/	까지	/kkaji/
괴다	/köda/	꾀다	/kköda/
기다	/kida/	끼다	/kkida/
갈다	/kalda/	깔다	/kkalda/
가다	/kada/	까다	/kkada/
개다	/kɛda/	깨다	/kkɛda/
개	/kɛ/	깨	/kkɛ/

ㅋ/k'/ This sound is a voiceless aspirated dorso-velar stop. It is very similar to the English /k/ sound, which usually occurs with a stressed vowel, as in 'kitchen,' 'kingdom,' 'cake,' etc. It is made by raising the back of your tongue against the soft palate with the air passage closing, then releasing it with a strong puff of air. This sound /k'/ is never voiced. See the following examples:

콩	/k'ong/	bean
코끼리	/k'okkiri/	elephant
키우다	/k'iuda/	to bring up
크다	/k'ŭda/	to be big
키	/k'i/	one's height
움켜쥐다	/umk'yəjüda/	to grip
경쾌	/kyəngk'we/	lightness
날카롭다	/nalk'aropta/	to be sharp
삼키다	/samk'ida/	to swallow

When it occurs in the final position and is not followed by a vowel, it is like an unreleased dorso-velar "ㄱ" sound. See the following examples:

부엌	/puək/	kitchen
새벽녘	/sɛbyəknyək/	around dawn
해질녘	/hɛjilnyək/	about sunset

Practice the difference between the Korean /k/ and /k'/.

공	/kong/	콩	/k'ong/
개다	/kɛda/	캐다	/k'ɛda/
겁	/kəp/	컵	/k'əp/
기	/ki/	키	/k'i/
근방	/kŭnbang/	큰방	/k'ŭnbang/

ㅈ/ch/ This sound is an unaspirated lamino-alveolar affricate. It stands for a sound approximately like the /ch/ or /tch/ in the English 'match,' which occurs with an unstressed vowel. This sound may cause German speakers trouble. You make it by touching the blade of your tongue to the gum ridge, somewhat in back of the usual position for /t/, then immediately release it with a friction, without a puff of breath. This sound /ch/, occurring as an initial sound of a syllable, is voiceless; it is pronounced with a very slight local aspiration. See the following examples:

지구	/chigu/	earth
저금	/chəgŭm/	savings
자동차	/chadongch'a/	car
잔치	/chanch'i/	feast
재료	/chɛryo/	material
주전자	/chujənja/	teakettle
지각	/chigak/	being late
자비	/chabi/	mercy

When it occurs between two voiced sounds, it is a voiced sound. The voiced "ㅈ" is phonetically transcribed by /j/. See the following examples:

우주	/uju/	universe
자주	/chaju/	frequently
저주	/chəju/	imprecation
가정	/kajəng/	home
아주	/aju/	very
제작	/chejak/	manufacture
전주	/chənju/	electric pole

When it occurs in the final position, and is not followed by a vowel, it is like an unreleased apico-alveolar "ㄷ" sound. See the following examples:

낮	/nat/	the daytime
젖	/chət/	milk
빚	/pit/	debt
찾다	/ch'atta/	to look for
꽂다	/kkotta/	to insert

Practice the difference between the Korean /ch/ and /cc/.

잠	/cham/	짬	/ccam/
재다	/chɛda/	째다	/ccɛda/
자다	/chada/	짜다	/ccada/
지다	/chida/	찌다	/ccida/
죄다	/chöda/	쬐다	/ccöda/

ㅊ/ch'/ This sound is a voiceless aspirated lamino-alveolar affricate. It is very similar to the English /ch/ sound, which usually occurs with a stressed vowel, as in 'charge,' 'choose,' etc. It is made by bringing the blade of your tongue to the gum ridge, somewhat in back of the usual position for /t/ ; then immediately release it with a friction and strong puff of breath. This sound /ch'/ is never voiced. See the following examples:

처녀	/ch'ənyə/	virgin, maid
채소	/ch'ɛso/	vegetables
찬송	/ch'ansong/	glorification
책상	/ch'ɛksang/	desk
청자	/ch'əngja/	celadon, blue pottery
기차	/kich'a/	train
눈치	/nunch'i/	tack, sense
기초	/kich'o/	basis
고추	/koch'u/	red pepper

When it occurs in the final position of a syllable and is not followed by a vowel, it is like an unreleased apico-alveolar "ㄷ" sound. See the following examples:

꽃	/kkot/	flower
빛	/pit/	light
숯	/sut/	charcoal
돛	/tot/	sail

Practice the difference between the Korean /ch/ and /ch'/.

장구	/changgu/	창구	/ch'anggu/
자다	/chada/	차다	/ch'ada/
절	/chəl/	철	/ch'əl/
조상	/chosang/	초상	/ch'osang/
종각	/chonggak/	총각	/ch'onggak/
주장	/chujang/	추장	/ch'ujang/
줍다	/chuptta/	춥다	/ch'uptta/
절하다	/chəlhada/	철하다	/ch'əlhada/
짐	/chim/	침	/ch'im/
진하다	/chinhada/	친하다	/ch'inhada/
주문	/chumun/	추문	/ch'umun/
주방	/chupang/	추방	/ch'upang/

ㅅ/s/ This sound is a voiceless apico-alveolar sibilant. It is very similar to the English /s/ sound, which usually occurs before consonants, as in 'street,' 'skate,' 'speed,' etc. You make it by bringing the tip of your tongue close to the gum ridge, (but without touching it) ; this forms a narrow passage through which air escapes with a hissing sound, due to a slight friction. The Korean sibilant "ㅅ" sound is a little softer than the English /s/. It is never voiced. See the following examples:

선생	/sənsɛng/	teacher
사냥	/sanyang/	hunting
신사	/sinsa/	gentleman
조사	/chosa/	investigation
수저	/sujə/	spoon and chopsticks
사람	/saram/	man
감사	/kamsa/	thanks
소식	/sosik/	news
세수	/sesu/	washing-up

When it occurs in the final position and is not followed by a vowel, it is like an unreleased apico-alveolar "ㄷ" sound. See the following examples:

갓	/kat/	Korean hat
곳	/kot/	place
못	/mot/	nail
빗	/pit/	comb
옷	/ot/	clothes
깃	/kit/	coat lapels

Practice the difference between the Korean /s/ and /ss/.

사다	/sada/	싸다	/ssada/
사전	/sajən/	싸전	/ssajən/
살살하다	/salsalhada/	쌀쌀하다	/ssalssalhada/
설다	/səlda/	썰다	/ssəlda/
솔다	/solda/	쏠다	/ssolda/
시	/si/	씨	/ssi/
살	/sal/	쌀	/ssal/
사리	/sari/	싸리	/ssari/
상방	/sangbang/	쌍방	/ssangbang/

ㅎ/h/ This sound is a voiceless glottal fricative. It is a very slight fricative sound, produced either by relaxed vocal bands or the walls of the pharynx with a puff of breath. The oral cavity is completely opened (unobstructed). It is very similar to the English /h/ sound as in 'heart.' See the following examples:

하루	/haru/	one day

가혹	/kahok/	harshness
호감	/hogam/	good impression
허영	/həyəng/	vanity
후회	/huhö/	contrition

When this sound /h/ is used with the diphthongs, (semivowel plus vowel), it is much more aspirated. It seems to cause American speakers some trouble. Here are some examples:

회의	/hwöi/	conference
휴가	/hyuga/	vacation
화요일	/hwayoil/	Tuesday
훨씬	/hwəlssin/	very much
휴지	/hyuji/	toilet paper
휴게실	/hyugesil/	recreation room
회사	/hwösa/	company
흉내	/hyungnɛ/	mimicry

When it occurs in the final position, it is like an unreleased apico-alveolar "ㄷ" sound.

히읗	/hiŭt/	the name of the letter "ㅎ"

The Final Compound Forms of Consonants :

When there are two different final consonants in a syllable, and they are not followed by a vowel, only one of them is pronounced. There is no rule as to which of them should be pronounced. See the following examples:

돐	/tol/	one full year
삶	/sam/	life
넋	/nək/	soul
닭	/tak/	domestic fowl
앉다	/antta/	to sit down
굵다	/kuktta/	to be thick
짧다	/ccaltta/	to be short
옮다	/omtta/	to move
핥다	/haltta/	to lick

RHYTHM :

English is spoken in a syncopated fashion, whereas Korean is spoken in a metronomic fashion. In English, you put a heavy stress on some syllables, and various weaker stresses on others. In Korean, however, each syllable is given moderate, approximately even stress, and has approximately equal length. Some syllables are heard more prominently than others. This prominence is mainly a matter of pitch. Therefore, in Korean, pitch is much more important than stress. You can hear stress in Korean, but it is because of certain consonants. Those consonants that are aspirated or glottalized are usually pronounced strongly. In English stress is the most important, but in Korean it is the least important. First of all, you should omit the English habit of syncopation. Try to time Korean syllables evenly, giving them equal stress.

INTONATION AND FINAL CONTOURS :

There are, generally speaking, four significant pitch levels in the Korean intonation : 1) high ; 2) medium-high ; 3) neutral ; 4) low. High and medium-high refer to accented levels ; neutral and low refer to unaccented levels. In English, accent indicates the way in which the four levels of stress occur. In Korean, the accent refers to the way in which pitch levels occur. In normal speech, Korean is spoken with neutral and low pitches. When emphasizing a certain word or phrase, or in an exclamatory expression, we speak with high and medium-high pitches. When there is a particle or conjunctive ending in a sentence, the intonation of the particle or conjunctive ending must be pronounced with low pitch. English speakers have a tendency to pronounce them with a rising pitch. So, it is extremely important to master the intonation of the Korean particle and conjunctive ending. In this book pitch levels are indicated at the end of phrases and sentences by one of the following pitches : rising pitch↗, falling pitch↘, dipping pitch⌒, sustaining pitch ¬, and double pitch (or high-low pitch) ↗. This latter indicates a kind of persuasive effort on the speaker's part, or a certain sweet reasonableness with which he/she hopes to win agreement, or a kind of obvious (needless-to-say) explanation.

AN INTRODUCTORY COURSE IN KOREAN

UNIT 1 인사 Greetings (1)

BASIC SENTENCES: MEMORIZE

인사	greeting
안녕	peace, well-being
박 선생님	Mr. Park
김 영 백	
1. 안녕하세요?↗ 박 선생님!	How are you, Mr. Park?
예	yes
김 선생님	Mr. Kim
박 용 득	
2. 예, 안녕하세요?↗ 김 선생님!	Fine (thank you), Mr. Kim, and you?
참	really, truly
오래간 만이에요	it's been a long time (since we've met)
김 영 백	
3. 참 오래간 만이에요.↷	It's really been a long time since we've met.
박 용 득	
4. 예, 오래간 만이에요.↷	Yes, it is.
요즈음	these days, nowadays
어떻게	how, in what, what manner
지내세요	(how) are you getting along
김 영 백	
5. 요즈음 어떻게 지내세요?↷	How are you getting along these days?
그저	just
그래요	so-so
박 용 득	
6. 그저 그래요.↷	(Just) so-so.

NOTES ON THE BASIC SENTENCES

1. 안녕하세요?↗ means literally 'Are you in peace?' This expression is an informal greeting used when addressing a superior, or in any situation requiring a salutation. It is interchangeable with 안녕하십니까? which is a formal greeting with no difference in meaning. It may be used at any time of the day. The English equivalent of this expression is 'How are you?,' 'Good morning,' 'Good afternoon,' 'Good evening.'
   박 선생님: 박 is the family name. 선생 means 'teacher' and 'doctor,' in both the medical and non-medical senses. As a term of address, it may be used independently, or attached to the family name. It is used to express respect and deference for the persons spoken to, but never used for oneself. -님 is the honorific suffix indicating reverence.
2. 예 'yes' is habitually pronounced 네. It is pronounced as it is written, however, in some areas such as Ch'ungchəng and Chəlla provinces. It is used as a regular response to a knock at the door, or the calling of one's name, or when one is greeted. The opposite word of 예 is 아니오 'no.' 아니오 is used in negative replies to questions, in contradictions and denials, and as an informal reply to apologies, expressions of thanks, and compliments.
3. 참 is the abbreviated form of 참으로 'really,' 'truly,' 'very.' 오래간 만이에요 means 'It's been a long time since we've met.' 오래간 means '(for) a long time' and 만 followed by the verb of identification -이에요 indicates passage of time. -만이에요 corresponds to the English 'after or since (the passage of such-and-such a stretch of time).'
5. 요즘 어떻게 지내세요?⌒ means 'How are you getting along these days?' 어떻게 means 'how?' or 'in what way?' When the final consonant -ㅎ of 어떻 is followed by the consonant -ㄱ in the following syllable, -ㄱ is pronounced as -ㅋ: like 어떠케.
6. 그저 그래요 is used when nothing particularly new has taken place or when something is not particularly good or bad.

DRILLS

ADDITIONAL VOCABULARY

대사님	ambassador	교수님	professor
신부님	Father, Catholic priest	목사님	pastor, minister

A. Substitution Drill

1. 안녕하세요? ↗ 박 선생님! — How are you, Mr. Park?
2. 안녕하세요? ↗ 김 선생님! — How are you, Mr. Kim?
3. 안녕하세요? ↗ 대사님! — How are you, Mr. Ambassador?
4. 안녕하세요? ↗ 신부님! — How are you, Father?
5. 안녕하세요? ↗ 김 교수님! — How are you, Professor Kim?
6. 안녕하세요? ↗ 목사님! — How are you, Pastor?

B. Substitution Drill

1. 오래간 만이에요, ⌒ 박 선생님! — It's been a long time since we've met, Mr. Park!
2. 오래간 만이에요, ⌒ 김 선생님! — It's been a long time since we've met, Mr. Kim!
3. 오래간 만이에요, ⌒ 대사님! — It's been a long time since we've met, Mr. Ambassador!
4. 오래간 만이에요, ⌒ 신부님! — It's been a long time since we've met, Father!
5. 오래간 만이에요, ⌒ 교수님! — It's been a long time since we've met, Professor!
6. 오래간 만이에요, ⌒ 목사님! — It's been a long time since we've met, Pastor!

C. Substitution Drill

1. 요즈음 어떻게 지내세요? ⌒ — How have you been, lately?
2. 김 선생님, 어떻게 지내세요? ⌒ — How have you been, Mr. Kim?
3. 박 선생님, 어떻게 지내세요? ⌒ — How have you been, Mr. Park?
4. 대사님, 어떻게 지내세요? ⌒ — How have you been, Mr. Ambassador?
5. 목사님, 어떻게 지내세요⌒? — How have you been, Pastor?
6. 교수님, 어떻게 지내세요? ⌒ — How have you been, Professor?
7. 신부님, 어떻게 지내세요? ⌒ — How have you been, Father?

D. Response Drill

1. 요즈음 어떻게 지내세요? ⌒ — 그저 그래요. ⌒
2. 김 선생님, 어떻게 지내세요? ⌒ — 그저 그래요. ⌒
3. 박 선생님, 어떻게 지내세요? ⌒ — 그저 그래요. ⌒
4. 대사님, 어떻게 지내세요? ⌒ — 그저 그래요. ⌒
5. 목사님, 어떻게 지내세요? ⌒ — 그저 그래요. ⌒
6. 교수님, 어떻게 지내세요? ⌒ — 그저 그래요. ⌒
7. 신부님, 어떻게 지내세요? ⌒ — 그저 그래요. ⌒

Korean Proverb :

시작이 반이다. Well begun is half done.

Notes :

It is difficult to find the time, the means or the courage to start a new project. If a task is once begun, it will probably be carried through. What is worth doing is worth doing promptly. Where there is no beginning, there is no ending.

UNIT 2 인사 Greetings (2)

BASIC SENTENCES : MEMORIZE

박 용 득

1. 김 선생님 아니세요 ? ↗ — Aren't you Mr. Kim ?

아니	Oh ! Good heavens !
이게	this
웬일	what matter, what reason
정말	really, truly
반갑다	to be glad

김 영 백

2. 아니 ! 이게 웬일이세요 ? ↗ 정말 반갑습니다. ↷ — Oh ! What's happening ? I am really glad to see you again.

가족	family

박 용 득

3. 가족들도 안녕하시구요 ? ↗ — Is your family well ?

덕택	favor, grace
잘	well
있다	to be

김 영 백

4. 예, 모두 덕택에 잘 있어요. ↷ — Yes, they are all well (thank you for your interest).

형님	older brother
-한테	to
안부	regards, best wishes
전하다	to convey, to pass

박 용 득

5. 형님한테 안부 전해 주세요. ↷ — Please give my best regards to your brother.

김 영 백

6. 예, 전해 드리지요. ↷ — I certainly will.

NOTES ON THE BASIC SENTENCES

2. 아니 is an exclamatory form expressing surprise, disbelief, annoyance, or merely emphasis. It corresponds to the English 'Dear me!,' 'What!,' 'Good heavens!,' 'Well!,' 'Oh my!,' or 'Why!' See the following examples:

아니 이게 웬 일이에요?	Good heavens! What happened?
아니 또 왔어요?	What! Did you come again?
아니 뭘 하세요?	Oh my! What are you doing?

이게 is a contraction of 이것이. 이것 means 'this thing' and -이 is the subject particle. See the following examples:

이게 (이것이) 뭐에요?	What's this?
그게 (그것이) 책이에요.	That is a book.
저게 (저것이) 좋아요.	That over there is good.

웬일이세요: 웬 means 'what'; 일 means 'a matter,' 'an affair,' or 'a work,' etc.; -이세요 is the verb ending. Therefore, it means 'What's all this?,' 'What's the matter?,' 'What's got into you?,' 'What's up?,' 'What's happening?' It is used when you meet a friend or a well-known person unexpectedly.

3. 가족들도: 가족 means 'members of a family'; -들 is the pluralizing suffix; -도 is the particle meaning 'also,' 'too.' 안녕하시구요 is slightly less formal than 안녕하시고요. -고 is the coordinate non-final ending meaning 'and.' (You will study this pattern later in detail).

4. 덕택에 indicates the speaker's appreciation for interest shown in his/her personal affairs: 'thanks for asking,' 'thanks to you,' or appreciation for assistance that has been received. It always implies pleasant or favorable information.

5. The particle -한테 'to (a person),' following a noun referring to animate beings, is used to indicate the receiver of an action, or the one for whom something is done or exists.
   전해 주세요 means literally 'Please pass...'
   The pattern -아(-어, -여) 주다 is used when a speaker requests something for himself, or when he does something for an inferior or an equal.

6. 전해 드리지요 is the polite answer to the above request. The pattern -아(-어, -여) 드리다 is used when a speaker does something for a person whose social status is superior or equal to his, or to anyone present to whom one is being polite.

DRILLS

A. Substitution Drill

1. 김 선생님 아니세요? ↗	Aren't you Mr. Kim?
2. <u>박 선생님</u> 아니세요? ↗	Aren't you Mr. Park?
3. <u>신부님</u> 아니세요? ↗	Aren't you the Father?
4. <u>목사님</u> 아니세요? ↗	Aren't you the Pastor?
5. <u>김 교수님</u> 아니세요? ↗	Aren't you Professor Kim?
6. <u>대사님</u> 아니세요? ↗	Aren't you the Ambassador?

B. Substitution Drill

1. 김 선생님, 이게 웬일이세요? ⌒	Mr. Kim! What a surprise!
2. <u>박 선생님</u>, 이게 웬일이세요? ⌒	Mr. Park! What a surprise!
3. <u>신부님</u>, 이게 웬일이세요? ⌒	Father! What a surprise!
4. <u>목사님</u>, 이게 웬일이세요? ⌒	Pastor! What a surprise!
5. <u>김 교수님</u>, 이게 웬일이세요? ⌒	Professor Kim! What a surprise!
6. <u>대사님</u>, 이게 웬일이세요? ⌒	Mr. Ambassador! What a surprise!

C. Substitution Drill

1. 김 선생님, 반갑습니다. ⌒	I'm glad to meet you, Mr. Kim!
2. <u>박 선생님</u>, 반갑습니다. ⌒	I'm glad to meet you, Mr. Park!
3. <u>대사님</u>, 반갑습니다. ⌒	I'm glad to meet you, Mr. Ambassador!
4. <u>목사님</u>, 반갑습니다. ⌒	I'm glad to meet you, Pastor!
5. <u>신부님</u>, 반갑습니다. ⌒	I'm glad to meet you, Father!
6. <u>교수님</u>, 반갑습니다. ⌒	I'm glad to meet you, Professor!

D. Substitution Drill

1. 가족들도 안녕하시구요? ⌒	And how is your family?
2. <u>대사님</u>도 안녕하시구요? ⌒	And how is the Ambassador?
3. <u>목사님</u>도 안녕하시구요? ⌒	And how is the Pastor?
4. <u>김 교수님</u>도 안녕하시구요? ⌒	And how is the Professor Kim?
5. <u>신부님</u>도 안녕하시구요? ⌒	And how is the Father?
6. <u>김 선생님</u>도 안녕하시구요? ⌒	And how is Mr. Kim?

E. Substitution Drill

1. 형님한테 안부 전해 주세요. ⌒	Please give my best regards to your brother.
2. <u>박 선생님</u>한테 안부 전해 주세요. ⌒	Please give my best regards to Mr. Park.

3. 김 선생님한테 안부 전해 주세요.↷ Please give my best regards to Mr. Kim.
4. 신부님한테 안부 전해 주세요.↷ Please give my best regards to Father.
5. 목사님한테 안부 전해 주세요.↷ Please give my best regards to Pastor.
6. 교수님한테 안부 전해 주세요.↷ Please give my best regards to Professor.
7. 대사님한테 안부 전해 주세요.↷ Please give my best regards to Ambassador.

F. Response Drill

1. 형님한테 안부 전해 주세요.↷ 예, 전해 드리지요.↷
2. 박 선생님한테 안부 전해 주세요.↷ 예, 전해 드리지요.↷
3. 김 선생님한테 안부 전해 주세요.↷ 예, 전해 드리지요.↷
4. 신부님한테 안부 전해 주세요.↷ 예, 전해 드리지요.↷
5. 목사님한테 안부 전해 주세요.↷ 예, 전해 드리지요.↷
6. 교수님한테 안부 전해 주세요.↷ 예, 전해 드리지요.↷
7. 대사님한테 안부 전해 주세요.↷ 예, 전해 드리지요.↷

UNIT 3 김치 Kimch'i

BASIC SENTENCES: MEMORIZE

배추김치	paech'ugimch'i (pickled cabbages)
있어요?	do you have? or does it exist?
박 용 득	
1. 배추김치 있어요? ↗	Do you have paech'ugimch'i?
미안합니다	I'm sorry.
없어요	do not have or does not exist
김 영 백	
2. 미안합니다. ⌐배추김치가 없어요. ⌒	I am sorry. We don't have any.
그럼	well then, or if that is true
박 용 득	
3. 그럼, 깍두기 있어요? ↗	Well then, do you have kkaktugi?
예	yes
김 영 백	
4. 예, 깍두기 있어요. ⌒	Yes, we have kkaktugi.
좀	some or a little
주세요	please give (me)
박 용 득	
5. 깍두기 좀 주세요. ⌒	Give me some kkaktugi.
잠깐	a little while
기다려 주세요	please wait
김 영 백	
6. 잠깐 기다려 주세요. ⌒	Just a moment. (lit. Please wait for a while.)

NOTES OT THE BASIC SENTENCES

1. 배추김치 'white cabbage kimch'i' is generally eaten in the winter.
   김치 'kimch'i' : In preparing kimch'i, cabbages are washed thoroughly, sprinkled with salt and left to soak overnight until they soften. Then they are washed again several times and mixed with other ingredients such as garlic, red pepper, celery, green onions, sliced fresh turnips, ginger, salted fish and oysters. The mixture is put into big jars which are kept in a place away from severe heat and cold. There are various kinds of kimch'i : 열무김치 'young radish kimch'i' and 오이김치 'cucumber kimch'i' are eaten in the summer. 동치미 'chopped radishes pickled in salt water' is yet another kind of kimch'i.
2. 미안합니다 is used to make an apology or to express feelings of sorrow or regret.
   배추김치가 : -가 is the subject particle. You will study it in detail soon.
3. 깍두기 : 'hot pickles of chopped radishes.' It is eaten year round.
4. 잠깐 기다려 주세요 'Just a moment,' (Lit. 'Wait a moment, please.'), is a polite request. Just remember it as a useful expression. This pattern will be studied in detail later.

STRUCTURE NOTES

I. Styles of Speech :

There are many kinds of speech styles in the Korean language, namely, 1) the informal-polite style ; 2) the formal-polite style ; 3) the plain style ; 4) the intimate style ; 5) the authoritative style ; 6) the familiar style. It is not easy for a foreigner to choose the appropriate speech style for any given situation, nor is it easy for him to determine the basis for social superiority and inferiority in the Korean social system. The longer a person is associated with the Korean language, the easier it will become to recognize appropriate speech styles. This requires, however, a thorough knowledge of the Korean social structure, as well as a sufficient amount of practice. The style of speech to be used is determined by the formality of the situation, the individuals involved, and one's personal relationship to these individuals. It is best for the foreigner to use the (formal or informal) polite style of speech, except when addressing children. In conversation between people occupying different positions in the Korean social structure, (for example, superior and inferior, employer and employee, teacher and student, customer and salesgirl, etc.), the person of lower position normally uses a more polite and formal style of speech. Generally speaking, men use the formal speech style more often than the informal speech style. On the other hand, women use the informal speech style more frequently. People of equal status in the Korean social system use the formal-polite speech style in conversation, unless they have a more friendly relationship.

II. The Informal-Polite Style:

We have introduced the informal-polite style (yo-style) first because not only is it widely used, especially in the Seoul and Kyongki area, but it is also simple and colloquial. When the Korean war broke out in 1950, the majority of displaced people from Seoul took refuge in other regions of the country. Consequently, the Seoul dialect (yo-style) spread out all over the country and has become the standard dialect used in Korea. The informal-polite style is most commonly used when speaking to people of a higher social status than the speaker. For example, this style is used with teachers, doctors, priests, high officials, parents, grandparents, elder brothers and sisters, etc., or in any situation where the speaker wishes to talk politely, but informally. The informal-polite style is interchangeable with the formal-polite style, without diminishing politeness.

1. When the final vowel of the verb stem (not necessarily the final letter) is ㅏ or ㅗ, it takes -아요. Here are some examples:

Stem:	Ending:	Original form:	Contraction:
가	-아요	(가아요)	가요
오	-아요	(오아요)	와요
싸	-아요	(싸아요)	싸요
좋	-아요	좋아요	(absent)

2. When the final vowel of the stem is any other vowel, or when the past or future tense infixes have been attached to the stem, it takes -어요. Here are some examples:

Stem:	Ending:	Original form:	Contraction:
가르치	-어요	가르치어요	가르쳐요
읽	-어요	읽어요	(absent)
먹	-어요	먹어요	(absent)
갔	-어요	갔어요	(absent)
왔	-어요	왔어요	(absent)
먹겠	-어요	먹겠어요	(absent)

하겠	-어요	하겠어요	(absent)

3. When the verb is a -하다 verb, it takes -여요. Here are some examples:

Stem:	Ending:	Original form:	Contraction:
일하	-여요	일하여요	일해요
사랑하	-여요	사랑하여요	사랑해요
말하	-여요	말하여요	말해요

Note:

In colloquial speech, the contracted forms are used more frequently than the original forms.

III. Korean Verbs:

English verbs change according to person and number ('I go,' 'he goes,' 'they go'). This is not so in Korean. Korean verbs are impersonal, do not change according to number, and always occur at the end of sentences. They indicate the occurrence of an action or the existence of a state without grammatical reference to a subject and can occur by themselves as complete standard sentences. For example, 가요 can mean: 'I go,' 'He goes,' 'They go,' 'We go,' etc. As a general rule, however, Korean verbs refer to the speaker in a statement or the person addressed in a question, unless the person is indicated through other means. For example: 김치 있어요? 'Do you have kimch'i?' 예, 김치 있어요 'Yes, I (we) have kimch'i.' In general, Korean verbs are classified into four kinds of verbs:

1. Action Verbs:

Action verbs indicate action or movement performed by the grammatical subject represented by the verb. In other words, they bring out the idea that 'SOMEONE DOES SOMETHING' or 'SOMETHING TAKES PLACE.'

2. Description verbs:

Description verbs indicate the quality or condition of the grammatical subject. In other words, they bring out the idea that 'SOMEONE OR SOMETHING IS A CERTAIN WAY.'

3. The Verb of Existence:

The verb of existence indicates existence, location, or possession. In other words, it is a verb used to say that '(SOMETHING) EXISTS,' or '(SOMEONE OR SOMETHING) IS LOCATED (in a place), 'or '(SOMEONE) HAS (SOMETHING).'

4. The Verb of Identification:

The verb of identification is a COPULAR linking the subject with its predicate. It is a verb used to indicate equality.

IV. The Verb 있다 :

The verb 있다 indicates existence, location or possession. It is used to say that '(something) exists,' or '(something) is located (in a place),' or '(somebody) has (something).' Its opposite verb is 없다 '(something) does not exist,' etc. It is extremely important to distinguish between the use of 있다 and 이다. The verb 이다 'equal' will be studied soon.

Examples :

김치 있어요?	Do you have kimch'i? or Is there kimch'i?
김치 없어요.	We have no kimch'i. or There is no kimch'i.
찬물 있어요?	Do you have cold water? or Is there cold water?
찬물 없어요.	We have no cold water. or There is no cold water.

DRILLS

ADDITIONAL VOCABULARY

더운 물	hot water	포도	grapes
끓인 물	boiled water	사과	apple(s)
홍차	black tea	복숭아	peach(es)
설탕	sugar	수박	watermelon
코피	coffee	참외	melon

A. Substitution Drill

1. 물 있어요? ↗	Do you have water?
2. 더운 물 있어요? ↗	Do you have hot water?
3. 찬물 있어요? ↗	Do you have cold water?
4. 끓인 물 있어요? ↗	Do you have boiled water?
5. 홍차 있어요? ↗	Do you have black tea?
6. 설탕 있어요? ↗	Do you have sugar?
7. 코피 있어요? ↗	Do you have coffee?
8. 포도 있어요? ↗	Do you have grapes?
9. 복숭아 있어요? ↗	Do you have peaches?

B. Substitution Drill

1. 예, ⌒물 있어요. ⌒	Yes, we have water.
2. 예, ⌒찬물 있어요. ⌒	Yes, we have cold water.
3. 예, ⌒더운 물 있어요. ⌒	Yes, we have hot water.
4. 예, ⌒참외 있어요. ⌒	Yes, we have melon.
5. 예, ⌒복숭아 있어요. ⌒	Yes, we have peaches.
6. 예, ⌒수박 있어요. ⌒	Yes, we have watermelon.
7. 예, ⌒사과 있어요. ⌒	Yes, we have apples.
8. 예, ⌒설탕 있어요. ⌒	Yes, we have sugar.

C. Substitution Drill

1. 아니오, ⌒김치 없어요. ⌒	No, we have no kimch'i.
2. 아니오, ⌒끓인 물 없어요. ⌒	No, we have no boiled water.
3. 아니오, ⌒홍차 없어요. ⌒	No, we have no black tea.
4. 아니오, ⌒설탕 없어요. ⌒	No, we have no sugar.
5. 아니오, ⌒포도 없어요. ⌒	No, we have no grapes.
6. 아니오, ⌒사과 없어요. ⌒	No, we have no apples.
7. 아니오, ⌒복숭아 없어요. ⌒	No, we have no peaches.
8. 아니오, ⌒수박 없어요. ⌒	No, we have no watermelon.

D. Substitution Drill

1. 찬물 좀 주세요. ⌒	Give me some cold water, please.
2. 더운 물 좀 주세요. ⌒	Give me some hot water, please.
3. 끓인 물 좀 주세요. ⌒	Give me some boiled water, please.
4. 설탕 좀 주세요. ⌒	Give me some sugar, please.
5. 코피 좀 주세요. ⌒	Give me some coffee, please.
6. 수박 좀 주세요. ⌒	Give me some watermelon, please.
7. 사과 좀 주세요. ⌒	Give me some apples, please.
8. 복숭아 좀 주세요. ⌒	Give me some peaches, please.

E. Response Drill

1. 찬물 있어요? ↗	예, 찬물 있어요. ⌒
2. 더운 물 있어요? ↗	예, 더운 물 있어요. ⌒
3. 끓인 물 있어요? ↗	예, 끓인 물 있어요. ⌒
4. 설탕 있어요? ↗	예, 설탕 있어요. ⌒
5. 코피 있어요? ↗	예, 코피 있어요. ⌒
6. 수박 있어요? ↗	예, 수박 있어요. ⌒
7. 사과 있어요? ↗	예, 사과 있어요. ⌒

8. 복숭아 있어요? ↗ — 예, 복숭아 있어요. ⌒

F. Response Drill

1. 찬물 있어요? ↗ — 아니오, 찬물 없어요. ⌒
2. 더운 물 있어요? ↗ — 아니오, 더운 물 없어요. ⌒
3. 끓인 물 있어요? ↗ — 아니오, 끓인 물 없어요. ⌒
4. 설탕 있어요? ↗ — 아니오, 설탕 없어요. ⌒
5. 코피 있어요? ↗ — 아니오, 코피 없어요. ⌒
6. 깍두기 있어요? ↗ — 아니오, 깍두기 없어요. ⌒
7. 김치 있어요? ↗ — 아니오, 김치 없어요. ⌒
8. 복숭아 있어요? ↗ — 아니오, 복숭아 없어요. ⌒

UNIT 4 한국말 Korean Language

BASIC SENTENCES : MEMORIZE

이것	this
무슨	what (kind of)
책	book
곽 상 훈	
1. 이것이 무슨 책이에요 ? ⌒	What (kind of a) book is this ?
한국말	Korean (language)
로 빈 슨	
2. 한국말 책이에요. ⌒	It's a Korean language book.
그럼	well (then), if that is so
공부하다	to study
곽 상 훈	
3. 그럼, 한국말을 공부하세요 ? ↗	So, are you studying Korean ?
그럼요	sure
그런데	but
어렵다	to be difficult
로 빈 슨	
4. 그럼요, 그런데 한국말이 어려워요. ⌒	Sure, but Korean is difficult.
어디	where
-에서	at, in
곽 상 훈	
5. 어디에서 공부하세요 ? ⌒	Where are you studying ?
대사관	embassy
로 빈 슨	
6. 대사관에서 공부해요. ⌒	I'm studying at the embassy.

NOTES ON THE BASIC SENTENCES

1. 이 것 means literally 'this thing.' 이- is a demonstrative modifying the dependent noun (bound noun) -것. It occurs only as a modifier of the following noun. 이 것 indicates a thing or things close to the speaker, i.e. 'this thing (here).'

그것 (a) indicates a thing or things removed from the speaker but close to the person addressed, i.e. 'near you.'

(b) It is also used to refer to a thing or things within sight but slightly removed from both speaker and person addressed, i.e. neither 'here' nor 'there.'

(c) Sometimes it is also used to indicate that thing or those things already under discussion.

저것 indicates a thing or things 'over there,' i.e. relatively far removed from both the speaker and the person addressed.

이것	'this thing'	이분	'this person'
그것	'that thing' or 'it'	그분	'that person,' 'he,' 'she'
저것	'that thing over there'	저분	'that person over there,' 'he, she (over there)'

무슨- means 'what (kind of),' 'some (kind of).' It occurs only as a modifier of a subsequent noun or bound form. However, 무엇 'what,' 'something' is always followed by function words such as the subject particle -가/-이, the object particle -를/을, or the verb of identification -이다. Here are some examples.

그것이 무슨 책이에요?	What (kind of a) book is that?
무엇이 좋아요?	What is good?
무엇을 공부하세요?	What do you study?
이것이 무엇이에요?	What's this?

4. 그럽요 is used when you agree with someone's statement or when you answer in the affirmative. It corresponds to the English 'You are right,' 'That's right,' 'That's what it is,' 'So it is,' 'Of course.'

어렵(다) means 'to be difficult,' 'to be hard.' Its opposite word is 쉽(다) 'to be easy.' 어렵(다) and 쉽(다) are irregular verbs. The final consonant -ㅂ of the stem, when followed a vowel, changes into 우. Study the following examples.

어려워요.	It's difficult
쉬워요.	It's easy.

The -ㅂ irregular verbs will be studied in detail later. Do not be too concerned about it now.

STRUCTURE NOTES

I. The Particle -가/-이 :

In English, the order in which you put words determines the meaning of the sentence. For instance, 'Philip likes Helen' and 'Helen likes Philip' both contain three words, but the meaning is quite different. Therefore, in English the word-order is very important. In Korean, however, the little words called PARTICLES indicate relations between words. Some Korean particles (such as -가/-이, -를/-을, or -는/-은) indicate a particular word order or stress-intonation pattern in English. For example, the particle -가/-이 is used to indicate the SUBJECT of a sentence. Study the following examples:

이것이 책이에요.	THIS is a book.
김치가 좋아요.	KIMCH'I is good.

Notes:

1. Korean particles never occur at the beginning of words, but are directly attached to the preceding noun.
2. Korean particles are never preceded by a pause, but are rather pronounced as part of the word to which they are attached.
3. -이 is used after a word ending in a consonant;
   -가 is used after a word ending in a vowel.

II. The verb 이다 :

This verb -이다 is the COPULA which links a subject with its predicate. It is used to indicate equality or identification. The English equivalent of this verb is 'equal.' Whenever an English sentence containing 'is' makes sense if you substitute 'equal' for 'is,' the Korean equivalent is -이 다. It is extremely important to distinguish between the use of 있다 'exist' and -이다 'equal.'

Examples:

이것이 책이에요.	This is a book (This=a book).
저분이 김 선생님이에요.	He (over there) is Mr. Kim (He=Mr. Kim).
그것이 물이에요.	That is water (That=water).
그것이 사과에요..	That is an apple (That=an apple).

그것이 홍차에요. That is black tea (That=black tea).

Notes:

1. This verb -이다 is never preceded by a pause, but is rather pronounced as part of the word to which it is attached.
2. After a vowel, the verb -이- may be dropped in colloquial speech, as well as in writing. In the beginning, however, it is better to practice with -이- even after a vowel.
3. This verb -이다 is ordinarily preceded by a noun or pronoun.

III. The object Particle -를/-을 :

We studied the particle -가/-이 which indicates the subject of a sentence. However, the particle -를/-을 indicates that the word to which it is attached is the DIRECT OBJECT of a transitive verb.

Examples:

한국말을 공부해요.	I study Korean.
옷을 입으세요.	Put on your clothes, please.
책을 읽어요.	I am reading a book.
개를 봐요.	I see a dog.

Notes:

1. This particle -를/-을 is never preceded by a pause, but is rather pronounced as part of the word to which it is attached.
2. -를 is used after words ending in a vowel;
   -을 is used after words ending in a consonant.

IV. The Particle -에서… : 'at,' 'in'

The particle -에서, depending on the context or situation, has two quite different meanings. One is 'at' or 'in,' indicating the place where an action takes place. The particle -에서 is attached to a noun, and is always followed by an action verb. It is used when you DO something in a place.

Examples:

학교에서 공부해요.	I study at school.
방에서 놀아요.	I play in the room.
마당에서 산책해요.	I take a walk in the garden.
사무실에서 일해요.	I work in the office.
식당에서 먹어요.	I eat in the dining room.

Another meaning is 'from,' indicating a starting point, separation, source, cause, etc.

Examples :

그분이 미국에서 와요.	He is coming from America.
세 시에 집에서 떠나요.	I leave (from) my house at three o'clock.

V. The Honorific Infix -(으)시- :

The infix -(으)시- is used to indicate respect and reverence on the part of the speaker for the person spoken to. This infix is used whenever one addresses or refers to persons of superior social standing, (for example : teachers, doctors, priests, high officials, parents, grandparents, elder brothers and sisters, etc.). It is also used to express reverence in addressing strangers and casual aquaintances, but never used for oneself.

Examples :

그분이 가세요.	He is going.
그분이 오세요.	He is coming.
그분이 옷을 입으세요.	He is getting dressed.
저분이 누구세요 ?	Who is that person over there ?
안녕하세요 ?	How are you ?

Notes :

2. The honorific is formed by inserting the infix -(으)시- between the verb stem and the endings, (such as -아(-어, -여)요, -ㅂ니다, -ㅂ니까 ? and -ㅂ시오, etc.).

2. -시- is used after verb stems ending in a vowel ;
   -으시- is used after verb stems ending in a consonant.

DRILLS

ADDITIONAL VOCABULARY

공책	notebook	일하다	to work
책상	desk	산책하다	to take a walk
연필	pencil	쉬다	to rest
분필	chalk	누가	who
만년필	fountain pen	영어	English
가르치다	to teach	편지	letter

읽다 to read
쓰다 to write
보다 to see

학교 school
사무실 office
마당 garden
방 room

A. Substitution Drill

1. 이것이 무엇이에요? ↷ What's this (thing)?
2. 그것이 무엇이에요? ↷ What's that (thing)?
3. 저것이 무엇이에요? ↷ What's that (thing) over there?

B. Substitution Drill

1. 그것이 책이에요. ↷ That's a book.
2. 그것이 공책이에요. ↷ That's a notebook.
3. 그것이 한국말 책이에요. ↷ That's a Korean language book.
4. 그것이 책상이에요. ↷ That's a desk.
5. 그것이 연필이에요. ↷ That's a pencil.
6. 그것이 분필이에요. ↷ That's a piece of chalk.
7. 그것이 만년필이에요. ↷ That's a fountain pen.

C. Substitution Drill

1. 무엇을 공부하세요? ↷ What do you study?
2. 무엇을 가르치세요? ↷ What do you teach?
3. 무엇을 읽으세요? ↷ What do you read?
4. 무엇을 쓰세요? ↷ What do you write?
5. 무엇을 보세요? ↷ What do you see?

D. Substitution Drill

1. 어디에서 공부하세요? ↷ Where do you study?
2. 어디에서 가르치세요? ↷ Where do you teach?
3. 어디에서 일하세요? ↷ Where do you work?
4. 어디에서 산책하세요? ↷ Where do you take a walk?
5. 어디에서 쉬세요? ↷ Where do you rest?

E. Substitution Drill

1. 누가 가르치세요? ↷ Who teaches (you)?
2. 누가 일하세요? ↷ Who is working?
3. 누가 산책하세요? ↷ Who takes a walk?
4. 누가 쉬세요? ↷ Who is resting?
5. 누가 공부하세요? ↷ Who is studying?

F. Response Drill

1. 무엇을 공부하세요? ↷	한국말을 공부해요. ↷
2. 무엇을 가르치세요? ↷	영어를 가르쳐요. ↷
3. 무엇을 읽으세요? ↷	책을 읽어요. ↷
4. 무엇을 쓰세요? ↷	편지를 써요. ↷
5. 무엇을 보세요? ↷	이 책상을 보아요. ↷

G. Response Drill

1. 어디에서 공부하세요? ↷	대사관에서 공부해요. ↷
2. 어디에서 가르치세요? ↷	학교에서 가르쳐요. ↷
3. 어디에서 일하세요? ↷	사무실에서 일해요. ↷
4. 어디에서 산책하세요? ↷	마당에서 산책해요. ↷
5. 어디에서 쉬세요? ↷	방에서 쉬어요. ↷

H. Response Drill

1. 누가 가르치세요? ↷	선생님이 가르치세요. ↷
2. 누가 일하세요? ↷	목사님이 일하세요. ↷
3. 누가 산책하세요? ↷	대사님이 산책하세요. ↷
4. 누가 쉬세요? ↷	교수님이 쉬세요. ↷
5. 누가 공부하세요? ↷	신부님이 공부하세요. ↷

Notes:

누가 and 누구:

누가 'who' is always used as a subject, whereas 누구 'who' or 'whom' (in most cases 누구 means 'whom') is used with the verb -이다 indicating equality or identification. 누구 is also used with particles such as -를/-을 'object particle,' -한테 'to,' -한테서 'from,' -하고 같이 'with,' etc.

UNIT 5 거리에서 On the Street

BASIC SENTENCES : MEMORIZE

실례합니다	Excuse me
미국 대사관	American Embassy
이 현 숙	
1. 실례합니다. ⟶ 미국 대사관이 어디에 있어요 ? ⌒	Excuse me. Where is the American Embassy ?
광화문	Kwanghwa-mun
천 선 희	
2. 미국 대사관요 ? ↗	The American Embassy ?
광화문에 있어요. ⌒	It is at Kwanghwamun.
여기서	from here
멀다	to be far
이 현 숙	
3. 여기서 멀어요 ? ↗	Is it far from here ?
가깝다	to be near
택시로	by taxi
십 분쯤	about 10 minutes
걸리다	to take (time)
천 선 희	
4. 아니오, 가까워요. ⌒	No, it's nearby.
택시로 십 분쯤 걸려요. ⌒	It takes about 10 minutes by taxi
감사하다	to thank
이 현 숙	
5. 감사합니다. ⟶	Thank you.
천 선 희	
6. 천만에요. ⌒	You're welcome.

NOTES ON THE BASIC SENTENCES

1. 실례합니다 means literally 'I am commiting a rudeness.' It is used when you trouble someone, when you interrupt what someone is doing, when you excuse yourself from someone's presence for a short time.
2. 광화문 'The Gate of Transformation by Light.' At the time of Yi dynasty Kwanghwa-mun was located at the south end of the Kyongbok Palace area. In front of Kwanghwa-mun was a broad avenue lined on either side with the various goverment department buildings, leading up from the Chong-no intersection (which is also called 'Kwang-hwa mum,' but meaning Kwanghwa-mun Crossing.)
3. 여기서 is a contraction of 여기에서. 여기 is a place-word indicating 'this place' or 'here.' Let's study the following words referring to place, in comparison with words indicating thing. (저기 bears an obvious resemblance to 저것 'that thing over there').

여기	'this place' or 'here'	이것	'this thing'
거기	'that place' or 'there'	그것	'that thing'
저기	'that place over there' or 'over there'	저것	'that thing over there'

4. 십 분쯤 : When the classifier -분 is used with Chinese numbers, it indicates 'minute.' When it is used with Korean numbers, however, it indicates 'honored people.'

Examples :

일 분 'one minute'	한 분 'one person'
이 분 'two minutes'	두 분 'two persons'
삼 분 'three minutes'	세 분 'three persons'

Note particularly that 이분 can also mean 'this honored person.' The suffix -쯤 indicates 'approximation.' You will study the classifiers in detail in the following lesson.

5. 감사합니다↘ is used as a courteous expression of gratitude or appreciation. It is interchangeable with 고맙습니다, making no difference in meaning.
6. 천만에요⌒ is used as a formal reply to apologies, expressions of thanks, and formal, respectful recognition.

STRUCTURE NOTES

I. The Formal-Polite Style:

The formal-polite style is used in addressing strangers, casual acquaintances, superiors, and social inferiors in formal situations. A person would use polite words (honorifics), when referring to persons of equal or superior social standing.

Examples:

(A) Interrogative Sentences:

안녕하십니까? ↗	How are you? or Are you well?
김치 있습니까? ↗	Do you have kimch'i? or Is there kimch'i?
이것이 좋습니까? ↗	Is this good?

Notes:

-ㅂ니까 is used after verb stems (or the honorific infix -시-) ending in a vowel;

-습니까 is used after verb stems ending in a consonant.

(B) Declarative Sentences:

감사합니다.	Thank you.
물 없습니다.	There is no water.
이것이 좋습니다.	This is good.

Notes:

-ㅂ니다 is used after verb stems (or the honorific infix -시-) ending in a vowel;

-습니다 is used after verb stems ending in a consonant.

(C) Imperative Sentences:

찬물 좀 주십시오. ⌒	Give me some cold water, please.
가십시오. ⌒	Go, please.
오십시오. ⌒	Come (here), please.
옷을 입으십시오. ⌒	Get dressed, please.

Notes:

-십시오 is used after verb stems ending in a vowel;

-으십시오 is used after verb stems ending in a consonant.

(D) Propositive Sentences:

갑시다. ↘	Let's go.

옵시다. ↘	Let's come.
옷을 입읍시다. ↘	Let's get dressed.

Notes:
-ㅂ시다 is used after verb stems ending in a vowel;
-읍시다 is used after verb stems ending in a consonant.

II. The Particle -에… : 'at', 'in'

In the previous lesson, we studied the particle -에서, indicating the place where an action takes place. It is used when you do something in a place. However, this particle -에 'at' or 'in' indicates that something or someone is STATIONARY in a place. Therefore, this particle -에 is attached to nouns, and is always followed by inactive verbs, such as 있다 'to exist,' 없다 'do not exist,' 많다 'to be many,' 살다 'to live, etc.'

Examples:

그분이 사무실에 계십니다. ↘	He is in the office.
그 책상이 교실에 있습니다. ↘	That desk is in the classroom.
그 분이 서울에 삽니다. ↘	He lives in Seoul.
그 연필이 방에 없습니다. ↘	That pencil is not in the room.
휴게실에 사람이 많습니다. ↘	There are many people in the recreation room.

Notes:
This particle -에, depending on the context or situation, has many different meanings: 'to' indicating specific direction; 'at,' 'in' or 'on' indicating time; 'for' indicating reference or relation; 'by' or 'with' indicating agent; etc. Generally speaking, a place or time word to which the particle -에 is attached can be made more specific. They are taken up later.

III. The Particle -(으)로… : 'with,' 'by (means of)'

The particle -(으)로, preceded by a noun, indicates the means with which someone performs an action, or by which someone drives or moves about.

Examples:

만년필로 쓰십시오. ↘	Please write with a fountain pen.
칼로 끊으십시오. ↘	Please cut it with a knife.
무엇으로 가시겠습니까? ⌒	How will you go?
기차로 가겠습니다. ↘	I will go by train.

버스로 갑시다. ↘ Let's go by bus.

Notes :

1. -로 is used after nouns ending in a vowel or the consonant -ㄹ; -으로 is used after nouns ending in all consonants except -ㄹ.
2. There are other uses of -(으)로 which will be studied later.

IV. The Chinese Derived Numbers :

In Korea, there are two kinds of cardinal numbers which correspond to the English numbers: the native Korean numbers, and the Chinese numbers, (numbers of Chinese origin). Let's study the Chinese numbers first. The native Korean numbers will be introduced later. The Chinese numbers are used mostly counting money, telling time, etc. The higher numbers require special attention, since they frequently cause difficulties for English speakers.

0 영	10 십	20 이십	30 삼십	40 사십
1 일	11 십일	21 이십일	31 삼십일	41 사십일
2 이	12 십이	22 이십이	32 삼십이	42 사십이
3 삼	13 십삼	23 이십삼	33 삼십삼	43 사십삼
4 사	14 십사	24 이십사	34 삼십사	44 사십사
5 오	15 십오	25 이십오	35 삼십오	45 사십오
6 육	16 십육	26 이십육	36 삼십육	46 사십육
7 칠	17 십칠	27 이십칠	37 삼십칠	47 사십칠
8 팔	18 십팔	28 이십팔	38 삼십팔	48 사십팔
9 구	19 십구	29 이십구	39 삼십구	49 사십구

50 오십	60 육십	70 칠십	80 팔십	90 구십
51 오십일	61 육십일	71 칠십일	81 팔십일	91 구십일
52 오십이	62 육십이	72 칠십이	82 팔십이	92 구십이
53 오십삼	63 육십삼	73 칠십삼	83 팔십삼	93 구십삼
54 오십사	64 육십사	74 칠십사	84 팔십사	94 구십사
55 오십오	65 육십오	75 칠십오	85 팔십오	95 구십오
56 오십육	66 육십육	76 칠십육	86 팔십육	96 구십육
57 오십칠	67 육십칠	77 칠십칠	87 팔십칠	97 구십칠
58 오십팔	68 육십팔	78 칠십팔	88 팔십팔	98 구십팔
59 오십구	69 육십구	79 칠십구	89 팔십구	99 구십구

100 백	1,000 천	10,000 만	100,000 십만
200 이백	2,000 이천	20,000 이만	1,000,000 백만
300 삼백	3,000 삼천	30,000 삼만	10,000,000 천만
400 사백	4,000 사천	40,000 사만	100,000,000 억
500 오백	5,000 오천	50,000 오만	1,000,000,000 십억
600 육백	6,000 육천	60,000 육만	10,000,000,000 백억
700 칠백	7,000 칠천	70,000 칠만	100,000,000,000 천억
800 팔백	8,000 팔천	80,000 팔만	1,000,000,000,000 조
900 구백	9,000 구천	90,000 구만	

Notes :

1. The digits from 1 to 10 and the digits 100 (백), 1,000 (천), 10,000 (만), 100,000,000 (억), 1,000,000,000,000 (조) are words. All other numbers are merely combinations of these words.
2. Two-digit numbers are read in terms of the number of tens, and units. Study the following examples :
   25 이십 오 (lit. 2 tens, 5)
   32 삼십 이 (lit. 3 tens, 2)
   67 육십 칠 (lit. 6 tens, 7)
3. Three-digit numbers are read in terms of the number of hundreds, tens, and units. A zero is usually dropped in the spoken number, when it occurs within a written number. Study the following examples :
   375 삼백 칠십 오 (lit. 3 hundreds, 7 tens, 5)
   567 오백 육십 칠 (lit. 5 hundreds, 6 tens, 7)
   603 육백 삼 (lit. 6 hundreds, 3)
4. Four-digit numbers are read in terms of the number of thousands, hundreds, tens, and units. Study the following examples :
   2356 이천 삼백 오십 육 (lit. 2 thousands, 3 hundreds, 5 tens, 6)
   3781 삼천 칠백 팔십 일 (lit. 3 thousands, 7 hundreds, 8 tens, 1)
5. When the individual elements occur in certain compounds, their pronunciation may be slightly altered. See the following examples :
   십만 → 심만(one hundred thousand)
   백만 → 뱅만(one million)

DRILLS

ADDITIONAL VOCABULARY

교실	classroom	자동차	car
집	house	지하철	subway
화장실	rest room	자전거	bicycle
기차	train	비행기	airplane

A. Substitution Drill

1. 미국 대사관이 어디에 있어요? ⌒	Where is the American Embassy?
2. 김치가 어디에 있어요? ⌒	Where is the kimch'i?
3. 더운 물이 어디에 있어요? ⌒	Where is the hot water?
4. 끓인 물이 어디에 있어요? ⌒	Where is the boiled water?
5. 홍차가 어디에 있어요? ⌒	Where is the black tea?
6. 설탕이 어디에 있어요? ⌒	Where is the sugar?
7. 포도가 어디에 있어요? ⌒	Where are the grapes?
8. 사과가 어디에 있어요? ⌒	Where are the apples?

B. Substitution Drill

1. 그것이 사무실에 있어요. ⌒	That is in the office.
2. 그것이 학교에 있어요. ⌒	That is in the school.
3. 그것이 마당에 있어요. ⌒	That is in the garden.
4. 그것이 방에 있어요. ⌒	That is in the room.
5. 그것이 교실에 있어요. ⌒	That is in the classroom.
6. 그것이 집에 있어요. ⌒	That is in the house.
7. 그것이 대사관에 있어요. ⌒	That is in the Embassy.
8. 그것이 화장실에 있어요. ⌒	That is in the rest room.

C. Substitution Drill

1. 택시로 십 분쯤 걸려요. ⌒	It takes about 10 minutes by taxi.
2. 기차로 십 분쯤 걸려요. ⌒	It takes about 10 minutes by train.
3. 자동차로 십 분쯤 걸려요. ⌒	It takes about 10 minutes by car.
4. 지하철로 십 분쯤 걸려요. ⌒	It takes about 10 minutes by subway.
5. 자전거로 십 분쯤 걸려요. ⌒	It takes about 10 minutes by bicycle.
6. 비행기로 십 분쯤 걸려요. ⌒	It takes about 10 minutes by airplane.

D. Substitution Drill

1. 공부합시다. ↘	Let's study.

2. 기다립시다. ↘	Let's wait.
3. 만년필로 씁시다. ↘	Let's write with a fountain pen.
4. 일합시다. ↘	Let's work.
5. 산책합시다. ↘	Let's take a walk.
6. 쉽시다. ↘	Let's rest.

E. Substitution Drill

1. 공부하십시오. ↘	Please study.
2. 책을 읽으십시오. ↘	Please read a book.
3. 기다리십시오. ↘	Please wait.
4. 산책하십시오. ↘	Please take a walk.
5. 편지를 쓰십시오. ↘	Please write a letter.
6. 찬물 좀 주십시오. ↘	Please give me some cold water.

F. Response Drill

1. 반갑습니까? ↗	예, 반갑습니다. ↘
2. 미안합니까? ↗	예, 미안합니다. ↘
3. 어렵습니까? ↗	예, 어렵습니다. ↘
4. 책을 읽습니까? ↗	예, 책을 읽습니다. ↘
5. 편지를 씁니까? ↗	예, 편지를 씁니다. ↘
6. 산책합니까? ↗	예, 산책합니다. ↘

G. Response Drill

1. 실례합니다. ¬	천만에요. ⌒
2. 미안합니다. ¬	천만에요. ⌒
3. 감사합니다. ¬	천만에요. ⌒
4. 고맙습니다. ¬	천만에요. ⌒

UNIT 6 물건사기 Shopping

BASIC SENTENCES : MEMORIZE

어서	please
오다	to come
이 경 희	
1. 어서 오세요. →	Do come in, please.
얼마에요	how much is it
박 성 철	
2. 이 사과 얼마에요? ⌒	How much are these apples?
한 개에	per one
사백 원	400 won
이 경 희	
3. 한 개에 사백 원이에요. ⌒	They're four hundred won each.
아이구	Oh!, Oh my!
왜	why
이렇게	so, that much
비싸다	to be expensive
싸게	cheaply
박 성 철	
4. 아이구! 왜 이렇게 비싸요? ⌒	Oh! Why is it so expensive?
좀 싸게 합시다. ↘	Let's make it a little cheaper.
정찰제	a fixed price system
이 경 희	
5. 여기는 정찰제에요. ⌒	It's a fixed price system.
박 성 철	
6. 그래요? ↗ 사과 열 개 주세요. ⌒	Really? Ten apples, please.
고맙다	to be grateful
이 경 희	
7. 고맙습니다. → 안녕히 가세요. →	Thank you. Good bye.
박 성 철	
8. 안녕히 계세요. →	Good bye.

NOTES ON THE BASIC SENTENCES

1. 어서 오세요 means literally 'Do come in, please.' This expression is used when you greet a customer entering a store or restaurant, etc. hospitably and with courtesy or cordiality. It is also used to greet a guest or a new comer.
   오다 'to come' regularly indicates motion toward the speaker's position, whereas 가다 'to go' indicates motion away from the speaker's position. For example, while you are talking on the telephone (from outside) with someone in the office, 'I will come to the office tomorrow,' the Korean equivalent of it is 내일 사무실에 가겠어요 (Lit. 'I will go to the office tomorrow.'). When you are acturally in the office, you would say 내일 사무실에 오겠어요 (Lit. 'I will come to the office tomorrow.').
2. 이 사과 means 'this apple.' 이-, 그- and 저- are demonstratives which occur only as modifiers of a following noun or dependent noun, (bound noun). When these demonstratives 이-, 그- and -저 are used with the dependent nouns -것 and -분, they must be written together, like 이것, 그것, 저것, 이분, 그분, 저분; but when they are used with other nouns or other dependent nouns, they must be written separately. See the following examples:
   이 곳 'this place' 그 책상 'that desk'
   저 사람 'that man over there'
3. 한 개 means 'one piece,' 'one item.' The classifier -개 'a piece' is used with Korean numbers. Some Korean numbers are slightly altered when they occur as modifiers of subsequent classifiers. These are: 하나, 둘, 셋, 넷, and 스물. See the following examples:

Korean numbers:	Number+Classifier:	Meaning:
하나	한 분	'one person'
둘	두 분	'two persons'
셋	세 분	'three persons'
넷	네 분	'four persons'
스물	스무 분	'twenty persons'

   These same numbers may change again according to the classfiers used. See the Structure Notes of this lesson.
   -원 is a Korean money classifier. It is used always with the Chinese derived numbers. According to the currency exchange rate in effect at the time of publication of this book (1990), about 710 won equals one U.S. dollar.
4. 아이구 is a variant of 아이고. 아이구 is an exclamatory expression of pain,

complaint, grudge, hardship, surprise, etc. It is also a bewailing sound cry heard in a mourner's house when someone's parents or grandparents have died.

7. 고맙습니다 is used as a courteous expression of gratitude or appreciation. It is interchangeable with 감사합니다, making no difference in meaning.
안녕히 가세요 means literally : 'Please go in peace.' It is used as a concluding remark at parting.
   (a) When you meet someone on the street, both of you use 안녕히 가세요 to say good-bye.
   (b) When you are leaving after visiting someone, the person who stays at home or in the office says to you 안녕히 가세요.
8. 안녕히 계세요 means literally : 'Please stay in peace.' The person who leaves says to the person who stays behind : 안녕히 계세요.

STRUCTURE NOTES

I. The Native Korean Numbers :

We have already studied the Chinese numbers in the previous lesson. Here we introduce the native Korean numbers, which are used mostly when counting things, events or persons.

0 공	10 열	20 스물
1 하나	11 열 하나	30 서른
2 둘	12 열 둘	40 마흔
3 셋	13 열 셋	50 쉰
4 넷	14 열 넷	60 예순
5 다섯	15 열 다섯	70 일흔
6 여섯	16 열 여섯	80 여든
7 일곱	17 열 일곱	90 아흔
8 여덟	18 열 여덟	99 아흔 아홉
9 아홉	19 열 아홉	100 백

Notes :

The numbers from 하나 'one' to 아흔 아홉 'ninety nine' are of native Korean origin, and those from 백 'one hundred' on are of Chinese origin. Many Koreans, however, habitually count from one hundred by using a combination of the Chinese numbers and the native Korean numbers. For example : 백 하나 'one hundred and one.' 백 둘 'one hundred and two,' etc.

II. Classifiers:

The classifiers are words used with numerals to designate countable or measurable objects. In English, there are words for counting a certain number of people, paper, cigarettes, or for measuring a certain quantity of gasoline, time, money, distance, etc.: 'ten persons,' 'five sheets of paper,' 'three packs of cigarettes,' 'two gallons of gasoline,' 'five o'clock,' 'two hundred won,' 'one kilometer,' etc. These words which combine with numerals to NAME, COUNT or MEASURE objects are called classifiers. They do not occur as independent words, but are used always with numerals. The use of either Chinese or Korean numbers varies depending on the classifiers.

Used with Korean numbers:

-갑	'packs (of cigarettes)'	한 갑	두 갑	세 갑	네 갑
-개	'items,' 'units,' 'objects'	한 개	두 개	세 개	네 개
-권	'volumes'	한 권	두 권	세 권	네 권
-달	'months'	한 달	두 달	석 달	넉 달
-대	'vehicles,' 'machines'	한 대	두 대	세 대	네 대
-마리	'fish,' 'animals'	한 마리	두 마리	세 마리	네 마리
-말	'measure of about 18 litres'	한 말	두 말	서 말	너 말
-번	'times'	한 번	두 번	세 번	네 번
-병	'bottles'	한 병	두 병	세 병	네 병
-분	'honored people'	한 분	두 분	세 분	네 분
-사람	'people'	한 사람	두 사람	세 사람	네 사람
-살	'years of age'	한 살	두 살	세 살	네 살
-시	'o'clock'	한 시	두 시	세 시	네 시
-시간	'hours'	한 시간	두 시간	세 시간	네 시간
-자	'measure of about 33.3m'	한 자	두 자	석 자	넉 자
-자루	'small stick (pencil, brush, etc.)	한 자루	두 자루	세 자루	네 자루
-장	'thin, flat objects (sheets)'	한 장	두 장	석 장	넉 장
-채	'buildings,' 'houses'	한 채	두 채	세 채	네 채

Used with Chinese numbers:

-개월	'months'	일 개월	이 개월	삼 개월	사 개월
-년	'years'	일 년	이 년	삼 년	사 년
-도	'degrees'	일 도	이 도	삼 도	사 도
-배	'multiples'	배	이 배	삼 배	사 배
-번	'serial numbers'	일 번	이 번	삼 번	사 번
-번선	'track numbers'	일 번선	이 번선	삼 번선	사 번선

-번지	'lot numbers'	일 번지	이 번지	삼 번지	사 번지
-분	'minutes'	일 분	이 분	삼 분	사 분
-원	'won'	일 원	이 원	삼 원	사 원
-월	'months of the year'	일 월	이 월	삼 월	사 월
-인	'people'	일 인	이 인	삼 인	사 인
-인분	'portions'	일 인분	이 인분	삼 인분	사 인분
-일	'days of the month'	일 일	이 일	삼 일	사 일
-주일	'weeks'	일 주일	이 주일	삼 주일	사 주일
-층	'floors'	일 층	이 층	삼 층	사 층
-호실	'room numbers'	일 호실	이 호실	삼 호실	사 호실

Notes :

1. When the classifier -번 is used with Korean numbers, it indicates 'times.' But when it is used with Chinese numbers, it indicates 'serial numbers.' See the following examples :

한 번	'one time'	일 번	'number one'
두 번	'two times'	이 번	'number two'
세 번	'three times'	삼 번	'number three'
네 번	'four times'	사 번	'number four'

2. When the classifier -분 is used with Chinese numbers, it indicates time in 'minutes.' But when it is used with Korean numbers, it indicates 'person.' See the following examples :

한 분	'one person'	일 분	'one minute'
두 분	'two persons'	이 분	'two minutes'
세 분	'three persons'	삼 분	'three minutes'
네 분	'four persons'	사 분	'four minutes'

3. The classifier 주일 'weeks' may be used with both Korean numbers and Chinese numbers. It is used, however, mostly with Chinese numbers.

III. The Particle -에… : 'for,' 'per'

We have already studied the particle -에, when it indicates static location. The particle -에, depending on the context or situation, can also indicate proportion.

Examples :

그것을 3,000 원에 샀어요.	I bought it for three thousand won.
500 원에 팔아요.	We sell it for five hundred won.
이 책은 한 권에 10,000 원입니다.	This book is 10,000 won per volume.

두 달에 한번 거기에 가요.	I go there once every two months.
하루에 두번 먹어요.	I eat twice a day.
이 종이 한 장에 얼마에요?	How much is this paper per sheet?

IV. The Honorific Verbs:

We have studied the honorific infix -(으)시- and the honorific suffix -님, which indicate reverence and respect on the part of the speaker for the person spoken to. There are also honorific verbs which indicate reverence for the person spoken to. Like all honorifics, these verbs are used only in polite speech in reference to persons other than oneself. They are used whenever one addresses or refers to persons of superior social standing: older people, teachers, doctors, priests, high officials, parents, foreign guests, learned men, and so forth. The honorific verbs, however, are limited in number. If you memorize the following list of verbs, you can handle most of the honorific verbs. The honorific verbs are used mostly with the honorific suffixes -님 and -께서, (-께서 is the honorific form of the subject particle -가/이).

Plain:	Honorifics:	Meaning:
먹다	잡수시다	to eat
자다	주무시다	to sleep
있다	계시다	to exist, to be
말하다	말씀하다	to say, to tell

Notes:

말씀하다 'to say,' 'to tell' is the honorific verb of 말하다. Therefore, 말씀하다 is used to express respect and reverence for persons spoken to, but is never used for oneself. For example: 선생님이 그렇게 말씀하셨습니다 'The teacher said so,' 내가 그렇게 말했습니다 'I said so.' (말씀하다 is a combination of the noun 말씀 'word,' 'speech' and the verb 하다 'to do.') When the noun 말씀, however, is used with the humble verb 드리다 'to give' (the humble verbs will be studied in detail later), it can be used for one's own acts. For example: 제가 선생님한테 말씀드렸습니다 'I told it to my teacher.'

DRILLS

ADDITIONAL VOCABULARY

먹다	to eat	잡수시다	to eat
자다	to sleep	주무시다	to sleep

말하다	to say	말씀하다	to say
계시다	to exist, to be	동생	younger brother
담배	cigarettes	쉽다	to be easy
맥주	beer	크다	to be big
종이	paper	작다	to be small
생선	fish	싸다	to be cheap
좋다	to be good	맛있다	to be delicious

A. Substitution Drill

1. 이 사과 얼마에요? ↷	How much are these apples?
2. 이 설탕 얼마에요? ↷	How much is this sugar?
3. 이 참외 얼마에요? ↷	How much are these melons?
4. 이 수박 얼마에요? ↷	How much are these watermelons?
5. 이 책상 얼마에요? ↷	How much is this desk?
6. 이 만년필 얼마에요? ↷	How much is this fountain pen?
7. 이 연필 얼마에요? ↷	How much is this pencil?
8. 이 공책 얼마에요? ↷	How much is this notebook?

B. Substitution Drill

1. 담배 한 갑 주세요. ↷	Give me one pack of cigarettes, please.
2. 책 두 권 주세요. ↷	Give me two volumes of books, please.
3. 자동차 두 대 주세요. ↷	Give me two cars, please.
4. 맥주 세 병 주세요. ↷	Give me three bottles of beer, please.
5. 종이 석 장 주세요. ↷	Give me three sheets of paper, please.
6. 생선 네 마리 주세요. ↷	Give me four fish, please.
7. 집 두 채 주세요. ↷	Give me two houses, please.
8. 사과 세 개 주세요. ↷	Give me three apples, please.

C. Substitution Drill

1. 한 개에 400 원이에요. ↷	They're 400 won each.
2. 한 갑에 500 원이에요. ↷	It's 500 won for one pack (of cigarettes).
3. 한 권에 4,000 원이에요. ↷	It's 4,000 won per volume.
4. 한 장에 20 원이에요. ↷	It's 20 won for one sheet (of paper).
5. 한 마리에 1,000 원이에요. ↷	It's 1,000 won for one fish.
6. 한 병에 2,500 원이에요. ↷	It's 2,500 won for one bottle (of beer).

D. Substitution Drill

1. 왜 이렇게 비싸요? ↷	Why is it so expensive?

2. 왜 이렇게 <u>쉬워요</u>? ⌒ Why is it so easy?
3. 왜 이렇게 <u>커요</u>? ⌒ Why is it so big?
4. 왜 이렇게 <u>작아요</u>? ⌒ Why is it so small?
5. 왜 이렇게 <u>싸요</u>? ⌒ Why is it so cheap?
6. 왜 이렇게 <u>어려워요</u>? ⌒ Why is it so difficult?

E. Pattern Drill

Teacher: 좀 더 쌉니다. ↘ It's a little cheaper.
Student: 좀 더 싸게 합시다. ↘ Let's make it a little cheaper.

1. 좀 더 큽니다. ↘ 좀 더 크게 합시다. ↘
2. 좀 더 작습니다. ↘ 좀 더 작게 합시다. ↘
3. 좀 더 쉽습니다. ↘ 좀 더 쉽게 합시다. ↘
4. 좀 더 어렵습니다. ↘ 좀 더 어렵게 합시다. ↘
5. 좀 더 좋습니다. ↘ 좀 더 좋게 합시다. ↘
6. 좀 더 맛있습니다. ↘ 좀 더 맛있게 합시다. ↘
7. 좀 더 재미있습니다. ↘ 좀 더 재미있게 합시다. ↘
8. 좀 더 비쌉니다. ↘ 좀 더 비싸게 합시다. ↘

F. Response Drill

1. 무엇을 잡수십니까? ↘ <u>불고기</u>를 먹습니다. ↘
2. 어디에서 주무십니까? ↘ <u>방</u>에서 잡니다. ↘
3. 누가 방에 계십니까? ↘ <u>동생</u>이 방에 있습니다. ↘
4. 누가 그렇게 말씀하십니까? ↘ <u>학생</u>이 그렇게 말합니다. ↘

UNIT 7 몇 시에 What Time?

BASIC SENTENCES: MEMORIZE

몇 시에	(at) what time
집에서	from the house
떠나다	to leave

이 현 숙

1. 몇 시에 집에서 떠나세요? ⌒ What time do you leave the house?

곽 순

2. 일곱 시에 떠나요. ⌒ I leave at seven o'clock.

일찍	early
학교	school
얼마나 멀어요	how far is it

이 현 숙

3. 그렇게 일찍요? ↗ 집에서 학교까지 얼마나 멀어요? ⌒ So early? How far is it from the house to school?

자동차로	by car

곽 순

4. 자동차로 삼십 분쯤 걸려요. ⌒ It takes about 30 minutes by car.

몇 시부터	from what time
수업	class, lesson
시작하다	to begin

이 현 숙

5. 몇 시부터 수업을 시작하세요? ⌒ What time does class begin?

곽 순

6. 아홉 시에 수업을 시작해요. ⌒ Class begins at nine o'clock.

몇 시간	how many hours
하루에	a day

이 현 숙

7. 하루에 몇 시간 공부하세요? ⌒ How many hours do you study a day?

곽 순

8. 하루에 네 시간 공부해요. ⌒ I study four hours a day.

NOTES ON THE BASIC SENTENCES

1. 몇 시에 집에서 떠나세요? : 몇-, depending on the context or situation, has two different meanings: 'what' or 'how many.' It occurs only as a modifier of a subsequent noun or bound form. See the following examples:

몇 시에요?	What time is it?
선생님이 몇 분이에요?	How many teachers are there?

The classifier -시 'o'clock' is used always with Korean numbers. 떠나다 'to leave' is pure Korean, while 출발하다 'to leave' is derived from Chinese. Both verbs can be used with either of the two particles -에서 and -을/-를. Here are examples.

집에서 떠나요 (출발해요).	I leave the house.
집을 떠나요 (출발해요).	I leave the house.

3. 얼마나, depending on the context or situation, has different meanings: '(about) how much,' '(about) how long,' '(about) how many,' 'how...,' '(about) how far,' etc. When the particle -(이)나 is used with the word 몇 'how many' or 얼마 'how much (many),' it indicates 'approximation.' Study the following examples.

그것을 얼마나 주었어요?	How much did you pay for that?
한국말을 얼마나 공부하셨어요?	How long have you been studying Korean?
책이 얼마나 있으세요?	How many books do you have?
여기서 얼마나 멀어요?	How far is it from here?

5. 수업 : 수업을 하다 means 'to give lessons,' while 수업을 받다 means 'to take a lesson.' The verb 시작하다 'to begin' is used always with the object particle -을/-를.

7. 시간, as an independent word, means 'time.' However, when it is used with Korean numbers, it is a classifier meaning 'hour.' See the following examples:

시간이 있습니까? ↗	Do you have time?
두 시간 공부합니다. ↘	I study for two hours.

STRUCTURE NOTES

I. The Particle -에··· : 'at,' 'on,' 'in'

We have already studied the particle -에 which indicates that something or someone is STATIONARY in a place. The particle -에, depending on the context or situation, can also indicate the time at which something takes place. In general, time words are divided into two main groups : (a) those which are followed by the particle -에 : e.g., 한 시에 'at one o'clock,' (used with hours of the day), 월요일에 'on Monday,' (used with days of the week), 이월에 'in February,' 1990 년에 'in 1990,' (used with months and years) ; (b) those which occur without the particle -에 : e.g., 오늘 'today,' 내일 'tomorrow,' 모레 'the day after tomorrow,' '어제' 'yesterday,' 그저께 'the day before yesterday,' 지금 'now,' etc.

Examples :

한 시에 갑시다.↘	Let us go at one o'clock.
두 시 반에 끝납니다.↘	I finish at two thirty.
월요일에 공부합니다.↘	I study on Monday.
이월에 가십니까?↗	Do you go in February?
1990년에 했습니다.↘	I did it in 1990.

II. The Particle -까지… : 'until,' 'by,' 'to'

The particle -까지, preceded by a time expression, indicates a specific time to which an action or condition continues.

Examples :

두 시까지 공부했습니다.↘	I studied until two o'clock.
지금까지 가르쳤습니다.↘	I taught until now.
몇 시까지 일하셨습니까?⌒	Until what time did you work?
삼 월까지 있었습니다.↘	I stayed until March.
언제까지 계시겠습니까?⌒	Until when will you stay?
내일까지 오십시오.↘	Come by tomorrow.
거기에 세 시까지 있겠습니다.↘	I'll be there by three.
아침부터 저녁까지 잤습니다.↘	I slept from morning till night.

This particle -까지 is also attached to place words to mean 'as far as,' '(all the way) to.' See the following examples :

어디까지 가십니까?⌒	How far are you going?
부산까지 갑시다.↘	Let's go as far as Pusan.
여기서부터 저기까지 걸어가세요.↘	Please walk from here to there.

III. The Particle -부터… : 'from'

The particle -부터, following time or place words, indicates a starting point in time or a place from which a physical movement begins. It is used mostly with time words.

Examples :

아홉 시부터 공부합시다. ↘	Let's study from nine o'clock.
오늘부터 아주 바쁩니다. ↘	I am very busy from today.
몇 시부터 공부를 시작하세요 ? ⌒	What time do you start studying ?
세 시부터 여기 있었어요. ↘	I have been here since three o'clock.
그분은 아침부터 밤까지 일해요. ↘	He works from morning till night.
열 시부터 지금까지 잤어요. ↘	I slept from ten o'clock until now.
한국말부터 공부합시다. ↘	Let's study Korean first.
이것부터 잡수세요. ↘	Please eat this one first.
여기서부터 시작했어요. ↘	I began (from) here.

DRILLS

ADDITIONAL VOCABULARY

바쁘다	to be busy	세탁소	laundry
한가하다	to have spare time, to have leisure	일어나다	to get up
숙제를 하다	to do one's homework	시작하다	to begin
등산하다	to climb a mountain	반	half
남자	a man, a male	수영하다	to swim
외교관	a diplomat	여자	a woman, a girl

A. Substitution Drill

1. 몇 시에 집에서 떠나세요 ? ⌒	What time do you leave the house ?
2. 몇 시에 산책하세요 ? ⌒	What time do you take a walk ?
3. 몇 시에 주무세요 ? ⌒	What time do you sleep ?
4. 몇 시에 일하세요 ? ⌒	What time do you work ?
5. 몇 시에 책을 읽으세요 ? ⌒	What time do you read a book ?
6. 몇 시에 공부하세요 ? ⌒	What time do you study ?
7. 몇 시에 일어나세요 ? ⌒	What time do you get up ?
8. 몇 시에 일을 시작하세요 ? ⌒	What time do you start working ?

B. Substitution Drill

1. 몇 시간 공부하세요 ? ⌒	How many hours do you study ?
2. 몇 시간 주무세요 ? ⌒	How many hours do you sleep ?
3. 몇 시간 잡수세요 ? ⌒	How many hours do you eat ?
4. 몇 시간 가르치세요 ? ⌒	How many hours do you teach ?

5. 몇 시간 산책하세요? ↷	How many hours do you (take a) walk?
6. 몇 시간 일하세요? ↷	How many hours do you work?
7. 몇 시간 쉬세요? ↷	How many hours do you rest?
8. 몇 시간 책을 읽으세요? ↷	How many hours do you read a book?

C. Substitution Drill

1. 한 시에 공부합시다. ↘	Let's study at one o'clock.
2. 두 시 이십 분에 공부합시다. ↘	Let's study at two twenty.
3. 세 시 십오 분에 공부합시다. ↘	Let's study at three fifteen.
4. 네 시 사십 분에 공부합시다. ↘	Let's study at four forty.
5. 다섯 시 십 분에 공부합시다. ↘	Let's study at five ten.
6. 여섯 시 반에 공부합시다. ↘	Let's study at six thirty.
7. 일곱 시 십 분에 공부합시다. ↘	Let's study at seven ten.
8. 여덟 시 오십 분에 공부합시다. ↘	Let's study at eight fifty.

D. Substitution Drill

1. 학생이 모두 몇 분이에요? ↷	How many students are there altogether?
2. 선생님이 모두 몇 분이에요? ↷	How many teachers are there altogether?
3. 동생이 모두 몇 분이에요? ↷	How many younger brothers do you have?
4. 남자가 모두 몇 분이에요? ↷	How many men are there altogether?
5. 여자가 모두 몇 분이에요? ↷	How many women are there altogether?
6. 대사님이 모두 몇 분이에요? ↷	How many ambassadors are there altogether?
7. 외교관이 모두 몇 분이에요? ↷	How many diplomats are there altogether?
8. 교수님이 모두 몇 분이에요? ↷	How many professors are there altogether?

E. Substitution Drill

1. 여기서 학교까지 얼마나 멀어요? ↷	How far is it from here to school?
2. 여기서 집까지 얼마나 멀어요? ↷	How far is it from here to the house?
3. 여기서 사무실까지 얼마나 멀어요? ↷	How far is it from here to the office?
4. 여기서 교실까지 얼마나 멀어요? ↷	How far is it from here to the classroom?

5. 여기서 화장실까지 얼마나 멀어요? ↷ How far is it from here to the rest room?
6. 여기서 마당까지 얼마나 멀어요? ↷ How far is it from here to the garden?
7. 여기서 대사관까지 얼마나 멀어요? ↷ How far is it from here to the embassy?
8. 여기서 세탁소까지 얼마나 멀어요? ↷ How far is it from here to the laundry?

F. Response Drill

1. 몇 시부터 일하세요? ↷ 두 시부터 일해요. ↷
2. 몇 시부터 가르치세요? ↷ 아홉 시부터 가르쳐요. ↷
3. 몇 시부터 숙제하세요? ↷ 다섯 시부터 숙제해요. ↷
4. 몇 시부터 주무세요? ↷ 열 시부터 자요. ↷
5. 몇 시부터 잡수세요? ↷ 일곱 시부터 먹어요. ↷
6. 몇 시부터 등산하세요? ↷ 열 시부터 등산해요. ↷
7. 몇 시부터 바쁘세요? ↷ 여덟 시부터 바빠요. ↷
8. 몇 시부터 한가하세요? ↷ 여섯 시부터 한가해요. ↷

G. Response Drill

1. 몇 시까지 공부하세요? ↷ 한 시 반까지 공부해요. ↷
2. 몇 시까지 주무세요? ↷ 일곱 시까지 자요. ↷
3. 몇 시까지 일하세요? ↷ 열 두 시까지 일해요. ↷
4. 몇 시까지 쉬세요? ↷ 두 시까지 쉬어요. ↷
5. 몇 시까지 책을 읽으세요? ↷ 네 시까지 책을 읽어요. ↷
6. 몇 시까지 산책하세요? ↷ 세 시까지 산책해요. ↷
7. 몇 시까지 가르치세요? ↷ 다섯 시까지 가르쳐요. ↷
8. 몇 시까지 편지를 쓰세요? ↷ 여섯 시까지 편지를 써요. ↷

UNIT 8 음식점에서 In the Restaurant

BASIC SENTENCES: MEMORIZE

주문하다	to order
종 업 원	
1. 주문하셨어요? ↗	Have you ordered?
아직도	(not) yet
뭘	what
시키다	to order
이 승 표	
2. 아니오, 아직도요. ⌒	No, not yet.
김 선생님! 뭘 시킬까요? ⌒	Mr. Kim! What shall we order?
불고기	pulgogi
어때요	how (about)
김 영 백	
3. 불고기가 어때요? ⌒	How about pulgogi?
이 인분	two portions of
이 승 표	
4. 그럼, 불고기 이 인분 주세요. ⌒	Then, pulgogi for two, please
술	liquer
종 업 원	
5. 술은요? ↗	(What kind of) drink?
맥주	beer
한 병	one bottle of
이 승 표	
6. 맥주 한 병 주세요. ⌒	One bottle of beer, please.

NOTES ON THE BASIC SENTENCES

2. 아직도요 is an unfinished sentence of 아직도 시키지 않았어요 'I haven't ordered yet.' 아직도 is used always with the negative predicate.

뭘 is a contraction of 무엇을. 무엇, depending on the intonation and pitch, is [illegible] only as an interrogative pronoun, but also as an indefinite pronoun. When 무엇 is pronounced with a higher initial pitch, and the final intonation of the sentence is down, it is used as an interrogative pronoun. However, it can also be used as an indefinite pronoun; this use is indicated by a rising contour at the end of an otherwise normal pitch.

They are:

무엇	'what'	or	'something'
누가	'who'	or	'somebody'
어디	'where'	or	'somewhere'
언제	'when'	or	'sometime'
어떻게	'how'	or	'somehow'
어떤	'what kind of'	or	'a certain'
몇	'how many (much)'	or	'some,' 'several'

Study the following examples, and note particularly the initial pitch and the final contour of the intonation of each sentence.

무엇을 사셨어요? ↷	What did you buy?
무엇을 사셨어요? ↗	Did you buy something?
누가 왔어요? ↷	Who came?
누가 왔어요? ↗	Did somebody come?
어디 가세요? ↷	Where are you going?
어디 가세요? ↗	Are you going somewhere?
언제 드릴까요? ↷	When shall I give it to you?
언제 드릴까요? ↗	Shall I give it to you sometime?
어떻게 하셨어요? ↷	How did you do it?
어떻게 하셨어요? ↗	Did you do it somehow?
어떤 사람을 만나셨어요? ↷	What kind of people did you meet?
어떤 사람을 만나셨어요? ↗	Did you meet someone, (a certain)?

시키다: When the verb 시키다 is preceded by a noun which indicates food, it means to order (something from a person); When this verb 시키다, however, is preceded by a noun other than food, it is a causative verb. It corresponds to the English 'force (a person to do),' 'make (a person do).' Study the following examples:

불고기를 시킵시다.	Let's order pulgogi.
그분한테 일을 시키세요.	Please make him work.
선생님한테 노래를 시키세요.	Please have your teacher sing a song.
학생들한테 공부를 시켰어요.	I made the students study.

3. 불고기 means 'broiled beef.' It is a very famous, popular and delicious food in Korea. The slice beef is marinated in all kinds of condiments, such as garlic, soy sauce, sesame oil, green onions, sugar, etc. Then it is put aside for a few hours to allow the flavor to set in. When being served, the cooked beef is broiled on a grill over a clay fire pot, placed in the center of the table.
4. 이 인분 means 'two portions of….' The classifier -인분 is used always with Chinese numbers to name a helping of food.
5. The classifier -병 'a bottle of' is used always with Korean numbers.

STRUCTURE NOTES

I. The Past Tense Infix -았-(-었-, -였-) :

The past tense is used to indicate an action which took place in the past, or a quality or condition which existed formerly. The past tense is formed by inserting the infix -았-(-었-, -였-) between a verb stem and the endings, such as -ㅂ(습)니다, -ㅂ(습)니까?, etc.

1. When the final vowel of the verb stem (not necessarily and final letter) is ㅏ or ㅗ, it takes -았-. See the following examples:

Past Form:	Contraction:	Meaning:
(가았습니다)	갔습니다	(I) went
(오았습니다)	왔습니다	(I) came
보았습니다	봤습니다	(I) saw (it)
좋았습니다	absent	(It) was good
많았습니다	absent	(They) were many

2. When the final vowel of the stem is any other vowel, (such as ㅓ, ㅜ, ㅡ, ㅣ), it takes -었-. See the following examples:

먹었습니다	absent	(I) ate
웃었습니다	absent	(He) laughed
(쓰었습니다)	썼습니다	(He) wrote (it)
주무시었습니다	주무셨습니다	(He) slept
읽었습니다	absent	(I) read

3. When the verb is a -하다 verb, it takes -였-. See the following examples:

하였습니다	했습니다	(I) did
공부하였습니다	공부했습니다	(I) studied
산책하였습니다	산책했습니다	(I) took a walk
일하였습니다	일했습니다	(I) worked

Note:
In colloquial speech, the contracted forms are used more frequently than the full ones.

II. The Pattern -ㄹ(을)까요?…: 'Shall we (I)....?' or 'Will it be...?'

The pattern -ㄹ(을)까요? is used to ask someone's view, opinion or appraisal about a certain matter or fact. It is used with any verb.

Example:

같이 갈까요? ↗	Shall we go together?
쉴까요? ↗	Shall we rest?
점심을 먹을까요? ↗	Shall I eat lunch?
그것이 좋을까요? ↗	Will it be good? (What's your opinion?)
그것이 재미있을까요? ↗	Will it be interesting? (What's your opinion?)
그분이 선생님일까요? ↗	Will he be a teacher?

Notes:

1. -ㄹ(을) is a modifier suffix which indicates the future. -까 is an interrogative marker. -요 is a particle indicating politeness or respect.
2. This pattern -ㄹ(을)까요?, when used with action verbs, is always answered in the propositive or imperative. See the following examples:

지금 공부할까요? ↗	Shall we study now?
예, ⌒지금 공부합시다. ↘	Yes, let's study now. (propositive)
아니오, ↗지금 공부하지 맙시다. ↘	No, let's not study now.
예, ⌒지금 공부하십시오. ↘	Yes, please study now. (imperative)
아니오, ↗ 지금 공부하지 마십시오. ↘	No, please don't study now.

3. However, this pattern -ㄹ(을)까요?, when used with verbs other than action verbs, is answered usually with the pattern -(을)것 같다 'it seems to be...,' indicating likelihood or with the future infix -겠-. This pattern -ㄹ(을)것 같다 will be studied later. See the following examples:

그것이 좋을까요? ↗	Will it be good? (What's your opinion?)

그것이 좋을 것 같습니다.↘ It seems to be good.
그것이 좋겠습니다.↘ I think it will be good.

4. -ㄹ까요? is used after verb stems ending in a vowel;
-을까요? is used after verb stems ending in a consonant.

III. The Contrast Particle -는/-은:

We have studied the particle -가/-이, which indicates the subject of a sentence. For example: 그분이 재미있습니다 'He is interesting,' tells which person is interesting. The particle -는/-은, however, is used to indicate a comparison between topics which are being compared: 그분은 'He in comparison with others.' In other words, the particle -는/-은 would not be used if no comparison were being made with another subject or with a connotation of comparison. This particle -는/-은 can be attached to almost any part of a sentence. Study the following examples:

(a) Replacing the subject particle 가/이:

한국말은 재미있어요.↘	Korean (in comparison with other languages) is interesting.
그분은 좋아요.↘	He (in comparison with others) is good.
이것은 연필이에요.↘	This (in comparison with other things) is a pencil.

(b) Replacing the object particles -를/-을:

한국말은 공부해요.↘	I study KOREAN (I don't study other languages.)
책은 읽어요.↘	I read a BOOK (I don't do other things.)

(c) With other particles:

책상이 교실에는 있어요.⌒	The desk is IN THE CLASSROOM (not in other places.)
학교에서는 공부해요.⌒	I study AT SCHOOL (not in other places.)

(d) With negative forms:

그것을 보지는 않았어요.⌒	I didn't SEE it (even though I may have heard it or touched it.)
그것을 사지는 않겠어요.⌒	I don't intend to BUY it (even though I like it or even though I asked how much it is.)

Notes:

1. The contrast particle -는/-은 is NOT used when there is an interrogative word in the sentence, (like 무엇 'what,' '누가' 'who,' 어느 (것) 'which (one),' 무슨 'what kind of,' 언제 'when,' 어디 'where,' etc.), because our attention usually focuses on this part of the sentence. It is also NOT used with a word or phrase that answers an interrogative word in a preceding question. See the following examples, and note particularly the particles.

무엇이 좋습니까?↷	What is good?
책이 좋습니다.↘	The book is good.
누가 공부하십니까?↷	Who is studying?
학생이 공부합니다.↘	The student is studying.
어느 것이 큽니까?↷	Which one is big?
그것이 큽니다.↘	That one is big.
무슨 책이 좋습니까?↷	What kind of book is better?
한국말 책이 좋습니다.↘	A Korean language book is better.

If the question is 저분은 누구십니까? 'Who is that person over there?,' the attention focuses on 저분은 'that person over there,' so the response is 저분은 선생님입니다 'That person over there is a teacher.'

2. The particle -는/-은 is USED when there is a pattern indicating a comparison in a sentence by the two different subjects -지만 'but,' -아(-어, -여)도 'even though,' -고 'and,' etc. See the following examples:

   이것은 좋지만, ↷그것은 나쁩니다.↘
   This one is good, but that one is bad.
   이것은 좋아도, ↷그것은 나쁩니다.↘
   Even though this one is good, that one is bad.
   이것은 좋고, ↷그것은 나쁩니다.↘
   This one is good and that one is bad.

3. -는 is used after words ending in a vowel;
   -은 is used after words ending in a consonant.

4. When the affirmative question form is used with the particle -도 also, 'too,' the negative answer always takes the contrast particle -는/-은. Study the following examples:

책도 사십니까?	Are you buying a book as well?
아니오, 책은 사지 않습니다.	No, I am not buying a book.

DRILLS

ADDITIONAL VOCABULARY

고속버스	highway bus	사랑하다	to love
배	boat, ship	데리고 가다	to take (someone somewhere)
사다	to buy		
도와주다	to help	아침	breakfast
좋아하다	to like	점심	lunch

A. Substitution Drill

1. 뭘 시킬까요? ↷ — What shall we order?
2. 뭘 주문할까요? ↷ — What shall we order?
3. 뭘 가르칠까요? ↷ — What shall we teach?
4. 뭘 공부할까요? ↷ — What shall we study?
5. 뭘 볼까요? ↷ — What shall we see?
6. 뭘 잡수실까요? ↷ — What shall we eat?
7. 뭘 쓸까요? ↷ — What shall we write?
8. 뭘 읽을까요? ↷ — What shall we read?

B. Substitution Drill

1. 불고기가 어때요? ↷ — How about pulgogi?
2. 더운 물이 어때요? ↷ — How about hot water?
3. 홍차가 어때요? ↷ — How about black tea?
4. 끓인 물이 어때요? ↷ — How about boiled water?
5. 복숭아가 어때요? ↷ — How about peaches?
6. 수박이 어때요? ↷ — How about watermelons?
7. 포도가 어때요? ↷ — How about grapes?
8. 사과가 어때요? ↷ — How about apples?

C. Pattern Drill

Teacher : 갑니다. ↘ — I go.
Student : 갔습니다. ↘ — I went.

1. 옵니다. ↘ — 왔습니다. ↘
2. 봅니다. ↘ — 봤습니다. ↘
3. 좋습니다. ↘ — 좋았습니다. ↘
4. 많습니다. ↘ — 많았습니다. ↘
5. 먹습니다. ↘ — 먹었습니다. ↘
6. 맛있습니다. ↘ — 맛있었습니다. ↘

7. 읽습니다.↘ 읽었습니다.↘
8. 합니다.↘ 했습니다.↘
9. 공부합니다.↘ 공부했습니다.↘

D. Response Drill

Teacher : 고속버스로 갈까요?↗ Shall we go by highway bus?
Student : 예, 고속버스로 갑시다.↘ Yes, let's go by highway bus.

1. 배로 올까요?↗ 예, 배로 옵시다.↘
2. 동생을 데리고 갈까요?↗ 예, 동생을 데리고 갑시다.↘
3. 그분을 도와줄까요?↗ 예, 그분을 도와줍시다.↘
4. 책을 살까요?↗ 예, 책을 삽시다.↘
5. 등산할까요?↗ 예, 등산합시다.↘
6. 수영할까요?↗ 예, 수영합시다.↘
7. 시작할까요?↗ 예, 시작합시다.↘
8. 쉴까요?↗ 예, 쉽시다.↘

E. Response Drill

Teacher : 주문하셨어요?↗ Did you order?
Student : 아니오, 아직도요.⌒ No, not yet.

1. 편지를 쓰셨어요?↗ 아니오, 아직도요.⌒
2. 아침을 잡수셨어요?↗ 아니오, 아직도요.⌒
3. 점심을 잡수셨어요?↗ 아니오, 아직도요.⌒
4. 시작하셨어요?↗ 아니오, 아직도요.⌒
5. 산책하셨어요?↗ 아니오, 아직도요.⌒
6. 수영하셨어요?↗ 아니오, 아직도요.⌒

F. Intonation Drill

Teacher : 무엇을 사셨어요?⌒ What did you buy?
Student : 무엇을 사셨어요?↗ Did you buy something?

1. 누가 왔어요?⌒ 누가 왔어요?↗
2. 어디 가세요?⌒ 어디 가세요?↗
3. 언제 드릴까요?⌒ 언제 드릴까요?↗
4. 어떻게 하셨어요?⌒ 어떻게 하셨어요?↗
5. 어떤 사람을 만나셨어요?⌒ 어떤 사람을 만나셨어요?↗

G. Response Drill

Teacher : 공부할까요 ? ↗	Shall we study ?
Student : 아니오, 공부하지 맙시다. ↘	No, let's not study.
1. 일할까요 ? ↗	아니오, 일하지 맙시다. ↘
2. 기다릴까요 ? ↗	아니오, 기다리지 맙시다. ↘
3. 책을 읽을까요 ? ↗	아니오, 책을 읽지 맙시다. ↘
4. 동생을 데리고 갈까요 ? ↗	아니오, 동생을 데리고 가지 맙시다. ↘
5. 그분을 도와줄까요 ? ↗	아니오, 그분을 도와주지 맙시다. ↘
6. 그 여자를 사랑할까요 ? ↗	아니오, 그 여자를 사랑하지 맙시다. ↘
7. 등산할까요 ? ↗	아니오, 등산하지 맙시다. ↘
8. 수영할까요 ? ↗	아니오, 수영하지 맙시다. ↘

UNIT 9 전화 Telephone

BASIC SENTENCES : MEMORIZE

여보세요	hello
미 스 민	
1. 여보세요 ! ⌒	Hello !
이 경 희	
2. 아 ! 여보세요. ⌒ 미스 민 ! ↘ 김 선생님 계세요 ? ↗	Ah ! Hello ! Miss Min. Is Mr. Kim there ?
지금	now
미 스 민	
3. 김 선생님요 ? ↗ 그분이 지금 안 계세요. ⌒	Mr. Kim ? He is not here now.
멀리	far, a long way off
나가다	to go out
이 경 희	
4. 그분이 멀리 나가셨어요 ? ↗	Did he go far ?
곧	soon
돌아오다	to return
미 스 민	
5. 아니오, 멀리 나가지 않았어요. ⌒ 곧 돌아오실 거에요. ⌒	No, he didn't go far. He will be back soon.
조금 있다가	a little later
다시	again
전화하다	to telephone
이 경 희	
6. 그럼, 조금 있다가 다시 전화하겠어요. ⌒	Then, I will call him again a little later.

NOTES ON THE BASIC SENTENCES

1. 여보세요 'hello' is most commonly used on the telephone. It is also used to call or attract someone's attention, particularly when addressing strangers. In Korea, the person who places a call usually says 여보세요 first, when a click is heard at the other end of the line. It is sometimes used to show one's indignation when fighting. 여보 is used mainly between husband and wife.
2. 아 'Ah!,' 'Oh!' is an exclamatory expression of admiration, surprise, grief, disappointment, etc.

   멀리 is an adverb meaning 'a long way off,' 'far off (away),' or 'in the distance;' 멀다 is a description verb meaning 'to be far;' 먼 is its noun modifier; 멀지 않아 is a phrase meaning 'before long,' 'in the near future.' The opposite word of 멀리 is 가까이 'near (to, by),' 'close (to, by).' Study the following examples.

그분이 멀리 갔어요.	He went far (away).
그분이 멀리서 왔어요.	He came from afar.
여기서 집까지 멀어요.	My house is far from here.
그분은 먼 곳에 살아요.	He lives in the distance.
멀지 않아 봄이 와요.	Spring is coming soon.

   나가다 means 'to go (get, head) out,' 'to step out,' 'to get away,' 'to leave,' 'to work in.' Study the following words which are related to it.

나가다 'to go out'	들어가다 'to go in(to)'
나오다 'to come out'	들어오다 'to come in(to)'
밖에 나가세요.	Please go outside.
나오세요.	Please come out.
방으로 들어가세요.	Please go into the room.
들어오세요.	Please come in.

   돌아오다 means 'to come back,' or 'to return' to a place where one used to live, e.g., one's own home, hometown, office or home country. 돌아가다 means 'to go back' or 'to make a detour.' It can also mean 'to die.' Study the following examples:

한 시에 집에 돌아왔어요.	I came home at one o'clock.
그분이 집으로 돌아갔어요.	He went (back) home.
그분이 고향으로 돌아갔어요.	He returned to his native place.
아버지가 돌아가셨어요.	My father died.

STRUCTURE NOTES

I. The Negative Adverb 안-… : 'do not'

The adverb 안- is used to express the negative. This negative adverb 안-, (a kind of prefix), is used regularly with action verbs and the verb of existence in its honorific form (계시다).

Examples:

집에 안 갔습니다.↘	I did not go home.
집에 안 갑니다.↘	I do not go home.
집에 안 가겠습니다.↘	I will not go home.
아침을 안 먹었습니다.↘	I did not eat breakfast.
아침을 안 먹습니다.↘	I do not eat breakfast.
아침을 안 먹겠습니다.↘	I will not eat breakfast.
그분이 교실에 안 계십니다.↘	He is not in the classroom.
공부를 안 했습니다.↘	I did not study.
공부를 안 합니다.↘	I do not study.
공부를 안 하겠습니다.↘	I will not study.

Notes:

1. Notice that the negative adverb 안- is put before the verb, ordinarily. The situation changes, however, when the verb is a -하 다 verb. -하 다 verbs are a combination of a noun and the verb -하다, (such as 공부하다, 산책하다, 등산하다, etc.). 안- is usually placed before the -하다, as in the following examples:

안 공부했습니다.	(awkward)
공부를 안 했습니다.	I did not study (correct).
안 산보하겠습니다.	(awkward)
산보를 안 하겠습니다.	I will not take a walk (correct).

2. 안- is a contraction of 아 니. However, the contracted form 안- is almost exclusively used in preference to the full form 아니.

II. Negative Constructions of Verbs:

(1) The verb of identification -이다:

We have studied the verb of identification -이다, which indicates equality. The verb -이다 is attached directly to a noun, and pronounced as part of the word to which it is attached. For example, 이것이 책입니다 'This is a book,' or 그것이 연필입니다 'That is a pencil.' In the negative construction of the verb -이다, however, the subject particle -가/-이 is attached directly to the noun, and then followed by the negative verb 아니다.

Examples :

이것이 책이 아닙니다.↘	This is not a book.
그것이 물이 아닙니다.↘	That is not water.
그것이 연필이 아닙니다.↘	That is not a pencil.
이것이 사과가 아닙니다.↘	This is not an apple.
그분이 학생이 아닙니다.↘	He is not a student.
이분이 한국사람이 아닙니다.↘	This person is not a Korean.
그분이 형님이 아니었습니다.↘	He was not my older brother.
그것이 화장실이 아니었습니다.↘	That was not a rest room.
그것이 분필이 아니었습니다.↘	That was not chalk.
그분이 학생이 아니었습니다.↘	He was not a student.

(2) **The verb of existence 있다 :**

We have also studied the verb 있다, which indicates existence, location or possession. The negative construction of the verb 있다 is 없다 '(something) does not exist,' '(someone or something) is not located (in a place),' '(someone) does not have (something).'

Examples :

교실에 책상이 없습니다.↘	There is no desk in the classroom.
지금 시간이 없습니다.↘	I have no time now.
학생이 여기에 없습니다.↘	The student is not here.
나는 책이 없었습니다.↘	I had no book.
학생이 교실에 없었습니다.↘	The student was not in the classroom.
거기에 찬물이 없었습니다.↘	There was no cold water there.

(3) **Action verbs and description verbs :**

The negative constructions of action verbs and description vers are formed by attaching the negative marker -지 않다 to the verb stems.

Examples :

그것이 좋지 않습니다.↘	That is not good.
그것이 크지 않습니다.↘	That is not big.
이것이 작지 않습니다.↘	This is not small.
그분이 공부하지 않습니다.↘	He does not study.
점심을 먹지 않습니다.↘	I do not eat lunch.

그것이 어렵지 않았습니다. ↘	That was not difficult.
그것이 쉽지 않았습니다. ↘	That was not easy.
공부하지 않았습니다. ↘	I did not study.
가지 않겠습니다. ↘	I will not go.
먹지 않겠습니다. ↘	I will not eat.

III. The Sentence-Final Ending -ㄹ(을)거에요… : 'will probably do'

The pattern -ㄹ(을) 거에요 is an informal form of -ㄹ(을) 것이에요. The suffix -ㄹ(을) indicates prospective future, and -것 'a thing.' Therefore, its literal meaning is 'it's a thing that is to be,' or 'it's a thing that one is to do.' This pattern is used with any verb, and indicates likelihood or probability.

Examples :

제가 내일 갈 거에요. ⌒	I'll probably go tomorrow.
지금 공부할 거에요. ⌒	I'll probably study now.
그 친구를 만날 거에요. ⌒	I'll probably see that friend.
그것이 비쌀 거에요. ⌒	It's probably expensive.
그것이 어려울 거에요. ⌒	It must be difficult.
그분이 교실에 계실 거에요. ⌒	He'll probably be in the classroom.
그분이 돈이 있을 거에요. ⌒	He'll probably have money.
그분이 학생일 거에요. ⌒	He'll probably be a student.
그분이 도착했을 거에요. ⌒	He must have arrived.

IV. The Future Tense Infix -겠- :

The future tense -겠- is used to indicate an action which is going to take place in the future, or a condition or quality which will exist at some other time. The future tense is formed by inserting the infix -겠- between a verb stem and the endings, (such as -ㅂ(습)니다, -ㅂ(습)니까?, etc.).

Examples :

무엇을 하시겠습니까? ↘	What will you do?
한국말을 공부하겠습니다. ↘	I'll study Korean.
몇 시에 잡수시겠습니까? ↘	What time will you eat?
여덟 시에 먹겠습니다. ↘	I'll eat at eight o'clock.
언제 오시겠습니까? ↘	When will you come?
모레 오겠습니다. ↘	I'll come the day after tomorrow.
몇 시간 가르치시겠습니까? ↘	How many hours will you teach?
세 시간 가르치겠습니다. ↘	I'll teach three hours.

This infix -겠-, depending on the context or situation, may also indicate a speaker's supposition or conjecture, but this will be studied later.

DRILLS

ADDITIONAL VOCABULARY

도착하다	to arrive	돈	money

A. Substitution Drill

1. 그분이 곧 돌아오실 거에요. ↷	He will probably be back soon.
2. 그분이 내일 갈 거에요. ↷	He will probably go tomorrow.
3. 그분이 지금 공부할 거에요. ↷	He will probably study now.
4. 그것이 비쌀 거에요. ↷	It is probably expensive.
5. 그것이 어려울 거에요. ↷	It is probably difficult.
6. 그분이 돈이 있을 거에요. ↷	He will probably have money.
7. 그분이 학생일 거에요. ↷	He will probably be a student.
8. 그분이 도착했을 거에요. ↷	He must have arrived.

B. Substitution Drill

1. 조금 있다가 다시 전화하겠어요. ↷	I'll call him again a little later.
2. 조금 있다가 다시 오겠어요. ↷	I'll come again a little later.
3. 조금 있다가 다시 수영하겠어요. ↷	I'll swim again a little later.
4. 조금 있다가 다시 시작하겠어요. ↷	I'll start again a little later.
5. 조금 있다가 다시 일하겠어요. ↷	I'll work again a little later.
6. 조금 있다가 다시 공부하겠어요. ↷	I'll study again a little later.
7. 조금 있다가 다시 도와주겠어요. ↷	I'll help again a little later.
8. 조금 있다가 다시 가르치겠어요. ↷	I'll teach again a little later.

C. Pattern Drill

Teacher: 집에 갔어요. ↷	I went home.
Student: 집에 안 갔어요. ↷	I didn't go home.
1. 아침을 먹었어요. ↷	아침을 안 먹었어요. ↷
2. 한국말을 가르쳤어요. ↷	한국말을 안 가르쳤어요. ↷
3. 숙제를 했어요. ↷	숙제를 안 했어요. ↷
4. 등산을 했어요. ↷	등산을 안 했어요. ↷
5. 수영을 했어요. ↷	수영을 안 했어요. ↷
6. 방에서 잤어요. ↷	방에서 안 잤어요. ↷
7. 편지를 썼어요. ↷	편지를 안 썼어요. ↷

8. 책을 읽었어요. ↷	책을 안 읽었어요. ↷

D. Pattern Drill

Teacher : 책이에요. ↷	It's a book.
Student : 책이 아니에요. ↷	It's not a book.
1. 찬물이에요. ↷	찬물이 아니에요. ↷
2. 연필이에요. ↷	연필이 아니에요. ↷
3. 사과에요. ↷	사과가 아니에요. ↷
4. 복숭아에요. ↷	복숭아가 아니에요. ↷
5. 참외에요. ↷	참외가 아니에요. ↷
6. 학생이에요. ↷	학생이 아니에요. ↷
7. 포도에요. ↷	포도가 아니에요. ↷
8. 화장실이에요. ↷	화장실이 아니에요. ↷

E. Pattern Drill

Teacher : 갔어요. ↷	I went.
Student : 가지 않았어요. ↷	I didn't go.
1. 공부했어요. ↷	공부하지 않았어요. ↷
2. 쉬었어요. ↷	쉬지 않았어요. ↷
3. 말씀했어요. ↷	말씀하지 않았어요. ↷
4. 일어났어요. ↷	일어나지 않았어요. ↷
5. 사랑했어요. ↷	사랑하지 않았어요. ↷
6. 좋아했어요. ↷	좋아하지 않았어요. ↷
7. 데리고 갔어요. ↷	데리고 가지 않았어요. ↷
8. 책을 샀어요. ↷	책을 사지 않았어요. ↷

F. Pattern Drill

Teacher : 집에 가겠어요. ↷	I'll go home.
Student : 집에 가지 않겠어요. ↷	I won't go home.
1. 아침을 먹겠어요. ↷	아침을 먹지 않겠어요. ↷
2. 산책하겠어요. ↷	산책하지 않겠어요. ↷
3. 일을 시작하겠어요. ↷	일을 시작하지 않겠어요. ↷
4. 내일 등산하겠어요. ↷	내일 등산하지 않겠어요. ↷
5. 그 여자를 사랑하겠어요. ↷	그 여자를 사랑하지 않겠어요. ↷
6. 그분을 도와주겠어요. ↷	그분을 도와주지 않겠어요. ↷
7. 동생을 데리고 가겠어요. ↷	동생을 데리고 가지 않겠어요. ↷
8. 복숭아를 사겠어요. ↷	복숭아를 사지 않겠어요. ↷

G. Response Drill

Teacher: 그것이 좋아요? ↗	Is it good?
Student: 아니오, 그것이 좋지 않아요. ⌒	No, it's not good.
1. 그것이 책이에요? ↗	아니오, 그것이 책이 아니에요. ⌒
2. 그분이 바빴어요? ↗	아니오, 그분이 바쁘지 않았어요. ⌒
3. 내일 가시겠어요? ↗	아니오, 내일 가지 않겠어요. ⌒
4. 주무셨어요? ↗	아니오, 자지 않았어요. ⌒
5. 잡수시겠어요? ↗	아니오, 먹지 않겠어요. ⌒
6. 지금 숙제를 하세요? ↗	아니오, 지금 숙제를 하지 않아요. ⌒
7. 편지를 쓰시겠어요? ↗	아니오, 편지를 쓰지 않겠어요. ⌒
8. 그분을 도와주시겠어요? ↗	아니오, 그분을 도와주지 않겠어요. ⌒

H. Pattern Drill

Teacher: 방에 책이 있어요. ⌒	There is a desk in the room.
Student: 방에 책이 없어요. ⌒	There isn't a book in the room.
1. 지금 시간이 있어요. ⌒	지금 시간이 없어요. ⌒
2. 나는 책이 있었어요. ⌒	나는 책이 없었어요. ⌒
3. 그것이 교실에 있었어요. ⌒	그것이 교실에 없었어요. ⌒
4. 돈이 있었어요. ⌒	돈이 없었어요. ⌒
5. 거기에 학생이 있어요. ⌒	거기에 학생이 없어요. ⌒
6. 집에 돈이 있어요. ⌒	집에 돈이 없어요. ⌒
7. 마당에 동생이 있어요. ⌒	마당에 동생이 없어요. ⌒
8. 그것이 사무실에 있어요. ⌒	그것이 사무실에 없어요. ⌒

UNIT 10 시간 Time

BASIC SENTENCES: MEMORIZE

박 성 영

1. 지금 몇 시에요? ↷ — What time is it now?

   반 — half

곽 상 훈

2. 열 두시 반이에요. ↷ — It's twelve thirty.

   벌써 — already
   점심 — lunch
   때 — time, an hour
   되다 — to become

박 성 영

3. 아이구! 벌써 점심 먹을 때가 되었군요! ↷ — Oh my! It's lunch time already.

   한턱 — a treat
   내다 — to give

곽 상 훈

4. 오늘은 내가 한 턱 내겠어요. ↷ 저하고 같이 나갑시다. ↷ — Today I'll give you a treat. Let's go out together.

박 성 영

5. 그래요? ↗ 무슨 좋은 일이 있으세요? ↗ — Really? What's the good news?

   딸 — daughter
   대학 — college, university
   입시 — an entrance exam
   합격하다 — to pass

곽 상 훈

6. 딸이 대학 입시에 합격했어요. ↷ — My daughter has passed her university entrance exam.

   축하하다 — to congratulate

박 성 영

7. 아이구! 축하합니다. ↘ — Oh! Congratulations.

NOTES ON THE BASIC SENTENCES

3. 벌써 점심 먹을 때가 되었군요 means literally 'It's already time to eat lunch.' When the suffix -ㄹ(을) is used either with action or description verbs, it indicates the future tense. You will study the suffix -ㄹ(을) in detail later. 점심 means 'lunch.' 아침 can mean 'morning' or 'breakfast.' 저녁 can mean 'evening' or 'supper.' However, there is only one meaning for 점심 'lunch.'
4. 오늘 'today' is a time word occurring without the particle -에 'at' or 'on.' But it may be used with the contrast particle -는/-은. Let us study some other time words as well.

내일	'tomorrow'	어제	'yesterday'
모레	'the day after tomorrow'	그저께	'the day before yesterday'
글피	'two days after tomorrow'	그끄저께	'two days before yesterday'
그글피	'three days after tomorrow'		

내가 한턱 내겠어요 : 한턱 means 'a treat' and 내다 'to serve (provide),' 'to treat (a person) to.' Therefore, 내가 한턱 내겠어요 means 'I'll give you a treat.' 한턱 내세요 'Give us a treat' is frequently heard when someone is promoted or engaged to be married.
5. 무슨 좋은 일이 있으세요? means literally 'Do you have anything in mind?' 무슨 is a noun modifier 'what (kind of).' However, when 무슨 is pronounced with normal initial pitch, and the final contour of the intonation of the sentence is up (↗), it is used an indefinite pronoun meaning 'something (anything).'
6. 입시 is a contraction of 입학 시험 'an entrance exam.' In Korea, competition in university entrance exams is so keen that when someone passes it is an achievement which warrants congratulation.
7. 축하합니다 'congratulations' is used to express sympathetic pleasure on account of success or good fortune.

STRUCTURE NOTES

I. The Particle -하고 같이… : 'together with'

The particle -하고 같이, preceded by nouns, indicates accompaniment, association, relation or harmony. The particle -하고 means 'with,' 'in company with'; 같이, as an independent word, means 'together.' The word 같이 in this pattern -하고 같이 can be dropped, making no difference in meaning. In the beginning stage, however, it is better to practice this pattern with the word 같이.

Examples:

누구하고 같이 잡수셨습니까? ↷ — Witn whom did you eat?
친구하고 같이 먹었습니다. ↷ — I ate with my friend.
아버지하고 같이 가겠습니다. ↷ — I will go with my father.
누구하고 같이 공부하십니까? ↷ — With whom do you study?
그분하고 같이 공부합니다. ↷ — I study with him.
남동생하고 같이 왔습니다. ↷ — I came with my younger brother.
형님하고 같이 일하겠습니다. ↷ — I will work with my older brother.

II. The Particle -하고… : 'and'

The particle -하고, (without the word 같이), is also used to link nouns in coordination. The last noun is usually followed by the subject particle -가/-이 or the object particle -를/-을, etc. This particle -하고 never links verbs, adjectives or adverbs.

Examples:

책하고 연필을 샀습니다. ↘ — I bought a book and a pencil.
한국말하고 영어가 재미있습니다. ↘ — Korean and English are interesting.
그분하고 내가 갔습니다. ↘ — He and I went.

III. The Exclamatory Ending -(는)군요:

The sentence-final ending -(는)군 요 is used with any verb, and indicates delight, wonder, astonishment or surprise.

Examples:

그분이 학교에 가는군요! — He is going to school!
그분이 학교에 갔군요! — He went to school!
그분이 학교에 가겠군요! — I think he will go to school!
그것이 예쁘군요! — That's beautiful!
그것이 예뻤군요! — That's was beautiful!
그것이 예쁘겠군요! — I think that will be beautiful!
그분이 한국 사람이군요! — He is Korean!
그분이 한국 사람이었군요! — He was Korean!
그분이 한국 사람이겠군요! — I think he is Korean!
그 책이 여기 있군요! — That book is here!

그 책이 여기 있었군요! That book was here!
그 책이 여기 있겠군요! I think that book is here!

Note:
-는군요 is attached to action verb stems in the present tense;
-군요 is attached to all other cases.

IV. The Particle -에… : 'to'

We have already studied the particle -에, which indicates that something or someone is STATIONARY in a place. For example, 그것이 교실에 있습니다 'That is in the classroom,' 그것이 집에 없습니다 'That is not at home.' We have also studied the particle -에, when it indicates the time at which something takes place. For example, 두 시 반에 갑시다 'Let's go at two thirty,' 세 시에 끝납니다 'I finish at three o'clock.' When this particle -에, however, is attached directly to a place word and is followed by 가다 or 오다, or their compounds, it indicats a specific destination.

Examples:

서울에 갑시다.↘ Let's go to Seoul.
학교에 왔습니다.↘ I came to school.
교실에 가겠습니다.↘ I will go to the classroom.
사무실에 오십시오.↘ Please come to the office.
그분이 휴게실에 갔습니다.↘ He went to the recreation room.

DRILLS

ADDITIONAL VOCABULARY

집사람	wife	글피	two days after tomorrow
남편	husband	그글피	three days after tomorrow
친구	friend	어제	yesterday
내일	tomorrow	그저께	the day before yesterday
모레	the day after tomorrow	그끄저께	two days before yesterday

A. Substitution Drill

1. 책하고 연필을 샀습니다.↘ I bought a book and a pencil.
2. 홍차하고 설탕을 샀습니다.↘ I bought black tea and sugar.
3. 포도하고 사과를 샀습니다.↘ I bought grapes and apples.
4. 복숭아하고 수박을 샀습니다.↘ I bought peaches and watermelons.

5. 참외하고 커피를 샀습니다. ↘ I bought melons and coffee.
6. 책하고 공책을 샀습니다. ↘ I bought a book and a notebook.
7. 연필하고 만년필을 샀습니다. ↘ I bought a pencil and a fountain pen.
8. 집하고 자동차를 샀습니다. ↘ I bought a house and a car.

B. Substitution Drill

1. 그분이 학교에 가시는군요! ⌒ He is going to school!
2. 그분이 공부하시는군요! ⌒ He is studying!
3. 그분이 점심을 잡수시는군요! ⌒ He is eating lunch!
4. 그분이 방에서 주무시는군요! ⌒ He is sleeping in the room!
5. 그분이 숙제를 하시는군요! ⌒ He is doing his homework!
6. 그분이 수영하시는군요! ⌒ He is swimming!
7. 그분이 일을 시작하시는군요! ⌒ He is starting working!
8. 그분이 산책하시는군요! ⌒ He is taking a walk!

C. Substitution Drill

1. 집에 갑시다. ↘ Let's go home.
2. 학교에 갑시다. ↘ Let's go to school.
3. 세탁소에 갑시다. ↘ Let's go to the laundry.
4. 대사관에 갑시다. ↘ Let's go to the Embassy.
5. 화장실에 갑시다. ↘ Let's go to the rest room.
6. 사무실에 갑시다. ↘ Let's go to the office.
7. 방에 갑시다. ↘ Let's go to the room.
8. 마당에 갑시다. ↘ Let's go to the garden.

D. Pattern Drill

Teacher: 그것이 좋아요⌒ It's good.
Student: 그것이 좋군요! ⌒ It's good!

1. 영어가 어려워요. ⌒ 영어가 어렵군요! ⌒
2. 그것이 쉬워요. ⌒ 그것이 쉽군요! ⌒
3. 그것이 커요. ⌒ 그것이 크군요! ⌒
4. 그것이 작아요. ⌒ 그것이 작군요! ⌒
5. 그것이 싸요. ⌒ 그것이 싸군요! ⌒
6. 그것이 좋아요. ⌒ 그것이 좋군요! ⌒
7. 그것이 나빠요. ⌒ 그것이 나쁘군요! ⌒
8. 그분이 바빠요. ⌒ 그분이 바쁘군요! ⌒

E. Response Drill

1. 누구하고 같이 잡수셨어요? ↷ — 친구하고 같이 먹었어요. ↷
2. 누구하고 같이 주무셨어요? ↷ — 집사람하고 같이 잤어요. ↷
3. 누구하고 같이 수영하셨어요? ↷ — 형님하고 같이 수영했어요. ↷
4. 누구하고 같이 산책하셨어요? ↷ — 대사님하고 같이 산책했어요. ↷
5. 누구하고 같이 일하셨어요? ↷ — 외교관하고 같이 일했어요. ↷
6. 누구하고 같이 등산하셨어요? ↷ — 동생하고 같이 등산했어요. ↷
7. 누구하고 같이 기다리셨어요? ↷ — 김 선생님하고 같이 기다렸어요. ↷
8. 누구하고 같이 공부하셨어요? ↷ — 남편하고 같이 공부했어요. ↷

F. Pattern Drill

Teacher: 점심을 먹어요. ↷ — I'm eating lunch.

Student: 벌써 점심을 먹을 때가 되었군요! ↷ — It's lunch time already!

1. 학교에 가요. ↷ — 벌써 학교에 갈 때가 되었군요! ↷
2. 공부해요. ↷ — 벌써 공부할 때가 되었군요! ↷
3. 가르쳐요. ↷ — 벌써 가르칠 때가 되었군요! ↷
4. 자요. ↷ — 벌써 잘 때가 되었군요! ↷
5. 수영해요. ↷ — 벌써 수영할 때가 되었군요! ↷
6. 배가 도착해요. ↷ — 벌써 배가 도착할 때가 되었군요! ↷
7. 일해요. ↷ — 벌써 일할 때가 되었군요! ↷
8. 일어나요. ↷ — 벌써 일어날 때가 되었군요! ↷

G. Pattern Drill

Teacher: 좋은 일이 있어요. ↷ — I have a good news.

Student: 무슨 좋은 일이 있으세요? ↗ — What's the good news? Or: Do you have anything in mind?

1. 어려운 일이 있어요. ↷ — 무슨 어려운 일이 있으세요? ↗
2. 큰 일이 있어요. ↷ — 무슨 큰 일이 있으세요? ↗
3. 나쁜 일이 있어요. ↷ — 무슨 나쁜 일이 있으세요? ↗
4. 바쁜 일이 있어요. ↷ — 무슨 바쁜 일이 있으세요? ↗
5. 반가운 일이 있어요. ↷ — 무슨 반가운 일이 있으세요? ↗
6. 재미있는 일이 있어요. ↷ — 무슨 재미있는 일이 있으세요? ↗

UNIT 11 택시 Taxi

BASIC SENTENCES : MEMORIZE

타다	to get in, to ride
운 전 사	
1. 어서 타세요. ↷ 어디로 갈까요? ↷	Please get in. Where shall we go?
손 님	
2. 광화문으로 갑시다. ↘	Let's go to Kwanghwa-mun.
날씨	weather
참	really, very
운 전 사	
3. 날씨가 참 좋지요? ↗	It's very fine weather, isn't it?
손 님	
4. 그럼요, ↷ 좋고 말고요. ↷ 가을인데요, 뭐! ↗	Of course, it's fine weather. It's fall.
다	all
운 전 사	
5. 다 왔어요. ↷ 광화문이에요. ↷	We've arrived. This is Kwanghwa-mun.
요금	fare
손 님	
6. 요금이 얼마지요? ↗	How much is the fare?
운 전 사	
7. 삼천 오백 원이에요. ↷	3,500 won.
손 님	
8. 수고하셨어요. ↷ 돈 여기 있어요. ↷	Thank you. Here is the money.

NOTES ON THE BASIC SENTENCES

1. 타다 means 'to ride (a horse),' 'to take (a train),' 'to take a ride in (a car),' 'to get on [into] (a train, a plane).' The opposite of 타다 is 내리다 'to get off,' 'to get out of.' study the following examples:

말을 타고 가겠어요.	I'll go on horseback.
기차를 탑시다.	Let's get into a train.
비행기를 탑시다.	Let's get aboard an airplane.
기차에서 내리세요.	Get off a train, please.

3. 날씨 'weather' is a pure Korean, while 일기 'weather' is derived from Chinese. 기후 means 'climate,' (such as oceanic or continental climate). Study the following examples:

날씨가 아주 좋아요.	It's very fine weather.
일기가 좋지 않아요.	It's not good weather.
기후가 좋아요.	The climate is good.

4. 뭐 is an exclamatory expression of admiration, surprise or a child's winning ways. It corresponds to the English 'what!' 'but anyway,' 'somehow or other.' Study the following examples:

뭐 그분이 죽었어요?	What! Is he dead?
뭐 얼마요?	What! How much did you say it is?
뭐 괜찮아요.	Never mind.

5. 다 means (1) 'all,' 'everything,' 'everybody,' (2) 'almost,' 'nearly,' (3) 'completely,' 'indeed.' Study the following examples:

다 같이 갑시다.	Let us go all together.
다 왔어요.	We've arrived. or All of us have come. or All are here.
그분이 다 죽어 가요.	He is almost to die.
별 말씀을 다 하십니다.	Don't mention it. or Not at all.
별 것 다 봤어요.	Now, I've seen everything.

6. 요금 means '(the amount of) a charge,' 'a fare,' 'a rate,' e.g., 수도요금 'water rate,' 전기요금 'power rate.'

8. 수고하셨어요 (past tense) means literally 'You took great pains.' This expression is used to show appreciation for what someone has done for you. 수고하십니다 (present tense) means literally 'You are taking great pains,' or 'It is toilsome on your part.' This expression is used to greet someone who is working hard. 수고하세요 or 수고 하십시오 is used when you part from someone who is actually working.

STRUCTURE NOTES

I. The Particle -(으)로 … : 'to'

We have studied the particle -(으)로, which indicates a means with which someone performs an action, or by which someone drives or moves about. For example, 만년필로 썼습니다 'I wrote with a fountain pen,' 버스로 갑시다 'Let's go by bus.' It indicates a specific destination, however, when the particle -(으)로 is attached directly to a place word.

Examples:

교실로 갔습니다.	I went to the classroom.
서울로 갑시다.	Let's go to Seoul.
사무실로 오십시오.	Please come to the office.
학교로 왔습니다.	I came to school.
집으로 돌아왔습니다.	I returned home.
방으로 들어갑시다.	Let's go into the room.

Notes:

1. -로 is used after noun ending in a vowel or the consonant -ㄹ; -으로 is used after nouns ending in all consonants except -ㄹ.
2. The particle -(으)로 'to' is interchangeable with -에 'to,' making no difference in meaning. Study the following examples:

서울로 갑시다.	Let's go to Seoul.
서울에 갑시다	Let's go to Seoul.

II. The Sentence-Final Ending -지요:

The sentence-final ending -지요 is used with any verb. It can be used in casual questions, statements, propositions and commands, and usually invites confirmation or agreement. The English equivalent of this pattern is 'I suppose (guess, think),' 'I daresay,' 'you know,' 'if I am not mistaken,' 'I bet,' etc.

(1) In questions: -지요 is used frequently as a tag-ending with a rising intonation, and indicates doubt or supposition.

그것이 참 좋지요?↗	That's very good, isn't it?
그분이 학생이지요?↗	He's a student, isn't he?
이 책이 재미있지요?↗	This book is interesting, I suppose.
그분이 누구지요?↗	Who is he?

이것이 무엇이지요? ↗ What is this?

(2) In statements: -지요 is used frequently for giving information, and has a falling intonation.

그분도 참 크지요. ⌒ He is also very big.
그것도 참 재미있지요. ⌒ That's also very interesting.
그분은 사무실에 있지요. ⌒ He is in the office.
나도 들었지요. ⌒ I also heard about it.

(3) In propositions and commands: -지 요, when used as an insistent suggestion or command, has a loud quick fall on the last syllable.

여기 앉으시지요. ↘ Let's sit down here. (propositive)
한국말을 공부하시지요. ↘ Study Korean, please. (imperative)

Note:

When the -지요 form is used with interrogative pronouns, the final contour is always a rising pitch. (When the interrogative pronoun is in a sentence without the -지 요 form, the final contour is usually a falling pitch.)

III. The Sentence-Final Ending -고 말고요…: 'of course'

The pattern -고 말고요 is used with any verb, and corresponds to the English 'there is no doubt about it that...,' 'it is needless to say that...,' 'it is a matter of course that...,' etc.

Examples:

그 여자가 예쁘고 말고요. There is no doubt that she is beautiful.
이 책이 좋고 말고요. It is needless to say that this book is good.

내일 가고 말고요. Of course I will go tomorrow.
돈이 있고 말고요. Of course I have money.
그분이 부자이고 말고요. Of couse he is a rich man.

IV. The Exclamatory Ending -ㄴ(은)데요/-는데요:

The sentence-final ending -ㄴ(은)데요/-는데요 may be used with any verb. It indicates interest, surprise, delight, astonishment, wonder, etc. This exclamatory ending is used mostly when a speaker is wondering about the reactions or feelings of the hearer, while showing his own interest, delight or astonishment about a certain fact, event or occurrence.

Examples.

그 여자가 참 예쁜데요 !	She is very beautiful !
그 책이 아주 좋은데요 !	That book is very good !
그것이 사무실인데요 !	That is an office !
그분이 학교에 가는데요 !	He is going to school !
그분이 학교에 갔는데요 !	He went to school !
그분이 학교에 가겠는데요 !	I think he will go to school !
사람이 많았는데요 !	There were many people !
사람이 많겠는데요 !	I think there will be many people !
그분이 한국 사람이었는데요 !	He was a Korean !
그분이 한국 사람이겠는데요 !	I think he will be a Korean !
그 책이 내 방에 있는데요 !	That book is in my room !
그 책이 내 방에 있었는데요 !	That book was in my room !
그 책이 내 방에 있겠는데요 !	I think that book will be in my room !

Notes :

1. -ㄴ(은)데요 is attached to description verb stems in the present tense, and to the verb of identification 이다 in the present tense. -ㄴ데요 is used after verb stems ending in a vowel ; -은데요 is used after verb stems ending in a consonant.
2. -는데요 is attached to all other cases.
3. The final contour of the intonation, depending on the speaker's emotion or feelings, can rise or fall.

DRILLS

ADDITIONAL VOCABULARY

들어가다	to go in	일찍	early
들어오다	to come in	빨리	quickly
예쁘다	to be beautiful	천천히	slowly

A. Substitution Drill

1. 그것이 사무실인데요 ! ⌒ — That is an office !
2. 그분이 외교관인데요 ! ⌒ — He is a diplomat !
3. 그것이 세탁소인데요 ! ⌒ — That is a laundry !
4. 그분이 대사님인데요 ! ⌒ — He is an Ambassdor !
5. 그분이 신부님인데요 ! ⌒ — He is a Father !
6. 그분이 목사님인데요 ! ⌒ — He is a Pastor !

7. 그것이 지하철인데요! ⌒ That is a subway!
8. 그것이 화장실인데요! ⌒ That is a rest room!

B. Pattern Drill

Teacher: 집에 갑시다. ↘ Let's go home.
Student: 집으로 갑시다. ↘ Let's go home.

1. 사무실에 갔어요. ⌒ 사무실로 갔어요. ⌒
2. 화장실에 가겠어요. ⌒ 화장실로 가겠어요. ⌒
3. 학교에 가요. ⌒ 학교로 가요. ⌒
4. 마당에 가겠어요. ⌒ 마당으로 가겠어요. ⌒
5. 대사관에 왔어요. ⌒ 대사관으로 왔어요. ⌒
6. 방에 들어갔어요. ⌒ 방으로 들어갔어요. ⌒
7. 교실에 들어왔어요. ⌒ 교실로 들어왔어요. ⌒
8. 세탁소에 갑시다. ↘ 세탁소로 갑시다. ↘

C. Pattern Drill

Teacher: 그분이 편지를 썼군요! ⌒
He wrote a letter!
Student: 그분이 편지를 썼는데요! ⌒
He wrote a letter!

1. 그분이 부산에 갔군요! ⌒ 그분이 부산에 갔는데요! ⌒
2. 그분이 아침을 잡수셨군요! ⌒ 그분이 아침을 잡수셨는데요! ⌒
3. 그분이 방에서 주무셨군요! ⌒ 그분이 방에서 주무셨는데요! ⌒
4. 그분이 등산하셨군요! ⌒ 그분이 등산하셨는데요! ⌒
5. 그분이 일을 시작하셨군요! ⌒ 그분이 일을 시작하셨는데요! ⌒
6. 그분이 동생을 사랑하셨군요! ⌒ 그분이 동생을 사랑하셨는데요! ⌒
7. 그분이 그렇게 말씀하셨군요! ⌒ 그분이 그렇게 말씀하셨는데요! ⌒
8. 그분이 학교에 계셨군요! ⌒ 그분이 학교에 계셨는데요! ⌒

D. Pattern Drill

Teacher: 그분이 편지를 쓰는군요! ⌒
He is writing a letter!
Student: 그분이 편지를 쓰는데요! ⌒
He is writing a letter!

1. 그분이 공부하는군요! ⌒ 그분이 공부하는데요! ⌒
2. 그분이 산책하는군요! ⌒ 그분이 산책하는데요! ⌒
3. 그분이 숙제하는군요! ⌒ 그분이 숙제하는데요! ⌒
4. 그분이 수영하는군요! ⌒ 그분이 수영하는데요! ⌒

5. 그분이 일찍 일어나는군요! ↷ 그분이 일찍 일어나는데요! ↷
6. 그분이 학생을 도와주는군요! ↷ 그분이 학생을 도와주는데요! ↷
7. 그분이 한국을 좋아하는군요! ↷ 그분이 한국을 좋아하는데요! ↷
8. 그분이 동생을 데리고 가는군요! ↷ 그분이 동생을 데리고 가는데요! ↷

E. Pattern Drill

Teacher : 한국말이 쉽군요! ↷ Korean is easy!
Student : 한국말이 쉬운데요! ↷ Korean is easy!

1. 영어가 어렵군요! ↷ 영어가 어려운데요! ↷
2. 참 반갑군요! ↷ 참 반가운데요! ↷
3. 정말 미안하군요! ↷ 정말 미안한데요! ↷
4. 그분이 크군요! ↷ 그분이 큰데요! ↷
5. 그 여자가 작군요! ↷ 그 여자가 작은데요! ↷
6. 택시요금이 싸군요! ↷ 택시요금이 싼데요! ↷
7. 불고기가 비싸군요! ↷ 불고기가 비싼데요! ↷
8. 그분이 바쁘군요! ↷ 그분이 바쁜데요! ↷

F. Response Drill

Teacher : 날씨가 참 좋지요? ↗ It's very fine weather, isn't it?
Student : 그럼요, 좋고 말고요. ↷ Of course, it's fine weather.

1. 그 여자가 예쁘지요? ↗ 그럼요, ↷ 예쁘고 말고요. ↷
2. 정말 반갑지요? ↗ 그럼요, ↷ 반갑고 말고요. ↷
3. 한국말이 어렵지요? ↗ 그럼요, ↷ 어렵고 말고요. ↷
4. 영어가 쉽지요? ↗ 그럼요, ↷ 쉽고 말고요. ↷
5. 그분이 한가하지요? ↗ 그럼요, ↷ 한가하고 말고요. ↷
6. 그 여자가 작지요? ↗ 그럼요, ↷ 작고 말고요. ↷
7. 요즈음 바쁘지요? ↗ 그럼요, ↷ 바쁘고 말고요. ↷
8. 김치가 맛있지요? ↗ 그럼요, ↷ 맛있고 말고요. ↷

G. Pattern Drill

Teacher : 한국말을 공부하세요. ↷ Study Korean, please.
Student : 한국말을 공부하시지요. ↘ Study Korean, please.

1. 여기서 기다리세요. ↷ 여기서 기다리시지요. ↘
2. 그분을 도와주세요. ↷ 그분을 도와주시지요. ↘
3. 빨리 시작하세요. ↷ 빨리 시작하시지요. ↘
4. 여기서 주무세요. ↷ 여기서 주무시지요. ↘
5. 천천히 잡수세요. ↷ 천천히 잡수시지요. ↘
6. 책을 읽으세요. ↷ 책을 읽으시지요. ↘

7. 한국말을 가르치세요. ↷ 한국말을 가르치시지요. ↘
8. 일찍 일어나세요. ↷ 일찍 일어나시지요. ↘

I. Pattern Drill

Teacher : 그분이 책이 있군요 ! ↷ He has a book !
Student : 그분이 책이 있는데요 ! ↷He has a book !

1. 그분이 돈이 있군요 ! ↷ 그분이 돈이 있는데요 ! ↷
2. 거기에 사람이 없군요 ! ↷ 거기에 사람이 없는데요 ! ↷
3. 김치가 맛있군요 ! ↷ 김치가 맛있는데요 ! ↷
4. 사과가 맛없군요 ! ↷ 사과가 맛없는데요 ! ↷
5. 방에 수박이 있군요 ! ↷ 방에 수박이 있는데요 ! ↷
6. 그것이 마당에 없군요 ! ↷ 그것이 마당에 없는데요 ! ↷

BOOK I

UNIT 12 시장 Market

BASIC SENTENCES : MEMORIZE

시장	market
같이	together
박 성 철	
1. 시장에 같이 안 가시겠어요?	Won't we go to the market together?
지금	now
최 인 숙	
2. 예, 지금 못 가겠어요.	That's right. I cannot go now.
몇 시	what time
몇 시쯤	about what time
박 성 철	
3. 몇 시쯤 가시겠어요?	About what time will you go?
저	I
네 시쯤	about four o'clock
최 인 숙	
4. 전 네 시쯤 가겠어요.	I'll go about four o'clock.
어느	which
박 성 철	
5. 어느 시장에 가시겠어요?	Which market will you go to?
남대문	the Great South-Gate
최 인 숙	
6. 남대문 시장에 가겠어요.	I'll go to the Great South-Gate market.

USEFUL EXPRESSIONS : MEMORIZE

1. 따라 하세요.	Please repeat after me.
2. 잘 들어 보세요.	Please listen well.
3. 알아 들으셨어요?	Did you understand me? Or: Did you get the meaning?

NOTES ON THE BASIC SENTENCES

4. 전 is a contraction of 저는, 'I (in comparison with others).' 전 'I' is used always with the contrast particle -는 (저는), while 제, also meaning 'I,' is used always with the subject particle -가 (제가). 저(는) and 제(가) are used to indicate reverence or respect on the part of the speaker for the person spoken to. In other words, 저는 and 제가 are words used by the speaker to demonstrate or express his own humility and, at the same time, to show his respect for the person with whom he is speaking.

   나 and 내 also mean 'I.' 나 is used regularly with the contrast particle -는 (나는), whereas 내 is used always with the subject particle -가 (내가). 나(는) and 내(가) are common words used when speaking to social inferiors or to persons of equal status in the Korean social system. However, these days, there is a tendency for people not to distinguish between 저 and 나, 제 and 내.
5. 어느 'which' is a noun modifier, and is therefore followed always by a noun.
6. 남대문 (Great South-Gate) is located in the vicinity of Seoul Station. It is designated National Treasure #1. It was constructed by Yi t'aejo, the founder of the Yi Dynasty in 1396. The present structure was built in 1448 during the reign of Sejong, (the 4th King), and is the oldest wooden structure in Seoul. Three Chinese characters, Sung Ye Mun, meaning 'Admire Virtue Gate,' were written for the gate by Prince Yangyong, elder brother of King Sejong.

STRUCTURE NOTES

I. Answers to Negative Question:

The word 예 is used to mean 'what you've said is correct,' whereas the word 아니오 is used to mean 'what you've said is incorrect.' Therefore, when you ask a negative question, the standard Korean answers 예 and 아니오 turn out to be completely opposite from the English 'yes' and 'no.' The English answers 'yes' and 'no' to negative questions are used to affirm or deny the facts themselves, rather than the statement about the fact.

Examples:

공부하지 않습니까?	Aren't you studying?
예, 공부하지 않습니다.	That's right. I'm not studying.

아니오, 공부합니다.	That's not right. I'm studying.
피곤하지 않습니까?	Aren't you tired?
예, 피곤하지 않습니다.	That's right. I'm not tired.
아니오, 피곤합니다.	That's not right. I'm tired.

Warning:

The Korean usage of 예 and 아니오 in response to negative questions is as foreign for an American studying Korean, as the English usage of 'yes' and 'no' is for a Korean studying English. When a Korean does not speak English fluently, and you state a question in a negative way, like 'Won't you go?,' a single-word answer 'Yes' from many Koreans means 'Yes, I won't go.'

II. The Adverb 못-… : 'can't,' 'won't,' 'not (possible)'

This adverb 못- is used mostly with action verbs, and indicates impossibility, strong denial or refusal, or the quality or state of being impossible. It corresponds to the English 'can't,' 'won't,' 'not (possible),' 'under no circumstances,' 'definitely not,' etc., depending on the context or situation.

Examples:

못 먹겠습니다.	I can't eat. Or: I won't eat. Or: I refuse to eat.
그 책은 못 샀습니다.	I couldn't buy that book.
어젯밤에 못 잤습니다.	I couldn't sleep last night.
이 책을 못 읽겠습니다.	I can't read this book. Or: I won't read this book. Or: I refuse to read this book.
못 도와주겠습니다.	I can't help you. Or: I won't help you. Or: I refuse to help you.

Notes:

1. There are two ways of using the adverb 못-: 못-+action verb, or action verb stem+-지 못하다. It makes no difference in meaning. See the following examples:

못 가겠습니다	I can't go.
가지 못하겠습니다	
못 읽었습니다.	I couldn't read.
읽지 못했습니다.	

2. The adverb 못- is not placed before verbs such as 공부하다 or 등산하다, which are a combination of a noun and the verb -하다. 못- is always placed directly before -하다, immediately following its noun component, as in the following examples:

못 공부했습니다. (awkward)
공부를 못 했습니다. (correct) I could not study.
공부를 하지 못했습니다. (correct) I could not study.

3. An exception to the meaning of 못- occurs when it is used with description verbs, such as 좋다 or 예쁘다. In these instances, the meaning is simply negative, and doesn't imply impossibility, refusal or any of the other meanings that it has when used with action verbs. See the following examples:

그분은 좋지 못합니다. He is not good.
그 아가씨는 예쁘지 못합니다. That lady is not beautiful.

III. The Suffix -쯤… : 'about'

The suffix -쯤 is attached to time, place or quantity expression, which ask or answer the questions: 'what time?,' 'when?,' 'how long?,' 'how far?,' 'how much?,' 'where?,' etc. It indicates an approximate point in time, place or quantity.

Examples:

몇 시쯤 가시겠습니까?	About what time will you go?
네 시쯤 가겠습니다.	I'll go about four o'clock.
언제쯤 떠나시겠습니까?	About when will you leave?
모레쯤 떠나겠습니다.	I'll leave about the day after tomorrow.
얼마쯤 계시겠습니까?	About how long will you stay?
사흘쯤 있겠습니까?	I'll stay about three days.
몇 분쯤 오셨습니까?	About how many people came?
다섯 분쯤 왔습니다.	About five people came.
어디쯤 있습니까?	About where is it?

Notes:

The suffix -쯤, when followed by the expression 문제 없다 'no problem,' is also used to tease someone about something. See the following examples:

이 책쯤은 문제 없습니다. This book is no problem.
돈쯤은 문제 없습니다. Money is no problem.

DRILLS

ADDITIONAL VOCABULARY

앉다	to sit (down)	옷	clothes, costume
서다	to stand (up)	듣다	to listen

구경하다	to watch (with interest), to sightsee
피곤하다	to be tired
떠나다	to leave
말하다	to speak
노래를 부르다	to sing a song
모르다	to do not know, to be unware of

A. Substitution Drill

1. 어느 분이 재미있어요?	Which person is interesting?
2. 어느 분이 좋아요?	Which person is better?
3. 어느 분이 커요?	Which person is bigger?
4. 어느 분이 작아요?	Which person is smaller?
5. 어느 분이 바빠요?	Which person is busier?
6. 어느 분이 한가해요?	Which person is unoccupied?
7. 어느 분이 괜찮아요?	Which person is alright?
8. 어느 분이 몰라요?	Which person doesn't know it?

B. Substitution Drill

1. 몇 시쯤 가시겠어요?	About what time will you go?
2. 몇 시쯤 떠나시겠어요?	About what time will you leave?
3. 몇 시쯤 구경하시겠어요?	About what time will you go sight-seeing?
4. 몇 시쯤 일어나시겠어요?	About what time will you get up?
5. 몇 시쯤 수영하시겠어요?	About what time will you swim?
6. 몇 시쯤 등산하시겠어요?	About what time will you go mountain-climbing?
7. 몇 시쯤 산보하시겠어요?	About what time will you take a walk?
8. 몇 시쯤 공부하시겠어요?	About what time will you study?

C. Pattern Drill

Teacher: 집에 갔습니다.	I went home.
Student: 집에 안 갔습니다.	I did not go home.
1. 아침을 먹었습니다.	아침을 안 먹었습니다.
2. 그 일을 마쳤습니다.	그 일을 안 마쳤습니다.
3. 두 시에 일어났습니다.	두 시에 안 일어났습니다.
4. 열 시에 잤습니다.	열 시에 안 잤습니다.
5. 편지를 썼습니다.	편지를 안 썼습니다.
6. 책을 읽었습니다.	책을 안 읽었습니다.
7. 노래를 불렀습니다.	노래를 안 불렀습니다.
8. 집에서 기다렸습니다.	집에서 안 기다렸습니다.

D. Pattern Drill

Teacher : 공부하겠습니다.	I will study.
Student : 공부를 안 하겠습니다.	I won't study.
1. 산보하겠습니다.	산보를 안 하겠습니다.
2. 시작하겠습니다.	시작을 안 하겠습니다.
3. 숙제하겠습니다.	숙제를 안 하겠습니다.
하겠습니다.	등산을 안 하겠습니다.
5. 일하겠습니다.	일을 안 하겠습니다.
6. 구경하겠습니다.	구경을 안 하겠습니다.
7. 수영하겠습니다.	수영을 안 하겠습니다.
8. 말하겠습니다.	말을 안 하겠습니다.

E. Pattern Drill

Teacher : 도와주겠습니다.	I will help you.
Student : 못 도와주겠습니다.	I can't help you. Or : I refuse to help you. Or : I won't help you.
1. 가르치겠습니다.	못 가르치겠습니다.
2. 기다리겠습니다.	못 기다리겠습니다.
3. 내일 뵙겠습니다.	내일 못 뵙겠습니다.
4. 두 시에 끝내겠습니다.	두 시에 못 끝내겠습니다.
5. 내가 데리고 가겠습니다.	내가 못 데리고 가겠습니다.
6. 책을 읽겠습니다.	책을 못 읽겠습니다.
7. 여기에 앉겠습니다.	여기에 못 앉겠습니다.
8. 서겠습니다.	못 서겠습니다.

F. Pattern Drill

Teacher : 못 갑니다.	I can't go.
Student : 가지 못합니다.	I can't go.
1. 못 듣습니다.	듣지 못합니다.
2. 못 앉습니다.	앉지 못합니다.
3. 못 섭니다.	서지 못합니다.
4. 노래를 못 부릅니다.	노래를 부르지 못합니다.
5. 책을 못 읽습니다.	책을 읽지 못합니다.
6. 편지를 못 씁니다.	편지를 쓰지 못합니다.
7. 지금 못 쉽니다.	지금 쉬지 못합니다.
8. 옷을 못 입습니다.	옷을 입지 못합니다.

G. Pattern Drill

Teacher : 공부를 못 했어요.	I couldn't study.
Student : 공부를 하지 못했어요.	I couldn't study.

1. 산보를 못 했어요.	산보를 하지 못했어요.
2. 시작을 못 했어요.	시작을 하지 못했어요.
3. 숙제를 못 했어요.	숙제를 하지 못했어요.
4. 등산을 못 했어요.	등산을 하지 못했어요.
5. 수영을 못 했어요.	수영을 하지 못했어요.
6. 구경을 못 했어요.	구경을 하지 못했어요.
7. 일을 못 했어요.	일을 하지 못했어요.
8. 말을 못 했어요.	말을 하지 못했어요.

H. Response Drill

Teacher : 공부하지 않습니까?	Aren't you studying?
Student : 예, 공부하지 않습니다.	That's right. I'm not studying.
1. 가르치지 않습니까?	예, 가르치지 않습니다.
2. 수고하지 않습니까?	예, 수고하지 않습니다.
3. 좋지 않습니까?	예, 좋지 않습니다.
4. 한가하지 않습니까?	예, 한가하지 않습니다.
5. 바쁘지 않습니까?	예, 바쁘지 않습니다.
6. 크지 않습니까?	예, 크지 않습니다.
7. 피곤하지 않습니까?	예, 피곤하지 않습니다.
8. 어렵지 않습니까?	예, 어렵지 않습니다.

I. Response Drill

Teacher : 공부하지 않습니까?	Aren't you studying?
Student : 아니오, 공부합니다.	That's not right. I'm studying.
1. 쉽지 않습니까?	아니오, 쉽습니다.
2. 미안하지 않습니까?	아니오, 미안합니다.
3. 그분을 좋아하지 않습니까?	아니오, 그분을 좋아합니다.
4. 그분을 사랑하지 않습니까?	아니오, 그분을 사랑합니다.
5. 쉬지 않습니까?	아니오, 쉽니다.
6. 편지를 쓰지 않습니까?	아니오, 편지를 씁니다.
7. 일하지 않습니까?	아니오, 일합니다.
8. 옷을 입지 않습니까?	아니오, 옷을 입습니다.

SHORT STORIES

1. 친구하고 같이 시장에 갔습니다.
   시장에 사람이 많았습니다.
   그래서 참 복잡했습니다.

많다	to be many, to be much
그래서	therefore, so
복잡하다	to be complicated, to be crowded

2. 학교에서 한국말을 공부합니다.

한국말이 참 재미있습니다.
아홉 시부터 공부를 시작합니다.
세 시 반에 공부가 끝납니다.

3. 그분이 지금 시장에 갑니다.
그런데 나는 못 가겠습니다.
왜냐하면 지금 아주 바쁩니다.

그런데	but, and (yet)
왜냐하면	because
아주	very, entirely

READING

저는 학생입니다. 한국말을 공부합니다. 한국말이 재미있습니다. 그러나 한국말이 어렵습니다. 학교에서 공부합니다. 아홉 시에 공부를 시작합니다. 오후 세 시 반에 공부가 끝납니다. 하루에 다섯 시간 공부합니다. 네 시쯤 집에 갑니다. 버스로 집에 갑니다. 집에서 한 시간쯤 쉽니다. 그리고 숙제를 합니다. 그런데 숙제가 많습니다. 여섯 시에 저녁을 먹습니다. 그리고 열 한 시까지 공부합니다. 열 두 시에 잡니다.

그러나	but	하루에	in a day
오후	the afternoon, the p.m.	그리고	and

BRIEFING

I am a student. I am studying Korean. Korean is interesting. But Korean is difficult. I am studying at school. I start studying at 9. It ends at 3 : 30 in the afternoon. I study five hours a day. I go home about 4 o'clock. I go home by bus. I rest about one hour at home. And I do my homework. But I have a lot of homework. I eat supper at 6. And I study until 11. I go to bed at 12.

Korean Porverb :

잘 되면 제탓 못되면 조상탓

If he succeeds, man praises himself; if he fails, he blames his ancestors.

Notes :

A man claims merit for himself when getting good results, but blames other people when getting bad results in any undertaking.

UNIT 13 얼마에요? How Much Is It?

BASIC SENTENCES: MEMORIZE

저것	that thing over there
얼마	how much
박 성 철	
1. 저것이 얼마에요?	How much is that over there?
오만 원	fifty thousand won
최 인 숙	
2. 오만 원이에요.	It's fifty thousand won.
왜	why
비싸다	to be expensive
좀	a little
깎다	to come down
박 성 철	
3. 왜 그렇게 비싸요? 좀 깎읍시다.	Why is it so expensive? Let's cut the price a little.
사만	forty thousand
오천	five thousand
최 인 숙	
4. 그럼, 사만 오천 원만 주세요.	Then, please give me only forty five thousand won.
더	more
제(가)	I
옷	clothes
사다	to buy
박 성 철	
5. 좀 더 싸게 합시다. 제가 이 옷도 사겠어요.	Let's reduce the price a little bit more. I'll buy these clothes too.
최 인 숙	
6. 그럼, 사만 원만 주세요.	Then, please give me only forty thousand won.

USEFUL EXPRESSIONS : MEMORIZE

1. 물어 보세요. Please ask (me).
2. 대답하세요. Please answer.
3. 다시 해 보세요. Please try to say (do) it again.

NOTES ON THE BASIC SENTENCES

2. -원 is a Korean money classifier. It is used always with the Chinese derived numbers. According to the currency exchange rate in effect at the time of publication of this book, (1990), about 710 won equals one U.S. dollar.
3. 주세요 'please give (me such-and-such)' is the informal-polite style of 주십시오, which is the formal-polite style.
5. 더 means 'more,' 'longer.' Its opposite word is 덜 'less,' 'incompletely.'

STRUCTURE NOTES

I. Independent Nouns and Dependent Nouns :

Korean nouns are classified into two groups : i.e., independent nouns and dependent nouns. Independent nouns are nouns that function as free forms by themselves, without requiring or relying on other words for support. On the other hand, dependent nouns do require or rely on other words for support.

Examples :

Independent Nouns :		Dependent Nouns :	
학생	student	-것	thing
공책	notebook	-분	person
만년필	fountain pen	-데	place

Notes :

1. Dependent nouns are always preceded by some other words, such as demonstratives or modifiers. See the following examples :

이것	this thing	이분	this person
그것	that thing	그분	that person
저것	that thing over there	저분	that person over there
좋은 데	good place		

2. A dependent noun and its preceding modifier function together as an independent noun.

II. The Particle -만… : 'only'

The particle -만 can be attached to almost any word of a sentence. It refers always to the word to which it is attached, and indicates exclusiveness. It can replace the subject particles -가/-이 or the object particles -를/-을. It can be used along with other particles. Study the following examples:

(a) **Replacing the subject particles -가/-이** :

그분만 가르칩니다.	He is the only one teaching.
선생님만 집에 갔습니다.	Only the teacher went home.
한국말만 재미있습니다.	Only Korean is interesting.

(b) **Replacing the object particles -를/-을** :

저는 한국말만 가르칩니다.	I teach only Korean.
이 옷만 사겠습니다.	I'll buy only these clothes.
이 책만 읽었습니다.	I read only this book.

(c) **With other particles:**

책상이 교실에만 있습니다.	Desks are in the classroom only.
그분이 학교에서만 가르칩니다.	He teaches only at school.
나는 밤에만 일합니다.	I work only at night.
학교까지만 갑시다.	Let's go only as far as the school.

III. The Particle -도… : 'also,' 'too,' 'even,' 'indeed'

Like the particle -만 'only,' the particle -도 can also be attached to almost any word of a sentence. The particle -도 refers always to the word to which it is attached. Study the following examples:

(a) **Replacing the subject particle -가/-이** :

나도 한국말을 가르칩니다.	I also teach Korean.
선생님도 집에 갔습니다.	The teacher also went home.
이 책도 좋습니다.	This book also is good.

(b) **Replacing the object particles -를/-을** :

한국말도 공부합니다.	I study Korean too.
불고기도 좋아합니다.	I like pulgogi too.
책도 샀습니다.	I bought a book too.

(c) **With other particles:**

집에서도 공부합니다.	I study at home too.
밤에도 일합니다.	I work at night too.
그분이 교실에서도 잡니다.	He sleeps in the classroom too.

Notes:

1. As we have seen in the above examples, the particle 도 'also' can replace the subject particles -가/-이 and the object particles -를/-을. It can be used with other particles as well.
2. The particle 도, when used with negative forms, places emphasis on the

negative form itself, or has the meaning of 'even.' See the following examples:

그분이 학교에 가지도 않습니다.	He does not even go to school.
그분이 공부를 하지도 않습니다.	He does not even study.
사람이 그리 많지도 않습니다.	There are not so many people.

3. The particle -도, when used with an adverb, indicates admiration or places emphasis on the adverb itself. See the following examples:

그분이 잘도 잡니다.	He sleeps very well.
이 책이 너무도 어렵습니다.	This book is too difficult.
그분이 아직도 가르칩니다.	He is still teaching.

IV. Adverbs:

In Korean, as in any language, adverbs serve as modifiers of verbs, adjectives, other adverbs, clauses or whole sentences. Most description verbs can be changed into adverbs by attaching the suffix -게 to the verb stem.

Examples:

예쁘게	beautifully	크게	greatly, exceedingly
재미있게	in an interesting way	싸게	cheaply

Some of the most frequently occurring adverbs are:

가끔	occasionally	아주	very (much)
그러나	but, however	아직	still
그런데	but, and (yet)	아침마다	every morning
그리고	and	앞으로	in the future
꽤(제법)	quite	자주	frequently
너무	too (much)	잘	well
늘	always	저녁마다	every evening
다시	again	적어도	at least
대개	usually	점점	gradually
대단히	very (much)	정신없이	absent-mindedly
드디어	finally	조금	a little bit
때때로	sometimes	주로	mostly
많이	lots	참	really
벌써	already	천천히	slowly
보통	ordinarily	퍽	very
빨리	quickly	흔히	frequently
상당히	considerably	항상	always

DRILLS

ADDITIONAL VOCABULARY

친절하다	to be kind	멀다	to be far
불친절하다	to be unkind	가깝다	to be near, to be close

A. Substitution Drill

1. 저것이 얼마에요?	How much is that over there?
2. 이 책이 얼마에요?	How much is this book?
3. 이 공책이 얼마에요?	How much is this notebook?
4. 그 연필이 얼마에요?	How much is that pencil?
5. 이 분필이 얼마에요?	How much is this chalk?
6. 이 만년필이 얼마에요?	How much is this fountain pen?
7. 이 복숭아가 얼마에요?	How much is this peach?
8. 이 수박이 얼마에요?	How much is this watermelon?

B. Substitution Drill

1. 그것은 오천 원이에요.	It's five thousand won.
2. 그것은 삼천 원이에요.	It's three thousand won.
3. 그것은 이천 원이에요.	It's two thousand won.
4. 그것은 육천 원이에요.	It's six thousand won.
5. 그것은 칠천 원이에요.	It's seven thousand won.
6. 그것은 팔천 원이에요.	It's eight thousand won.
7. 그것은 구천 원이에요.	It's nine thousand won.
8. 그것은 만 원이에요.	It's ten thousand won.

C. Pattern Drill

Teacher: 그분이 친절해요.	He is kind.
Student: 그분도 친절해요.	He also is kind.
1. 그분이 불친절해요.	그분도 불친절해요.
2. 거기가 멀어요.	거기도 멀어요.
3. 여기가 가까워요.	여기도 가까워요.
4. 이 책이 좋아요.	이 책도 좋아요.
5. 이것이 복잡해요.	이것도 복잡해요.
6. 복숭아가 맛있어요.	복숭아도 맛있어요.
7. 그분이 한가해요.	그분도 한가해요.

D. Pattern Drill

Teacher: 한국말을 공부해요.	I study Korean.
Student: 한국말도 공부해요.	I study Korean too.

1. 불고기를 좋아해요. 불고기도 좋아해요.
2. 책을 샀어요. 책도 샀어요.
3. 한국말을 가르쳐요. 한국말도 가르쳐요.
4. 일을 해요. 일도 해요.
5. 책을 읽어요. 책도 읽어요.
6. 편지를 써요. 편지도 써요.
7. 사과를 먹어요. 사과도 먹어요.
8. 개를 봐요. 개도 봐요.

E. Pattern Drill

Teacher: 집에서 공부해요. I study at home.
Student: 집에서도 공부해요. I study at home too.

1. 밤에 일해요. 밤에도 일해요.
2. 학교에서 가르쳐요. 학교에서도 가르쳐요.
3. 마당에서 산보해요. 마당에서도 산보해요.
4. 휴게실에서 쉬어요. 휴게실에서도 쉬어요.
5. 교실에서 책을 읽어요. 교실에서도 책을 읽어요.
6. 방에서 편지를 써요. 방에서도 편지를 써요.
7. 사무실에서 일해요. 사무실에서도 일해요.
8. 학교에 가요. 학교에도 가요.

F. Pattern Drill

Teacher: 학교에 가지 않아요. I don't go to school.
Student: 학교에 가지도 않아요. I don't even go to school.

1. 한국말을 공부하지 않아요. 한국말을 공부하지도 않아요.
2. 그분이 친절하지 않아요. 그분이 친절하지도 않아요.
3. 그분이 일하지 않아요. 그분이 일하지도 않아요.
4. 그분이 듣지 않아요. 그분이 듣지도 않아요.
5. 그분이 말하지 않아요. 그분이 말하지도 않아요.
6. 그분이 떠나지 않아요. 그분이 떠나지도 않아요.
7. 그분이 일어나지 않아요. 그분이 일어나지도 않아요.
8. 그분이 기다리지 않아요. 그분이 기다리지도 않아요.

G. Pattern Drill

Teacher: 한국말이 재미있어요. Korean is interesting..
Student: 한국말만 재미있어요. Only Korean is interesting.

1. 그분이 불친절해요. 그분만 불친절해요.
2. 거기가 멀어요. 거기만 멀어요.
3. 여기가 가까워요. 여기만 가까워요.

4. 그분이 가르쳐요. 그분만 가르쳐요.
5. 이 책이 비싸요. 이 책만 비싸요.
6. 그 분필이 싸요. 그 분필만 싸요.
7. 불고기가 맛있어요. 불고기만 맛있어요.
8. 여기가 복잡해요. 여기만 복잡해요.

H. Pattern Drill

Teacher: 한국말을 가르쳐요. I teach Korean.
Student: 한국말만 가르쳐요. I teach only Korean.

1. 그분이 일을 해요. 그분이 일만 해요.
2. 책을 샀어요. 책만 샀어요.
3. 불고기를 좋아해요. 불고기만 좋아해요.
4. 한국말을 공부해요. 한국말만 공부해요.
5. 책을 읽어요. 책만 읽어요.
6. 편지를 써요. 편지만 써요.
7. 사과를 먹어요. 사과만 먹어요.
8. 옷을 입어요. 옷만 입어요.

I. Pattern Drill

Teacher: 그분이 학교에서 가르쳐요.
He teaches at school.
Student: 그분이 학교에서만 가르쳐요.
He teaches only at school.

1. 책상이 교실에 있어요. 책상이 교실에만 있어요.
2. 밤에 일해요. 밤에만 일해요.
3. 학교까지 갑시다. 학교까지만 갑시다.
4. 마당에서 산보해요. 마당에서만 산보해요.
5. 휴게실에서 쉬어요. 휴게실에서만 쉬어요.
6. 사무실에서 일해요. 사무실에서만 일해요.
7. 교실에서 공부해요. 교실에서만 공부해요.
8. 학교에 가요. 학교에만 가요.

J. Pattern Drill

Teacher: 좀 더 쌉니다. It's a little cheaper.
Student: 좀 더 싸게 합시다. Let's make it a little cheaper.

1. 좀 더 큽니다. 좀 더 크게 합시다.
2. 좀 더 작습니다. 좀 더 작게 합시다.
3. 좀 더 좋습니다. 좀 더 좋게 합시다.
4. 좀 더 재미있습니다. 좀 더 재미있게 합시다.

5. 좀 더 쉽습니다. 좀 더 쉽게 합시다.
6. 좀 더 어렵습니다. 좀 더 어렵게 합시다.
7. 좀 더 복잡합니다. 좀 더 복잡하게 합시다.
8. 좀 더 맛있습니다. 좀 더 맛있게 합시다.

SHORT STORIES

1. 어제 오후에 백화점에 갔어요.
   백화점에 물건이 많았어요.
   그런데 물건이 비쌌어요.

   백화점 department store
   물건 a thing, goods

2. 오늘 아침에 늦게 일어났어요.
   그래서 아침도 먹지 못했어요.
   지금 배가 고파요.

   늦게 late
   배가 고프다 to be hungry

3. 그분이 학교에서만 가르쳐요.
   집에서는 가르치지 않아요.
   집에서는 아이들하고 재미있게 놀아요.

   아이들 children
   놀다 to play

READING

어제 시내에 갔습니다. 자동차로 갔습니다. 시내까지 그리 멀지 않았습니다. 그런데 시내에 사람이 아주 많았습니다. 자동차도 아주 많았습니다. 그래서 아주 복잡했습니다. 백화점에 들어갔습니다. 점원이 참 친절했습니다. 나는 옷을 샀습니다. 만년필도 샀습니다. 만년필이 쌌습니다. 그런데 만년필이 참 좋았습니다. 나는 옷하고 만년필만 샀습니다. 다른 것은 사지 않았습니다. 일곱 시쯤 집에 돌아왔습니다.

들어가다 to go in
점원 a salesman, a saleswoman
다른 another, other
돌아오다 to come back, to return

BRIEFING

I went downtown yesterday. I went by car. Downtown was not so far. But there were many people downtown. There were also many cars. So it was very crowded. I went into the department store. Salesgirls were very kind. I bought clothes. I also bought a fountain pen. Other than those items, I didn't buy anything else. I came back home about 7 o'clock.

UNIT 14 누구한테서 From Whom?

BASIC SENTENCES: MEMORIZE

누구한테서	from whom
편지	letter
박 성 철	
1. 누구한테서 편지가 왔어요?	From whom did the letter come?
어머님	mother
최 인 숙	
2. 어머님한테서 편지가 왔어요.	The letter came from my mother.
언제	when
어머님한테	to (your) mother
답장하다	to answer (a letter)
박 성 철	
3. 언제 어머님한테 답장하시겠어요?	When will you answer your mother?
오늘 저녁에	this evening
답장	a reply letter
최 인 숙	
4. 오늘 저녁에 답장하겠어요.	I'll write a reply this evening.
일 주일에	a week
몇 장	how many letters
쓰세요?	do you write?
박 성 철	
5. 일 주일에 편지를 몇 장 쓰세요?	How many letters do you write a week?
보통	usually, ordinarily
석 장쯤	about three letters
최 인 숙	
6. 보통 석 장쯤 써요.	I usually write about three letters.

USEFUL EXPRESSIONS: MEMORIZE

1. 다시 말씀해 주세요. — Say it again, please.
2. 한국말로 해 보세요. — Please try to speak in Korean.
3. 맞았어요. Or: 맞아요. — That's correct.
4. 틀렸어요. Or: 틀려요. — That's wrong.

FAMILY TERMS:

There are two kinds of family terms: NEUTRAL and EXALTED. The neutral terms, besides being used as general terms without reference to any particular individuals, are used when speaking to other people about yourself or members of your own family. Sometimes, the neutral terms are used in reference to anyone, without showing special deference. The exalted terms are used in reference to members of the families of others. It is customary to show deference to a person and his family by using exalted forms for kinship terms. When directly addressing a member of your family, you use the exalted term if the person is older. But you use the given name if the person is younger.

Neutral words:	Exalted words:	Meaning:
고조부	고조부님	great-great-grandfather
고조모	고조모님	great-great-grandmother
증조부	증조부님	great-grandfather
증조모	증조모님	great-grandmother
조부모	조부모님	grandparents
할아버지 (조부)	할아버님 (조부님)	grandfather
할머니 (조모)	할머님 (조모님)	grandmother
부모	부모님	parents
양친	——	both parents
아버지 (부친)	아버님 (춘부장)	father
어머니 (모친)	어머님 (자당)	mother
고모	고모님	father's sister
이모	이모님	mother's sister
아저씨 (숙부)	—— (숙부님)	uncle
외삼촌 (외숙부)	—— (외숙부님)	mother's brother
아주머니 (숙모)	아주머님 (숙모님)	aunt
외숙모	외숙모님	the wife of mother's brother
아들	아드님	son
딸	따님	daughter
남편	바깥어른 (바깥양반)	husband

아내 (처)	부인	wife
형제	형제분	brothers
자매	자매님	sisters
오누이	——	brother and sister
형	형님	older brother (man's)
형수	형수님	older brother's wife (man's)
오빠	오라버님	older brother (woman's)
올케	——(언니)	brother's wife (woman's)
누나	누님	older sister (man's)
매부	——	sister's husband (man's)
매형	——	older sister's husband (man's)
매제	——	younger sister's husband (man's)
언니	——	older sister (woman's)
형부	——	older sister's husband (woman's)
남동생	계씨	younger brother (both man's and woman's)
계수	계수씨	younger brother's wife (man's)
여동생	——	younger sister (both man's and woman's)
시아버지	시아버님	father-in-law (husband's father)
시어머니	시어머님	mother-in-law (husband's mother)
시아주버니 (시숙)	시아주버님 (시숙님)	husband's older brother
시동생	——	husband's younger brother
시누이	——	husband's sister
장인	장인어른	father-in-law (wife's father)
장모	장모님	mother-in-law (wife's mother)
사위	사위님	son-in-law (daughter's husband)
며느리 (자부)	며느님 (자부님)	daughter-in-law (son's wife)
처남	——	wife's brother
처형	——	wife's older sister
처제	——	wife's younger sister
조카	조카님	nephew
조카딸	조카따님	niece
손자	손자님	grandson
외손자	외손자님	grandson (by one's daughter)
손녀	손녀님	granddaughter
외손녀	외손녀님	granddaughter (by one's daughter)

Notes:

1. 아저씨 'uncle' is used not only as a family term, but to refer to a non-family male adult whose age is similar to the speaker's father. It is also used in reference to a male whose social status is lower than 선생님.
2. 아주머니 'aunt,' besides being used as a family term, is used to refer to any woman whose age is similar to the speaker's mother. It is also used in reference to a woman whose social status is lower than 사모님 or 여사. 사모님 'teacher's wife,' besides being used in addressing a teacher's wife, is used in reference to the wife of a person whose social status is higher than the speaker. -여사 is used in reference to married women who are very famous, or whose social status is very high. It is attached to a family name, or a family name plus a given name.
3. 형 'older brother,' besides being a family term, is used by men to address other men whose age is similar to themselves, to show deference of familiarity. It is attached directly to the family name of a male, like 박형, 김형, 최형.
4. 언니 'older sister' is not only a family term, but is also used by women when addressing women older than themselves, to show familiarity.
5. -씨 following a family name, or a family name plus a given name, may be used without distinction of age or sex, to express courtesy. It is less formal than 선생님, 사모님 or -여사.
6. -군 following a family name, a given name, or a family name plus a given name, is used mostly by men in addressing other men whose social status is similar or inferior to themselves, to show familiarity.
7. -양 following a family name, a given name, or family name plus a given name of unmarried girls is used to show familiarity.

NOTES ON THE BASIC SENTENCES

3. 답장 means 'a reply letter,' 답장하다 is an action verb meaning 'to answer (a letter).' 회답 is also used to indicate 'a reply letter.'
4. -주일 is a classifier meaning 'weeks.' It may be used both with Korean numbers and Chinese numbers. It is used, however, mostly with Chinese numbers. 주일 is used also to mean 'the Lord's Day.'
5. 몇 장 means 'how many (letters).' The classifier -장 'sheets' is used to indicate thin and flat objects.

STRUCTURE NOTES

I. The Particle -한테서… : 'from (a person)'

The particle -한 테 서, following a noun referring to animate beings, is used to indicate the source or starting point of an action.

Examples :

누구한테서 편지가 왔습니까?	From whom did the letter come?
어머님한테서 편지가 왔습니다.	The letter came from my mother.
친구한테서 들었습니다.	I heard it from my friend.
아버지한테서 받았습니다.	I received it from my father.
누구한테서 그것을 사셨습니까?	From whom did you buy it?

II. The Particle -한테… : 'to (a person)'

The particle -한 테, following a noun referring to animate beings, is used to indicate the receiver of an action, or the one for whom something is done or exists.

Examples :

친구한테 그것을 주었습니다.	I gave it to my friend.
누구한테 편지를 쓰셨습니까?	To whom did you write a letter?
어머님한테 편지를 썼습니다.	I wrote a letter to my mother.
학생한테 그 책을 주겠습니다.	I'll give that book to the student.
친구한테 물어 보십시오.	Please ask your friend.

III. Particles Used in Verb Phrases:

(1) Particles -가/-이 and -를/-을

The subject particle -가/-이 and the object particle -를/-을, when inserted into verb phrases, are regarded as formal constructions. So they don't add meaning.

Examples :

수영을 할 수가 없습니다.	I cannot swim.
수영을 하지를 않습니다.	I don't swim.
수영을 할 줄을 모릅니다.	I don't know how to swim.

(2) The Particle -도

The particle -도, when inserted into verb phrases, places emphasis on the verb phrase itself, or has the meaning of 'even, as studied in the previous lesson.

Examples :

수영을 할 수도 없습니다.	I cannot even swim.
수영을 하지도 않습니다.	I do not even swim.
수영을 할 줄도 모릅니다.	I don't even know how to swim.

(3) The Contrast Particle -는/-은

The particle 는-/-은, when inserted into verb phrases, indicates a comparison to the topc which follows it.

Examples :

수영을 할 수는 없습니다.	I cannot swim, (but…)
수영을 하지는 않습니다.	I don't swim, (but…)
수영을 할 줄은 모릅니다.	I don't know how to swim, (but…)

The patterns -ㄹ(을) 수 있다/없다 'can (can't) do' and ㄹ(을) 줄 알다/모르다 'one knows (doesn't know) how to do' will be studied in detail later.

IV. Gender :

There is no gender referring to human beings and animals in the Korean noun. For example, 그분 and 그이 are used as general terms for both male and female. If you want to express the sex of human beings or animals, special words implying the sex are added : (1) for human beings, 남- 'male,' 여- 'female' (2) for animals 수- 'male,' 암- 'female,' in general.

General term :		Masculine :	Feminine :
선생	teacher	남선생	여선생
학생	student	남학생	여학생
동생	younger brother or sister	남동생	여동생

In Korean, sex is indicated mostly by the words themselves :

신사	gentleman	숙녀	lady
총각	bachelor	처녀	virgin or unmarried girl
남자	male person	여자	female person

DRILLS

ADDITIONAL VOCABULARY

기쁘다	to be glad, to be happy	울다	to weep, to cry
슬프다	to be sad, to be sorrowful	다르다	to be different, to be unlike
웃다	to laugh, to smile	적다	to be of small quantity, to be of small number

A. Substitution Drill

1. 할아버지한테서 편지가 왔어요. — The letter came from my grandfather.
2. 할머니한테서 편지가 왔어요. — The letter came from my grandmother.
3. 아버지한테서 편지가 왔어요. — The letter came from my father.
4. 어머니한테서 편지가 왔어요. — The letter came from my mother.
5. 형님한테서 편지가 왔어요. — The letter came from my older brother.
6. 누님한테서 편지가 왔어요. — The letter came from my older sister.
7. 남동생한테서 편지가 왔어요. — The letter came from my younger brother.
8. 여동생한테서 편지가 왔어요. — The letter came from my younger sister.

B. Substitution Drill

1. 할아버지한테 편지를 써요. — I'm writing a letter to my grandfather.
2. 할머니한테 편지를 써요. — I'm writing a letter to my grandmother.
3. 아버지한테 편지를 써요. — I'm writing a letter to my father.
4. 어머니한테 편지를 써요. — I'm writing a letter to my mother.
5. 형님한테 편지를 써요. — I'm writing a letter to my older brother.
6. 누님한테 편지를 써요. — I'm writing a letter to my older sister.
7. 남동생한테 편지를 써요. — I'm writing a letter to my younger brother.
8. 여동생한테 편지를 써요. — I'm writing a letter to my younger sister.

C. Pattern Drill

Teacher: 수영을 하지 않아요. — I don't swim.

Student: 수영을 하지를 않아요. — I don't swim.

1. 기쁘지 않아요. — 기쁘지를 않아요.
2. 슬프지 않아요. — 슬프지를 않아요.
3. 웃지 않아요. — 웃지를 않아요.
4. 울지 않아요. — 울지를 않아요.

5. 다르지 않아요. 다르지를 않아요.
6. 같지 않아요. 같지를 않아요.
7. 적지 않아요. 적지를 않아요.
8. 멀지 않아요. 멀지를 않아요.

D. Pattern Drill

Teacher: 수영을 하지 않아요. I don't swim.
Student: 수영을 하지도 않아요. I don't even swim.

1. 울지 않아요. 울지도 않아요.
2. 웃지 않아요. 웃지도 않아요.
3. 듣지 않아요. 듣지도 않아요.
4. 말하지 않아요. 말하지도 않아요.
5. 구경하지 않아요. 구경하지도 않아요.
6. 도와주지 않아요. 도와주지도 않아요.
7. 좋아하지 않아요. 좋아하지도 않아요.
8. 숙제를 하지 않아요. 숙제를 하지도 않아요.

E. Response Drill (Review)

Teacher: 공부하지 않았어요? Didn't you study?
Student: 예, 공부하지 않았어요. That's right (No). I didn't study.

1. 책을 읽지 않았어요? 예, 책을 읽지 않았어요.
2. 편지를 쓰지 않았어요? 예, 편지를 쓰지 않았어요.
3. 노래를 부르지 않았어요? 예, 노래를 부르지 않았어요.
4. 그분을 사랑하지 않았어요? 예, 그분을 사랑하지 않았어요.
5. 등산을 하지 않았어요? 예, 등산을 하지 않았어요.
6. 일을 시작하지 않았어요? 예, 일을 시작하지 않았어요.
7. 산보하지 않았어요? 예, 산보하지 않았어요.
8. 일을 마치지 않았어요? 예, 일을 마치지 않았어요.

F. Response Drill (Review)

Teacher: 가지 않겠어요? Won't you go?
Student: 아니오, 가겠어요. That's not right (Yes). I'll go.

1. 들어가지 않겠어요? 아니오, 들어가겠어요.
2. 돌아오지 않겠어요? 아니오, 돌아오겠어요.
3. 답장하지 않겠어요? 아니오, 답장하겠어요.
4. 울지 않겠어요? 아니오, 울겠어요.
5. 웃지 않겠어요? 아니오, 웃겠어요.
6. 서지 않겠어요? 아니오, 서겠어요.

7. 앉지 않겠어요? 아니오, 앉겠어요.
8. 옷을 입지 않겠어요? 아니오, 옷을 입겠어요.

G. Response Drill (Review)

Teacher: 그것이 좋을까요? Will it be good? (What's your opinion?)

Student: 예, 그것이 좋겠습니다. Yes, I think it will be good.

1. 그것이 재미있을까요? 예, 그것이 재미있겠어요.
2. 그것이 복잡할까요? 예, 그것이 복잡하겠어요.
3. 그것이 비쌀까요? 예, 그것이 비싸겠어요.
4. 그것이 쌀까요? 예, 그것이 싸겠어요.
5. 그것이 다를까요? 예, 그것이 다르겠어요.
6. 그것이 같을까요? 예, 그것이 같겠어요.
7. 그것이 괜찮을까요? 예, 그것이 괜찮겠어요.
8. 그것이 맛있을까요? 예, 그것이 맛있겠어요.

H. Response Drill (Review)

Teacher: 같이 갈까요? Shall we go together?

Student: 예, 같이 갑시다. Yes, let's go together.

1. 같이 노래를 부를까요? 예, 같이 노래를 부릅시다.
2. 같이 산보할까요? 예, 같이 산보합시다.
3. 같이 읽을까요? 예, 같이 읽읍시다.
4. 같이 들어갈까요? 예, 같이 들어갑시다.
5. 같이 떠날까요? 예, 같이 떠납시다.
6. 같이 앉을까요? 예, 같이 앉읍시다.
7. 같이 수영할까요? 예, 같이 수영합시다.
8. 같이 등산할까요? 예, 같이 등산합시다.

SHORT STORIES

1. 오늘 아버지한테서 편지가 왔습니다.
   그래서 아주 기뻤습니다.
   오늘 저녁에 답장을 쓰겠습니다.

2. 어제 저녁에는 숙제를 했습니다.
   그리고 어머님한테 편지를 썼습니다.
   친구한테도 편지를 썼습니다.

3. 저는 한국말만 공부합니다.
   일본말은 공부하지 않습니다.

일본말 the Japanese language

중국말도 공부하지 않습니다. 중국말 the Chinese language

READING

일 주일 전에 어머니한테서 편지가 왔습니다. 그런데 요즘 대단히 바빴습니다. 그래서 답장을 쓰지 못했습니다. 오늘 저녁에 답장을 쓰겠습니다. 지금 어머니는 미국에 계십니다. 아버지도 미국에 계십니다. 어머니는 저한테 편지를 자주 하십니다. 그런데 아버지한테서는 편지가 가끔 옵니다. 저는 일 주일에 보통 편지를 석 장쯤 씁니다. 그런데 요즘은 숙제가 너무 많습니다. 그래서 일 주일에 한 장만 씁니다.

전에 ago
요즘 these days
대단히 very (much)
자주 frequently, often
가끔 occasionally
너무 too (much)

BRIEFING

A letter came from my mother a week ago. But these days I've been very busy. So I was not able to write an answer. I'm going to write an answer this evening. My mother is in America now. My father is also in America. My mother writes to me frequently. But my father doesn't write to me frequently (Letters from my father come occasionally.) I usually write three letters a week. But these days I have too much homework. So I write only one letter a week.

UNIT 15 백화점 Department

BASIC SENTENCES : MEMORIZE

누구와 같이	with whom
백화점	department store
박 성 철	
1. 누구와 같이 백화점에 가셨어요?	With whom did you go to the department store?
친구와 같이	with my friend
최 인 숙	
2. 친구와 같이 백화점에 갔어요.	I went to the department store with my friend.
무엇	what
사다	to buy
박 성 철	
3. 무엇을 사셨어요?	What did you buy?
치약	toothpaste
수건	towel
예쁜	beautiful
인형	doll
최 인 숙	
4. 치약과 수건을 샀어요. 그리고 예쁜 인형도 샀어요.	I bought toothpaste and a towel. And I also bought a beautiful doll.
곧	soon, immediately
돌아오다	to return
박 성 철	
5. 곧 집으로 돌아오셨어요?	Did you return home immediately?
창경궁	ch'anggyonggoong
최 인 숙	
6. 아니오, 친구하고 같이 창경궁에 갔어요.	No, I went to the ch'anggyonggoong with my friend.

USEFUL EXPRESSIONS : MEMORIZE

1. 따라 읽으세요. Please read after me.
2. 읽어 보세요. Read it, please.
3. 천천히 말씀해 주세요. Speak slowly, please.
4. 좀 더 크게 말씀하세요. Speak a little louder, please.

NOTES ON THE BASIC SENTENCES

1. 백화점 'department store' is a noun derived from the Chinese : 백 means 'hundred,' 화 'goods,' 'cargo,' and 점 'store.' Therefore, its meaning is 'a store keeping a wide variety of goods arranged in several departments.'

4. 치약 'toothpaste' is a noun derived from the Chinese : 치 means 'tooth' and 약 'medicine.' Therefore, its literal meaning is 'a medicine used for cleaning the teeth.'

   수건 'towel' is 'an absorbent cloth for wiping or drying,' whereas 손수건 'handkerchief' is 'a small square piece of cloth used for various purposes or as a costume accessory.'

   예쁜 is an adjective meaning 'beautiful,' 'pretty.' Its opposite word is 미운 'hateful' or 추한 'ugly.'

   인형 'doll' is a noun derived from the Chinese : 인 means 'human being' and 형 'form,' 'figure.' Therefore, its meaning is 'a small scale figure of a human being used especially as a child's plaything.' Korean dolls are exported to foreign countries a great deal these days. They are popular with foreigners because of their dress.

5. 돌아오다 'to return,' 'to come back' is a compound verb : 돌다 'to turn' and 오다 'to come.' 돌아가다 'to go back' is also a compound verb : 돌다 'to turn' and 가다 'to go.' Depending on the context or situation, 돌아가다 also can mean 'to die,' 'to pass away.'

6. 창경궁 means 'the Palace of Bright Rejoicing.' It was constructed in 1419, and first occupied by T'aejo, the founder of the Yi Dynasty. It is located to the east of 창덕궁. During the Hideyoshi invasion of 1592, most of the palace buildings were burned. They were reconstructed during the reign of Sunjo, (the 23rd king), in 1833. It is now a favorite recreational playground in the spring and fall. Usually during the cherry blossom festival, the palace is open late in the evening and attracts blossom viewers from all over the country.

STRUCTURE NOTES

I. The Particle -와/-과 같이… : 'together with'

The particle -와/-과 같이, preceded by nouns, indicates accompaniment, association, relation or harmony. 같이, as an independent word, means 'together,' 'along with,' 'with,' 'in company with.'

Examples :

누구와 같이 가셨습니까?	With whom did you go?
친구와 같이 갔습니다.	I went with my friend.
누구와 같이 하시겠습니까?	With whom will you do it?
아버지와 같이 하겠습니다.	I will do it with my father.
누구와 같이 잡수셨습니까?	With whom did you eat?
선생님과 같이 먹었습니다.	I ate with my teacher.
형님과 같이 산보했습니다.	I took a walk with my older brother.

Notes :

1. This particle -와/-과 같이 is interchangeable with -하고 같이, studied in Unit 10, Structure Notes I, making no difference in meaning. As we have already learned, the word 같이 may be dropped in the -하고 같이 pattern; likewise, it may be dropped in the -와/-과 같이 pattern.
2. -와 같이 is used after nouns ending in a vowel;
   -과 같이 is used after nouns ending in a consonant.

II. The Particle -와/-과… : 'and'

The particle -와/-과 is used to link nouns in coordination. The last noun is followed usually by the subject particle -가/-이, the object particle -를/-을, etc. This particle -와/-과 never links verbs, adjectives, or adverbs.

Examples :

친구와 내가 학교에 갔습니다.	My friend and I went to school.
그분과 내가 일했습니다.	He and I worked.
책과 연필을 샀습니다.	I bought a book and a pencil.
한국말과 영어가 재미있습니다.	Korean and English are interesting.
치약과 수건을 주십시오.	Please give me some toothpaste and a towel.

Notes :

1. The particle -와/-과 is interchangeable with -하고, making no difference in meaning.

2. -와 is used after nouns ending in a vowel;
   -과 is used after nouns ending in a consonant.

III. The Noun Modifiers: D.V.S. + -ㄴ(은)

In Korean, the noun modifier functions in the same way that an adjective or relative clause functions in English. The noun modifier is always put in front of the noun, and indicates a quality, quantity or degree of the noun it modifies. Description verbs can be changed into noun modifiers by attaching the suffix -ㄴ(은) to the verb stem. (Noun modifiers occurring with action verbs and the verb of existence will be studied in detail later.)

D.V.S.+Suffix:	**Noun Modifiers:**	**Meaning:**
크+ㄴ	큰	big
바쁘+ㄴ	바쁜	busy
복잡하+ㄴ	복잡한	complicated
좋+은	좋은	good
작+은	작은	small
같+은	같은	(the) same

Note:

-ㄴ is used after verb stems ending in a vowel;
-은 is used after verb stems ending in a consonant.

Some of the most frequently occurring noun modifiers are:

새	new	거짓	false
헌	old, worn-out	온	all, whole
첫	the first	각	each
헛	vain, fruitless	왼	left
옛	ancient	오른	right
윗	the upper, the above	딴	another, different
뒷	back, behind	외딴	isolated, out-of-the-way
다음	next, following	맞은	the opposite
외	only, single	갖은	all sorts of
단	only, single	온갖	all sorts of
참	real, true	뭇	all sorts of

Notes:

1. 외 'only,' 'single' is used mostly with the words 딸 'daughter,' and 아들 'son', but 단 'only,' 'single' is used mostly with the words 한번 'once,' and 한 사람 'one man.' Study the following examples:

외 딸	only daughter	단 한번	only once
외 아들	only son	단 한사람	only one man

2. 갖은 'all sorts of,' is interchangeable with 온갖, making no difference in meaning. 갖은 and 온갖 are used mostly with the words 고생 'hardship,' 생각 'thought,' and 욕 'abuse,' whereas 뭇 'all sorts of' is used mostly with the words 사람 'people,' 새 'birds,' and 짐승 'animals.' Study the following examples:

갖은 (온갖) 고생	all sorts of hardships
갖은 (온갖) 생각	all sorts of thoughts.
갖은 (온갖) 욕	all sorts of abuse
뭇 사람	all sorts of people
뭇 새	all sorts of birds
뭇 짐승	all sorts of animals

DRILLS

ADDITIONAL VOCABULARY

귀엽다	to be lovable, to be charming	더럽다	to be dirty, to be filthy
깨끗하다	to be clean, to be clear	이야기하다	to speak, to talk

A. Substitution Drill (Review)

1. 식당으로 갑시다.	Let's go to the dining room,
2. 화장실로 갑시다.	Let's go to the rest room.
3. 세탁소로 갑시다.	Let's go to the laundry.
4. 사무실로 갑시다.	Let's go to the office.
5. 마당으로 갑시다.	Let's go to the garden.
6. 학교로 갑시다.	Let's go to the school.
7. 휴게실로 갑시다.	Let's go to the recreation room.
8. 교실로 갑시다.	Let's go to the classroom.

B. Substitution Drill

1. 치약과 수건을 샀어요.	I bought toothpaste and a towel.
2. 설탕과 포도를 샀어요.	I bought sugar and grapes.
3. 사과와 복숭아를 샀어요.	I bought apples and peaches.
4. 수박과 참외를 샀어요.	I bought watermelon and a melon.
5. 책과 공책을 샀어요.	I bought a book and a notebook.
6. 책상과 연필을 샀어요.	I bought a desk and a pencil.

7. 인형과 만년필을 샀어요. I bought a doll and a fountain pen.
8. 자동차와 집을 샀어요. I bought a car and a house.

C. Pattern Drill

Teacher : 방이 깨끗합니다. The room is clean.
Student : 깨끗한 방입니다. It is clean room.

1. 사무실이 더러워요. 더러운 사무실이에요.
2. 아이들이 귀여워요. 귀여운 아이들이에요.
3. 학생이 커요. 큰 학생이에요.
4. 선생님이 좋아요. 좋은 선생님이에요.
5. 책상이 작아요. 작은 책상이에요.
6. 인형이 예뻐요. 예쁜 인형이에요.
7. 점원이 친절해요. 친절한 점원이에요.
8. 교실이 달라요. 다른 교실이에요.

D. Pattern Drill (Review)

Teacher : 식당에 갑시다. Let's go to the dining room.
Student : 식당으로 갑시다. Let's go to the dining room.

1. 교실에 들어갑시다. 교실로 들어갑시다.
2. 집에 돌아왔습니다. 집으로 돌아왔습니다.
3. 사무실에 가겠습니다. 사무실로 가겠습니다.
4. 마당에 갑시다. 마당으로 갑시다.
5. 학교에 오겠습니다. 학교로 오겠습니다.
6. 세탁소에 들어가십시오. 세탁소로 들어가십시오.
7. 휴게실에 갔습니다. 휴게실로 갔습니다.
8. 방에 들어가겠습니다. 방으로 들어가겠습니다.

E. Pattern Drill

Teacher : 치약하고 수건을 샀습니다.
I bought toothpaste and a towel.
Student : 치약과 수건을 샀습니다.
I bought toothpaste and a towel.

1. 수박하고 참외를 먹었어요. 수박과 참외를 먹었어요.
2. 그분하고 내가 일했어요. 그분과 내가 일했어요.
3. 책하고 연필을 사겠어요. 책과 연필을 사겠어요.
4. 친구하고 내가 등산했어요. 친구와 내가 등산했어요.
5. 복숭아하고 포도가 맛있어요. 복숭아와 포도가 맛있어요.
6. 설탕하고 치약을 샀어요. 설탕과 치약을 샀어요.

F. Response Drill

1. 누구와 같이 가셨어요?	친구와 같이 갔어요.
2. 누구와 같이 등산하셨어요?	아버지와 같이 등산했어요.
3. 누구와 같이 주무셨어요?	형님과 같이 잤어요.
4. 누구와 같이 잡수셨어요?	어머님과 같이 먹었어요.
5. 누구와 같이 산보하셨어요?	남동생과 같이 산보했어요.
6. 누구와 같이 이야기하셨어요?	여동생과 같이 이야기했어요.
7. 누구와 같이 수영하셨어요?	선생님과 같이 수영했어요.
8. 누구와 같이 구경하셨어요?	학생과 같이 구경했어요.

G. Pattern Drill (These are irregular verbs. Practice them as they are written. The grammatical explanation will be given later.)

Teacher: 어렵습니다..	It's difficult.
Student: 어려웠어요.	It was difficult.
1. 참 쉽습니다.	참 쉬웠어요.
2. 가깝습니다.	가까웠어요.
3. 귀엽습니다.	귀여웠어요.
4. 더럽습니다.	더러웠어요.
5. 바쁩니다.	바빴어요.
6. 기쁩니다.	기뻤어요.
7. 슬픕니다.	슬펐어요.
8. 다릅니다.	달랐어요.
9. 예쁩니다.	예뻤어요.
10. 큽니다.	컸어요.

SHORT STORIES

1. 친구와 같이 여행했습니다.
아주 재미있었습니다.
그런데 좀 피곤했습니다.

여행하다	to travel
아주	truly, very (much)
피곤하다	to be tired

2. 서점에 갔습니다.
한국말 책과 독일말 책을 샀습니다.
택시로 집에 돌아왔습니다.

서점	bookstore
독일말	German language

3. 어제 형님과 같이 시장에 갔습니다.
포도와 복숭아를 샀습니다.
그리고 곧 집으로 돌아왔습니다.

READING

저는 오늘 학교에 일찍 왔습니다. 친구와 같이 교실로 들어갔습니다. 그런데 교실이 더러웠습니다. 그래서 교실을 청소했습니다. 칠판도 더러웠습니다. 그래서 칠판도 지우개로 깨끗이 닦았습니다. 조금 후에 선생님이 들어오셨습니다. 아홉 시에 공부를 시작했습니다. 오늘은 한국말 공부가 참 재미있었습니다. 11시 50 분에 공부가 끝났습니다. 그래서 일찍 집으로 돌아왔습니다. 집에서 친구와 같이 재미있게 놀았습니다. 그리고 친구와 같이 포도와 사과도 먹었습니다.

일찍	early	깨끗이	cleanly
청소하다	to clean	닦다	to clean, to wipe, to polish,
칠판	blackboard	조금 후에	a little later
지우개	eraser		

BRIEFING

I came to school early today. I went into the classroom with my friend. But the classroom was dirty. So we cleaned the classroom. The blackboard was also dirty. Therefore, we also wiped the blackboard cleanly with an eraser. A little later my teacher came here. We started studying at 9. Today Korean language study was very interesting. We finished the study at 11 : 50. So I came back home early. I had fun with my friend. I ate both grapes and apples with my friend.

UNIT 16 오 원짜리 비행기 A Five Won Plane Ride

BASIC SENTENCES : MEMORIZE

박 성 철

1. 언제 한국에 오셨어요? When did you come to Korea?

두 달	two months
전에	ago

캐 네 디

2. 두 달 전에 한국에 왔어요. I came to Korea two months ago.

그런데	but
잘	well
하다	to do (here to speak)

박 성 철

3. 그런데, 한국말을 잘 하십니다. But, you speak Korean well.

천만에요	don't mention it, it is an undeserved compliment
조금	a little, a bit
밖	outside, outdoors

캐 네 디

4. 천만에요. 조금 밖에 몰라요. Not really. I speak only a little.

정말	the truth

박 성 철

5. 정말입니다. 참 잘 하십니다. I'm telling you the truth. You speak very well.

-짜리	worth, value
태우다	to let ride
이제	now
놀리다	to make fun of

캐 네 디

6. 오 원짜리 비행기 태우지 마세요. 이제 그만 놀리세요. I think you're kidding me. (lit. Don't take me on a five won plane ride.) Stop making fun of me now.

USEFUL EXPRESSIONS : MEMORIZE

1. 안녕히 주무셨어요 ?	Did you sleep well ? (Greeting used in the morning.)
2. 안녕히 주무세요.	Good night. (lit. Sleep in peace. It is a greeting used before going to sleep.)
3. 이리로 오세요.	Come here, please.

NOTES ON THE BASIC SENTENCES

2. 두달 means 'two months.' The classifier -달 (or -개월) 'months' is used to count an amout of months. -달 is always preceded by Korean numbers, whereas -개월 is always preceded by Chinese numbers. The classifier -월 is used to name the calendar months. It is always preceded by Chinese numbers. See the following examples :

한 달	or	일 개월	1 month	일월 (정월)	January
두 달	or	이 개월	2 months	이월	February
석 달	or	삼 개월	3 months	삼월	March
넉 달	or	사 개월	4 months	사월	April
다섯 달	or	오 개월	5 months	오월	May
여섯 달	or	육 개월	6 months	유월	June
일곱 달	or	칠 개월	7 months	칠월	July
여덟 달	or	팔 개월	8 months	팔월	August
아홉 달	or	구 개월	9 months	구월	September
열 달	or	십 개월	10 months	시월	October
열한 달	or	십일 개월	11 months	십일월	November
열두 달	or	십이 개월	12 months	십이월	December

Notes :

1. Some Korean numbers are altered slightly when they occur as modifiers of subsequent classifiers. Notice 석달 'three months,' 넉달 'four months,' 유월 'June,' and 시월 'October.'
2. In order to indicate duration of time, the suffix -동안 'for (three days, a week, a month, etc.,)' is attached normally to -달 'months,' whereas the suffix -간 'for' is attached to -개월 'months.' But they are optional. Study the following examples :

   한국말을 두 달동안 공부했습니다. I studied Korean for two months.

   한국말을 이 개월간 공부했습니다. I studied Korean for two months.
3. The classifier -월, used to name the calendar months, is habitually rein-

forced by -달 'months.' Study the following examples:

한국에 지난 팔월달에 왔어요. I came to Korea last August.
사월달에 갑시다. Let's go in April.

전(에) means 'ago,' 'before,' 'since.' Its opposite word is 후(에) 'after,' 'later (on),' 'afterwards.' Study the following examples:

한 시간 전에 왔습니다. I came (here) an hour ago.
두 시간 후에 갑시다. Let's go in two hours.

3. 한국말을 잘 하십시다 means 'You speak Korean well.' 하다 means 'to do,' but in this context it indicates 'to speak.'
4. 천만에요 'You're welcome,' or 'Don't mention it,' besides being used as a formal reply to apologies, expression of thanks, and formal and respectful recognition, is used when you don't expect something to happen.
5. 정말 means 'the truth,' 'reality.' Its synonym is 참말. The opposite word is 거짓말 'lie.' 거짓말하다 is a verb 'to tell a lie.' 정말 and 참말 are also used as adverbs, depending on the context or situation. See the following examples:

정말입니까? or 참말입니까? Is it true?
거짓말이 아닙니다. It is not a lie.
그분이 거짓말을 합니다. He is telling a lie.
정말 (참말) 좋습니다. It's really good.

6. 오 원 짜리 비행기 태우지 마세요: 오 원 짜리 means 'five won (worth),' 비행기 'an airplane,' and 태우다 'to take a ride on,' 'to let ride.' Therefore, its literal meaning is 'Don't take me on a five won plane ride.' A long time ago, kids enjoyed riding on toy airplanes in parks or palaces, which cost 5 won per ride. This expression is used when someone is kidding you, praising you too much, or is trying to fool you.

STRUCTURE NOTES

I. Noun + 밖에 + 없다 (or 모르다 or V.S. +-지 않다)…: 'there is no one (nothing) but…'

The word 밖, as an independent noun, means 'outside,' 'the exterior.' For example, 밖에 나갑시다 'Let's go out.' It indicates exclusiveness, however, when the word 밖에, preceded by a noun, is followed by a negative predicate.

Examples:

이것 밖에 없습니다. This is all I have.

사무실에 한 분 밖에 없습니다. There is only one person in the office.
조금 밖에 모릅니다. I know only a little.
집 밖에 보이지 않습니다. There is nothing in sight but the house.
한국말 밖에 공부하지 않습니다. I don't study any language but Korean.
이것 밖에 먹지 않겠습니다. The only thing I'll eat is this.
그분 밖에 가지 않습니다. Only that person goes.
그것 밖에 좋지 않습니다. That is the only good thing.

Note:

The pattern Noun + 밖에 + Negative Predicate is interchangeable with -만 'only,' making no difference in meaning.

II. The Suffix -짜리··· : '(a thing) worth'

The suffix -짜리, preceded by a figure plus the money classifier -원, indicates worth or value. It is followed usually by the name of the thing whose value or price is expressed.

Examples:

오만 원짜리 옷 50,000 won clothes
만 원짜리 만년필 10,000 won fountain pen
오천 원짜리 책 5,000 won book
이만 원짜리 구두 20,000 won shoes
천 원짜리 공책 1,000 won notebook

III. The Negative Imperative Form : A.V.S. +-지 말다··· : 'Dont't do···'

The word 말다, as an independent verb, means 'to stop,' 'to cease,' 'to quit,' 'to give up,' 'to refrain from.' The pattern -지 말다 is regularly preceded by action verb stems to indicate prohibition or dissuasion. It is used always as a negative imperative form, or a negative propositive form.

Examples:

지금 공부하지 마십시오. Please don't study now.
학교에 가지 마십시오. Please don't go to school.
일찍 주무시지 마십시오. Please don't sleep early.
지금 떠나지 맙시다. Let's not leave now.
그분을 도와주지 맙시다. Let's not help him.
옷을 입지 맙시다. Let's not put on clothes.

IV. The Negative Adverb 그만… : 'stop (doing)'

The adverb 그만- means 'that much and no more,' 'to that extent only,' 'no more than that,' etc. It is always placed before action verbs. It is used mostly as a negative imperative form, or a negative propositive form.

Examples:

그만 잡수십시오.	Stop eating.
그만 가십시오.	Stop going.
그만 일하십시오.	Stop working.
그만 잡시다.	Let's stop sleeping.
그만 닦읍시다.	Let's stop polishing.

DRILLS

ADDITIONAL VOCABULARY

팔다	to sell	살다	to live
가지고 오다	to bring (something somewhere)	깨다	to wake up
가지고 가다	to take or bring (something somewhere)		

A. Substitution Drill

1. 서울에 살지 마세요.	Please don't live in Seoul.
2. 그것을 팔지 마세요.	Please don't sell that.
3. 지금 청소하지 마세요.	Please don't clean now.
4. 이야기하지 마세요.	Please don't talk.
5. 울지 마세요.	Please don't weep (cry).
6. 웃지 마세요.	Please don't laugh.
7. 여기서 놀지 마세요.	Please don't play here.
8. 노래를 부르지 마세요.	Please don't sing a song.

B. Substitution Drill

1. 공부하지 맙시다.	Let's not study.
2. 들어가지 맙시다.	Let's not go in.
3. 그분을 도와주지 맙시다.	Let's not help him.
4. 여기서 수영하지 맙시다.	Let's not swim here.
5. 일찍 일어나지 맙시다.	Let's not get up early.
6. 지금 청소하지 맙시다.	Let's not clean now.
7. 등산하지 맙시다.	Let's not climb a mountain.

8. 그 책을 읽지 맙시다. Let's not read that book.

C. Substitution Drill

1. 만 원 짜리 옷을 샀어요. I bought clothes for 10,000 won.
2. 이 천 원짜리 책을 샀어요. I bought a book for 2,000 won.
3. 백 원짜리 공책을 샀어요. I bought a notebook for 100 won.
4. 삼백 원짜리 치약을 샀어요. I bought toothpaste for 300 won.
5. 오천 원짜리 인형을 샀어요. I bought a doll for 5,000 won.
6. 이만 원짜리 책상을 샀어요. I bought a desk for 20,000 won.
7. 이백 원짜리 수건을 샀어요. I bought a towel for 200 won.
8. 오백 원짜리 수박을 샀어요. I bought a watermelon for 500 won.

D. Substitution Drill

1. 한 시간 전에 여기에 왔어요. I came here an hour ago.
2. 두 시간 전에 여기에 왔어요. I came here two hours ago.
3. 석 달 전에 여기에 왔어요. I came here three months ago.
4. 넉 달 전에 여기에 왔어요. I came here four months ago.
5. 여섯 달 전에 여기에 왔어요. I came here six months ago.
6. 열 달 전에 여기에 왔어요. I came here ten months ago.
7. 여덟 달 전에 여기에 왔어요. I came here eight months ago.
8. 아홉 달 전에 여기에 왔어요. I came here nine months ago.

E. Substitution Drill

1. 한 시간 후에 갑시다. Let's go in an hour.
2. 두 시간 후에 갑시다. Let's go in two hours.
3. 세 시간 후에 갑시다. Let's go in three hours.
4. 네 시간 후에 갑시다. Let's go in four hours.
5. 한 달 후에 갑시다. Let's go in one month.
6. 두 달 후에 갑시다. Let's go in two months.
7. 석 달 후에 갑시다. Let's go in three months.
8. 넉 달 후에 갑시다. Let's go in four months.

F. Pattern Drill

Teacher: 한 달동안 공부했습니다.
I studied for one month.
Student: 일 개월간 공부했습니다.
I studied for one month.

1. 두 달동안 일했어요. 이 개월간 일했어요.
2. 석 달동안 놀았어요. 삼 개월간 놀았어요.

3. 넉 달동안 가르쳤어요.	사 개월간 가르쳤어요.
4. 다섯 달동안 기다렸어요.	오 개월간 기다렸어요.
5. 여섯 달동안 살았어요.	육 개월간 살았어요.
6. 일곱 달동안 여행했어요.	칠 개월간 여행했어요.
7. 여덟 달동안 공부했어요.	팔 개월간 공부했어요.
8. 아홉 달동안 청소했어요.	구 개월간 청소했어요.

G. Pattern Drill

Teacher: 책을 삽니다.	I am buying a book.
Student: 책 밖에 사지 않습니다.	I'm not buying anything but a book.
1. 그분을 도와줍니다.	그분 밖에 도와주지 않습니다.
2. 노래를 부릅니다.	노래 밖에 부르지 않습니다.
3. 책을 읽습니다.	책 밖에 읽지 않습니다.
4. 청소를 합니다.	청소 밖에 하지 않습니다.
5. 답장을 씁니다.	답장 밖에 쓰지 않습니다.
6. 등산을 합니다.	등산 밖에 하지 않습니다.
7. 수영을 합니다.	수영 밖에 하지 않습니다.
8. 구경을 합니다.	구경 밖에 하지 않습니다.

H. Pattern Drill

Teacher: 그분 밖에 가지 않아요.
Only that person goes.
Student: 그분 밖에 가지 않았어요.
Only that person went.

1. 이것 밖에 좋지 않아요.	이것 밖에 좋지 않았어요.
2. 이것 밖에 없어요.	이것 밖에 없었어요.
3. 한 분 밖에 없어요.	한 분 밖에 없었어요.
4. 공책 밖에 사지 않어요.	공책 밖에 사지 않았어요.
5. 그분 밖에 깨지 않아요.	그분 밖에 깨지 않았어요.
6. 책 밖에 팔지 않아요.	책 밖에 팔지 않았어요.
7. 두 분 밖에 살지 않아요.	두 분 밖에 살지 않았어요.
8. 비행기 밖에 없어요.	비행기 밖에 없었어요.

I. Pattern Drill

Teacher: 일합시다.	Let's work.
Student: 그만 일합시다.	Let's stop working.
1. 먹읍시다.	그만 먹읍시다.
2. 가르칩시다.	그만 가르칩시다.

3. 기다립시다. — 그만 기다립시다.
4. 여행합시다. — 그만 여행합시다.
5. 공부합시다. — 그만 공부합시다.
6. 청소합시다. — 그만 청소합시다.
7. 놉시다. — 그만 놉시다.
다. — 그만 잡시다.

J. Pattern Drill

Teacher : 오월에 갑시다. — Let's go in May.
Student : 오월달에 갑시다.. — Let's go in May.

1. 구월에 가겠습니다. — 구월달에 가겠습니다.
2. 사월부터 일합니다. — 사월달부터 일합니다.
3. 유월까지 공부합니다. — 유월달까지 공부합니다.
4. 일월이 춥습니다. — 일월달이 춥습니다.
5. 팔월이 덥습니다. — 팔월달이 덥습니다.
6. 칠월에 쉽니다. — 칠월달에 쉽니다.
7. 시월에 왔습니다. — 시월달에 왔습니다.
8. 이월에 놀았습니다. — 이월달에 놀았습니다.

SHORT STORIES

1. 석달 전에 한국에 왔어요.
그 때는 날씨가 아주 더웠어요.
그런데 요즘은 날씨가 선선해요.

그때	(at) that time
날씨	(the) weather
덥다	to be hot
선선하다	to be cool (refreshing)

2. 어제 친구하고 같이 백화점에 갔습니다.
친구는 물건을 많이 샀습니다.
그러나 나는 만년필 밖에 사지 않았습니다.

물건	thing

3. 지금은 날씨가 춥습니다.
그러니까 지금 가지 맙시다.
두 시간 후에 갑시다.

춥다	to be cold
그러니까	therefore

READING

석 달 전에 한국에 왔습니다. 비행기로 왔습니다. 그 때는 여름이었습니다. 그래서 참 더웠습니다. 나는 김포 공항에서 택시를 탔습니다. 오후 5시쯤 집에 도착했습니다. 집에서 목욕했습니다. 그리고 저녁을 먹었습니다. 나는 아주 피곤했습니다. 그래서 일찍 잤습니다.

다음 날 일곱 시쯤 잠이 깨었습니다. 그러나 나는 다시 잤습니다. 열 시쯤 일어났습니다. 이를 닦았습니다. 그리고 세수했습니다. 식당에 갔습니다. 거기서 아침을 먹었습니다. 그리고 친구하고 같이 이야기를 많이 했습니다.

여름	summer	다음 날	next day
김포공항	Kimpo airport	잠	sleep, slumber
타다	to ride, to get in, to get on	다시	again
		이를 닦다	to clean one's teeth
오후	afternoon, p.m.	세수하다	to wash up
도착하다	to arrive at (in)	많이	a great deal, lots
목욕하다	to take a bath		

BRIEFING

I came to Korea three months ago. I came by airplane. It was summer. So it was very hot. I took a taxi at Kimpo Airport. I arrived at home about 5 o'clock in the afternoon. I took a bath at home. And I ate supper. I was very tired. So I went to bed early. I woke up about 7 o'clock on the following day (next day). But I slept again. I got up about 10. I brushed my teeth. And I washed up. I went to the dining room. I ate breakfast there. And I talked a lot with my friend.

UNIT 17 바쁘세요? Are You Busy?

BASIC SENTENCES: MEMORIZE

지금 — now
바쁘다 — to be busy

박 성 철

1. 지금 바쁘세요? — Are you busy now?

그리 — so, to that extent

곽 상 흔

2. 아니오, 그리 바쁘지 않아요. — No, I'm not so busy.

그럼 — if that is so, well (then) if that is the case, then,
절 — me
돕다 — to help

박 성 철

3. 그럼, 절 좀 도와 주시겠어요? — Then, will you help me a little bit?

곽 상 흔

4. 예, 도와 드리지요 — Sure, I will.

깨끗이 — cleanly
씻다 — to wash

박 성 철

5. 이걸 좀 깨끗이 씻어 주세요. — Wash this cleanly, please.

곧 — right now, soon

곽 상 흔

6. 예, 곧 씻어 드리지요. — I'll wash it right now.

USEFUL EXPRESSIONS: MEMORIZE

1. 어디에 사세요? — Where do you live?
2. 이름이 무엇이에요? — What's your name?
3. 이것이 무슨 뜻이에요? — What does this mean?

NOTES ON THE BASIC SENTENCES

2. 그리 means 'so,' 'to that extent (degree),' 'in that way.' It is regularly used with the negative predicate. Its synonyms are 그렇게, 그다지 and 별로 (lit. 'in particular,' 'especially'). The word 그리, depending on the context or situation, also can mean 'that way,' 'that direction,' '(to) that place.' Let's study the following words referring to place, in comparison with words indicating thing.

이리 (여기)	'this way,' 'here,' '(to) this place'	이것	'this thing'
그리 (거기)	'that way,' 'there,' '(to) that place'	그것	'that thing'
저리 (저기)	'that way over there,' 'over there,'	저것	'that thing over there'

3. 그럼 is a contraction of 그러면 meaning 'if that is so,' 'if that is the case,' 'if that is true (right),' 'then,' 'well(then),' etc.
   절 is a contraction of 저를.
5. 이걸 is a contraction of 이것을.
   깨끗이 is an adverb meaning 'cleanly.' 깨끗하다 'to be clean' is a description verb. Its opposite word is 더럽다 'to be dirty.'
   씻다 'to wash' is used when washing one's hands, oneself or dishes.
   세수하다 'to wash' is used normally when washing one's face and hands.
   세탁하다 'to wash' is used when washing clothes, or laundering.

STRUCTURE NOTES

I. The Humble Verbs:

In general, humble verbs are used to indicate reverence or respect on the part of the speaker for the person spoken to. In other words, they are words used by the speaker to express his own humility and, at the same time, show his respect for the person with whom he is speaking. They regularly refer to one's own acts, when speaking to persons socially superior to the speaker — as a student to his professor. When two persons of approximately equal social status are talking, each may use the formal polite forms in reference to each other, unless they are on a friendly basis. (In this case, they use the intimate style or the plain style). Like honorific verbs, the humble verbs are limited in number. If you memorize the following list you can handle most of the humble verbs.

Plain :	**Humble :**	**Meaning :**
주다	드리다	to give
묻다 (말하다)	여쭈다	to ask, to tell
보다	뵙다	to see, to meet
데리고 가다	모시고 가다	to take along (someone somewhere)
알리다	아뢰다	to inform, to tell

Notes :

1. The plain word 주다 'to give' is used when a person gives to an inferior or to an equal. It is used regularly for giving to animals or to things, (as in 'give food to the dog').
2. The humble word 드리다 'to give' is used when a person gives to a superior or an equal, or to anyone present to whom one is being polite. It is never used for oneself i.e. 'give to me.' See the following examples :

   드릴까요? — Shall I give it to you?
   예, 주세요. — Yes, give it to me.

II. The Sentence-Final Ending -아(-어, -여) 주다 (or 드리다) :

If you study the plain word 주다 and the humble word 드리다 well, it is easy to learn this pattern -아(-어, -여) 주다 (or 드리다). It is always attached to an action verb stem. The pattern -아(-어, -여) 주다 is used when a speaker requests something for himself, or when he does something for an inferior or an equal.

Examples :

저를 도와 주시겠어요?	Would you be kind enough to help me? Or : Will you help me?
와 주세요.	Come here, please (for me).
그것을 읽어 주세요.	Please read it for me.
한국말을 가르쳐 주겠어요.	I'll teach you Korean (to an equal).
내가 도와 주겠어.	I'll help you (to an inferior).

The pattern -아(-어, -여) 드리다 is used, however, when a speaker does something for a person whose social status is superior or equal to his, or to anyone present to whom one is being polite.

Examples :

읽어 드릴까요?	Shall I read it for you?

도와 드리겠어요. — I'll help you.

그분한테 읽어 드리세요. — Please read it for him.

편지를 써 드리지요. — I'll write for you.

Notes:

Like the formation of the informal-polite style, when the final vowel of the verb stem is -ㅏ or -ㅗ, it takes -아 주다 (or 드리다); when the final vowel of the stem is any other vowel, it takes -어 주다 (or 드리다); when the verb is a -하다 verb, it takes -여 주다 (or 드리다).

DRILLS

ADDITIONAL VOCABULARY

만들다	to make	올라오다	to come up
친하다	to be intimate, to be close	내려가다	to go down
		내려오다	to come down
올라가다	to go up		

A. Substitution Drill

1. 저를 도와 주시겠어요? — Would you be kind enough to help me?
2. 그것을 읽어 주시겠어요? — Would you be kind enough to read it for me?
3. 한국말을 가르쳐 주시겠어요? — Would you be kind enough to teach me Korean?
4. 그것을 만들어 주시겠어요? — Would you be kind enough to make it for me?
5. 올라와 주시겠어요? — Would you be kind enough to come up (here)?
6. 내려가 주시겠어요? — Would you be kind enough to go down (there)?
7. 내려와 주시겠어요? — Would you be kind enough to come down (here)?
8. 노래를 불러 주시겠어요? — Would you be kind enough to sing a song for me?

B. Substitution Drill

1. 읽어 드릴까요? — Shall I read it for you?
2. 편지를 써 드릴까요? — Shall I write for you?
3. 노래를 불러 들릴까요? — Shall I sing a song for you?
4. 한국말을 가르쳐 드릴까요? — Shall I teach you Korean?
5. 이야기해 드릴까요? — Shall I tell it to you?
6. 이 방을 청소해 드릴까요? — Shall I clean this room for you?

7. 도와 드릴까요? — Shall I help you?
8. 그것을 씻어 드릴까요? — Shall I wash it for you?

C. Response Drill

Teacher: 좀 도와 주시겠어요? — Will you help me a little bit?
Student: 예, 도와 드리지요. — Sure, I will.

1. 편지를 써 주시겠어요? — 예, 편지를 써 드리지요.
2. 저를 태워 주시겠어요? — 예, 태워 드리지요.
3. 이것을 가지고 가 주시겠어요? — 예, 가지고 가 드리지요.
4. 청소해 주시겠어요? — 예, 청소해 드리지요.
5. 일찍 일어나 주시겠어요? — 예, 일찍 일어나 드리지요.
6. 이야기해 주시겠어요? — 예, 이야기해 드리지요.
7. 기다려 주시겠어요? — 예, 기다려 드리지요.
8. 들어가 주시겠어요? — 예, 들어가 드리지요.

D. Response Drill (Review)

Teacher: 그것이 참 좋지요? — That's very good, isn't it?
Student: 예, 그것이 참 좋아요. — Yes, it is very good.

1. 그것이 참 예쁘지요? — 예, 그것이 참 예뻐요.
2. 그것이 참 귀엽지요? — 예, 그것이 참 귀여워요.
3. 이 방이 깨끗하지요? — 예, 이 방이 깨끗해요.
4. 날씨가 덥지요? — 예, 날씨가 더워요.
5. 날씨가 선선하지요? — 예, 날씨가 선선해요.
6. 날씨가 춥지요? — 예, 날씨가 추워요.
7. 그분이 친절하지요? — 예, 그분이 친절해요.
8. 여기가 복잡하지요? — 예, 여기가 복잡해요.

E. Pattern Drill (Review)

Teacher: 여기 앉읍시다. — Let's sit down here.
Student: 여기 앉으시지요. — Let's sit down here.

1. 이 일을 끝냅시다. — 이 일을 끝내시지요.
2. 일찍 일어납시다. — 일찍 일어나시지요.
3. 노래를 부릅시다. — 노래를 부르시지요.
4. 들어갑시다. — 들어가시지요.
5. 올라갑시다. — 올라가시지요.
6. 올라옵시다. — 올라오시지요.
7. 내려갑시다. — 내려가시지요.
8. 내려옵시다. — 내려오시지요.

F. Response Drill (Review)

Teacher: 한국말을 공부하셨어요?
Did you study Korean?
Student: 예, 한국말을 공부했어요.
Yes, I studied Korean.

1. 청소하셨어요? 예, 청소했어요.
2. 이를 닦으셨어요? 예, 이를 닦았어요.
3. 답장하셨어요? 예, 답장했어요.
4. 잘 구경하셨어요? 예, 잘 구경했어요.
5. 목욕하셨어요? 예, 목욕했어요.
6. 세수하셨어요? 예, 세수했어요.
7. 그분하고 여행하셨어요? 예, 그분하고 여행했어요.
8. 어제 수영하셨어요? 예, 어제 수영했어요.

G. Response Drill (Review)

Teacher: 지금 바쁘세요? Are you busy now?
Student: 예, 지금 바빠요. Yes, I am busy now.

1. 한국말을 공부하세요? 예, 한국말을 공부해요.
2. 지금 산보하세요? 예, 지금 산보해요
3. 편지를 쓰세요? 예, 편지를 써요.
4. 노래를 부르세요? 예, 노래를 불러요.
5. 지금 떠나세요? 예, 지금 떠나요.
6. 이를 닦으세요? 예, 이를 닦아요.
7. 서울에 사세요? 예, 서울에 살아요.
8. 그분을 사랑하세요? 예, 그분을 사랑해요.

H. Response Drill (Review)

Teacher: 가시겠어요? Will you go?
Student: 아니오, 가지 않겠어요. No, I won't go.

1. 올라가시겠어요? 아니오, 올라가지 않겠어요.
2. 노래를 부르시겠어요? 아니오, 노래를 부르지 않겠어요.
3. 답장하시겠어요? 아니오, 답장하지 않겠어요.
4. 이야기하시겠어요? 아니오, 이야기하지 않겠어요.
5. 들어가시겠어요? 아니오, 들어가지 않겠어요.
6. 여행하시겠어요? 아니오, 여행하지 않겠어요.
7. 가지고 가시겠어요? 아니오, 가지고 가지 않겠어요.
8. 내려가시겠어요? 아니오, 내려가지 않겠어요.

I. Pattern Drill

Teacher : 그리 바쁘지 않아요.	I'm not so busy.
Student : 별로 바쁘지 않아요.	I'm not particularly busy.
1. 그리 좋지 않아요.	별로 좋지 않아요.
2. 그리 크지 않아요.	별로 크지 않아요.
3. 그리 어렵지 않아요.	별로 어렵지 않아요.
4. 그리 덥지 않아요.	별로 덥지 않아요.
5. 그리 춥지 않아요.	별로 춥지 않아요.
6. 그리 복잡하지 않아요.	별로 복잡하지 않아요.
7. 그리 예쁘지 않아요.	별로 예쁘지 않아요.
8. 그리 귀엽지 않아요.	별로 귀엽지 않아요.

J. Intonation Drill (Review)

Teacher : 이분이 누구에요 ? ⌒	Who is this person ?
Student : 이분이 누구지요 ? ↗	Who is this person ?
1. 누가 왔어요 ? ⌒	누가 왔지요 ? ↗
2. 무엇이 좋아요 ? ⌒	무엇이 좋지요 ? ↗
3. 무엇을 잡수세요 ? ⌒	무엇을 잡수시지요 ? ↗
4. 어디에서 공부하세요 ? ⌒	어디에서 공부하시지요 ? ↗
5. 몇 시에 주무세요 ? ⌒	몇 시에 주무시지요 ? ↗
6. 언제 사셨어요 ? ⌒	언제 사셨지요 ? ↗
7. 왜 오셨어요 ? ⌒	왜 오셨지요 ? ↗
8. 어떻게 하셨어요 ? ⌒	어떻게 하셨지요 ? ↗

SHORT STORIES

1. 친구가 아주 바빴어요.
   그래서 친구를 도와 주었어요.
   지금 좀 피곤해요.

2. 일년 전에 그분이 한국말을 몰랐어요.
   내가 그분한테 한국말을 가르쳐 주었어요.
   지금은 그분이 한국말을 잘 해요

   일년 전에 one year ago

3. 낮잠을 잤어요
   그런데 아주 시끄러웠어요.
   그래서 잠이 깨었어요.

   낮잠을 자다 to take a nap
   시끄럽다 to be noisy

READING

오늘도 친구와 같이 학교에서 공부했어요. 그런데 한국말이 아주 어려웠어요. 그래서 선생님한테 여쭤 보았어요. 선생님이 잘 설명해 주셨어요. 오늘은 네 시간 밖에 공부하지 않았어요. 그래서 일찍 집에 돌아왔어요. 오늘은 숙제가 많았어요. 그러나 나는 낮잠부터 잤어요. 그런데 잘 때 누가 떠들었어요. 아주 시끄러웠어요. 그래서 잠이 깨었어요. 좀 화가 났어요. 그러나 참았어요. 나는 친구와 같이 운동장에 나갔어요. 운동장에서 운동을 많이 했어요. 기분이 참 좋았어요.

여쭤 보다	to ask and see what it's like	떠들다	to make noise
		화가 나다	to get angry
설명하다	to explain	참다	to bear, to endure
낮잠부터 자다	I took a nap first	운동장	playground
잘 때	when I was sleeping	운동하다	to do excercise
누가	is an indefinite pronoun meaning 'somebody'	기분	feeling, mood, a frame of mind

BRIEFING

Today also, I studied at school with my friends. But Korean was very difficult. So I asked questions of my teacher. The teacher explained well. I studied only 4 hours today. So I came back home early. Today I had a lot of homework. But I took a nap first. While I was sleeping, somebody made a noise. It was very noisy. So I woke up. I got angry a little bit. But I put up with it. I went out to the playground with my friend. I exercised a lot at the playground. I felt very good.

UNIT 18 누구의 책? Whose Book?

BASIC SENTENCES: MEMORIZE

누구의 — whose

박 성 철

1. 이것이 누구의 책이에요? — Whose book is this?

내 — my

최 인 숙

2. 내 책이에요. — It's my book.

얼마에 — (for) how much

박 성 철

3. 얼마에 사셨어요? — How much did you pay for it?

구천 원 — nine thousand won

최 인 숙

4. 구천 원에 샀어요. — I paid nine thousand won for it.

서점 — bookstore

박 성 철

5. 이것을 서점에서 살 수 있어요? — Can you buy this in a bookstore?

팔다 — to sell
한 권 — one volume
드리다 — to give

최 인 숙

6. 아니오, 서점에서는 팔지 않아요. 내가 한 권 드릴께요. — No, they don't sell it in a bookstore. I will give you one volume.

USEFUL EXPRESSION: MEMORIZE

1. 어떻게 말합니까? — How do you say it?
2. 다 말씀해 보세요. — Say them all, please.
3. 어떻게 씁니까? — How do you write it?
4. 어떻게 발음합니까? — How do you pronounce it?

NOTES ON THE BASIC SENTENCES

1. 누구의 means 'whose.' When the particle 의 is used as a final syllable meaning 'of,' it is ordinarily pronounced 에.
2. 내, besides being used to mean 'I,' is a contraction of 나의 'my.'
3. 얼마 means 'how much.' 얼마 전에 'some time ago'; 얼마 후에 'some time later'; 얼마 동안 'for a while.' 얼마, depending on the intonation and pitch, is used not only as an interrogative pronoun, but also as an indefinite pronoun. When 얼마, is pronounced with a higher initial pitch, and the final intonation of the sentence is down, it is used as an interrogative pronoun. However, it can also be used as an indefinite pronoun; this use is indicated by a rising contour at the end of an otherwise normal pitch.
6. 한 권 means 'one book,' 'one volume.' When the classifier -권 is used with Korean numbers, it is used to specify an amount of books. It indicates serial numbers, however, when it is used with Chinese numbers.

   한 권 'one book' or 'one volume'

   일 권 'book one' or 'volume number one'

STRUCTURE NOTES

I. The Particle -의… :'of'

The particle -의 is equivalent to the English translation 'of,' but there is no exact equivalent to it as a single word in English. The particle -의, preceded by a noun, may indicate possession, relationship, origin, static location, etc., but in every instance, the preceding noun limits or modifies the noun following.

Examples:

나의 (내) 책입니다.	It is my book.
그분은 나의 (내) 친구입니다.	He is a friend of mine.
이것은 그분의 책상입니다.	This is his desk.
내 친구의 아버지가 오셨어요.	My friend's father came.
사람의 말은 재미있어요.	The way that man speaks is interesting.

II. The Potential -ㄹ(을) 수 있다 (없다)… : 'can (cannot) do'

The sentence-final ending -ㄹ(을) 수 있다 (없다) is used with action verbs and the verb 있다; it indicates ability, capability, or possibility.

Examples:

서점에서 살 수 있어요.	You can buy it in a bookstore.
서점에서 살 수 없어요.	You can't buy it in a bookstore.

지금 할 수 있어요.	I can do it now.
지금 할 수 없어요.	I can't do it now.
그분을 도와줄 수 있어요.	I can help him.
그분을 도와줄 수 없어요.	I can't help him.
교실에서 공부할 수 있어요.	You can study in the classroom.
교실에서 공부할 수 없어요.	You can't study in the classroom.
그럴 수 있어요.	Such things do happen.
그럴 수 없어요.	Such things don't happen.
내일 뵐 수 있어요?	Can I see you tomorrow?
내일 뵐 수 없어요?	Can't I see you tomorrow?
여기에 있을 수 있어요.	You can stay here.
여기에 있을 수 없어요.	You can't stay here.

The tense is expressed regularly in the final verb 있다 (없다), not in the preceding verb. Here are some examples.

그분을 도와줄 수 있었어요.	I was able to help him.
그분을 도와줄 수 없었어요.	I wasn't able to help him.

Notes:

-ㄹ 수 있다 (없다) is used after verb stems ending in a vowel;
-을 수 있다 (없다) is used after verb stems ending in a consonant.

III. The Intentional -ㄹ(을)께요…: 'will do'

The sentence-final ending -ㄹ(을)께요 is used with action verbs and the verb 있다; it indicates a speaker's intention or planning.

Examples:

내가 한 권 드릴께요.	I'll give you one volume.
내가 도와줄께요.	I'll help you.
내일 갈께요.	I'll go tomorrow.
여기서 일할께요.	I'll work here.
그분을 만날께요.	I'll meet him.
지금 공부할께요.	I'll study now.
여기에 있을께요.	I'll stay here.

Notes:

1. This pattern is used only with first person statements. It is never used with second person question.
2. -ㄹ께요 is used after verb stems ending in a vowel;
   -을께요 is used after verb stems ending in a consonant.

DRILLS

ADDITIONAL VOCABULARY

만나다	to meet	맥주	beer
나가다	to go out	이상하다	to be strange
생각하다	to think	찾다	to look for, to search for
무섭다	to be fearful, to be frightful	담배	cigarettes

A. Substitution Drill

1. 내가 한 권 드릴께요.	I'll give you one volume.
2. 내가 도와줄께요.	I'll help you.
3. 내가 내일 갈께요.	I'll go tomorrow.
4. 여기서 일할께요.	I'll work here.
5. 그분을 만날께요.	I'll meet him.
6. 지금 공부할께요.	I'll study now.
7. 여기에 있을께요.	I'll stay here.
8. 그것을 찾을께요.	I'll look for it.

B. Substitution Drill (Review)

1. 이 종이 한 장에 얼마에요?	How much is this paper per sheet?
2. 이 책 한 권에 얼마에요?	How much is this book per volume?
3. 이 책상 한 개에 얼마에요?	How much does this desk cost?
4. 이 공책 한 권에 얼마에요?	How much does this notebook cost?
5. 이 맥주 한 병에 얼마에요?	How much is this beer per bottle?
6. 이 연필 한 자루에 얼마에요?	How much are these pencils apiece?
7. 이 담배 한 갑에 얼마에요?	How much are these cigarettes per pack?
8. 이 자동차 한 대에 얼마에요?	How much does this car cost?

C. Substitution Drill (Review)

1. 사백 원에 샀어요.	I paid 400 won for it.
2. 오백 원에 샀어요.	I paid 500 won for it.
3. 육백 원에 샀어요.	I paid 600 won for it.
4. 칠백 원에 샀어요.	I paid 700 won for it.
5. 팔백 원에 샀어요.	I paid 800 won for it.
6. 구백 원에 샀어요.	I paid 900 won for it.
7. 천원에 샀어요.	I paid 1,000 won for it.

8. 삼천 원에 샀어요. I paid 3,000 won for it.

D. Substitution Drill

1. 그것은 그분의 책이에요. It is his book.
2. 그것은 내 책이에요. It is my book.
3. 그것은 선생님의 책이에요. It is the teacher's book.
4. 그것은 학생의 책이에요. It is the student's book.
5. 그것은 아버지의 책이에요. It is my father's book.
6. 그것은 어머니의 책이에요. It is my mother's book.
7. 그것은 형님의 책이에요. It is my older brother's book.
8. 그것은 동생의 책이에요. It is my younger brother's book.

E. Pattern Drill

Teacher : 지금 갈 수 있어요. I am able to go now.
Student : 지금 갈 수 없어요. I am unable to go now.

1. 그분을 만날 수 있어요. 그분을 만날 수 없어요.
2. 지금 나갈 수 있어요. 지금 나갈 수 없어요.
3. 참을 수 있어요. 참을 수 없어요.
4. 낮잠을 잘 수 있어요. 낮잠을 잘 수 없어요.
5. 내가 설명할 수 있어요. 내가 설명할 수 없어요.
6. 그것을 찾을 수 있어요. 그것을 찾을 수 없어요.
7. 그것을 만들 수 있어요. 그것을 만들 수 없어요.
8. 두 시에 도착할 수 있어요. 두 시에 도착할 수 없어요.

F. Pattern Drill

Teacher : 그 분을 도와줄 수 있었어요.
I was able to help him.
Student : 그분을 도와줄 수 없었어요.
I was unable to help him.

1. 여행할 수 있었어요. 여행할 수 없었어요.
2. 가지고 갈 수 있었어요. 가지고 갈 수 없었어요.
3. 청소할 수 있었어요. 청소할 수 없었어요.
4. 이야기할 수 있었어요. 이야기할 수 없었어요.
5. 그것을 깎을 수 있었어요. 그것을 깎을 수 없었어요.
6. 구경할 수 있었어요. 구경할 수 없었어요.
7. 들을 수 있었어요. 들을 수 없었어요.
8. 수영할 수 있었어요. 수영할 수 없었어요.

G. Pattern Drill

Teacher : 도와주겠어요. I'll help you.
Student : 도와줄께요. I'll help you.

1. 책을 읽겠어요. 책을 읽을께요.
2. 두 시까지 마치겠어요. 두 시까지 마칠께요.
3. 세 시에 일어나겠어요. 세 시에 일어날께요.
4. 내일 답장하겠어요. 내일 답장할께요.
5. 지금 숙제하겠어요. 지금 숙제할께요.
6. 한 시에 시작하겠어요. 한 시에 시작할께요.
7. 싸게 팔겠어요. 싸게 팔께요.
8. 내가 설명하겠어요. 내가 설명할께요.

H. Response Drill

1. 그것이 누구의 책이에요? 그것이 선생님의 책이에요.
2. 그분이 누구의 아버지에요? 그분이 친구의 아버지에요.
3. 그것을 얼마에 사셨어요? 그것을 500 원에 샀어요.
4. 하루에 몇 번 잡수세요? 하루에 두 번 먹어요.
5. 그분을 만날 수 있을까요? 예, 그분을 만날 수 있어요.
6. 이 책을 어디에서 팔아요? 책방에서 이 책을 팔아요.
7. 누구를 생각하세요? 친구를 생각해요.
8. 무엇이 무섭습니까? 개가 무섭습니다.
9. 무엇이 이상합니까? 한국말이 이상합니다.

I. Intonation Drill (Review)

Teacher : 무엇을 사셨어요? ↷ What did you buy?
Student : 무엇을 사셨어요? ↗ Did you buy something?

1. 누가 왔어요? ↷ 누가 왔어요? ↗
2. 어디 가세요? ↷ 어디 가세요? ↗
3. 언제 드릴까요? ↷ 언제 드릴까요? ↗
4. 어떤 사람을 만나시겠어요? ↷ 어떤 사람을 만나시겠어요? ↗
5. 몇 권 사셨어요? ↷ 몇 권 사셨어요? ↗

SHORT STORIES

1. 친구의 아버지가 저를 찾아왔어요.
그분은 아주 좋은 분이에요.
오늘은 그분하고 같이 점심을 먹었어요.

찾아오다 to visit, to come to see

2. 책방에서 이 책을 샀어요.
   이 책을 3,000 원에 샀어요.
   오늘 저녁부터 읽겠어요.

3. 지금은 아주 바빠요.
   그래서 지금은 갈 수 없어요.
   제가 두 시간 후에 갈께요.

4. 밤에 혼자서 산보했어요.
   그런데 갑자기 누가 불렀어요.
   나는 깜짝 놀랐어요.

혼자서	alone
갑자기	suddenly
부르다	to call
깜짝	with a start
놀라다	to be surprised

READING

어제 친구와 같이 책방에 갔어요. 책방에서 한국말 책을 한 권 샀어요. 그 책을 15,000 원에 샀어요. 그 책이 아주 좋은 책이었어요. 우리는 배가 고팠어요. 그래서 한식점에 들어갔어요. 거기서 저녁을 같이 먹었어요. 한식이 참 맛있었어요. 우리는 저녁을 먹은 다음에 극장에 갔어요. 그런데 극장에 사람이 굉장히 많았어요. 그래서 표를 살 수 없었어요. 할수없이 집에 돌아왔어요. 집에서 목욕한 다음에 숙제를 했어요. 그리고 텔레비전을 한 시간쯤 구경했어요. 열 한 시쯤 친구하고 같이 맥주를 마셨어요. 그리고 열두 시에 잤어요.

우리	we	굉장히	magnificently, awfully
한식점	Korean restaurant	표	ticket
한식	Korean food	할수없이	helplessly, reluctantly
먹은 다음에	after eating	텔레비전	television
극장	theater	마시다	to drink

BRIEFING

I went to the bookstore with my friend yesterday. I bought a Korean language book at the bookstore. I bought it for 15,000 won. It was a very good book. We were hungry. So we went into the restaurant. We ate supper there. Korean food was very delicious. After eating supper we went to the theater. But there were an awful lot of people in the theater. So we couldn't help but come back home. At home after taking a bath, I did my homework. I watched television about one hour. About 11 o'clock I drank beer with my friend. And I went to bed at twelve.

UNIT 19 코피를 마시면 If I Drink Coffee

BASIC SENTENCES: MEMORIZE

들다 — to eat, to drink, to have

최 인 숙

1. 무얼 드시겠어요? — What will you have?

우유 — milk

박 성 철

2. 우유 있어요? — Do you have milk?

아이구 — Oh My! My goodness

코피 — coffee

최 인 숙

3. 아이구! 우유가 없군요. — Oh My! We have no milk.
코피 드릴까요? — Shall I give you coffee?

마시다 — to drink

박 성 철

4. 코피는 마시고 싶지 않아요. — I don't want to drink coffee.

왜 — why

최 인 숙

5. 왜요? — Why?

배 — the stomach, the belly

아프다 — to be painful

박 성 철

6. 난 코피를 마시면 배가 아파요. — If I drink coffee, I'll get a stomachache.

USEFUL EXPRESSIONS: MEMORIZE

1. 책을 펴 주세요. — Open the book, please.
2. 책을 덮어 주세요. — Close the book, please.
3. 책을 보지 마세요. — Don't look at the book, please.

NOTES ON THE BASIC SENTENCES

1. 무얼 드시겠어요? means 'What will you have?' 무얼 is a contraction of 무엇을, and 들다 means 'to drink,' 'to eat,' 'to have.' The verb 들다 is an irregular verb. See Structure No. 1 of this Unit.

Words for eating and drinking are:

잡수시다 'to eat' (honorific)
들다 'to eat,' 'to drink' (honorific)
먹다 'to eat' (plain word)
마시다 'to drink'

많이 잡수세요.	Help yourself, please.
많이 드세요.	Help yourself, please.
아침을 잡수셨어요?	Did you have breakfast?
자 듭시다.	Let's begin eating.
참 잘 먹었습니다.	I've had enough, thank you.
물을 마시겠어요.	I'll drink water.

3. 아이구 is a variant of 아이고. 아이구 is an exclamatory expression of pain, complaint, grudge, hardship, surprise, etc. It is also a bewailing sound — a cry heard in a mourner's house, when someone's parents or grandparents have died. 코피 'coffee' is derived from English. Pay attention to the differences between the Korean and English pronunciations. In the Korean sound system, there is no labio-dental fricative, such as /f/, /v/.

6. 난 is a contration of 나는. 배, depending on the context or situation, means (1) 'the stomach,' 'the belly,' (2) 'a ship,' 'a boat,' (3) 'a pear.' Here are some examples:

나는 배가 고파요.	I am hungry.
배가 아파요.	I have a stomachache.
배로 갑시다.	Let's go by boat.
이 배가 맛있어요.	This pear is delicious.

It is also used to mean 'double,' 'times,' 'fold.'

배	two times, double	오 배	five times	팔 배	eight times
삼 배	three times	육 배	six times	구 배	nine times
사 배	four times	칠 배	seven times	십 배	ten times
				백 배	one hundred times

STRUCTURE NOTES

I. -ㄹ Irregular Verbs:

Some verbs ending in a final consonant -ㄹ are irregular.

Examples:

들다	to eat, to drink	살다	to live
팔다	to sell	울다	to cry
알다	to know	놀다	to play

1. The final consonant -ㄹ of the stem is dropped, when followed by the consonants -ㄴ, -ㅂ, -ㅅ or the vowel -오. See the following examples:

무엇을 파니?	What do you sell? (plain style)
수박을 팝니다.	I sell watermelon.
그것을 나한테 파세요.	Please sell that to me.
그분이 책을 파오.	He is selling books. (intimate style)

2. But the final consonant -ㄹ of the stem is not dropped, when followed by other consonants or vowels. See the following examples:

그것을 팔지 마세요.	Don't sell it, please.
그것을 팔겠습니다.	I'll sell it.
그것을 팔아야 합니다.	I have to sell it.
그것을 팔았습니다.	I sold it.

II. The Sentence-Final Ending -고 싶다/-고 싶어 하다…: 'want to (do)'

The pattern -고 싶다/-고 싶어 하다 is used with action verbs and the verb 있다 'to stay'; it indicates the desires of the subject.

1. The sentence-final ending -고 싶다 is used regularly with first person statements and second person questions. See the following examples:

가고 싶어요.	I want to go.
공부하고 싶어요.	I want to study.
코피를 한잔 마시고 싶어요.	I want to drink a cup of coffee.
여기에 있고 싶어요.	I want to stay here.
무엇을 사고 싶습니까?	What do you want to buy?
어디에 가고 싶으세요?	Where do you want to go?
누구를 만나고 싶으세요?	Whom do you want to meet?

The tense and/or negation are expressed regularly in the final verb 싶다.

See the following examples:

가고 싶어요.	I want to go.
가고 싶지 않아요.	I don't want to go.
가고 싶었어요.	I wanted to go.
가고 싶지 않았어요.	I did not want to go.

2. The sentence-final ending -고 싶어 하다 is used regularly with the third person. See the following examples:

그분이 가고 싶어 해요.	He wants to go.
그분이 일하고 싶어 해요.	He wants to work.
그분이 여기에 있고 싶어 해요.	He wants to stay here.

The tense and/or negation are expressed regularly in the final verb -하다. See the following examples:

그분이 가고 싶어 해요.	He wants to go.
그분이 가고 싶어 하지 않아요.	He doesn't want to go.
그분이 가고 싶어 했어요.	He wanted to go.
그분이 가고 싶어 하지 않았어요.	He didn't want to go.

III. The Conditional -(으)면…: 'if,' 'when'

The non-final ending -(으)면 is used with any verb, and indicates condition or stipulation. In Korean, the dependent clause precedes the main clause, whereas in English the order of the dependent and main clause doesn't matter. The pattern -(으)면 usually ends with a comma intonation.

Examples:

그것이 좋으면, 사겠어요.	If it's good, I'll buy it.
그 책이 재미있으면, 읽겠어요.	If that book is interesting, I'll read it.
그분이 오면, 갑시다.	If (when) he comes, let's go.
그분이 가면, 나도 가겠어요.	If he goes, I'll go too.
시간이 있으면, 가세요.	If (when) you have time, go.
돈이 있으면, 사세요.	If you have money, buy it.
공부하면, 피곤해요.	If I study, I get tired.

만일 (만약) 'supposing,' as an advance signal of the condition, may occur at the beginning of a conditional phrase. It places emphasis on its suppositional character.

만일 비가 오면, 가지 맙시다.	If it rains, let's not go.
만약 그분을 만나면, 말씀하세요.	If you see him, tell him.

Notes:

1. When the subject of the dependent clause (if-clause) is different from that of the main clause, it always takes the subject particle -가/-이.
   한국말이 재미있으면, 공부하겠어요. If Korean is interesting, I will study it.
2. When the subject of the dependent clause (if-clause) is the same as that of the main clause, it takes the contrast particle -는/-은.
   나는 그것을 마치면, 가겠어요. If I finish that, I'll go.
3. -면 is used after verb stems ending in a vowel or the consonant -ㄹ;
   -으면 is used after verb stems ending in all consonants except -ㄹ.

DRILLS

ADDITIONAL VOCABULARY

걸어가다	to go on foot, to walk	어둡다	to be dark
뛰어가다	to run, to rush	문	a door
넣다	to put (a thing) in, to pour in	열다	to open
		닫다	to close
꺼내다	to take (bring, pull) out	기쁘다	to be glad, to be pleased, to be delighted
밝다	to be bright		

A. Substitution Drill

1. 걸어가고 싶어요.	I want to walk.
2. 뛰어가고 싶어요.	I want to run.
3. 설탕을 넣고 싶어요.	I want to put sugar in.
4. 그것을 꺼내고 싶어요.	I want to take it out.
5. 그분을 찾아가고 싶어요.	I want to visit him.
6. 그분을 만나고 싶어요.	I want to meet him.
7. 나가고 싶어요.	I want to go out.
8. 낮잠을 자고 싶어요.	I want to take a nap.

B. Substitution Drill

1. 코피를 마시고 싶지 않아요.	I don't want to drink coffee.
2. 답장을 하고 싶지 않아요.	I don't want to answer the letter.
3. 웃고 싶지 않아요.	I don't want to laugh.
4. 울고 싶지 않아요.	I don't want to cry.
5. 노래를 부르고 싶지 않아요.	I don't want to sing a song.
6. 여기에 앉고 싶지 않아요.	I don't want to sit down here.

7. 여기에 서고 싶지 않아요. — I don't want to stand up here.
8. 그분을 사랑하고 싶지 않아요. — I don't want to love him.

C. Substitution Drill

1. 그분이 문을 열고 싶어 해요. — He wants to open the door.
2. 그분이 문을 닫고 싶어 해요. — He wants to close the door.
3. 그분이 설명하고 싶어 해요. — He wants to explain it.
4. 그분이 올라가고 싶어 해요. — He wants to go up.
5. 그분이 내려가고 싶어 해요. — He wants to go down.
6. 그분이 이를 닦고 싶어 해요. — He wants to clean his teeth.
7. 그분이 서울에 살고 싶어 해요. — He wants to live in Seoul.
8. 그분이 가지고 가고 싶어 해요. — He wants to take it along.

D. Substitution Drill (Review)

1. 그분이 학교에 가는군요! — He is going to school!
2. 그분이 공부하는군요! — He is studying now!
3. 그분이 교실을 청소하는군요! — He is cleaning the classroom!
4. 그분이 낮잠을 자는군요! — He is taking a nap!
5. 그분이 세수하는군요! — He is washing his face!
6. 그분이 그분을 도와주는군요! — He is helping him!
7. 그분이 쉬는군요! — He is taking a rest!
8. 그분이 수영하는군요! — He is swimming!

E. Pattern Drill

Teacher: 그분이 서울에 사십니다.
He lives in Seoul.

Student: 그분이 서울에 살지 않아요.
He does not live in Seoul.

1. 그분이 코피를 드십니다. — 그분이 코피를 들지 않아요.
2. 그분이 책을 파십니다. — 그분이 책을 팔지 않아요.
3. 그분이 문을 여십니다. — 그분이 문을 열지 않아요.
4. 그분이 우십니다. — 그분이 울지 않아요.
5. 그분이 노십니다. — 그분이 놀지 않아요.

F. Pattern Drill (Review)

Teacher: 그것이 예쁩니다. — That's beautiful.
Student: 그것이 예쁘군요 — That's beautiful!

1. 이 방이 밝습니다. — 이 방이 밝군요!
2. 이 방이 어둡습니다. — 이 방이 어둡군요!

3. 참 기쁩니다. 참 기쁘군요!
4. 이상합니다. 이상하군요!
5. 참 무섭습니다. 참 무섭군요!
6. 너무 시끄럽습니다. 너무 시끄럽군요!
7. 아주 춥습니다. 아주 춥군요!
8. 아주 덥습니다. 아주 덥군요!

G. Pattern Drill

Teacher: 가고 싶었어요. I wanted to go.
Student: 가고 싶지 않았어요. I didn't want to go.

1. 청소하고 싶었어요. 청소하고 싶지 않았어요.
2. 그것을 팔고 싶었어요. 그것을 팔고 싶지 않았어요.
3. 비행기를 타고 싶었어요. 비행기를 타고 싶지 않았어요.
4. 두 시에 도착하고 싶었어요. 두 시에 도착하고 싶지 않았어요.
5. 목욕하고 싶었어요. 목욕하고 싶지 않았어요.
6. 이를 닦고 싶었어요. 이를 닦고 싶지 않았어요.
7. 세수하고 싶었어요. 세수하고 싶지 않았어요.
8. 그분을 태우고 싶었어요. 그분을 태우고 싶지 않았어요.

H. Pattern Drill

Teacher: 그분이 가고 싶어 했어요.
He wanted to go.
Student: 그분이 가고 싶어 하지 않았어요.
He didn't want to go.

1. 그분이 팔고 싶어 했어요. 그분이 팔고 싶어 하지 않았어요.
2. 그분이 세수하고 싶어 했어요. 그분이 세수하고 싶어 하지 않았어요.
3. 그분이 만들고 싶어 했어요. 그분이 만들고 싶어 하지 않았어요.
4. 그분이 올라가고 싶어 했어요. 그분이 올라가고 싶어 하지 않았어요.
5. 그분이 올라오고 싶어 했어요. 그분이 올라오고 싶어 하지 않았어요.
6. 그분이 내려가고 싶어 했어요. 그분이 내려가고 싶어 하지 않았어요.
7. 그분이 내려오고 싶어 했어요. 그분이 내려오고 싶어 하지 않았어요.
8. 그분이 설명하고 싶어 했어요. 그분이 설명하고 싶어 하지 않았어요.

I. Integration Drill

Teacher: 그것이 좋아요. 사겠어요.
It's good. I'll buy it.
Student: 그것이 좋으면, 사겠어요.
If it's good, I'll buy it.

1. 아이들이 떠들어요. 자지 못해요.
   아이들이 떠들면, 자지 못해요.
2. 화가 나요. 공부할 수 없어요.
   화가 나면, 공부할 수 없어요.
3. 시끄러워요. 참을 수 없어요.
   시끄러우면, 참을 수 없어요.
4. 그것을 생각합니다. 기분이 나쁩니다.
   그것을 생각하면, 기분이 나쁩니다.
5. 편지가 옵니다. 답장을 하겠습니다.
   편지가 오면, 답장을 하겠습니다.
6. 운동을 합니다. 기분이 좋습니다.
   운동을 하면, 기분이 좋습니다.
7. 시간이 있습니다. 가겠습니다.
   시간이 있으면, 가겠습니다.
8. 시간이 없습니다. 뛰어가겠습니다.
   시간이 없으면, 뛰어가겠습니다.

SHORT STORIES

1. 눈을 감고 싶지 않았어요.
   눈을 뜨고 싶었어요.
   그런데 눈을 뜰 수 없었어요.

눈	an eye
뜨다	to open (eyes)
감다	to close (eyes)

2. 그 학생이 서울에 가고 싶어 했어요.
   내가 그 학생을 서울에 데리고 갔어요.
   그 학생이 아주 좋아했어요.

좋아하다	to be pleased with, to be glad, to like

3. 그것이 좋으면, 사겠어요.
   좋지 않으면, 사지 않겠어요.
   좋은 것을 보여 주세요.

보이다	to show

READING

여자 친구한테서 편지가 왔어요. 그 여자가 다방에서 만나자고 했어요. 그래서 기분이 참 좋았어요. 나는 목욕부터 했어요. 그리고 면도 했어요. 새 옷을 갈아입었어요. 새 넥타이도 매었어요. 택시를 타고 다방에 갔어요. 그런데 다방에 여자 친구가 없었어요. 누이 동생이 다방에 있었어요. 여자 친구가 나한테 편지를 쓰지 않았어요. 누이

동생이 장난으로 나한테 그런 편지를 썼어요. 화가 났지만 참았어요. 누이 동생을 데리고 극장에 갔어요. 영화가 참 재미있었어요.

다방	tea (coffee) house	넥타이	necktie
만나자고 했어요	She said (wrote) 'Let's meet…'	매다	to tie
		택시를 타고 다방에 갔어요.	I took a taxi and went to the tea house
면도하다	to shave oneself		
새 옷	new clothes	장난으로	for fun
갈아입다	to change (clothes)	영화	movie
그런	like that	누이동생	younger sister

BRIEFING

A letter came from my girl friend. She said, "Let's meet in the tea room." So I felt very good. I took a bath first. And I shaved. I changed into new clothes. I also tied a new tie. I took a taxi and went to the tearoom. But my girl friend was not in the tearoom. My younger sister was in the tearoom. My girl friend didn't write a letter to me. My younger sister wrote such a letter to me for fun. I got angry, but I put up with it. I went to the theater with my younger sister. The movie was very interesting.

UNIT 20 수영 Swimming

BASIC SENTENCES : MEMORIZE

수영하다	to swim
최 인 숙	
1. 같이 수영하러 갈까요?	Shall we go for a swim?
싫다	to dislike, to hate
박 성 철	
2. 오늘은 가기 싫어요. 피곤하기 때문에 쉬겠어요.	I really don't feel like going today. I'll rest because I'm tired.
푹	deeply, completely
최 인 숙	
3. 피곤하시면, 푹 쉬세요.	If you are tried, get a good rest.
문	a door
닫다	to close
박 성 철	
4. 미안하지만, 문 좀 닫아 주시겠어요?	I'm sorry, but will you please close the door?
최 인 숙	
5. 예, 그러지요.	Yes, I will.
잘	well
다녀오다	to go round to see (a person) and then return
박 성 철	
6. 어서 잘 다녀 오세요.	So long!
최 인 숙	
7. 그럼, 다녀 오겠어요.	So long!

USEFUL EXPRESSIONS : MEMORIZE

1. 마음대로 하세요.	Do as you please.
2. 그냥 두세요.	Leave it as it is.
3. 시간이 다 되었어요.	Time is up.

NOTES ON THE BASIC SENTENCES

1. 싫다 'to be unpleasant,' 'to dislike' is used always with the subject particle -가/-이, whereas 싫어하다 'to dislike,' 'to hate' is used with the object particle -를/-을. See the following examples, and note particularly the particles.

나는 과자가 싫어요.	I have no taste for sweets.
나는 과자를 싫어해요.	I don't like sweets.

2. 쉬다 means 'to rest.' '쉽다' means 'to be easy.' When they are followed by a vowel, however, pay attention to the slight difference in the pronunciation of these two words. See the following examples:

쉬어요.	I'm taking a rest.
쉬워요.	It's easy.
쉬었습니다.	I took a rest.
쉬웠습니다.	It was easy.

4. 좀, depending on the context or situation, means (1) 'some,' 'to some extent,' 'a little,' (2) 'please,' 'just.' See the following examples:

오늘은 기분이 좀 좋아요.	I feel a little better today.
내일 좀 공부하세요.	Please study tomorrow.

닫다 means 'to close.' Its opposite word is 열다 'to open.' Study the following words, which have to do with opening and closing.

열다≠닫다	'to open≠to close (a door, a lid, a cover, etc.)'
뜨다≠감다	'to open≠to close (eyes)'
벌리다≠다물다	'to open≠to close (mouth)'

문을 열어 주세요.	Please open the door.
문을 닫아 주세요.	Please close the door.
눈을 뜨세요.	Open your eyes.
눈을 감으세요.	Close your eyes.
입을 벌리세요.	Open your mouth.
입을 다무세요.	Close your mouth.

6. 잘 다녀 오세요 is a farewell given regularly by a person remaining behind to a person leaving his own home, his office, his town, city or country, etc.
7. 다녀 오겠어요 is a farewell given regularly by a person leaving his own home, his office, his town, city, or country etc., to a person remaining behind. It is used as a reply to the preceding sentence, #6.

STRUCTURE NOTES

I. The Ending -(으)러 : A.V.S. +-(으)러… : 'in order to'

The non-final ending -(으)러 is used with action verbs, and indicates the purpose of an action. This ending -(으)러 is followed always by either 가다, 오다 or their compounds, or any verb of movement.

Examples :

점심을 먹으러 왔어요.	I came to eat lunch.
그분을 만나러 갑시다.	Let's go to see him.
책을 사러 오겠어요.	I'll come to buy a book.
일하러 거기에 갔어요.	He went there to work.
수영하러 갈까요?	Shall we go for a swim?
공부하러 여기에 들어왔어요.	I came in here to study.
그분이 산보하러 나갔어요.	He went out to take a walk.
그분이 놀러 왔어요.	He came to play.
그분이 일하러 다닙니다.	He goes about working.

Notes :

1. The tense and/or negation are expressed regularly in the final verb, not in the verb with -(으)러. Study the following examples:

책을 사러 왔어요.	I came to buy a book.
책을 사러 와요.	I am coming to buy a book.
책을 사러 오겠어요.	I'll come to buy a book.
책을 사러 오지 않겠어요.	I won't come to buy a book.

2. -러 is used after verb stems ending in a vowel and the consonant -ㄹ; -으러 is used after verb stems ending in all consonants except -ㄹ.

II. Verbal Noun Formations :

In Korean, verbal nouns are made with the nominalizing suffixes -기 and -ㅁ/-음. (There are many ways of making verbal nouns out of verbs, but -기 and -ㅁ/-음 are the most common.

The Nominalizing Suffix -기… : '-ing,' 'to (do)'

In Korean, most verbs can be changed into verbal nouns by attaching the nominalizing suffix -기 to the verb stem. The verbal nouns made in this way -기 indicate activity, quality, quantity, extent, or state of being, concretely. The English equivalent of this pattern is '-ing,' or the infinitive 'to (do).'

Verb:		V.S.	Suffix:	V.N.	Meaning:
공부하다	to study	공부하-	-기	공부하기	studying
가르치다	to teach	가르치-	-기	가르치기	teaching
일하다	to work	일하-	-기	일하기	working
읽다	to read	읽-	-기	읽기	reading
크다	to be big	크-	-기	크기	bigness, size

Notes:

1. When a verbal noun made with the suffix -기 is used as a subject, it takes the particle -가/-이. (However, the partcle -가/-이 can be dropped in lively conversation.) Here are some examples:

가르치기가 쉽습니다.	It is easy to teach. Or: Teaching is easy.
그분을 만나기가 어렵습니다.	It is difficult to meet him. Or: Meeting him is difficult.
공부하기가 싫어요.	Studying is hateful.

2. When a verbal noun made with the suffix -기 is used as an object, it takes the particle -를/-을. (The particle -를/-을 can be dropped, however, in lively conversation.) Here are some examples:

그분은 일하기를 싫어해요.	He doesn't like to work.
나가기를 싫어해요.	I hate to go out.
먹기를 좋아해요.	I like to eat.
공부하기를 시작했어요.	I began to study.
내일 날씨가 좋기를 바랍니다.	I hope the weather will be nice tomorrow.

The Nominalizing Suffix -ㅁ/-음:

Other verbal nouns are made by attaching the nominalizing suffix -ㅁ/-음 to the verb stem. Verbal nouns made with the suffix -ㅁ/-음 usually indicate activity or state of being, abstractly.

Verb:		V.S.	Suffix:	V.N.	Meaning:
보다	to see	보-	-ㅁ	봄	seeing
가르치다	to teach	가르치-	-ㅁ	가르침	teaching
그리다	to draw	그리-	-ㅁ	그림	drawing
꾸다	to dream	꾸-	-ㅁ	꿈	dreaming
싸우다	to fight	싸우-	-ㅁ	싸움	fighting
살다	to live	살-	-ㅁ	삶	living, life

얼다	to freeze	얼-	-음	얼음	ice
자다	to sleep	자-	-ㅁ	잠	sleeping
죽다	to die	죽-	-음	죽음	death
지다	to carry	지-	-ㅁ	짐	luggage
찾다	to find	찾-	-음	찾음	finding
추다	to dance	추-	-ㅁ	춤	dancing

Notes:

1. -ㅁ is used after verb stems ending in a vowel and the word 살;
   -음 is used after verb stems ending in a consonant, except in the word 살.
2. Some verbal nouns made with the suffix -ㅁ/-음, are used to complement objects of some other verb forms of the same roots.

잠(을) 자다	to sleep	그림(을) 그리다	to draw
꿈(을) 꾸다	to dream	뜀(을) 뛰다	to jump
춤(을) 추다	to dance	숨(을) 쉬다	to breathe

3. There are many other ways to form verbal nouns, but most of them are irregular. It is better to memorize them one at a time, as they occur.

III. The Causal Ending -기 때문에…: 'so,' 'therefore,' 'because'

The non-final ending -기 때문에 may be used with any verb, and indicates cause or reason. The English equivalent of this pattern -기 때문에 is 'so,' 'therefore,' or 'because,' but it is convenient to translate this pattern as 'so,' since this word fits into the English syntax in about the same way that -기 때문에 fits into the Korean syntax. The main difference is in the pause: English speaker before 'so,' but Korean after -기 때문에.

Examples:

내일 가기 때문에, 오늘 가지 않겠어요.	I'm going tomorrow, so today I won't go.
시간이 없었기 때문에, 갈 수 없었어요.	I had no time, so I could not go.
지금 피곤하기 때문에, 쉬고 싶어요.	I'm tired now, so I want to rest.
날씨가 좋지 않기 때문에, 집에 있겠어요.	The weather is not good, so I'll stay home.
춥기 때문에, 못 갔어요.	It was cold, so I could not go.
한국 사람이기 때문에, 김치를 좋아해요.	I'm Korean, so I like kimchi.

선생이 아니기 때문에, 가르칠 수 없어요.	I'm not a teacher, so I can't teach.

Notes :

1. The tense infixes (-았-, -겠-) can be used in the dependent clause (because-clause) if necessary, but the tense is expressed normally in the main clause. Here are some examples :

춥기 때문에 갔어요.	Because it was cold, I went.
춥기 때문에 갑니다.	Because it is cold, I go.
춥기 때문에 가겠어요.	Because it is cold, I will go.

2. Sometimes it can be used with the polite particle <u>-요</u> as an unfinished sentence. Here are some examples :

왜 가지 않으세요 ?	Why aren't you going ?
춥기 때문에요.	Because it is cold……

3. The form <u>-때문에,</u> (without the suffix -기), may be used with nouns to mean 'because of,' 'on account of.' See the following examples :

나 때문에 그분이 못 갔어요.	He couldn't go because of me.
무엇 때문에 찾아오셨어요 ?	Why did you visit me ?
그분 때문에 못 잤어요.	I could not sleep because of him.
그 일 때문에 여기에 왔어요.	I came here because of that work.

IV. <u>The Contrastive Ending -지만… : 'but'</u>

The non-final ending <u>-지만</u> is used with any verb, and connects two clauses which are in contrast to each other. In this pattern, <u>-지 만</u> ends regularly with a comma intonation.

Examples :

좋지만, 사지 않겠어요.	It is good, but I won't buy it.
공부했지만, 잘 모르겠어요.	I studied, but I don't understand it well.
가고 싶었지만, 시간이 없었어요.	I wanted to go, but I had no time.
비가 왔지만, 갔어요.	It rained, but I went.
시간이 있지만, 안 가겠어요.	I have time, but I will not go.
그분은 공부하지 않지만, 나는 공부해요.	He doesn't study, but I study.
그분이 한국 사람이지만, 영어를 가르쳐요.	He is Korean, but he teaches English.
기분이 나쁘겠지만, 참으세요.	I think you feel bad, but please be patient.

Notes:

1. The tense infixes (-았-, -겠-) can be used in the dependent clause.
2. Sometimes it can be used as an unfinished sentence.

   돈이 있지만, …… I have money, but…

DRILLS

ADDITIONAL VOCABULARY

들리다	to be heard, to be audible
즐겁다	to be delightful, to be joyful
멀다	to be far
가깝다	to be close, to be near
잊어버리다	to forget
잃어버리다	to lose
뚱뚱하다	to be fat
홀쭉하다	to be thin, to be slim

A. Substitution Drill

1. 그분 때문에 못 갔어요. I couldn't go because of him.
2. 돈 때문에 못 갔어요. I couldn't go because of money.
3. 그 일 때문에 못 갔어요. I couldn't go because of that work.
4. 숙제 때문에 못 갔어요. I couldn't go because of my homework.
5. 옷 때문에 못 갔어요. I couldn't go because of my clothes.
6. 공부 때문에 못 갔어요. I couldn't go because of my studies:
7. 선생님 때문에 못 갔어요. I couldn't go because of my teacher.
8. 그 여자 때문에 못 갔어요. I couldn't go because of that woman.

B. Substitution Drill

1. 그분을 만나기가 어려워요. It is difficult to meet him.
2. 공부하기가 어려워요. It is difficult to study.
3. 잊어버리기가 어려워요. It is difficult to forget it.
4. 설명하기가 어려워요. It is difficult to explain it.
5. 낮잠을 자기가 어려워요. It is difficult to take a nap.
6. 참기가 어려워요. It is difficult to endure it.
7. 그것을 만들기가 어려워요. It is difficult to make it.
8. 그것을 꺼내기가 어려워요. It is difficult to take it out.

C. Substitution Drill

1. 방에서 잠을 잤습니다. I slept in the room.
2. 방에서 꿈을 꾸었습니다. I dreamed in the room.
3. 방에서 춤을 추었습니다. I danced in the room.

4. 방에서 그림을 그렸습니다. I drew a picture in the room.
5. 방에서 뜀을 뛰었습니다. I jumped in the room.
6. 방에서 숨을 쉬었습니다. I took a breath in the room.

D. Substitution Drill

1. 공부하기 싫어요. I hate to study.
2. 운동하기 싫어요. I hate to exercise.
3. 세수하기 싫어요. I hate to wash my face.
4. 그것을 보이기 싫어요. I hate to show it.
5. 장난하기 싫어요. I hate to play tricks.
6. 면도하기 싫어요. I hate to shave.
7. 옷을 갈아입기 싫어요. I hate to change my clothes.
8. 가르치기 싫어요. I hate to teach.

E. Substitution Drill

1. 그분이 일하기 싫어해요. He doesn't like to work.
2. 그분이 도와주기 싫어해요. He doesn't like to help you.
3. 그분이 눈을 감기 싫어해요. He doesn't like to close his eyes.
4. 그분이 넣기 싫어해요. He doesn't want to put it in.
5. 그분이 걸어가기 싫어해요. He doesn't want to walk.
6. 그분이 청소하기 싫어해요. He doesn't want to clean.
7. 그분이 그것을 팔기 싫어해요. He doesn't want to sell it.
8. 그분이 목욕하기 싫어해요. He doesn't like to take a bath.

F. Substitution Drill

1. 그분을 만나러 갑시다. Let's go to see him.
2. 점심을 먹으러 갑시다. Let's go to eat lunch.
3. 일하러 갑시다. Let's go to work.
4. 수영하러 갑시다. Let's go to swim.
5. 공부하러 갑시다. Let's go to study.
6. 산보하러 갑시다. Let's go to take a walk.
7. 놀러 갑시다. Let's go to play.
8. 옷을 입으러 갑시다. Let's go to dress.

G. Integration Drill

Teacher: 지금 피곤합니다. 쉬고 싶어요.
I'm tired now. I want to rest.

Student: 지금 피곤하기 때문에, 쉬고 싶어요.
I'm tired now, so I want to rest.

1. 한국 사람입니다. 김치를 좋아합니다.
   한국 사람이기 때문에, 김치를 좋아합니다.
2. 선생님이 아닙니다. 가르칠 수 없습니다.
   선생님이 아니기 때문에, 가르칠 수 없습니다.
3. 아주 멀었습니다. 못 갔습니다.
   아주 멀었기 때문에, 못 갔습니다.
4. 바빴습니다. 잊어버렸습니다.
   바빴기 때문에, 잊어버렸습니다.
5. 아주 가깝습니다. 같이 갔어요.
   아주 가깝기 때문에, 같이 갔어요.
6. 시간이 없습니다. 갈 수 없습니다.
   시간이 없기 때문에, 갈 수 없습니다.
7. 복잡했습니다. 그것을 잃어버렸습니다.
   복잡했기 때문에, 그것을 잃어버렸습니다.
8. 멀었습니다. 잘 들리지 않았습니다.
   멀었기 때문에, 잘 들리지 않았습니다.

H. Integration Drill

Teacher : 가고 싶었습니다. 시간이 없었습니다.
I wanted to go. I had no time.
Student : 가고 싶었지만, 시간이 없었습니다.
I wanted to go, but I had no time.

1. 좋지 않았습니다. 샀습니다.
   좋지 않았지만, 샀습니다.
2. 공부했습니다. 잘 모르겠습니다.
   공부했지만, 잘 모르겠습니다.
3. 뚱뚱합니다. 조금 밖에 먹지 않습니다.
   뚱뚱하지만, 조금 밖에 먹지 않습니다.
4. 홀쭉합니다. 많이 먹습니다.
   홀쭉하지만, 많이 먹습니다.
5. 그분은 즐겁습니다. 나는 즐겁지 않습니다.
   그분은 즐겁지만, 나는 즐겁지 않습니다.
6. 기분이 나빴습니다. 참았습니다.
   기분이 나빴지만, 참았습니다.
7. 여기는 가깝습니다. 거기는 멉니다.
   여기는 가깝지만, 거기는 멉니다.
8. 나는 홀쭉합니다. 그분은 뚱뚱합니다.

나는 홀쭉하지만, 그분은 뚱뚱합니다.

SHORT STORIES

1. 점심을 먹으러 식당에 갔습니다.
   그런데 점심을 먹기가 싫었습니다.
   그래서 먹지 않았습니다.

   Expansion Drill

   점심을 먹으러 식당에 갔지만, 점심을 먹기가 싫었기 때문에, 먹지 않았습니다.

2. 영어를 배우기가 어렵습니다. 배우다 to learn
   미국에 가고 싶습니다.
   열심히 공부합니다. 열심히 ardently

   Expansion Drill

   영어를 배우기가 어렵지만, 미국에 가고 싶기 때문에, 열심히 공부합니다.

3. 그 일 때문에 여기에 왔습니다.
   그분이 아주 바쁩니다.
   내일 다시 오겠습니다.

   Expansion Drill

   그 일 때문에 여기에 왔지만, 그분이 아주 바쁘기 때문에, 내일 다시 오겠습니다.

READING

어떤 외국사람이 은단을 사러 약방에 갔습니다. 그런데 은단이라는 단어를 잊어버렸습니다. 약방 주인한테 연탄이 있느냐고 물었습니다. 약방 주인이 그 말을 듣고 이상하게 생각했습니다. 약방에서는 연탄을 팔지 않는다고 했습니다. 연탄을 사고 싶으면 연탄가게로 가라고 했습니다. 연탄가게에서는 연탄을 마음대로 살 수 있다고 했습니다. 그래서 이 외국사람은 약방 주인한테 다시 물었습니다. 먹는 연탄 있지 않느냐고 했습니다. 약방 주인이 이 말을 듣고 깜짝 놀랐습니다. 연탄을 잡수시느냐고 물었습니다. 이 외국사람은 연탄을 잘 먹는다고 대답했습니다.

어떤	a certain	이상하게	strangely

외국사람	foreigner	연탄가게	briquette store
약방	drugstore	마음대로	as one wishes (pleases)
단어	word, vocabulary	대답하다	to answer
-라는 단어	the word for (it)	먹는 연탄	edible briquette
주인	the owner, the master	깜짝 놀라다	to be startled suddenly
연탄	briquette		
묻다	to ask		
*은단	flavor pellets which are taken after a meal or smoking to freshen the breath.		

BRIEFING

A certain foreigner went to the drugstore to buy 은단. But he forgot the word for 은단. He asked the owner of the drugstore if he had briquettes. The owner of the drugstore heard the word "연탄" and thought it very strange. He said that they didn't sell 연탄 in the drugstore. He said that if you wanted to buy briquettes, go to the briquette store. He said that in the briquette store you can buy as many briquettes as you want. So this foreigner asked the owner of the drugstore again. He asked, "Don't you have edible briquettes?" The owner of the drugstore heard the word 먹는 연탄 (edible briquette) and was startled suddenly. He asked if he ate briquettes. This foreigner said that he ate 연탄 very well.

UNIT 21 날씨 Weather

BASIC SENTENCES : MEMORIZE

시원하다	to be refreshing, to be cool
박 성 철	
1. 오늘은 어제보다 시원하지요 ?	Today is cooler than yesterday, isn't it ?
같다	to be the same
최 인 숙	
2. 예, 좀 시원한 것 같군요.	Yes, it seems a little cooler.
지난	last
여름	summer
무척	terribly, exceedingly
덥다	to be hot
박 성 철	
3. 지난 여름은 무척 더웠지요 ?	Last summer was terribly hot, wasn't it ?
재작년	the year before last
최 인 숙	
4. 예, 더웠어요. 그러나 재작년 만큼은 덥지 않았어요.	Yes, it was. But it was not as hot as the year before last.
박 성 철	
5. 재작년이 그렇게 더웠어요 ?	Was the year before last that hot ?
제일	the first, number one
최 인 숙	
6. 그럼요, 제일 더웠어요.	It sure was. It was the hottest (of the three).

USEFUL EXPRESSIONS : MEMORIZE

1. 죄송합니다.	I am sorry.
2. 별 말씀을 다 하세요.	Don't mention it. Or : Not at all.
3. 신경(을) 쓰지 마세요.	Don't worry about it. Or : Don't strain your nerves. Or : Don't pay any attention to it.

NOTES ON THE BASIC SENTENCES

1. 시원하다, depending on the context or situation, means (1) 'to be refreshing,' 'to be cool,' (2) 'to feel good,' 'to be a relief.' See the following examples:

날씨가 시원합니다.	The weather is cool.
시원한 바람이 불어요.	A refreshing breeze is blowing.
그분이 여기에 없기 때문에, 속이 시원합니다.	Because he is not here, I feel better. (I'm relieved.)

Words for the weather are:

시원하다	to be refreshing, to be cool.
쌀쌀하다	to be chilly, to be rather cold
따뜻하다	to be warm, to be mild
덥다	to be hot
춥다	to be cold
무덥다	to be humid, to be sultry, to be hot and damp

3. 지난 'last' is a noun modifier derived from 지나다 'to pass by,' 'to go past,' 'to pass through.' Study the following words:

지난 날	days gone by, bygone days.
지난 번에	the other day, the last time, some time ago
지난 밤에	last night
지난 달에	last month
지난 해에	last year

덥다 'to be hot' is an irregular verb. When the final consonant -ㅂ of the stem is followed by a vowel, -ㅂ changes into 우. This irregular verb -ㅂ will be studied later.

4. 재작년 means 'the year before last.' Study the following words, which have to do with the year.

Chinese words:		**Pure Korean words:**	**Meaning:**
작년에	or	지난 해(에)	last year
금년에	or	올해(에)	this year
내년에	or	다음 해(에)	next year

As we have seen in the above examples, the Chinese words may be used with the particle -에, whereas the pure Korean words can be used either with the particle -에, or without it.

STRUCTURE NOTES

I. The Comparison -보다… : '(more) than'

The particle -보다 '(more) than' is used as a standard of comparison, when both items of comparison are mentioned. It is attached normally to the second noun of a comparison, and oftentimes accompanied by 더 'more.'

Examples :

한국말이 영어보다 (더) 어려워요.	Korean is more difficult than English.
개가 고양이보다 (더) 커요.	Dogs are bigger than cats.
이 집이 그 집보다 (더) 작아요.	This house is smaller than that house.
오늘은 어제보다 (더) 시원해요.	Today is cooler than yesterday.
기차는 차보다 (더) 빨라요.	The train is faster than the car.
이것이 그것보다 (더) 예뻐요.	This is prettier than that.

The phrase ending with -보다 may occur before the subject of a sentence, making no difference in meaning, other than a slight change in emphasis. See the following examples, and note particularly the words to which the particle -보다 is attached.

이것이 그것보다 더 예뻐요.	This is prettier than that.
그것보다 이것이 더 예뻐요.	This is prettier than that.
개가 고양이보다 더 커요.	Dogs are bigger than cats.
고양이보다 개가 더 커요.	Dogs are bigger than cats.

When only one thing or one quality is mentioned, and the other item of comparison is omitted, the word 더 'more' is normally used. See the following examples :

이것이 더 좋아요.	This is better.
이것이 더 비싸요.	This is more expensive.
한국말이 더 어려워요.	Korean is more difficult.
꽃을 더 좋아해요.	I prefer flowers.
택시로 가는 것이 더 좋아요.	It's better to go by taxi.

When a comparison of two items is requested via an interrogative pronoun, an appropriate particle is added.

1. If the interrogative pronoun 어느 것 (분, 쪽) 'which thing (person, side)' is used as a subject, it takes the particle -가/-이 ; at the same time, the second of the two nouns in the comparison takes the contrast particle -는/-은. Study the following examples :

   이 책과 그 책은 어느 것이 더 좋습니까?

Which book is better —— this book or that one?
이것과 그것은 어느 것이 더 예쁩니까?
Which is prettier —— this one or that one?
이 학생과 저 학생은 누가 더 큽니까?
Who is bigger —— this student or that student?
한국말과 영어는 어느 쪽이 더 어렵습니까?
Which language is more difficult —— Korean or English?

2. If the interrogative pronoun 어느 것 (분, 쪽) 'which thing (person, side)' is used as an object, it takes the particle -를/-을; at the same time, the second of the two nouns in the comparison takes the particle -중에 'between,' 'of,' 'among,' 'out of.' Study the following examples:
이 여자와 그 여자 중에 어느 분을 더 좋아하십니까?
Which girl do you like better —— this girl or that one?
이분과 저분 중에 어느 분을 더 잘 아십니까?
Which one do you know better —— this person or that one?
형님과 누님 중에 누구를 더 사랑하십니까?
Whom do you love more —— your older brother or your older sister?

II. The Sentence-Final Ending -ㄴ(-은) 것 같다… : 'it seems to be'

The pattern -ㄴ(은) 것 같다 is used with description verbs and the verb -이다, and indicates resemblance or likeness. 같다, as an independent word, means 'to be like,' 'to be similar,' 'to be as.'

Examples:

그것이 좋은 것 같아요.	It seems to be good. Or: It's like a good one.
좀 시원한 것 같아요.	It seems a little cooler.
날씨가 추운 것 같아요.	The weather seems to be cold.
그분이 큰 것 같아요.	He seems to be big.
그분이 선생님인 것 같아요.	He seems to be a teacher.
그분이 학생인 것 같아요.	He seems to be a student.

Notes:

1. -ㄴ 것 같다 is used after verb stems ending in a vowel;
-은 것 같다 is used after verb stems ending in a consonant.
2. This pattern can be used with action verbs. This usage will be studied in detail later.
3. The tense is expressed regularly in the final verb 같다, not in the main verb with -ㄴ(은). Study the following examples:

그것이 좋은 것 같았어요. It seemed to be good.
그것이 좋은 것 같지 않았어요. It didn't seem to be good.

4. The negation is expressed either in the final verb 같다 or in the main verb with -ㄴ(은). However, there is a slight difference in meaning. Study the following examples:

그것이 좋은 것 같지 않아요. It does not seem to be good.
그것이 좋지 않은 것 같아요. It seems that it is not good.

III. The Particle -만큼… : 'to the extent of,' 'as much as'

The particle -만큼 is attached to nouns, and indicates extent or degree. The English equivalent of this pattern is 'to the extent of,' 'as much as,' 'equal to,' etc.

Examples:

저도 그분만큼 할 수 있어요. I can do as well as he.
이 책도 그 책만큼 비싸요. This book also is as expensive as that book.
이것도 그것만큼 어려워요. This is as difficult as that.
이것도 그것만큼 좋아요. This is as good as that.
나도 그분만큼 돈이 있어요. I have as much money as he does.

This particle -만큼 'to the extent of' is used also in negative comparisons. Study the following examples:

이것은 그것만큼 예쁘지 않아요. This is not as pretty as that. (lit. This is not pretty to the extent of that.)
이 책은 그 책만큼 좋지 않아요. This book is not as good as that book.
이분은 김 선생님만큼 크지 않아요. This person is not as big as Mr. Kim.
선생님만큼 먹지 않았어요. I did not eat as much as my teacher.
이것은 그것만큼 비싸지 않아요. This one is not as expensive as that one.

This particle -만큼 is used also in questions where a negative answer is expected. See the following examples:

그분이 이분만큼 커요? Is he as big as this person?
아니오, 그분이 이분만큼 크지 않아요. No, he is not as big as this person.
영어가 한국말만큼 어려워요? Is English as difficult as Korean?
아니오, 영어가 한국말만큼 어렵지 않아요. No, English is not as difficult as Korean.

IV. The Superlative Marker 제일 (or 가장)… : 'the most'

The word 제일 is originally an ordinal number meaning 'the first' 'number one.' The superlative marker 제일 or 가장 'to the greatest degree' is used when three or more items of comparison are mentioned. It is regularly put before description verbs, noun modifiers or adverbs.

Examples:

어제가 제일 더웠습니다.	Yesterday was the hottest.
이 책이 제일 재미있어요.	This book is the most interesting.
그분이 제일 커요.	He is the biggest one.
그것이 제일 예뻐요.	That one is the prettiest.
제일 어려운 것은 그것이에요.	The most difficult one is that one.
이것이 제일 작은 책상이에요	This is the smallest desk.
그분이 제일 잘 가르쳐요.	He teaches best of all.

Note:

제일 is interchangeable with 가장, making no difference in meaning. 제일 is used, however, more than 가장.

DRILLS

ADDITIONAL VOCABULARY

따뜻하다	to be warm, to be mild	넓다	to be wide, to be broad
무덥다	to be humid, to be sultry	좁다	to be narrow
높다	to be high	길다	to be long
낮다	to be low	짧다	to be short

A. Substitution Drill

1. 날씨가 추운 것 같아요.	The weather seems to be cold.
2. 날씨가 따뜻한 것 같아요.	The weather seems to be warm.
3. 날씨가 무더운 것 같아요.	The weather seems to be humid.
4. 날씨가 시원한 것 같아요.	The weather seems to be cool.
5. 날씨가 쌀쌀한 것 같아요.	The weather seems to be chilly.
6. 날씨가 더운 것 같아요.	The weather seems to be hot.
7. 날씨가 좋은 것 같아요.	The weather seems to be good.
8. 날씨가 나쁜 것 같아요.	The weather seems to be bad.

B. Substitution Drill

1. 이것이 제일 재미있어요.	This is the most interesting.
2. 이것이 제일 어려워요.	This is the most difficult.

3. 이것이 제일 예뻐요. This is the most beautiful.
4. 이것이 제일 커요. This is the biggest one.
5. 이것이 제일 길어요. This is the longest one.
6. 이것이 제일 짧아요. This is the shortest one.
7. 이것이 제일 작아요. This is the smallest one.
8. 이것이 제일 높아요. This is the highest one.

C. Substitution Drill

1. 이것이 그것만큼 짧지 않아요. This is not as short as that.
2. 이것이 그것만큼 넓지 않아요. This is not as wide as that.
3. 이것이 그것만큼 좋지 않아요. This is not as good as that.
4. 이것이 그것만큼 길지 않아요. This is not as long as that.
5. 이것이 그것만큼 예쁘지 않아요. This is not as pretty as that.
6. 이것이 그것만큼 낮지 않아요. This is not as low as that.
7. 이것이 그것만큼 높지 않아요. This is not as high as that.
8. 이것이 그것만큼 비싸지 않아요. This is not as expensive as that.

D. Substitution Drill

1. 이것이 더 좋아요. This is better.
2. 이것이 더 비싸요. This is more expensive.
3. 이것이 더 어려워요. This is more difficult.
4. 이것이 더 예뻐요. This is more beautiful.
5. 이것이 더 나빠요. This is worse.
6. 이것이 더 넓어요. This is wider.
7. 이것이 더 길어요. This is longer.
8. 이것이 더 짧아요. This is shorter.

E. Pattern Drill

Teacher: 이것이 그것만큼 어려워요.
This is as difficult as that.
Student: 이것이 그것보다 어려워요.
This is more difficult than that.

1. 이 책이 그 책만큼 비싸요. 이 책이 그 책보다 비싸요.
2. 이것이 그것만큼 좋아요. 이것이 그것보다 좋아요.
3. 이분이 그분만큼 재미있어요. 이분이 그분보다 재미있어요.
4. 이분이 그분만큼 예뻐요. 이분이 그분보다 예뻐요.
5. 여기가 거기만큼 복잡해요. 여기가 거기보다 복잡해요.
6. 이분이 그분만큼 뚱뚱해요. 이분이 그분보다 뚱뚱해요.

7. 여기가 거기만큼 시끄러워요. 여기가 거기보다 시끄러워요.
8. 오늘이 어제만큼 더워요. 오늘이 어제보다 더워요.

F. Pattern Drill

Teacher: 이것이 그것보다 예뻐요.
This is prettier than that.
Student: 그것보다 이것이 예뻐요.
This is prettier than that.

1. 이것이 그것보다 짧아요. 그것보다 이것이 짧아요.
2. 이 책이 그 책보다 좋아요. 그 책보다 이 책이 좋아요.
3. 한국말이 영어보다 쉬워요. 영어보다 한국말이 쉬워요.
4. 오늘이 어제보다 따뜻해요. 어제보다 오늘이 따뜻해요.
5. 여기가 거기보다 멀어요. 거기보다 여기가 멀어요.
6. 이분이 그분보다 친절해요. 그분보다 이분이 친절해요.
7. 이 방이 그 방보다 밝아요. 그 방보다 이 방이 밝아요.
8. 이 교실이 그 교실보다 깨끗해요. 그 교실보다 이 교실이 깨끗해요.

G. Response Drill

Teacher: 이 책과 그 책은 어느 것이 더 좋아요?
Which book is better —— this book or that one?
Student: 이 책이 그 책보다 더 좋아요.
This book is better than that one.

1. 한국말과 영어는 어느 것이 더 재미있습니까?
   한국말이 영어보다 더 재미있습니다.
2. 이 여자와 그 여자는 누가 더 예쁩니까?
   이 여자가 그 여자보다 더 예쁩니다.
3. 이 방과 저 방은 어느 방이 더 밝습니까?
   이 방이 저 방보다 더 밝습니다.
4. 이분과 그분은 어느 분이 더 친절합니까?
   이분이 그분보다 더 친절합니다.
5. 만년필과 연필은 어느 것이 더 비쌉니까?
   만년필이 연필보다 더 비쌉니다.
6. 복숭아와 참외는 어느 것이 더 맛있습니까?
   복숭아가 참외보다 더 맛있습니다.
7. 이분과 그분은 누가 더 바쁩니까?
   이분이 그분보다 더 바쁩니다.
8. 이것과 저것은 어느 것이 더 깨끗합니까?
   이것이 저것보다 더 깨끗합니다.

H. Response Drill

Teacher: 이분과 저분 중에 어느 분을 더 잘 아십니까?
Which one do you know better —— this person or that one?
Student: 이분보다 저분을 더 잘 압니다.
I know this person better than that one?

1. 이 여자와 그 여자 중에 어느 분을 더 사랑하십니까?
이 여자보다 그 여자를 더 사랑합니다.
2. 수박과 복숭아 중에 어느 것을 더 좋아하십니까?
수박보다 복숭아를 더 좋아합니다.
3. 이 남자와 그 남자 중에 누구를 더 싫어하십니까?
이 남자보다 그 남자를 더 싫어합니다.
4. 이 교실과 저 교실 중에 어느 교실을 더 좋아하십니까?
이 교실보다 저 교실을 더 좋아합니다.
5. 이분과 저분 중에 어느 분을 더 좋아하십니까?
이분보다 저분을 더 좋아합니다.
6. 형님과 누님 중에 어느 분을 더 좋아하십니까?
형님보다 누님을 더 좋아합니다.

SHORT STORIES

1. 오늘은 어제보다 따뜻해요.
그러나 그저께만큼은 따뜻하지 않아요.
날씨가 좀 추운 것 같아요.

그저께 the day before yesterday

Expansion Drill

오늘은 어제보다 따뜻한지만, 그저께만큼은 따뜻하지 않아요. 날씨가 좀 추운 것 같아요.

2. 어제 제일 친한 친구가 찾아왔어요.
그래서 그분하고 같이 늦게까지 술을 마셨어요.
오늘 아침에 좀 피곤한 것 같아요.

친하다 to be intimate, to be close　　늦게까지 until late

Expansion Drill

어제 제일 친한 친구가 찾아왔기 때문에, 그분하고 같이 늦게까지 술을 마셨어요. 오늘 아침에 좀 피곤한 것 같아요.

3. 같이 가고 싶지만 피곤합니다.
오늘은 집에서 쉬겠습니다.
내일 시간이 있으면 같이 갑시다.

Expansion Drill

같이 가고 싶지만 피곤하기 때문에, 오늘은 집에서 쉬겠습니다.
내일 시간이 있으면 같이 갑시다.

READING

어떤 외국 사람이 석 달 전에 한국에 왔습니다. 요즘 그분은 날마다 학교에서 한국말을 공부합니다. 그러나 한국말은 조금 밖에 모릅니다. 그저께는 치약을 하나 사고 싶었습니다. 그래서 운전기사한테 부탁했습니다. 치약을 하나 사 달라고 했습니다. 그런데 발음을 잘못했습니다. 그래서 이 운전기사는 쥐약으로 알아들었습니다. 운전기사는 쥐약을 사 가지고 왔습니다. 이 외국 사람은 그것으로 이를 닦으려고 했습니다. 그러나 그것이 좀 이상했습니다. 그래서 한국 사람한테 물어 보았습니다. 알고 보니, 그것이 치약이 아니었습니다. 그것은 쥐약이었습니다. 그래서 그때부터 이 외국 사람은 발음을 열심히 공부하기 시작했습니다.

석 달 전에	three months ago
날마다	everyday
치약	toothpaste
운전기사	driver
부탁하다	to ask (one's favor)
발음	pronunciation
잘못하다	to do wrong
쥐약	rat poison
알아 듣다	to comprehend, to understand
물어 보다	to ask and see what it's like
알고 보니	(finally) he found out that···
그 때부터	from that time on
열심히	eagerly, zealously

BRIEFING

A certain foreigner came to Korea three months ago. These days he is studying Korean at school everday. But he knows Korean only a little. The day before yesterday he wanted to buy toothpaste. So he asked his driver, as a favor, to buy toothpaste. But he pronounced it the wrong way. So this driver thought that the man had said "rat poison." The driver bought the rat poison and brought it home. The foreigner was going to brush his teeth with it, but it looked strange. So he asked some Korean people about it. He found out that it was not toothpaste. It was rat poison. Therefore, from that time on, the foreigner eagerly started to study pronunciation.

UNIT 22 얼마나 멀어요? How Far Is It?

BASIC SENTENCES: MEMORIZE

시청	the City Hall
얼마나	about what distance, about how far

박 성 철

1. 여기서 시청까지 얼마나 멀어요?	How far is it from here to City Hall?
택시로	by taxi
이십 분쯤	about 20 minutes
걸리다	to take (time)

최 인 숙

2. 택시로 이십 분쯤 걸려요.	It takes about twenty minutes by taxi.
그리로	to that place, in that direction

박 성 철

3. 그리로 가는 버스는 없어요?	Doesn't any bus go there?
있고 말고요	of course there is
십 분마다	every ten minutes

최 인 숙

4. 있고 말고요. 십 분마다 하나씩 있어요.	Of course there is (a bus that goes there). One comes every ten minutes.
타다	to ride, to take to take a ride, to get in

박 성 철

5. 어디서 탈 수 있어요?	Where would I be able to get it?
저기서	over there

최 인 숙

6. 저기서 타세요.	Get it over there.

USEFUL EXPRESSIONS : MEMORIZE

1. 시간이 너무 걸려요. — It takes too much time.
2. 누구(의) 차례에요? — Whose turn is it?
3. 알려 드리겠어요. — I'll let you know.

NOTES ON THE BASIC SENTENCES

1. 여기서 is a contraction of 여기에서 'from here.' Let's review the particle -에서 'from.'

   그분이 미국에서 왔어요. — He came from America.
   그분이 일본에서 돌아왔어요. — He returned from Japan.
   기차에서 내렸어요. — I got off the train.

   얼마나 means 'about how far.' When the particle -나 is used with an interrogative pronoun indicating distance or quantity, such as 'how far?,' 'how many?,' or 'how old?,' it indicates approximation. This particle -나 will be studied in detail later.

2. 택시 'taxi' is derived from English.

   걸리다, depending on the context or situation, has many different meanings: (1) 'to take (time),' (2) 'to be hung,' (3) 'to have a (telephone) call (from),' 'to get through,' (4) 'to be attached (seized, afflicted) with,' etc. Study the following examples:

   시간이 걸립니다. — It takes time.
   벽에 그림이 걸려 있어요. — A picture is hanging on the wall.
   전화가 안 걸렸어요. — I didn't get my call through.
   감기에 걸렸어요. — I caught a cold.

3. 그리로 means 'to that place,' 'in that direction.' The place words 이리, 그리 and 저리 always take the particle -로 when indicating destination, whereas 여기, 거기 and 저기 can be used with the particles -로 and -에. Study the following examples:

   이리로 오세요. — Please come this way (here).
   여기로 오세요.
   여기에 오세요.

   그리로 갑시다. — Let's go there.
   거기로 갑시다.
   거기에 갑시다.

   저리로 가세요. — Please go over there.

저기로 가세요.
저기에 가세요.

5. 어디서 is a contraction of 어디에서.
6. 저기서 is a contraction of 저기에서.

STRUCTURE NOTES

I. Noun Modifiers:

We have studied the noun modifier -ㄴ(은) used with description verbs to indicate quality, quantity or extent of the noun it modifies, (see Unit 15, S.N. III). Now let's study noun modifiers that occur with action verbs and the verb of existence.

a. The Suffix -는:

When the suffix -는 is attached directly to action verb stems and 있-, it indicates the present tense. It functions in the same way as a relative clause in English. The English equivalent of this pattern describes a present, existing condition. It is equivalent to '—ing' in English, (e.g., buying, bringing, raining, having, etc.) Study the following examples:

책을 사는 분이 내 학생입니다.	The person who is buying the book is my student.
한국말을 가르치는 분이 누구입니까?	Who is that person teaching Korean?
비가 오는 것 같아요.	It looks like it is raining.
저기 있는 책을 가지고 오세요.	Bring those books (which are) over there.
돈이 있는 분이 지금 와요.	The man who has money is coming now.

b. The Suffix -ㄴ(은):

When the suffix -ㄴ(은) is attached directly to action verb stems, it indicates the past tense. Study the following examples:

책을 산 분이 내 학생이에요.	The person who bought the book is my student.
여기서 구두를 닦은 분이 저기 있어요.	The person who shined my shoes here is over there.

Notes:

1. -ㄴ is used after verb stems ending in a vowel;
   -은 is used after verb stems ending in a consonant.
2. The suffix -ㄴ(은) is used also with description verbs, as we have already studied.

c. The Suffix -ㄹ(을) :

When the suffix -ㄹ(을) is used either with action or description verbs, it indicates the future tense. Study the following examples:

부산에 갈 분이 지금 와요.	The person who will go to Pusan is coming now.
여기서 공부할 분이 내 동생이에요.	The person who will study here is my younger brother.
비가 올 것 같아요.	It looks like it will rain.
그것이 비쌀 것 같아요.	I think it will be expensive.
어느 것이 좋을지 모르겠어요.	I don't know which one will be better.

Note:

-ㄹ is used after verb stems ending in a vowel;

-을 is used after verb stems ending in a consonant.

II. The Particle -마다… : 'every'

The particle -마다 may be attached directly to any noun, and means 'every,' 'each,' 'all (inclusive).

Examples:

그분이 날마다 학교에 가요.	He goes to school everyday.
사람마다 달라요.	Everybody is different.
학생마다 그분을 좋아해요.	Every student likes him.
그분이 저녁마다 나가요.	He goes out every evening.
집집마다 아이가 있어요.	There are children in (each and) every house.
곳곳마다 집이 있어요.	There are houses everywhere.
버스가 십 분마다 와요.	A bus comes every ten minutes.
일요일마다 교회에 가요.	I go to church every Sunday.
두 시간마다 하나 잡수세요.	Take one every two hours.

III. The Suffix -씩… : 'apiece,' 'respectively,' 'each'

The suffix -씩 is attached directly to a number, or to any number made with a classifier (counter) ; it indicates distribution.

조금씩 공부하세요.	Study little by little.
하나씩 잡수세요.	Please eat (them) one by one.
날마다 여덟 시간씩 일해요.	I work 8 hours everyday.
학생이 둘씩 와요.	The students come by twos.

하루에 세 번씩 먹었어요. I ate three times a day.
한 사람한테 천 원씩 주세요. Give them 1,000 won each.

DRILLS

ADDITIONAL VOCABULARY

미국	America	독일	Germany
영국	England	대만	Taiwan
일본	Japan	소련	the Soviet Union
불란서	France	중공	People's Republic of China

A. Substitution Drill

1. 한국에서 미국까지 얼마나 멀어요? How far is it from Korea to America?
2. 한국에서 영국까지 얼마나 멀어요? How far is it from Korea to England?
3. 한국에서 일본까지 얼마나 멀어요? How far is it from Korea to Japan?
4. 한국에서 불란서까지 얼마나 멀어요? How far is it from Korea to France?
5. 한국에서 독일까지 얼마나 멀어요? How far is it from Korea to Germany?
6. 한국에서 대만까지 얼마나 멀어요? How far is it from Korea to Taiwan?
7. 한국에서 소련까지 얼마나 멀어요? How far is it from Korea to the Soviet Union?
8. 한국에서 중공까지 얼마나 멀어요? How far is it from Korea to People's Republic of China?

B. Substitution Drill

1. 택시로 20 분쯤 걸려요. It takes about twenty minutes by taxi.
2. 택시로 30 분쯤 걸려요. It takes about thirty minutes by taxi.
3. 택시로 10 분쯤 걸려요. It takes about ten minutes by taxi.
4. 택시로 15 분쯤 걸려요. It takes about fifteen minutes by taxi.
5. 택시로 한 시간쯤 걸려요. It takes about an hour by taxi.
6. 택시로 두 시간쯤 걸려요. It takes about two hours by taxi.
7. 택시로 세 시간쯤 걸려요. It takes about three hours by taxi.
8. 택시로 네 시간쯤 걸려요. It takes about four hours by taxi.

C. Substitution Drill (Review)

1. 그 여자가 예쁘고 말고요. Of course she is beautiful.
2. 한국말이 재미있고 말고요. Of course Korean is interesting.

3. 그 책이 좋고 말고요. — Of course that book is good.
4. 그 방이 어둡고 말고요. — Of course that room is dark.
5. 그 방이 밝고 말고요. — Of course that room is bright.
6. 그분이 친절하고 말고요. — Of course he is kind.
7. 그분이 뚱뚱하고 말고요. — Of course he is fat.
8. 그분이 홀쭉하고 말고요. — Of course he is thin (slim).

D. Substitution Drill

1. 비가 오는 것 같아요. — It looks like it is raining.
2. 그분이 공부하는 것 같아요. — It looks like he is studying.
3. 그분이 학교에 가는 것 같아요. — It looks like he is going to school.
4. 그분이 오는 것 같아요. — It looks like he is coming.
5. 그분이 숙제를 하는 것 같아요. — It looks like he is doing his homework.
6. 그분이 목욕하는 것 같아요. — It looks like he is taking a bath.
7. 그분이 산보하는 것 같아요. — It looks like he is taking a walk.
8. 그분이 세수하는 것 같아요. — It looks like he is washing his face.

E. Pattern Drill

Teacher: 비가 오는 것 같아요. — It looks like it is raining.
Student: 비가 온 것 같아요. — It looks like it rained.

1. 그분이 걸어가는 것 같아요. — 그분이 걸어간 것 같아요.
2. 뛰어가는 것 같아요. — 뛰어간 것 같아요.
3. 그것을 넣는 것 같아요. — 그것을 넣은 것 같아요.
4. 그것을 꺼내는 것 같아요. — 그것을 꺼낸 것 같아요.
5. 문을 여는 것 같아요. — 문을 연 것 같아요.
6. 문을 닫는 것 같아요. — 문을 닫은 것 같아요.
7. 눈을 뜨는 것 같아요. — 눈을 뜬 것 같아요.
8. 눈을 감는 것 같아요. — 눈을 감은 것 같아요.

F. Pattern Drill

Teacher: 비가 오는 것 같아요. — It looks like it is raining.
Student: 비가 올 것 같아요. — It looks like it will rain.

1. 면도하는 것 같아요. — 면도할 것 같아요.
2. 옷을 갈아입는 것 같아요. — 옷을 갈아입을 것 같아요.
3. 넥타이를 매는 것 같아요. — 넥타이를 맬 것 같아요.
4. 그분이 장난하는 것 같아요. — 그분이 장난할 것 같아요.
5. 그분이 운동을 하는 것 같아요. — 그분이 운동을 할 것 같아요.
6. 그분이 낮잠을 자는 것 같아요. — 그분이 낮잠을 잘 것 같아요.

7. 그것을 가지고 가는 것 같아요.	그것을 가지고 갈 것 같아요.
8. 그분이 웃는 것 같아요.	그분이 웃을 것 같아요.

G. Pattern Drill

Teacher : 책을 사는 분이 내 학생입니다.
The person who is buying the book is my student.
Student : 책을 산 분이 내 학생입니다.
The person who bought the book is my student.

1. 공부하는 분이 와요.	공부한 분이 와요.
2. 편지를 쓰는 분이 형님이에요.	편지를 쓴 분이 형님이에요.
3. 여행하는 분이 친구에요.	여행한 분이 친구에요.
4. 일하는 분이 한국 사람이에요.	일한 분이 한국 사람이에요.
5. 일어나는 분이 학생이에요.	일어난 분이 학생이에요.
6. 그것을 만드는 분이 동생이에요.	그것을 만든 분이 동생이에요.
7. 이를 닦는 분이 선생님이에요.	이를 닦은 분이 선생님이에요.
8. 지금 말하는 분이 친구에요.	지금 말한 분이 친구에요.

H. Response Drill

1. 날마나 학교에 가시지요?	예, 날마다 학교에 가요.
2. 버스가 몇 분마다 와요?	버스가 십 분마다 와요.
3. 저녁마다 어디에 가세요?	저녁마다 극장에 가요.
4. 학생마다 다르지요?	예, 학생마다 달라요.
5. 곳곳마다 무엇이 있어요?	곳곳마다 자동차가 있어요.
6. 집집마다 무엇이 있어요?	집집마다 개가 있어요.
7. 아침마다 무엇을 하세요?	아침마다 산책합니다.
8. 몇 시간마다 먹을까요?	세 시간마다 잡수세요.

I. Response Drill

1. 조금씩 공부할까요?	예, 조금씩 공부하세요.
2. 하나씩 먹을까요?	예, 하나씩 잡수세요.
3. 하루에 몇 번씩 먹을까요?	하루에 세 번씩 잡수세요.
4. 날마다 몇 시간씩 일하세요?	날마다 여덟 시간씩 일해요.
5. 한 분한테 얼마씩 줄까요?	한 분한테 1,000 원씩 주세요.
6. 하루에 몇 시간씩 공부하세요?	하루에 다섯 시간씩 공부해요.
7. 하루에 몇 시간씩 주무세요?	하루에 일곱 시간씩 자요.
8. 하루에 몇 시간씩 운동하세요?	하루에 두 시간씩 운동해요.

SHORT STORIES

1. 저는 아침마다 30분씩 산책합니다
그리고 학교에 갈 때에 걸어갑니다. — 갈 때에: when I go
걸어서 이십 분쯤 걸립니다. — 걸어서: on foot

2. 오늘 아침에 비가 올 것 같았어요.
그래서 우산을 가지고 왔어요. — 우산: an umbrella
그러나 비가 오지 않았어요.

3. 여기서 공부한 분은 친구입니다.
그리고 지금 들어오는 분은 선생님입니다.
내일 미국에 갈 분은 저 여자입니다.

READING

저는 지금 한국말을 공부하는 학생입니다. 아침마다 버스로 학교에 갑니다. 집에서 학교까지 삼십 분쯤 걸립니다. 그런데 버스를 타기가 아주 힘들어요. 그리고 버스에 사람을 많이 태워요. 그래서 버스가 참 복잡합니다. 오늘 아침에도 겨우 버스를 탔습니다. 그런데 버스가 가다가 갑자기 멎었습니다. 그래서 나는 어떤 숙녀 앞에 넘어졌습니다. 나는 그분한테 정중하게 "물좀 주세요"하고 말했습니다. 버스 안에 있는 사람들이 모두 웃었습니다. "미안합니다"라는 말을 깜빡 잊어버렸습니다.

힘들다	to be difficult, to be laborious	앞에	in front of, before
겨우	barely	넘어지다	to fall down, to tumble down
가다가	while going	정중하게	politely, with courtesy
갑자기	suddenly	사람들	people
멎다	to stop	깜빡	completely, entirely
숙녀	lady	안	inside

BRIEFING

I am a Korean language student now. I go to school by bus every morning. It takes about thirty minutes from my house to school. It's very difficult to take a bus. They take too many people on board. So the bus is very crowded. I got on the bus with difficulty this morning also. The bus was going but suddenly stopped. As a result, I fell down in front of a certain lady. I said to her politely, 'Give me some water.' All the people in the bus laughed. I forgot completely the expression 'I am sorry.'

UNIT 23 기후 Climate

BASIC SENTENCES: MEMORIZE

지난 밤에 — last night
비 — a rain

박 성 철

1. 지난 밤에 비가 온 것 같지요? — It looks like it rained last night, doesn't it?

정말 — truly, really
많이 — a lot

최 인 숙

2. 예, 정말 비가 많이 왔는데요! — Yes, it really rained a lot!

오늘도 — today also

박 성 철

3. 오늘도 비가 올 것 같지요? — It looks like it will rain today too, doesn't it?

글쎄요 — well!
개다 — to clear up

최 인 숙

4. 글쎄요. 잘 모르겠어요. 날씨가 개었으면 좋겠어요. — Well! I don't know. I wish the weather would clear up.

박 성 철

5. 요즘 주말마다 비가 오는데요! — These days it rains every weekend!

어쩌면 (아마) — perhaps, possibly, by any possibility
오후에 — in the afternoon
등산 가다 — to go mountain-climbing

최 인 숙

6. 어쩌면 오후엔 갤 것 같아요. 날씨가 개면, 난 등산 갈래요. — Perhaps the weather will clear up this afternoon. If the weather clears up, I will go mountain-climbing.

USEFUL EXPRESSIONS: MEMORIZE

1. 관심이 있으세요? — Are you interested in it?

2. 관심이 없어요. I'm not interested in it.
3. 문제 없어요. There is no problem.

NOTES ON THE BASIC SENTENCES

1. 비, depending on the context or situation, means (1) '(a) rain,' (2) 'a broom.' Study the following examples:

비가 와요.	It is raining.
비가 올 것 같아요.	It looks like rain.
비로 쓸었어요.	I swept with a broom.

2. 정말 'the truth,' 'reality,' besides being used as a noun, is also an adverb meaning 'truly,' 'really.' Its synonym is 참말. Its opposite word is 거짓말 'a lie.' 거짓말하다 means 'to tell a lie.' Study the following examples:

정말입니까? 참말입니까?	Is that true?
정말입니다. 참말입니다.	It's true (Believe me).
그분은 정말 좋은 학생이에요.	He is really a good student.
그것이 거짓말입니다.	That's a lie.
거짓말하지 마세요.	Don't tell a lie.

4. 글쎄요 means 'well,' 'let me see,' or 'ah.' It is used as an expression of doubt or uncertainty, or when hesitating to do something.

5. 주말 means 'the weekend.' -말 indicates 'the end,' 'the close.' Study the following examples:

주말 the weekend
월말 the end of the month
연말 the end of the year

그분은 주말 여행을 떠났어요.	He went away for the weekend.
월말에는 바빠요.	I'm busy at the end of the month.
연말에 드리겠어요.	I'll give it to you at the end of the year.

6. 오후 'the afternoon,' besides being used as a conversational term, is a technical term for 'p.m.' Its opposite word is 오전 'the forenoon,' 'the morning' which is also used as a technical term for 'a.m.' 난 is a contraction of 나는. 등산 가다 means 'to go mountain-climbing.' When the verb 가다 is preceded by nouns such as 등산 'a mountain-climb,' 목욕 'a bath,' 산책 'a walk,' 소풍 'a picnic,' 여행 'a trip,' 사냥 'a hunt,' etc., it indicates the purpose of an action. Study the following examples:

등산(을) 가다 to go mountain-climbing

목욕(을) 가다 to go to a bath-house
산책(을) 가다 to go for a walk
소풍(을) 가다 to go on a picnic
여행(을) 가다 to go traveling
사냥(을) 가다 to go on a hunt
낚시질(을) 가다 to go fishing

STRUCTURE NOTES

I. V.S. +-았(-었, -였)으면 좋겠다… : 'I wish so-and-so would happen'

The pattern -았(-었, -였)으면 좋겠다 may be used with any verb, and indicates a speaker's hope or desire.

Examples:

날씨가 개었으면 좋겠어요. I wish the weather would clear up. (lit. If the weather would clear up, it would be good.)

그분이 여기에 왔으면 좋겠어요. I wish he could come here. (lit. If he could come here, it would be good.)

미국에 갔으면 좋겠어요. I wish I could go to America. (lit. If I could go to America, it would be good.)

그분을 만났으면 좋겠어요. I wish I could see him. (lit. .If I could see him, it would be good.)

한국말을 잘 했으면 좋겠어요. I wish I could speak Korean well. (lit. If I could speak Korean well, it would be good.)

지금 수영했으면 좋겠어요. I wish I could swim now, (lit. If I could swim now, it would be good.)

Although the past tense infix is used in this pattern, the meaning is in the present tense. Thererfore, the pattern -았(-었, -였)으면 좋겠다 is interchangeable with -(으)면 좋겠다, (without the past tense infix), making no difference in meaning. The pattern with the past tense infix is, however, more euphemistic. Study the following examples:

집에 갔으면 좋겠어요. I hope I can go home, (lit. If I could go home, it would be good.)

집에 가면 좋겠어요. I hope I can go home, (lit. If I can go home, it will be good.)

II. The Intentional -ㄹ(을)래요… : 'will do,' 'intend to do'

The sentence-final ending -ㄹ(을)래요 is used with action verbs and the verb 있다; it indicates a speaker's intention or planning.

Examples :

부산에 가실래요?	Will you go to Pusan?
예, 부산에 갈래요.	Yes, I'll go to Pusan.
아니오, 부산에 가지 않을래요.	No, I won't go to Pusan.
내일 공부하실래요?	Will you study tomorrow?
예, 내일 공부할래요.	Yes, I'll study tomorrow.
아니오, 내일 공부하지 않을래요.	No, I won't study tomorrow.
오늘 저녁에 집에 계실래요?	Will you stay at home this evening?
예, 오늘 저녁에 집에 있을래요.	Yes, I'll stay at home this evening.
아니오, 오늘 저녁에 집에 있지 않을래요.	No, I won't stay at home this evening.

Notes :

1. The sentence-final ending -ㄹ(을)래요 is used regularly with first person statements and second person questions.
2. -ㄹ래요 is used after verb stems ending in a vowel;
   -을래요 is used after verb stems ending in a consonant.
3. Notice that the pattern -(을)께 요, studied in Unit 18, S.N. III, is used only with first person statements.

III. The Ordinal Numbers :

In Korean, there are two kinds of ordinal numbers; i.e., Korean ordinal numbers and Chinese ordinal numbers.

a. Korean Ordinal Numbers :

One way to express 'first, second, third,' etc., is to attach the suffix -째 to Korean cardinal numbers, with the exception of the word 'first.' Study the following examples :

첫째	first	넷째	fourth	일곱째	seventh
둘째	second	다섯째	fifth	여덟째	eighth
셋째	third	여섯째	sixth	아홉째	ninth
				열째	tenth

Notes :

The suffix -째 can also be attached to any number made with the classifier (counter). Study the following examples :

첫 번째	the first time	이 일째	the second day
두 번째	the second time	삼 일째	the third day
세 번째	the third time	사 일째	the fourth day

이 권째	the second book	두 시간째	the second hour
삼 권째	the third book	세 시간째	the third hour

b. Chinsese Ordinal Numbers:

Another way to express 'first, second, third', etc., is to prefix 제- to Chinese numbers. The Chinese ordinal numbers are used less commonly than Korean ordinal numbers. Study the following examples.

제 일	first	제 사	fourth	제 칠	seventh
제 이	second	제 오	fifth	제 팔	eighth
제 삼	third	제 육	sixth	제 구	ninth
				제 십	tenth

Examples:

그분이 반에서 첫째를 했어요.	He became first in his class.
첫째 배가 고파요.	First (of all), I feel hungry.
제 일과가 어려워요.	The first lesson is difficult.

DRILLS

ADDITIONAL VOCABULARY

눈	snow	태풍	a typhoon
소나기	a shower	구름	a cloud
바람	a wind	끼다	to cloud up
불다	to blow	흐리다	to be cloudy
번개	(a bolt of) lightning	가물다	to be dry, to become parched
치다	to flash	장마	the rainy season

A. Substitution Drill

1. 날씨가 개었으면 좋겠어요. — I wish the weather would clear up.
2. 소나기가 왔으면 좋겠어요. — I wish a shower would come.
3. 바람이 불었으면 좋겠어요. — I wish a wind would blow.
4. 태풍이 불었으면 좋겠어요. — I wish a typhoon would blow.
5. 번개가 쳤으면 좋겠어요. — I wish lightning would flash.
6. 날씨가 흐렸으면 좋겠어요. — I wish the weather were cloudy.
7. 한국말을 잘 했으면 좋겠어요. — I wish I could speak Korean well.
8. 수영했으면 좋겠어요. — I wish I could swim.

B. Substitution Drill (Review)

1. 그분이 한국 사람인데요! — He is a Korean!

2. 그분이 미국 사람인데요!	He is an American!
3. 그분이 영국 사람인데요!	He is an Englishman!
4. 그분이 일본 사람인데요!	He is a Japanese!
5. 그분이 불란서 사람인데요!	He is a Frenchman!
6. 그분이 독일 사람인데요!	He is a German!
7. 그분이 소련 사람인데요!	He is a Russian!
8. 그분이 중국 사람인데요!	He is a Chinese man!

C. Substitution Drill

1. 그분이 등산 갔어요.	He went mountain-climbing.
2. 그분이 목욕 갔어요.	He went to the bathhouse.
3. 그분이 산책 갔어요.	He went for a walk.
4. 그분이 소풍 갔어요.	He went for a picnic.
5. 그분이 여행 갔어요.	He went traveling.
6. 그분이 사냥 갔어요.	He went hunting.

D. Substitution Drill

1. 구름이 낄 것 같아요.	It seems to be getting cloudy.
2. 날씨가 갤 것 같아요.	It seems that the weather will clear up.
3. 소나기가 올 것 같아요.	It seems that a shower will come.
4. 태풍이 불 것 같아요.	It seems that a typhoon will blow.
5. 바람이 불 것 같아요.	It seems that a wind will blow.
6. 날씨가 흐릴 것 같아요.	The weather seems to be getting cloudy.
7. 번개가 칠 것 같아요.	It seems that lightning will flash.
8. 날씨가 가물 것 같아요.	It seems to be getting dry.

E. Substitution Drill

1. 낮잠을 잘래요.	I will take a nap.
2. 이를 닦을 래요.	I will clean my teeth.
3. 등산 갈래요.	I will go mountain-climbing.
4. 목욕 갈래요.	I will go to the bathhouse.
5. 산책 갈래요.	I will go for a walk.
6. 소풍 갈래요.	I will go on a picnic.
7. 사냥 갈래요.	I will go on a hunt.
8. 여행 갈래요.	I will go traveling.

F. Pattern Drill (Review)

Teacher: 그 여자가 예쁘군요!	She is very beautiful!
Student: 그 여자가 예쁜데요!	She is very beautiful!

1. 날씨가 춥군요! 날씨가 추운데요!
2. 날씨가 덥군요! 날씨가 더운데요!
3. 날씨가 선선하군요! 날씨가 선선한데요!
4. 날씨가 무덥군요! 날씨가 무더운데요!
5. 날씨가 따뜻하군요! 날씨가 따뜻한데요!
6. 날씨가 시원하군요! 날씨가 시원한데요!
7. 날씨가 쌀쌀하군요! 날씨가 쌀쌀한데요!
8. 날씨가 나쁘군요! 날씨가 나쁜데요!

G. Pattern Drill (Review)

Teacher: 그분이 학교에 가는군요!
He is going to school!
Student: 그분이 학교에 가는데요!
He is going to school!

1. 비가 오는군요! 비가 오는데요!
2. 그분이 부탁하는군요! 그분이 부탁하는데요!
3. 그분이 가기 싫어하는군요! 그분이 가기 싫어하는데요!
4. 그분이 장난하는군요! 그분이 장난하는데요!
5. 옷을 갈아입는군요! 옷을 갈아입는데요!
6. 그분이 눈을 뜨는군요! 그분이 눈을 뜨는데요!
7. 그분이 뛰어가는군요! 그분이 뛰어가는데요!
8. 그분이 걸어가는군요! 그분이 걸어가는데요!

H. Response Drill

Teacher: 부산에 가실래요? Will you go to Pusan?
Student: 아니오, 부산에 가지 않을래요. No, I won't go to Pusan.

1. 운동을 하실래요? 아니오, 운동을 하지 않을래요.
2. 목욕하실래요? 아니오, 목욕하지 않을래요.
3. 면도하실래요? 아니오, 면도하지 않을래요.
4. 세수하실래요? 아니오, 세수하지 않을래요.
5. 여행하실래요? 아니오, 여행하지 않을래요.
6. 구경하실래요? 아니오, 구경하지 않을래요.
7. 도와주실래요? 아니오, 도와주지 않을래요.
8. 가지고 가실래요? 아니오, 가지고 가지 않을래요.

I. Pattern Drill

Teacher: 이것이 첫 번째입니다. This is the first time.
Student: 이것이 첫 시간째입니다. This is the first hour.

1. 이것이 두 번째입니다. 이것이 두 시간째입니다.
2. 이것이 세 번째입니다. 이것이 세 시간째입니다.
3. 이것이 네 번째입니다. 이것이 네 시간째입니다.
4. 이것이 다섯 번째입니다. 이것이 다섯 시간째입니다.
5. 이것이 여섯 번째입니다. 이것이 여섯 시간째입니다.
6. 이것이 일곱 번째입니다. 이것이 일곱 시간째입니다.
7. 이것이 여덟 번째입니다. 이것이 여덟 시간째입니다.
8. 이것이 아홉 번째입니다. 이것이 아홉 시간째입니다.

SHORT STORIES

1. 지난 밤에 두 시간 밖에 자지 못 했습니다.
   그래서 지금 굉장히 피곤합니다.
   집에서 푹 쉬었으면 좋겠습니다.

   굉장히 magnificently, awfully

   Expansion Drill

   지난 밤에 두 시간 밖에 자지 못했기 때문에, 지금 굉장히 피곤합니다. 집에서 푹 쉬었으면 좋겠습니다.

2. 날씨가 흐렸어요.
   오후에 비가 오지 않을 것 같아요.
   나는 친구하고 같이 사냥 갈래요.

   Expansion Drill

   날씨가 흐렸지만, 오후에 비가 오지 않을 것 같아요. 나는 친구하고 같이 사냥 갈래요.

3. 봄에는 따뜻하지만, 여름에는 덥습니다.
   가을에는 선선합니다.
   겨울에는 춥습니다.

   봄 spring
   가을 fall, autumn
   겨울 winter

READING

어제 시내에서 친구를 만났어요. 그분을 십 년 만에 만났어요. 아주 반가웠어요. 나는 친구하고 같이 술집에 들어갔어요. 술집에서 술을 열 두 시까지 마셨어요. 술에 취해서 돌아올 수 없었어요. 우리는 새벽 네 시까지 계속해서 술을 마셨어요. 다섯 시쯤 친구하고 같이 택시를 타고 집에 돌아왔어요. 우리는 초인종을 눌렀어요. 그러나 부인이 문을 열어 주지 않았어요. 한 이십 분 후에 부인이 문을 열어 주었어요. 그러나 부인한테 아주 혼났어요.

십 년 만에	after ten years (This pattern -만에 will be studied later)
반갑다	to be glad, to be delighted (to meet)
술집	a bar, a tavern
지나다	to pass by, to pass through
새벽	dawn
계속해서	continuously
취하다	to get drunk (intoxicated)
타고	to ride and
초인종	a (call) bell
누르다	to press
부인	a wife (honorific)
한	about
혼나다	to have a hard time, to get a hard time

BRIEFING

I met a friend downtown yesterday. I met him for the first time in ten years. I was very glad to see him. I went into the bar with my friend. We drank until 12 o'clock midnight in the bar. We got drunk, so we were not able to come back home. We kept drinking until 4 o'clock in the morning. We took a taxi about 5 o'clock and got home. We pressed the bell. But my wife didn't open the door for us. A little while later my wife opened the door for us. But my wife gave me a hard time.

UNIT 24 영화 Movies

BASIC SENTENCES : MEMORIZE

영화	the movies
박 성 철	
1. 지금 영화를 보러 가실 거에요?	Will you go to see a movie now?
숙제	homework
최 인 숙	
2. 아니오, 숙제를 하고 갈 거에요.	No, I'll do my homework and then go.
갈 때	when you go
들르다	to stop by, to drop in
박 성 철	
3. 갈 때 내 방에 들러 주세요. 같이 갑시다.	Please drop by my room when you go. Let's go together.
끝날 때까지	until it is finished
기다리다	to wait
최 인 숙	
4. 숙제가 끝날 때까지 기다리시겠어요?	Will you wait until my homework is finished?
언제쯤	about when
박 성 철	
5. 언제쯤 끝날 것 같아요?	About when do you think it will be finished?
최 인 숙	
6. 아마 한 시간쯤 걸릴 거에요.	It will probably take about an hour.

USEFUL EXPRESSIONS : MEMORIZE

1. 주말 잘 지내세요.	Have a nice weekend.
2. 할 수 없어요.	It can't be helped.
3. 만나 뵈어 반갑습니다.	I'm glad to see you. Or : Pleased to meet you.

NOTES ON THE BASIC SENTENCES

1. 지금 'now' is used both with non-past tense verbs and past tense verbs. When it is used with a non-past verb, it indicates immediate future ; but when it is used with a past verb, it indicates immediate past. 방금 'just now,' 'a moment ago' is used, however, always with a past verb, and indicates immediate past. Study the following examples :

지금 왔어요.	I just came.
지금 가겠어요.	I'll go now.
방금 먹었어요.	I ate just now.

영화 means 'a motion picture,' 'a movie.' When the consonant ㅎ with a vowel occurs as a final syllable, the aspirated sound is not pronounced, habitually. But when it occurs in the initial syllable, the aspirated sound is pronounced clearly. Study the following examples :

영화	a movie	화요일	Tuesday
전화	a telephone	회사	a company
회화	a conversation	회의	a meeting

가실 거에요? is an informal form of 가실 것이에요? (See Unit 9, Structure Notes III.)

3. 내 방에 들러 주세요 means 'Please drop by my room.' The verb 들르다 'to stop by,' 'to drop in' is an irregular verb. The final vowel -으 is dropped when followed by the vowel -어. This irregular verb, ending in a final vowel -으, will be studied later.

4. 기다리시겠어요? means 'Will you wait?' The question form, with the future tense, is sometimes used as an euphemistic expression to ask someone's favor. Study the following examples :

찬물 좀 주세요.	Give me some cold water, please.
찬물 좀 주시겠어요?	Will you give me some cold water? (euphemistic)

STRUCTURE NOTES

I. The Coordinate Non-Final Ending -고… : 'and'

We have studied the particles -하고 and -와/-과 meaning 'and,' used to link nouns in coordination. For example, 책하고 연필을 샀어요 'I bought a book and a pencil.' '치약과 수건을 주세요' 'Please give me some toothpaste and a towel.' This pattern -고 is used, however, to link two clauses in coordination.

Examples:

숙제를 하고, 가겠어요.	I'll do my homework and (then) go.
문을 열고, 들어오세요.	Open the door and come in.
나는 공부하고, 그분은 자요.	I'm studying and he's sleeping.
바람이 불고, 비가 와요.	The wind is blowing and it's raining.
이것이 싸고, 좋아요.	This is cheap and good.
그분은 크고, 나는 작아요.	He is tall and I am short.
나는 학생이고, 그분은 선생님이에요.	I'm a student and he is a teacher.

Notes:

1. When this pattern -고 is used with negative constructions, like -지 않고 or -지 말고, it indicates the rejection of one action in favor of another. Study the following examples:

숙제를 하지 않고, 그분을 도와주겠어요.	I'm not going to do my homework I'm going to help him.
그분을 만나지 않고, 돌아 왔어요.	Without seeing him, I came back.
먹지 말고, 갑시다.	Let's go without eating.
일하지 말고, 공부하세요.	Don't work, (but) study.

   Later, you will study this pattern -고 used with the negative construction in detail.

2. This pattern -고 may be used with any verb, and the subjects of the two clauses can be the same or different.

3. When the subjects of the two clauses are different, they usually take the contrast particle -는/-은. Study the following examples:

이것은 좋고, 그것은 나빠요.	This is good and that is bad.
한국말은 재미있고, 영어는 어렵습니다.	Korean is interesting and English is difficult.

II. The Non-Final Ending -ㄹ(을) 때…: 'when,' 'while'

The pattern -ㄹ(을) 때 may be used with any verb, and indicates a time when something takes place or exists. The English equivalent of this pattern is 'when,' or 'while.' It ends regularly with a comma intonation.

Examples:

주무실 때, 불을 끄세요.	When you go to bed, turn off the light, please.
여기에 오실 때, 가지고 오세요.	When you come here, bring that.
그분이 갈 때, 나도 가겠어요.	When he leaves, I'll go too.

날씨가 따뜻할 때, 가겠어요.	When the weather is warm, I'll go.
시간이 있을 때, 같이 갑시다.	When you have time, let's go together.
내가 일할 때, 그분이 왔어요.	When I was working, he came.
내가 산보할 때, 그분이 떠났어요.	When I was taking a walk, he left.

Notes:

1. This pattern -ㄹ(을) 때 can be used with any verb. But it cannot be used with the verb -이다 in the present tense. Study the following examples:

내가 선생이었을 때, 거기에 갔어요.	When I was a teacher, I went there.
내가 선생일 때, …	(not used)

2. When the actions of the two clauses take place at the same time, the past tense infix (-았-) is not needed in this pattern -ㄹ(을) 때, as you have seen in the above examples. But when the action of the main clause takes place before the action of the dependent clause, the past tense infix may be used within the pattern -ㄹ(을) 때. Study the following examples:

그분을 만났을 때, 그 이야기를 했어요.	When I saw him, I told him about it.
교실에 들어갔을 때, 불이 꺼져 있었어요.	When I entered the classroom, the light was off.
한국에 왔을 때, 아주 더웠어요.	When I came to Korea, it was very hot.
학교에 갔을 때, 그분이 안 계셨어요.	When I went to school, he was not there.

3. This pattern -ㄹ(을) 때 can be followed by any particle, such as -가/-이, -를/-을, -에, -도, -마다, -부터, -까지, etc. Study the following examples:

저녁을 먹을 때가 되었어요.	It's time to eat supper. (lit. The time that we eat supper came.)
어렸을 때를 생각하세요.	Think of the time when you were a child.
학교에 갈 때에, 그분을 만났어요.	On the way to school, I met him.
학교에 갈 때도, 그분을 만났어요.	I met him again as I was going to school.
한국에 올 때마다, 그분을 만나요.	Every time I come to Korea, I see him.
이 일을 시작할 때부터, 기분이 나빴어요.	From the time that I began this work, I felt bad.
그분이 돌아올 때까지 기다리세요.	Wait until he comes back.

4. -ㄹ 때 is used after verb stems ending in a vowel;
-을 때 is used after verb stems ending in a consonant.

DRILLS

ADDITIONAL VOCABULARY

예습하다	to prepare one's lesson	내다보다	to look out
복습하다	to review	들여다보다	to look in (through), to peep into (through)
연습하다	to practice	자라다	to grow, to grow up
쳐다보다	to look up, to stare	굵다	to be thick (tree)
내려다보다	to look down	가늘다	to be thin (tree)

A. Substitution Drill (Review)

1. 그것이 비쌀 거에요. — It must be expensive.
2. 그것이 재미있을 거에요. — It must be interesting.
3. 그것이 어려울 거에요. — It must be difficult.
4. 그것이 굵을 거에요. — (The tree) must be thick.
5. 그것이 가늘 거에요. — (The tree) must be thin.
6. 그것이 길 거에요. — It must be long.
7. 그것이 짧을 거에요. — It must be short.
8. 그것이 넓을 거에요. — It must be wide.

B. Substitution Drill (Review)

1. 그분이 교실에 계실 거에요. — He'll probably be in the classroom.
2. 그분이 물을 거에요. — He'll probably ask you.
3. 그분이 대답할 거에요. — He'll probably answer.
4. 그분이 부탁할 거에요. — He'll probably ask you a favor.
5. 그분이 싫어할 거에요. — He'll probably dislike it.
6. 그분이 장난할 거에요. — He'll probably play a trick.
7. 그분이 낮잠을 잘 거에요. — He'll probably take a nap.
8. 그분이 잊어버릴 거에요. — He'll probably forget it.

C. Substitution Drill

1. 숙제를 하고 가겠어요. — I'll do my homework and then go.
2. 공부를 하고 가겠어요. — I'll study and then go.
3. 세수를 하고 가겠어요. — I'll wash my face and then go.
4. 목욕을 하고 가겠어요. — I'll take a bath and then go.
5. 구경을 하고 가겠어요. — I'll sightsee and then go.
6. 이를 닦고 가겠어요. — I'll clean my teeth and then go.
7. 옷을 갈아입고 가겠어요. — I'll change my clothes and then go.
8. 이 방을 청소하고 가겠어요. — I'll clean this room and then go.

D. Substitution Drill

1. 그분을 만나지 않고 돌아왔어요.	Without seeing him, I came back.
2. 일하지 않고 돌아왔어요.	Without working, I came back.
3. 그분을 도와주지 않고 돌아왔어요.	Without helping him, I came back.
4. 연습하지 않고 돌아왔어요.	Without practicing, I came back.
5. 복습하지 않고 돌아왔어요.	Without reviewing, I came back.
6. 쳐다보지 않고 돌아왔어요.	Without looking up, I came back.
7. 내려다보지 않고 돌아왔어요.	Without looking down, I came back.
8. 내다보지 않고 돌아왔어요.	Without looking out, I came back.

E. Substitution Drill

1. 저녁을 먹을 때가 되었어요.	It's time to eat supper.
2. 한국말을 공부할 때가 되었어요.	It's time to study Korean.
3. 일어날 때가 되었어요.	It's time to get up.
4. 복습할 때가 되었어요.	It's time to review.
5. 연습할 때가 되었어요.	It's time to practice.
6. 예습할 때가 되었어요.	It's time to prepare our lessons.
7. 운동을 할 때가 되었어요.	It's time to exercise.
8. 산보를 할 때가 되었어요.	It's time to take a walk.

F. Integration Drill

Teacher: 이것은 좋아요. 그것은 나빠요.
This is good. That is bad.
Student: 이것은 좋고, 그것은 나빠요.
This is good and that is bad.

1. 이 나무는 굵어요. 저 나무는 가늘어요.
   이 나무는 굵고, 저 나무는 가늘어요.
2. 이분은 뚱뚱해요. 저분은 홀쭉해요.
   이분은 뚱뚱하고, 저분은 홀쭉해요.
3. 이것은 길어요. 저것은 짧아요.
   이것은 길고, 저것은 짧아요.
4. 이 방은 넓어요. 저 방은 좁아요.
   이 방은 넓고, 저 방은 좁아요.
5. 이 교실은 깨끗해요. 저 교실은 더러워요.
   이 교실은 깨끗하고, 저 교실은 더러워요.
6. 여기는 멀어요. 거기는 가까워요.
   여기는 멀고, 거기는 가까워요.
7. 이 사무실은 밝아요. 저 사무실은 어두워요.

이 사무실은 밝고, 저 사무실은 어두워요.

8. 한국말은 쉬워요. 영어는 어려워요.
   한국말은 쉽고, 영어는 어려워요.

G. Integration Drill

Teacher : 주무세요. 불을 끄세요.
Go to bed. Turn off the light.

Student : 주무실 때, 불을 끄세요.
When you go to bed, turn off the light.

1. 여기에 오세요. 그것을 가지고 오세요.
   여기에 오실 때, 그것을 가지고 오세요.
2. 나가세요. 들러 주세요.
   나가실 때, 들러 주세요.
3. 낮잠을 주무세요. 문을 닫으세요.
   낮잠을 주무실 때, 문을 닫으세요.
4. 목욕을 하세요. 이것을 가지고 가세요.
   목욕을 하실 때, 이것을 가지고 가세요.
5. 학교에 가세요. 그분을 만나세요.
   학교에 가실 때, 그분을 만나세요.
6. 교실에 들어가세요. 문을 여세요.
   교실에 들어가실 때, 문을 여세요.
7. 밖에 나가세요. 그것을 보세요.
   밖에 나가실 때, 그것을 보세요.
8. 부산에 내려가세요. 그것을 주세요.
   부산에 내려가실 때, 그것을 주세요.

H. Integration Drill

Teacher : 그분이 와요. 기다리세요.
He is coming. Wait.

Student : 그분이 올 때까지, 기다리세요.
Wait until he comes.

1. 그분이 갑니다. 일하겠습니다.
   그분이 갈 때까지, 일하겠습니다.
2. 공부가 끝납니다. 기다리세요.
   공부가 끝날 때까지, 기다리세요.
3. 내가 일을 마칩니다. 주무세요.
   내가 일을 마칠 때까지, 주무세요.
4. 내가 올라갑니다. 공부하세요.

내가 올라갈 때까지, 공부하세요.

5. 내가 나갑니다. 구경하세요.
   내가 나갈 때까지, 구경하세요.
6. 공부가 끝납니다. 책을 읽으세요.
   공부가 끝날 때까지, 책을 읽으세요.
7. 잘 할 수 있습니다. 연습하세요.
   잘 할 수 있을 때까지, 연습하세요.
8. 내가 도착합니다. 복습하세요.
   내가 도착할 때까지, 복습하세요.

I. Integration Drill

Teacher: 한국에 옵니다. 그분을 만납니다.
I come to Korea. I see him.

Student: 한국에 올 때마다, 그분을 만납니다.
Every time I come to Korea, I see him.

1. 시간이 있습니다. 거기에 갑니다.
   시간이 있을 때마다, 거기에 갑니다.
2. 그분이 옵니다. 내가 바쁩니다.
   그분이 올 때마다, 내가 바쁩니다.
3. 극장에 갑니다. 사람이 많습니다.
   극장에 갈 때마다, 사람이 많습니다.
4. 그분을 만납니다. 이야기하겠습니다.
   그분을 만날 때마다, 이야기하겠습니다.
5. 그것을 봅니다. 화가 납니다.
   그것을 볼 때마다, 화가 납니다.
6. 그분이 미국에 갑니다. 부탁하겠습니다.
   그분이 미국에 갈 때마다, 부탁하겠습니다.
7. 한국에 옵니다. 날씨가 춥습니다.
   한국에 올 때마다, 날씨가 춥습니다.
8. 문을 닫습니다. 시끄럽습니다.
   문을 닫을 때마다, 시끄럽습니다.

J. Integration Drill

Teacher: 이 일을 시작했습니다. 기분이 나빴습니다.
I began this work. I felt bad.

Student: 이 일을 시작할 때부터, 기분이 나빴습니다.
From the time that I began this work, I felt bad.

1. 한국에 왔습니다. 바빴습니다.
   한국에 올 때부터, 바빴습니다.
2. 교실에 들어왔습니다. 이상했습니다.
   교실에 들어올 때부터, 이상했습니다.
3. 공부를 시작했습니다. 배가 고팠습니다.
   공부를 시작할 때부터, 배가 고팠습니다.
4. 일을 시작했습니다. 피곤했습니다.
   일을 시작할 때부터, 피곤했습니다.
5. 아침을 먹었습니다. 그분이 웃었습니다.
   아침을 먹을 때부터, 그분이 웃었습니다.
6. 여기에 왔습니다. 화가 났습니다.
   여기에 올 때부터, 화가 났습니다.
7. 일을 했습니다. 사람이 많았습니다.
   일을 할 때부터, 사람이 많았습니다.
8. 그분이 떠났습니다. 울기 시작했습니다.
   그분이 떠날 때부터, 울기 시작했습니다.

SHORT STORIES

1. 지금 점심을 먹을 때가 되었습니다.
   점심을 먹고 가겠습니다.
   내가 갈 때까지 기다리세요.

   Expansion Drill

   지금 점심을 먹을 때가 되었기 때문에, 점심을 먹고 가겠습니다.
   내가 갈 때까지 기다리세요.

2. 내가 시간이 있을 때 같이 갑시다.
   지금은 바쁘기 때문에, 못 가겠습니다.
   내일은 아마 시간이 있을 거에요.

3. 어제 그분을 찾아갔을 때, 그분이 집에 안 계셨습니다.
   그분을 찾아갈 때마다, 그분은 집에 안 계십니다.
   그분이 요즘 아주 바쁜 것 같습니다.

READING

나는 <u>의사</u>입니다. 지금 <u>병원</u>에서 <u>일하고 있습니다.</u> 어제는 큰 <u>교통 사고</u>가 <u>났습</u>니다. 그래서 어떤 여자가 <u>얼굴</u>을 많이 <u>다쳤</u>습니다. 나는 두 시간 동안 그 여자를 수술했습니다. 다행히 그 여자는 죽지 않고 살았습니다. 그런데 오늘 아침에 그 여자의 이름을 보고, 나는 깜짝 놀랐습니다. 그 여자는 옛날의 내 약혼자였습니다. 내가 대학교 삼 학년 때였습니다. 우리 동네에 아주 예쁜 여학생이 있었습니다. 우리는 서로 사랑했습니다. 나중에 약혼했습니다. 그런데 그 여자는 내 친구한테 시집갔습니다. 왜냐하면 내 친구는 아주 부잣집 아들이었기 때문입니다.

의사	a (medical) doctor	이름	a name
병원	a hospital	옛날	ancient times, old days
일하고 있다	I'm working	약혼자	an engaged person
교통 사고	a traffic accident	대학교	a college
나다	to happen, to break out	삼 학년	the third grade, junior
		동네	a village
얼굴	a face	여학생	a girl student
다치다	to get hurt	서로	each other
두 시간 동안	for two hours	나중에	in the end, finally
수술	a surgical operation	약혼하다	to get engaged
수술하다	to operate	시집가다	to get married (to)
다행히	fortunately	부잣집	a rich man's house
죽다	to die	아들	a son

BRIEFING

I'm a medical doctor. I'm working at the hospital now. Yesterday a big traffic accident happened. A certain woman's face was seriously injured. I performed a surgical operation on her for two hours. Fortunately the woman survived. This morning I saw her name, and I was completely surprised. She was my old fiancee when I was a junior in college. There was a very beautiful girl student in my village. We loved each other. Finally we got engaged. But she got married to my friend because my friend was the son of a very rich man.

UNIT 25 괜찮아요? Is It Alright?

BASIC SENTENCES: MEMORIZE

들어가도	even though I go in
괜찮아요?	is it alright?
최 인 숙	
1. 들어가도 괜찮아요?	May I go in?
어서	without hesitation, without delay
박 성 철	
2. 예, 어서 들어오세요.	Yes sure. Come on in.
청소하다	to clean
최 인 숙	
3. 지금 이 방을 청소할까요?	Shall I clean this room now?
끝난 다음에	after it is finished
박 성 철	
4. 지금은 공부해야 해요. 공부가 끝난 다음에 하세요.	I have to study now. Please clean it after I finish studying.
조금 있다가	a little later
최 인 숙	
5. 그럼, 조금 있다가 올까요?	Then, shall I come a little later?
약	about
박 성 철	
6. 예, 약 삼십 분 후에 오세요.	Yes, please come back in about thirty minutes.

USEFUL EXPRESSIONS: MEMORIZE

1. 염려하지 마세요.	Don't worry, please.
2. 편히 앉으세요.	Make yourself comfortable.
3. 어떻게 되었어요?	How did it turn out?
4. 잘 되었어요.	It turned out well.

NOTES ON THE BASIC SENTENCES

1. 들어가다, depending on the context or situation, can mean (1) 'to go in (into),' (2) 'to enter (a company, a school),' (3) 'to contain,' 'to include,' (4) 'to be spent,' (5) 'to become hollow,' etc. Study the following examples:

그분이 방으로 들어갔어요.	He went into the room.
그분이 학교에 들어갔어요.	He entered the school.
이 과자에는 우유가 들어갔어요.	This candy contains (has) milk.
이 책에 돈이 많이 들어갔어요.	Much money was spent for this book.
배가 고프기 때문에, 눈이 푹 들어갔어요.	Your eyes grow hollow with hunger.

3. 청소하다 means 'to clean,' 'to sweep.' Study the following words.
청소부 'a cleaner,' 'a sweeper,' 'a street cleaner,' 'a garbage-man'
청소차 'a scavenger's cart,' 'a garbage wagon'
전기 청소기 or 진공 청소기 'a vacuum cleaner'

6. 약- 'about' is a prefix indicating an approximate point in time or quantity. So it is always put before time and/or quantity expressions. 약- 'about' is interchangeable with the prefix 한- 'about,' making no difference in meaning. Oftentimes, 약- and 한- are used together with the suffix -쯤 'about,' as an emphatic expression. Study the following examples:

약 두 시간 공부했어요.	I studied about two hours.
약 두 시간쯤 공부했어요.	I studied about two hours. (emphatic)
약 열 개 먹었어요.	I ate about ten of them.
약 열개쯤 먹었어요.	I ate about ten of them. (emphatic)
한 십 분 걸려요.	It takes about ten minutes.
한 십 분쯤 걸려요.	It takes about ten minutes. (emphatic)
한 열 개 샀어요.	I bought about ten.
한 열 개쯤 샀어요.	I bought about ten. (emphatic)

STRUCTURE NOTES

I. The Concessive Ending -아(-어, -여)도… : 'even if' 'even though'

The non-final ending -아(-어, -여)도 is used with any verb, except 이다. The English equivalent of this pattern is 'even if it is so-and-so,' 'even if someone does so-and-so,' or 'even being or doing so-and-so.' 아(-어, -여)도 regularly ends with a comma intonation.

Examples:

맛있어도, 먹지 않겠어요.	Even though it's delicious, I won't eat it.
맛이 없어도, 잡수세요.	Even if it's not delicious, eat it.
재미있어도, 보고 싶지 않아요.	Even though it's interesting, I don't want to see it.
재미없어도, 공부하세요.	Even if it's not interesting, study it.
날씨가 추워도, 가겠어요.	Even though the weather is cold, I'll go (there).
비싸도, 사겠어요.	Even if it's expensive, I'll buy it.
들어도, 모르겠어요.	Even if I listen, I don't understand.
읽고 싶어도, 너무 어려워요.	Even if I want to read it, it's too difficult.
연습해도, 잘 되지 않아요.	Even if I practice it, it doesn't go well (it's not successful).
나는 가지 않아도, 그분은 가요.	Even though I don't go, he goes.

When this pattern -아(-어, -여)도 is followed, however, by the word 좋다 'it's good,' 'it's OK,' or 괜찮다 'it's all right,' 'it doesn't matter,' it is used for asking or giving permission. In other words, for the expression 'someone MAY do something,' this pattern -아(-어, -여)도 좋다 (괜찮다) is used. Its literal meaning is 'even being or doing so-and-so, it's all right.' Study the following examples:

들어가도 좋습니까 (괜찮습니까)?	May I go in?
들어가도 좋아요.	You may go in.
학교에 가도 괜찮습니까?	May I go to school?
학교에 가도 괜찮아요.	You may go to school.
사지 않아도 좋습니까?	Is it alright even if I don't buy it?
사지 않아도 좋습니다.	It's alright even if you don't buy it. Or: You don't have to buy it.
내일 다시 와도 괜찮습니까?	May I come again tomorrow?
내일 다시 와도 괜찮습니다.	You may come again tomorrow.
시끄러워도 괜찮습니까?	Is it alright even if it's noisy?
시끄러워도 괜찮아요.	It doesn't matter even if it's noisy.
멀어도 좋습니까?	Is it alright even if it's far?
멀어도 좋습니다.	It doesn't matter even if it's far.

The negative answer to a request for permission depends on whether the request is affirmative or negative.

1. In denying permission, a statement of prohibition is used: -(으)면 안 되다 'someone must not do something,' (lit. 'if someone does something, it

won't do') ; or the negative imperative form -지 말다 'Don't do.' Study the following examples:

그것을 사도 좋습니까?	May I buy it?
그것을 사면 안 됩니다.	You must not buy it.
그것을 사지 마세요.	Don't buy it, please.
그것을 사지 말아 주세요.	Don't buy it, please. (polite)

2. In denying permission, the obligatory pattern -아(-어, -여)야 하다 is used: 'someone must or has to do something'; -지 않으면 안 되다 'if someone doesn't do something, it won't do'; or the affirmative imperative form -(으)십시오 'Please do it.' Study the following examples:

그것을 사지 않아도 좋습니까?	Is it alright even if I don't buy it?
그것을 사야 합니다.	You must buy it.
그것을 사지 않으면 안 됩니다.	You must buy it, (lit. If you don't buy it, it won't do).
그것을 사십시오 (사세요).	Please buy it.
그것을 사 주십시오 (사 주세요).	Please buy it. (polite)

Notes:

-아도 is used after -아 and 오;

-어도 is used after any other vowel;

-여도 is used after 하-, or the stem of the verb 하다 'to do.'

II. The Obligatory Ending -아(-어, -여)야 하다… : 'must,' 'have to'

There are several ways of expressing obligation in Korean: i.e.— 'someone must do something.' One of the most common ways is the use of the pattern -아(-어, -여)야 하다. It may be used with any verb, and indicates obligation and/or necessity.

Examples:

지금 공부해야 합니다.	I have to study now.
그것을 잊어버려야 합니다.	You must forget it.
이 책을 읽어야 합니다.	I have to read this book.
그것이 좋아야 합니다.	It has to be good.
그것이 깨끗해야 합니다.	It has to be clean.
돈이 있어야 합니다.	You must have money.
그것이 연필이어야 합니다.	It has to be a pencil.

Notes :

1. The tense is expressed regularly in the final verb 하다. Study the following examples :

집에 가야 합니다.	I must go home.
집에 가야 했습니다.	I had to go home.
집에 가야 하겠습니다.	I'll have to go home.

2. The negation is expressed regularly in the main verb. Study the following examples :

집에 가야 합니다.	You must go home.
집에 가지 않아야 합니다.	You should not go home.
집에 안 가야 합니다.	You should not go home.
집에 가지 말아야 합니다.	You must not go home. (stronger)

3. The rules for attaching this ending to verb stems are the same as for -아 (-어, -여)도 of this Unit, S.N. No. I.

Another way of saying that 'someone must or has to do something' is to use the pattern -지 않으면 안 되다. The English equivalent of this pattern is 'if someone doesn't do something, it won't do, (lit. it doesn't become),' or 'unless someone does something, it won't do.'

Examples :

지금 공부하지 않으면 안 됩니다.	I have to study now, (lit. If I don't study now, it won't do.)
이 책을 읽지 않으면 안 됩니다.	I must read this book, (lit. If I don't read this book, it won't do.)
학교에 가지 않으면 안 됩니다.	I must go to school, (lit. If I don't go to school, it won't do.)

Notes :

The tense is expressed regularly in the final verb 되다. Study the following examples :

가지 않으면 안 됩니다	I must go.
가지 않으면 안 되었습니다.	I had to go.
가지 않으면 안 되겠습니다.	I'll have to go.

These pattern -아(-어, -여)야 하다 and -지 않으면 안 되다 occur frequently as strong negative replies to questions which ask, 'Is it alright (even) if I don't······?' (See this Unit, S.N. 1). Study the following examples :

그것을 사지 않아도 좋습니까?	Is it alright even if I don't buy it?
그것을 사야 합니다.	You must buy it.

그것을 사지 않으면, 안 됩니다. You must buy it, (lit. If you don't buy it, it won't do.)

To deny obligation, i.e.— 'someone need not or does not have to do something, 'the pattern -지 않아도 좋다 is used. It means 'even if someone doesn't do something, it's alright.' Study the following examples:

그것을 사야 합니까? Must I buy it?

그것을 사지 않아도 좋습니다. You don't have to buy it, (lit. Even if you don't buy it, it's alright.)

Other ways of expressing obligation will be studied later.

III. A.V.S. +-ㄴ(은) 다음에…: 'after doing'

The word 다음 is a noun meaning 'later'; the particle -에 'at,' 'on,' 'in' indicates time or place. This non-final ending -ㄴ(은) 다음에 is used to say 'after something happens' or 'after something happened.'

Examples:

공부가 끝난 다음에, 가겠어요. I'll go after I finish studying.

산보한 다음에, 자고 싶어요. I want to go to bed after taking a walk.

일한 다음에, 잡수세요. Please eat after working.

그분을 만난 다음에, 집에 왔어요. I came home after I met him.

전화한 다음에, 오세요. Please come after you phone me.

그것을 들은 다음에, 갔어요. After I heard it, I went (there).

그 책을 산 다음에, 저녁을 먹읍시다. Let's eat supper after buying that book.

그분하고 이야기한 다음에, 숙제를 했어요. I did my homework after I talked with him.

Notes:

1. This pattern -ㄴ(은) 다음에 is used always with action verbs, and the subjects of the two clauses can be the same or different.
2. The tense and/or negation is expressed in the final (main) clause, not in the dependent clause. Study the following examples, and note particularly the tense of the verb in the final clause.

   산보한 다음에 잡니다. I go to bed after taking a walk.

   산보한 다음에 잤습니다. I went to bed after taking a walk.

   산보한 다음에 자겠습니다. I'll go to bed after taking a walk.

   산보한 다음에 자지 않겠습니다. I won't go to bed after taking a walk.
3. -ㄴ 다음에 is used after verb stems ending in a vowel;
   -은 다음에 is used after verb stems ending in a consonant.

4. When the subject (of the dependent clause and the main clause) is the same, and the verb of the dependent clause is 가다/오다 or their compounds, this pattern -ㄴ(은) 다음에 CAN'T be used. See the following examples:

내가 집에 간 다음에 공부하겠어요.	(never used)
내가 집에 가서 공부하겠어요.	I'll go home and study. (This pattern will be studied in the following Unit).

DRILLS

ADDITIONAL VOCABULARY

행복하다	to be happy	얇다	to be thin (paper, book, etc.)
불행하다	to be unhappy, to be unfortunate	깊다	to be deep
두껍다	to be thick (paper, book, etc.)	얕다	to be shallow

A. Substitution Drill

1. 들어가도 좋습니까?	May I go in?
2. 부탁해도 좋습니까?	May I ask you a favor?
3. 눈을 떠도 좋습니까?	May I open my eyes?
4. 눈을 감아도 좋습니까?	May I close my eyes?
5. 옷을 갈아입어도 좋습니까?	May I change my clothes?
6. 문을 열어도 좋습니까?	May I open the door?
7. 문을 닫아도 좋습니까?	May I close the door?
8. 뛰어가도 좋습니까?	May I run?

B. Substitution Drill

1. 그것을 잊어 버려야 합니다.	You have to forget it.
2. 그것을 설명해야 합니다.	You have to explain it.
3. 낮잠을 자야 합니다.	You have to take a nap.
4. 운동을 해야 합니다.	You have to exercise.
5. 잘 생각해야 합니다.	You have to think it over well.
6. 그것을 찾아야 합니다.	You have to search for it.
7. 이 일을 계속해야 합니다.	You have to continue this work.
8. 지금 세수해야 합니다.	You have to wash your face now.

C. Substitution Drill

1. 공부하지 않으면 안 됩니다.	You have to study.
2. 이 책을 읽지 않으면 안 됩니다.	You have to read this book.

3. 이 일을 마치지 않으면 안 됩니다. You have to finish this work.
4. 숙제를 하지 않으면 안 됩니다. You have to do your homework.
5. 그분의 말을 듣지 않으면 안 됩니다. You have to listen to his words.
6. 이를 닦지 않으면 안 됩니다. You have to clean your teeth.
7. 이것을 씻지 않으면 안 됩니다. You have to wash this.
8. 그것을 만들지 않으면 안 됩니다. You have to make it.

D. Pattern Drill

Teacher : 재미있지만, 보고 싶지 않아요.
It's interesting, but I don't want to see it.

Student : 재미있어도, 보고 싶지 않아요.
Even though it's interesting, I don't want to see it.

1. 날씨가 춥지만, 가겠어요. 날씨가 추워도, 가겠어요.
2. 피곤하지만, 공부해야 해요. 피곤해도, 공부해야 해요
3. 배가 고프지만, 참아야 합니다. 배가 고파도, 참아야 합니다.
4. 시끄럽지만, 기다려 주세요. 시끄러워도, 기다려 주세요.
5. 이 방이 깨끗하지만, 좋지 않아요. 이 방이 깨끗해도, 좋지 않아요.
6. 그것이 어렵지만, 해야 합니다. 그것이 어려워도, 해야 합니다.
7. 더럽지만, 지금 청소할 수 없어요. 더러워도, 지금 청소할 수 없어요.
8. 가깝지만, 가고 싶지 않아요. 가까워도, 가고 싶지 않아요.

E. Integration Drill

Teacher : 공부가 끝납니다. 가겠습니다.
I finish studying. I'll go.

Student : 공부가 끝난 다음에, 가겠습니다.
I'll go after I finish studying.

1. 운동을 합니다. 숙제를 하겠습니다.
운동을 한 다음에, 숙제를 하겠습니다.
2. 초인종을 누릅니다. 들어가겠습니다.
초인종을 누른 다음에, 들어가겠습니다.
3. 면도합니다. 사냥을 가겠습니다.
면도한 다음에, 사냥을 가겠습니다.
4. 낮잠을 잡니다. 소풍을 가겠습니다.
낮잠을 잔 다음에, 소풍을 가겠습니다.
5. 점심을 먹습니다. 계속하겠습니다.
점심을 먹은 다음에, 계속하겠습니다.
6. 운동을 합니다. 그 일을 시작하겠습니다.

운동을 한 다음에, 그 일을 시작하겠습니다.

7. 지금 듣습니다. 대답하겠습니다.
   지금 들은 다음에, 대답하겠습니다.
8. 목욕합니다. 그분을 만나겠습니다.
   목욕한 다음에, 그분을 만나겠습니다.

F. Response Drill

Teacher:	그것을 사야 합니까?	Must I buy it?
Student:	그것을 사지 않아도 괜찮아요.	You don't have to buy it.

1. 지금 공부해야 합니까? — 지금 공부하지 않아도 괜찮아요.
2. 그분한테 부탁해야 합니까? — 그분한테 부탁하지 않아도 괜찮아요.
3. 지금 답장해야 합니까? — 지금 답장하지 않아도 괜찮아요.
4. 노래를 불러야 합니까? — 노래를 부르지 않아도 괜찮아요.
5. 내일 떠나야 합니까? — 내일 떠나지 않아도 괜찮아요.
6. 그분한테 물어야 합니까? — 그분한테 묻지 않아도 괜찮아요.
7. 문을 닫아야 합니까? — 문을 닫지 않아도 괜찮아요.
8. 이 차에 태워야 합니까? — 이 차에 태우지 않아도 괜찮아요.

G. Response Drill

Teacher: 그것을 사지 않아도 괜찮아요?
Is it alright even if I don't buy it?

Student: 아니오, 그것을 사야 합니다.
No, you must buy it.

1. 면도하지 않아도 괜찮아요? — 아니오, 면도해야 합니다.
2. 답장하지 않아도 괜찮아요? — 아니오, 답장해야 합니다.
3. 그분한테 묻지 않아도 괜찮아요? — 아니오, 그분한테 물어야 합니다.
4. 운동을 하지 않아도 괜찮아요? — 아니오, 운동을 해야 합니다.
5. 걸어가지 않아도 괜찮아요? — 아니오, 걸어가야 합니다.
6. 그것을 찾지 않아도 괜찮아요? — 아니오, 그것을 찾아야 합니다.
7. 이를 닦지 않아도 괜찮아요? — 아니오, 이를 닦아야 합니다.
8. 그분한테 여쭈지 않아도 괜찮아요? — 아니오, 그분한테 여쭤야 합니다.

H. Response Drill

Teacher:	시끄러워도 좋습니까?	Is it alright even if it's nosiy?
Student:	아니오, 시끄러우면 안 됩니다.	No, it won't do if it's noisy.

1. 두꺼워도 좋습니까? — 아니오, 두꺼우면 안 됩니다.

2. 얇아도 좋습니까? 아니오, 얇으면 안 됩니다.
3. 깊어도 좋습니까? 아니오, 깊으면 안 됩니다.
4. 얕아도 좋습니까? 아니오, 얕으면 안 됩니다.
5. 불행해도 좋습니까? 아니오, 불행하면 안 됩니다.
6. 불친절해도 좋습니까? 아니오, 불친절하면 안 됩니다.
7. 어두워도 좋습니까? 아니오, 어두우면 안 됩니다.
8. 멀어도 좋습니까? 아니오, 멀면 안 됩니다.

SHORT STORIES

1. 여기서 약 한 시간쯤 걸려요.
   그러니까 지금 떠나지 않아도 괜찮아요.
   약 세 시간 후에 떠나세요.

   Expansion Drill

   여기서 약 한 시간쯤 걸리기 때문에, 지금 떠나지 않아도 괜찮아요. 약 세 시간 후에 떠나세요.

2. 그것을 읽고 싶어도 너무 어려워요.
   한국말을 공부한 다음에 읽겠어요.
   아마 내년에는 읽을 수 있을 것 같아요.

   Expansion Drill

   그것을 읽고 싶어도 너무 어렵기 때문에, 한국말을 공부한 다음에 읽겠어요. 아마 내년에는 읽을 수 있을 것 같아요.

3. 지금 시내에 가도 괜찮아요.
   그러나 세 시까지 여기에 와야 합니다.
   그렇지 않으면 이 일을 끝낼 수 없어요. 그렇지 않으면 otherwise

   Expansion Drill

   지금 시내에 가도 괜찮지만, 세 시까지 여기에 와야 합니다. 그렇지 않으면 이 일을 끝낼 수 없어요.

READING

6·25 동란 때의 이야기입니다. 남편은 싸움터에서 전사했습니다. 그런데 부인은 애기를 낳을 날이 가까웠습니다. 성탄절이 되었습니다. 부인은 다른 사람의 도움이 필요했습니다. 이웃 동네에 친한 친구가 있었습니다. 그 친구는 신자였습니다. 부인은 그 친구를 만나러 갔습

니다. 그런데 가다가 배가 아프기 시작했습니다. 도저히 더 갈 수 없었습니다. 마침 돌다리가 있었습니다. 부인은 그 돌다리 밑에서 애기를 낳았습니다. 눈이 오고 바람이 불었습니다. 아주 추운 겨울이었습니다. 그런데 애기를 덮어 줄 것이 아무 것도 없었습니다. 그래서 부인은 자기의 옷을 벗었습니다. 그 옷으로 애기를 감싸 주었습니다. 찬 바람이 몹시 불었습니다.

6·25 동란	The Korean War (1950-1953)	가다가	when she was going
이야기	a story	도저히	(not) at all, by no means
남편	a husband	마침	fortunately
싸움터	a battlefield	돌다리	a stone bridge
전사하다	to be killed in action	밑(에서)	under, underneath
애기를 낳다	to give birth to a child	덮다	to cover (with)
날	a day	아무것도 없다	to have nothing
성탄절	Christmas	자기	oneself, one's (own)
필요하다	to be necessary	벗다	to take off
이웃 동네	neighboring village	감싸다	to shield
친하다	to be familiar (close)	찬 바람	cold wind
신자	a believer	몹시	exceedingly, awfully

BRIEFING

This story takes place during the Korean War. Her husband was killed in action on the battlefield. The day for her to give birth to their child was near. It was Christmas. She needed someone to help her. There was an intimate friend in the neighborhood. The friend was a Christian. She went to see her friend. But while she was on her way, she began to go into labor. She was not able to travel further. Fortunately there was a stone bridge. She gave birth to her child under that stone bridge. It was snowing and windy. It was a very cold winter. There was nothing with which to cover the child. So she took off her own clothes. She protected that child with her clothes. The cold wind was blowing hard.

UNIT 26 담배 Cigarettes

BASIC SENTENCES: MEMORIZE

교실에서	in the classroom
담배	a cigarette
피우다	to smoke

박 성 철

1. 교실에서 담배를 피워도 괜찮아요?	May I smoke in the classroom?
피우면	if you smoke
안 돼요	it won't be good

최 인 숙

2. 아니오, 여기서 피우면 안 돼요. 밖에 나가서 피우세요.	No, you should not smoke here. Please go outside and smoke.
잠깐	for a while

박 성 철

3. 그럼, 잠깐 나갔다가 들어 오겠어요.	Then, I'll go out for a while and then come back.
곧	soon
수업	a class, a lesson
시작하다	to begin

최 인 숙

4. 어서 갔다 오세요. 그러나 곧 수업을 시작하겠어요.	Please do so. However, we will begin class very soon.
시작하기 전에	before it begins
들어올께요	I'll come in

박 성 철

5. 수업을 시작하기 전에 들어 올께요.	I'll come back in before the class begins.

USEFUL EXPRESSIONS: MEMORIZE

1. 또 만났군요.	It's good to see you again.
2. 그렇게 나쁘지 않아요.	It's not that bad.

3. 내 잘못이 아니에요　　It's not my fault.

4. 믿을 수 없어요.　　It's unbelievable. Or : I cannot believe it.

NOTES ON THE BASIC SENTENCES

1. 담배 means 'cigarette.' Korean cigarettes are comparatively popular with foreigners because of their taste. They are exported to foreign countries a great deal these days. Traditionally, it's rude for young people to smoke in front of their fathers, superiors or old men. Middle and high school students are not allowed to smoke. If they do, they are punished.

   피우다, depending on the context or situation, can mean, (1) 'to smoke (a cigarette),' (2) 'to burn,' 'to kindle,' (3) 'to emit (a scent),' 'to send out (an odor),' etc. Study the following examples :

   담배를 피우지 마세요.　　Don't smoke cigarettes.

   불을 피우지 마세요.　　Don't make a fire.

   냄새를 피우지 마세요.　　Don't make a bad smell.

2. 여기서 is a contraction of 여기에서 'at this place.'

   안 돼요 is a contraction of 안 되어요 'it won't do, (lit. it doesn't become').

4. 곧, depending on the context or situation, can mean (1) 'at once,' 'immediately,' (2) 'easily,' 'readily,' (3) 'the same as,' 'the very,' 'that is,' 'namely,' etc. Study the following examples :

   지금 곧 가겠어요.　　I'm coming right away.

   곧 배울 수 있어요.　　You can learn it easily.

   이것이 곧 그분이 산 것이에요.　　This is the very thing which he bought.

   수업 means 'class work,' 'a lesson.' Study the following words :

   수업시간 중에 'during school hours,' 'in class'

   수업료 'a school (tuition) fee'

STRUCTURE NOTES

I. The Non-Final Ending -아(-어, -여)서… : '(someone) does and does'

This pattern -아(-어, -여)서 is used when one subject performs one action and then a second one. It is attached directly to the stem of the first action verb, and is then followed by a second verb. This pattern -아(-어, -여)서 regularly ends with a comma intonation.

Examples :

시내에 가서, 저녁을 먹겠어요.　　I'll go downtown and eat supper.

학교에 가서, 공부하겠어요.　　I'll go to school and study.

집에 와서, 잤어요. I came home and slept.
들어와서, 기다리세요. Please come in and wait.
방에 들어가서, 이야기합시다. Let's go into the room and talk.
이 책을 가지고 가서, 읽겠어요. I'll take this book with me and read it.
그것을 가지고 와서, 먹겠어요. I'll bring that (here) and eat it.
이 길을 건너가서, 기다리세요. Please cross this street and wait.
서서, 말씀하세요. Please stand up and talk.
앉아서, 잡수세요. Please sit down here and eat.
일어나서, 세수했어요. I got up and washed my face.

Notes:

1. As you have seen in the above examples, this pattern -아(-어, -여)서 is used regularly with some verb indicating movement or change of posture in the first verb, such as 가다, 오다 (or their compounds), 서다 'to stand up,' 앉다 'to sit down,' (or their compounds), 일어나다 'to get up,' etc.
2. The tense is expressed in the final (main) verb, not with -아(-어, -여)서. Study the following examples:
   학교에 가서 공부합니다. I go to school and study.
   학교에 가서 공부했습니다. I went to school and studied.
   학교에 가서 공부하겠습니다. I'll go to school and study.
3. This pattern -아(-어, -여)서 is used also with action verbs other than 가다, 오다, etc. Study the following examples:
   편지를 써서 부치겠습니다. I'll write a letter and mail it.
   그분을 만나서 이야기합시다. Let's meet him and talk (to him).
   돈을 벌어서 집을 사겠어요. I'll make money and buy a house.
   이 차를 팔아서 새 차를 사겠어요. I'll sell this car and buy a new one.
   이것을 구워서 먹겠어요. I'll roast this and eat it.
   씻어서 잡수세요. Please wash it and eat it.
   끓여서 잡수세요. Please boil it and eat it.

Let's compare this pattern -아(-어, -여)서 with the coordinate non-final ending -고, studied in Unit 13, S.N. No II.

1. Verbs such as 가다, 오다, etc., can't be used with the coordinate non-final ending -고, when the subject of two verbs is the same. Study the following examples:
   학교에 가고, 공부하겠어요. (never used)
   학교에 가서, 공부하겠어요. (correct)
2. However, when the subjects of the two verbs are different, the coordinate

non-final ending -고 can be used with the contrast particle -는/-은. Study the following examples:

나는 집에 가고, 그분은 학교에 가요.	I'm going home and he is going to school.
나는 올라가고, 그분은 내려와요.	I'm going up and he is coming down.

3. If the subject of the two verbs is the same, and the verbs are not 가다, 오다, etc., the coordinate non-final ending -고 is used. Study the following examples:

공부하고 잤어요.	I studied and slept
먹고 일했어요.	I ate and worked.
문을 열고 들어오세요.	Open the door and come in.

4. This pattern -아(-어, -여)서 indicates a certain continuity from the first action to the second, whereas the pattern -고 indicates a discontinuity between the first action and the second. Compare the following minimal pair sentences.

편지를 써서 드리겠어요.	I'll write this letter and give it to you.
편지를 쓰고 드리겠어요.	I'll give it (for example, the book you've asked for) to you after I have finished writing this letter.
그분을 만나서 이야기합시다.	Let's meet him and talk (to him).
그분을 만나고 이야기합시다.	Let's meet him and talk, (the two of us).

II. The Transferentive Ending -다(가): A.V.S. +-다(가)

The non-final ending -다(가) is attached directly to the stems of action verbs, and indicates change or shift of action.

1. When the patten -다(가) is used in the present tense, it indicates an interruption or discontinuation of an action.

시장에 가다가 와요.	I was on my way to the market, but am coming back.
시장에 가다가 왔어요.	I was on my way to the market, but came back.
시장에 가다가 들르겠어요.	I'll drop in (there) when I go to the market.
공부하다가 잤어요.	When I was studying, I slept.
더 노시다가 가세요.	Please stay a bit more before going.
조금 있다가 주무세요.	Please go to bed after a little while.
학교에 가다가 그분을 만났어요.	I met him when I was going to school. Or: On my way to school, I met him.

복숭아를 먹다가 사과를 먹어요.	I was eating a peach, but now I'm eating an apple.
영어를 공부하다가 불어를 공부해요.	I was studying English, but now I'm studying French.
구두를 신다가 끈이 끊어졌어요.	When I was tying my shoes, my shoestring broke.

2. However, when this pattern -다(가) is used with the past tense (-았-), it indicates reversal, nullification, or unanticipated consequence, following the completion of the first action.

Examples :

학교에 갔다가 와요.	I went to school and am on my way back.
학교에 갔다가 왔어요.	I've been to school. Or : I went to school and then came back.
학교에 갔다가 들르겠어요.	I'll go to school and then drop in (there).
교실에 들어갔다가 나오세요.	Please go into the classroom and then come out.
불을 켰다가 껐어요.	I turned on the light and turned it off again.
신을 신었다가 벗었어요.	I put on my shoes and took them off again.
시계를 샀다가 팔았어요.	I bought a watch and sold it again.

3. When two past transferentives are followed by a form of the verb 하다, it indicates alternation. The alternatives are usually opposites, (contrastives).

Examples :

사람이 갔다 왔다 해요.	People keep coming and going.
사람이 갔다 왔다 했어요.	People kept coming and going.
그분이 불을 켰다 껐다 해요.	He keeps turning the lights on and off.
그분이 불을 켰다 껐다 했어요.	He kept turning the lights on and off.
그분이 웃었다 울었다 해요.	He keeps laughing and crying.
그분이 웃었다 울었다 했어요.	He kept laughing and crying.

Notes :

The subject of the two verbs must be the same ; the particle -가 is optional.

III. A.V.S. +-기 전에… : 'before doing'

The word 전 is a noun meaning 'time before' or 'place in front' ; the particle -에 'at,' 'on,' 'in' indicates time or place. This non-final ending -기 전에 is used for the expression 'before something happens' or 'before something happened.'

Examples :

주무시기 전에 불을 끄세요.	Before you go to bed, turn off the light.
학교에 가기 전에 여기에 오세요.	Please come here before you go to school.
기차가 떠나기 전에 그것을 샀어요.	I bought it before the train left.
그분이 돌아오기 전에 집에 가세요.	Go home before he comes back.
세수하기 전에 이를 닦았어요.	I brushed my teeth before I washed my face.
일하기 전에 잡수세요.	Please eat before you start working.
잊어버리기 전에 지금 주세요.	Give it to me now before you forget.

Notes :

1. This pattern -기 전에 is used always with action verbs ; the subject of the two clauses can be the same or different.
2. The tense and/or negation is expressed regularly in the main clause.
   Study the following examples :

자기 전에 불을 끕니다.	Before I go to bed, I turn off the light.
자기 전에 불을 껐습니다.	Before I went to bed, I turned off the light.
자기 전에 불을 끄겠습니다.	Before I go to bed, I'll turn off the light.
자기 전에 불을 끄지 않아요.	Before I go to bed, I don't turn off the light.

DRILLS

ADDITIONAL VOCABULARY

돈	money	끓이다	to boil (water)
벌다	to make (money)	깎다	to peel
굽다	to roast	삶다	to boil (something solid)

A. Substitution Drill

1. 나가서 기다리세요.	Please go out and wait.
2. 들어가서 기다리세요.	Please go in and wait.
3. 들어와서 기다리세요.	Please come in and wait.
4. 올라가서 기다리세요.	Please go up and wait.
5. 내려가서 기다리세요.	Please go down and wait.
6. 올라와서 기다리세요.	Please come up and wait.
7. 내려와서 기다리세요.	Please come down and wait.

8. 앉아서 기다리세요. — Please sit down and wait.

B. Substitution Drill

1. 예습하고 가겠어요. — I'll prepare my lessons and go.
2. 복습하고 가겠어요. — I'll review and go.
3. 연습하고 가겠어요. — I'll practice it and go.
4. 쳐다보고 가겠어요. — I'll look up and go.
5. 내려다보고 가겠어요. — I'll look down and go.
6. 내다보고 가겠어요. — I'll look out and go.
7. 들여다보고 가겠어요. — I'll look in and go.
8. 면도하고 가겠어요. — I'll shave and go.

C. Substitution Drill

1. 미국에 갔다 와요. — I went to America, and am on my way back.
2. 영국에 갔다 와요. — I went to England, and am on my way back.
3. 일본에 갔다 와요. — I went to Japan, and am on my way back.
4. 불란서에 갔다 와요. — I went to France, and am on my way back.
5. 독일에 갔다 와요. — I went to Germany, and am on my way back.
6. 대만에 갔다 와요. — I went to Taiwan, and am on my way back.
7. 소련에 갔다 와요. — I went to the Soviet Union and am on my way back.
8. 중공에 갔다 와요. — I went to the Peoples' Republic of (Red) China, and am on my way back.

D. Substitution Drill

1. 시장에 갔다 왔어요. — I went to the market, and came back.
2. 다방에 갔다 왔어요. — I went to the tearoom, and came back.
3. 약방에 갔다 왔어요. — I went to the drugstore, and came back.
4. 책방에 갔다 왔어요. — I went to the bookstore, and came back.
5. 백화점에 갔다 왔어요. — I went to the department store, and came back.
6. 사무실에 갔다 왔어요. — I went to the office, and came back.
7. 병원에 갔다 왔어요. — I went to the hospital, and came back.
8. 세탁소에 갔다 왔어요. — I went to the laundry, and came back.

E. Integration Drill

Teacher : 편지를 쓰겠어요. 부치겠어요.

I'll write a letter. I'll mail it.

Student : 편지를 써서 부치겠어요.

I'll write a letter and mail it.

1. 그분을 만나겠어요. 이야기 하겠어요. 그분을 만나서 이야기하겠어요.
2. 돈을 벌겠어요. 집을 사겠어요. 돈을 벌어서 집을 사겠어요.
3. 이것을 팔겠어요. 새 차를 사겠어요. 이것을 팔아서 새 차를 사겠어요.
4. 이것을 굽겠어요. 먹겠어요. 이것을 구워서 먹겠어요.
5. 씻겠어요. 먹겠어요. 씻어서 먹겠어요.
6. 끓이겠어요. 먹겠어요. 끓여서 먹겠어요.
7. 깎겠어요. 먹겠어요. 깎아서 먹겠어요.
8. 삶겠어요. 먹겠어요. 삶아서 먹겠어요.

F. Integration Drill

Teacher : 시장에 가요. 들르겠어요.

I go to the market. I'll drop in (there).

Student : 시장에 가다가 들르겠어요.

I'll drop in (there) when I go to the market.

1. 조금 더 있겠어요. 가겠어요. 조금 더 있다가 가겠어요.
2. 더 놀겠어요. 공부하겠어요. 더 놀다가 공부하겠어요.
3. 복숭아를 먹겠어요. 사과를 먹겠어요. 복숭아를 먹다가 사과를 먹겠어요.
4. 가르치겠어요. 가겠어요. 가르치다가 가겠어요.
5. 공부하겠어요. 자겠어요. 공부하다가 자겠어요.
6. 일하겠어요. 책을 읽겠어요. 일하다가 책을 읽겠어요.
7. 영화를 보겠어요. 오겠어요. 영화를 보다가 오겠어요.
8. 수영하겠어요. 산보하겠어요. 수영하다가 산보하겠어요.

G. Integration Drill

Teacher : 주무세요. 불을 끄세요.

Go to bed. Turn off the light.

Student : 주무시기 전에, 불을 끄세요.

Before you go to bed, turn off the light.

1. 학교에 가세요. 여기에 오세요.
   학교에 가기 전에, 여기에 오세요.
2. 일하세요. 잡수세요.
   일하기 전에, 잡수세요.

3. 잊어버리세요. 지금 주세요.
   잊어버리기 전에, 지금 주세요.
4. 그분이 돌아오세요. 집에 가세요.
   그분이 돌아오기 전에, 집에 가세요.
5. 그분이 가세요. 그것을 사세요.
   그분이 가기 전에, 그것을 사세요.
6. 그분이 일어나세요. 떠나세요.
   그분이 일어나기 전에, 떠나세요.
7. 그분이 도착하세요. 일을 끝내세요.
   그분이 도착하기 전에, 일을 끝내세요.
8. 그분이 말씀하세요. 그분한테 여쭈세요.
   그분이 말씀하기 전에, 그분한테 여쭈세요.

H. Pattern Drill

Teacher: 사람이 갔다 왔다 해요.
People keep coming and going.
Student: 사람이 갔다 왔다 했어요.
People kept coming and going.

1. 불을 켰다 껐다 해요.	불을 켰다 껐다 했어요.
2. 그분이 웃었다 울었다 해요.	그분이 웃었다 울었다 했어요.
3. 올라갔다 내려왔다 해요.	올라갔다 내려왔다 했어요.
4. 들어갔다 나왔다 해요.	들어갔다 나왔다 했어요.
5. 그분이 섰다 앉았다 해요.	그분이 섰다 앉았다 했어요.
6. 옷을 입었다 벗었다 해요.	옷을 입었다 벗었다 했어요.
7. 문을 열었다 닫았다 해요.	문을 열었다 닫았다 했어요.
8. 눈을 떴다 감았다 해요.	눈을 떴다 감았다 했어요.

SHORT STORIES

1. 공부를 많이 했기 때문에, 피곤했어요.
   내 방에 들어가서 쉬었어요.
   그리고 밖에 나가서 산보했어요.
2. 지금은 돈이 없기 때문에, 집을 살 수 없어요.
   돈을 벌어서 집을 사겠어요.
   부인이 애기를 낳기 전에, 살 수 있을 것 같아요.
3. 학교에 가다가 친구를 만났어요.
   그 친구하고 같이 다방에 들어갔어요.
   그런데 복잡했기 때문에, 들어갔다가 나왔어요.

READING

그때 그 다리 위를 지나가는 어떤 외국 선교사가 있었습니다. 그 선교사는 다리 밑에서 애기가 우는 소리를 들었습니다. 그래서 다리 밑으로 내려가 봤습니다. 갓난 애기가 엄마 품에 안겨 있었습니다. 그러나 어머니는 이 세상 사람이 아니었습니다. 그 선교사는 그 애기를 안고 집으로 돌아왔습니다. 그 애기는 건강하게 잘 자랐습니다. 한 해가 가고 두 해가 가고 10년이 지났습니다. 이 소년은 자꾸 선교사한테 부모님에 대해서 물었습니다. 소년은 열 두 살이 되었습니다. 또 다시 성탄절이 되었습니다. 선교사는 이 소년한테 모든 이야기를 다 해 주었습니다. 그리고 어머니의 산소를 찾아갔습니다. 소년은 울었습니다. 그리고 소년은 옷을 벗어서 어머님의 산소를 덮어 주었습니다. "어머님 참 추우셨지요?"

위	the avove, on	건강하게	healthfully
지나가다	to pass by	한 해	one year
외국 선교사	a foreign missionary	열 두 살	twelve years old
소리	a voice	지나다	to go by
내려가 보다	to go down and see	소년	a boy
갓난 애기	a newborn baby	자꾸	repeatedly
엄마	mom	부모님에 대해서	about one's parents
품	the bosom, the breast	다시	again
안기다	to be held in one's arms	모든	whole, all
세상	the world	다	all, everything.
안다	to hold in one's arms	산소	a grave

BRIEFING

At that time a certain foreign missionary was passing on that bridge. The missionary heard a baby's cry from under the bridge. So he went down there. The mother held a new-born baby in her arms. But the mother had died. The missionary took the baby in his arms and returned home. The baby grew up to be healthy. One year, two years and ten years went by. This boy constantly asked the missionary about his parents. The boy became twelve years old. Christmas came again. The missionary told him everything. And the boy visited his mother's grave. The boy was crying. The boy took off his clothes and covered his mother's grave with them. "Mother, don't you feel very cold?"

UNIT 27 무슨 뜻입니까? What does it mean?

BASIC SENTENCES: MEMORIZE

어려워서	because it is difficult
잘	well
모르겠어요.	(I) don't know
뜻	a meaning

박 성 철

1. 이것이 어려워서, 잘 모르겠어요. 이것이 무슨 뜻입니까? — I don't understand this well because it is difficult. What does this mean?

선생님께	to the teacher

최 인 숙

2. 선생님께 물어 보세요. — Please ask the teacher.

아무	any person, anyone, anybody

박 성 철

3. 지금 선생님이 아무도 안 계세요. — There isn't any teacher here now.

연습하다.	to practice

최 인 숙

4. 그럼, 아는 것부터 연습하세요. — Then, begin by practicing what you know.

무조건	unconditionally
외다	to memorize

박 성 철

5. 무조건 외어 볼까요? — Shall I memorize (them) unconditionally?

암기하다	to memorize

최 인 숙

6. 암기할 수 있으면, 암기하세요. — If you can memorize them, do so.

USEFUL EXPRESSIONS : MEMORIZE

1. 전화가 왔어요. There is a phone call for you.
2. 통화 중이에요. The line is busy.
3. 잘못 거셨어요. You got the wrong number.
4. 그런 것 같아요. I think so.

NOTES ON THE BASIC SENTENCES

1. 어려워서 means 'because it's difficult.' 어렵다 'to be difficult' is an irregular verb. When the final consonant -ㅂ of the stem is followed by a vowel, -ㅂ changes into -우. This irregular verb, ending in the final consonant -ㅂ, will be studied later in detail.
   이것이 무슨 뜻입니까? means 'What does this mean?' 무슨, depending on the intonation and pitch, means (1) 'what,' 'what kind of,' (2) 'something.' It occurs only as a modifier of a subsequent noun or bound form.
   Study the following examples:
   무슨 일이 일어났습니까?↘ What happened?
   무슨 일이 일어났습니까?↗ Did something happen?
2. 물어 보세요 means literally 'Please ask(him) and see (what it's like).
   묻다 is an irregular verb. When the final consonant -ㄷ of the stem is followed by a vowel, -ㄷ, will be studied later in detail.
4. 아는 것부터 means literally 'from the thing (that) you know.'
   알다 is an irregular verb. When the final consonant -ㄹ of the stem is followed by the consonants -ㄴ, -ㅂ, -ㅅ, or the vowel -오, the final consonant -ㄹ is dropped. This will be studied later in detail.
5. 무조건 'uncondition,' besides being used as a noun, is an adverb: 'unconditionally.' 무-, as a prefix, means 'un-,' '-less,' 'non-,' 'not having,' 'lacking,' etc.
   외다 'to memorize' is a standard word. But 외우다, which is a dialect, is used more frequently in colloquial speech. Its synonym is 암기하다 'to memorize,' which is derived from Chinese.

STRUCTURE NOTES

I. The Causal Non-Final Ending -아(-어, -여)서… : 'so,' 'because'

In the previous unit, we studied the pattern -아(-어, -여)서, which is used when the same subject performs one action and then a second one. This pattern -아(-어, -여)서, depending on the context or situation, can also indicate cause or reason.

Examples :

시끄러워서, 좋지 않아요.	It's noisy, so it's not good. Or : Because it's noisy, it's not good.
어두워서, 보이지 않아요.	It's dark, so I can't see it. Or : Because it's dark, I can't see it.
피곤해서, 쉬었어요.	I was tired, so I took a rest.
추워서, 집에 있겠어요.	It's cold, so I'll stay at home.
아주 바빠서, 갈 수 없었어요.	I was very busy, so I couldn't go. Or : Because I was very busy, I couldn't go.
눈이 와서, 추워요.	It snowed, so it's cold. Or : Because it snowed, it's cold.
돈이 없어서, 못 갔어요.	I had no money, so I couldn't go. Or : Because I had no money, I couldn't go.
시간이 없어서, 숙제를 못 했어요.	I had no time, so I couldn't do my homework.

Notes :

1. When this pattern -아(-어, -여)서 indicates cause or reason, it is used mostly with description verb ; the above examples are exceptions, when used with verbs such as 오다, 없다, etc.
2. When the final (main) clause is an imperative or propositive, this pattern is not used ; instead, another causal non-final ending -(으)니까 is used. -(으)니까 will be studied later. Study the follwing examples :

좋아서, 삽시다.	(never used)
좋아서, 사세요.	(never used)
좋으니까, 삽시다.	Because it is good, let's buy it. (correct)
좋으니까, 사세요.	Because it is good, please buy it. (correct)

3. The tense and/or negation is expressed in the final (main) clause, not in the first (dependent) clause with -아(-어, -여)서. Study the following examples :

피곤해서, 자요.	Because I'm tired, I am going to bed.
피곤해서, 잤어요.	Because I was tired, I went to bed.
피곤해서, 자겠어요.	Because I'm tired, I will go to bed.
피곤해서, 일하지 않겠어요.	Because I'm tired, I won't work.

4. Sometimes, it can be used with the polite particle -요 as an unfinished sentence, or if the over-all meaning is clear from the context. Study the

following examples:

왜 안 가세요?	Why aren't you going to go?
피곤해서요.	Because I'm tired···

II. The Particles -께서 and -께:

1. The Particle-께서

This is the honorific form of the subject particle -가/-이. It is used to indicate reverence and respect on the part of the speaker for the person spoken to, or about. This particle -께서 is used whenever one addresses or refers to a person of superior social standing: older persons, teachers, parents, priests, high officials, and so forth. It is never used for oneself. It is attached directly to (personal) nouns or pronouns, (with or without -님).

Examples:

할아버지께서 그렇게 말씀하셨어요.	My grandfather told me so.
우리 선생님께서 오셨어요.	Our teacher came.
어머님께서 춤을 추셨어요.	My mother danced.
형님께서 오실 것 같아요.	I think my older brother will come.
누님께서 나한테 부탁하셨어요.	My older sister asked me a favor.

2. The Particle -께···: 'to (a person)'

This is the honorific form of the particle -한테 'to,' and its usage is the same. It is attached directly to (personal) nouns and pronouns, and indicates the receiver of an action or the one for whom something is done or exists. It is never used for oneself.

Examples:

선생님께 물어 보세요.	Please ask the teacher.
어머님께 편지를 썼어요.	I wrote a letter to my mother.
형님께 부탁하세요.	Please ask your older brother a favor.

III. A.V.S. +-아(-어, -여) 보다···: '(someone) tries doing (so-and-so)'

The word 보다, as an independent verb, means 'to see,' 'to look.' This pattern -아(-어, -여) 보다 is used to convery: 'someone does something and finds out,' 'someone tries doing something (to see how it will turn out),' or 'someone does something to see (how it will turn out).'

Examples:

이 음식을 잡숴 보세요.	Please try eating this food.
한식을 먹어 봤어요.	I tried eating Korean food.
다시 전화해 보세요.	Please try calling again.

그분을 만나 보겠어요.	I'll meet him and see.
여기서 기다려 보세요.	Please wait here and see.
한식점에서 먹어 볼까요?	Shall we try eating at a Korean restaurant?
어느 백화점에 가 볼까요?	Which department store shall we try going to?
한국 말로 말해 보고 싶어요.	I want to try speaking in Korean.
지금 거기에 가 보세요.	Please go there now and see.
그분한테 물어 보겠어요.	I'll ask him and see.
문을 열어 봅시다.	Let's open the door and find out.

IV. 아무도 + negative… : 'nobody does…' 'nobody is…'

The word 아무, as an independent noun, means 'any person,' 'anyone,''anybody.' It is used also as a noun prefix meaning 'any.'
For example, 아무라도 할 수 있어요 'anyone can do it.' 아무한테나 물어 보세요 'Please ask anyone about it.' 아무때나 오세요 'Come and see me any time.' However, 아무도 is followed always by a negative predicate and means 'nobody does…,' 'no one is…,' etc.

Examples:

아무도 그것을 몰라요.	Nobody knows that.
아무도 가지 않아요.	No one is going.
아무도 먹고 싶어하지 않아요.	No one wants to eat it.
아무도 일하지 않았어요.	Nobody worked.
아무도 사무실에 없어요.	There is nobody in the office.
아무도 한가하지 않아요.	No one has free time.
아무도 아프지 않아요.	No one is sick.

아무 것도 + negative means 'nothing.' Study the following examples:

아무 것도 먹지 않겠어요.	I won't eat anything.
아무 것도 하지 않았어요.	I did nothing.
아무 것도 사고 싶지 않아요.	I don't want to buy anything.
아무 것도 주지 않겠어요.	I won't give anything.
아무 것도 보지 않았어요.	I didn't see anything.

DRILLS

A. Substitution Drill

1. 암기할 수 있으면, 암기하세요. If you can memorize them, do so.
2. 복습할 수 있으면, 복습하세요. If you can review them, do so.
3. 연습할 수 있으면, 연습하세요. If you can practice them, do so.
4. 예습할 수 있으면, 예습하세요. If you can prepare your lesson, do so.
5. 계속할 수 있으면, 계속하세요. If you can continue it, do so.
6. 들를 수 있으면, 들르세요. If you can drop in there, do so.
7. 사냥갈 수 있으면, 사냥가세요. If you can go hunting, do so.
8. 소풍갈 수 있으면, 소풍가세요. If you can go for a picnic, do so.

B. Substitution Drill

1. 선생님께 물어 보세요. Please ask the teacher.
2. 아버님께 물어 보세요. Please ask your father.
3. 어머님께 물어 보세요. Please ask your mother.
4. 할아버님께 물어 보세요. Please ask your grandfather.
5. 할머님께 물어 보세요. Please ask your grandmother.
6. 아저씨께 물어 보세요. Please ask your uncle.
7. 아주머니께 물어 보세요. Please ask your aunt.
8. 형님께 물어 보세요. Please ask your older brother.

C. Pattern Drill

Teacher: 시끄럽기 때문에, 좋지 않아요.
It's noisy, so it's not good.
Student: 시끄러워서, 좋지 않아요.
It's noisy, so it's not good.

1. 어둡기 때문에, 보이지 않아요. 어두워서, 보이지 않아요.
2. 피곤하기 때문에, 쉬겠어요. 피곤해서, 쉬겠어요.
3. 춥기 때문에, 안 가겠어요. 추워서, 안 가겠어요.
4. 바쁘기 때문에, 못 했어요. 바빠서, 못 했어요.
5. 무겁기 때문에, 가기 싫어요. 무거워서, 가기 싫어요.
6. 더럽기 때문에, 청소해요. 더러워서, 청소해요.
7. 무섭기 때문에, 못 가겠어요. 무서워서, 못 가겠어요.
8. 덥기 때문에, 놀았어요. 더워서, 놀았어요.

D. Pattern Drill

Teacher: 아버님이 오셨어요. My father came.
Student: 아버님께서 오셨어요. My father came.

1. 형님이 가셨어요.	형님께서 가셨어요.
2. 누님이 춤을 추셨어요.	누님께서 춤을 추셨어요.
3. 김 선생님이 부탁하셨어요.	김 선생님께서 부탁하셨어요.
4. 어머님이 말씀하셨어요.	어머님께서 말씀하셨어요.
5. 할아버님이 주무셨어요.	할아버님께서 주무셨어요.
6. 할머님이 일하셨어요.	할머님께서 일하셨어요.
7. 아저씨가 우셨어요.	아저씨께서 우셨어요.
8. 아주머님이 장난하셨어요.	아주머님께서 장난하셨어요.

E. Pattern Drill

Teacher : 이것을 잡수세요.	Please eat this.
Student : 이것을 잡숴 보세요.	Please try this.
1. 다시 전화하세요.	다시 전화해 보세요.
2. 그분을 만나세요.	그분을 만나 보세요.
3. 여기서 기다리세요.	여기서 기다려 보세요.
4. 지금 가세요.	지금 가 보세요.
5. 그분한테 부탁하세요.	그분한테 부탁해 보세요.
6. 문을 여세요.	문을 열어 보세요.
7. 한국말로 말하세요.	한국말로 말해 보세요.
8. 영어를 가르치세요.	영어를 가르쳐 보세요.

F. Response Drill

Teacher : 누가 공부하십니까?	Who studies?
Student : 아무도 공부하지 않아요.	No one studies.
1. 누가 잡수십니까?	아무도 먹지 않아요.
2. 누가 주무십니까?	아무도 자지 않아요.
3. 누가 쳐다보십니까?	아무도 쳐다보지 않아요.
4. 누가 내려다보십니까?	아무도 내려다보지 않아요.
5. 누가 연습하십니까?	아무도 연습하지 않아요.
6. 누가 복습하십니까?	아무도 복습하지 않아요.
7. 누가 예습하십니까?	아무도 예습하지 않아요.
8. 누가 약혼하십니까?	아무도 약혼하지 않아요.

G. Response Drill

Teacher : 무엇을 잡수시겠읍니까?
What will you eat?

Student : 아무 것도 먹지 않겠어요.
I won't eat anything.

1. 무엇을 씻으시겠습니까? 아무 것도 씻지 않겠어요.
2. 무엇을 쓰시겠습니까? 아무 것도 쓰지 않겠어요.
3. 무엇을 가르치시겠습니까? 아무 것도 가르치지 않겠어요.
4. 무엇을 하시겠습니까? 아무 것도 하지 않겠어요.
5. 무엇을 설명하시겠습니까? 아무 것도 설명하지 않겠어요.
6. 무엇을 읽으시겠습니까? 아무 것도 읽지 않겠어요.
7. 무엇을 도와주시겠습니까? 아무 것도 도와주지 않겠어요.
8. 무엇을 만드시겠습니까? 아무 것도 만들지 않겠어요.

H. Pattern Drill

Teacher: 피곤해서, 잡니다. Because I'm tired, I am going to bed.
Student: 피곤해서, 자겠읍니다. Because I'm tired, I will go to bed.

1. 화가 나서, 갑니다. 화가 나서, 가겠습니다.
2. 뚱뚱해서, 못 들어갑니다. 뚱뚱해서, 들어가겠습니다.
3. 추워서, 갑니다. 추워서, 가겠습니다.
4. 어려워서, 안 합니다. 어려워서, 안 하겠습니다.
5. 더러워서, 청소합니다. 더러워서, 청소하겠습니다.
6. 더워서, 집에 있어요. 더워서, 집에 있겠어요.
7. 무서워서, 안 갑니다. 무서워서, 안 가겠습니다.
8. 재미가 없어서, 안 봅니다. 재미가 없어서, 안 보겠습니다.

SHORT STORIES

1. 피곤해서, 일찍 집에 가겠어요.
   집에 가서 쉬고 싶어요.
   선생님께 잘 말씀해 주세요.

   Expansion Drill

   피곤해서 일찍 집에 가서 쉬고 싶어요. 선생님께 잘 말씀해 주세요.

2. 김 선생님께서 놀러 오셨어요.
   그런데 그분하고 같이 너무 많이 이야기했어요.
   지금 피곤해서 아무 것도 하고 싶지 않아요.

   Expansion Drill

   김 선생님께서 놀러 오셨어요. 그런데 그분하고 같이 너무 많이 이야기했기 때문에 지금 피곤해서 아무 것도 하고 싶지 않아요.

3. 친구를 찾아 갔어요.
   그런데 집에 아무도 안 계셨어요.
   기다려 봤지만, 아무도 오지 않았어요.

Expansion Drill

친구를 찾아갔지만, 집에 아무도 안 계셨어요. 기다려 봤지만, 아무도 오지 않았어요.

READING

오늘은 일찍 집에 돌아왔습니다. 나는 피곤해서 잤습니다. 그런데 자다가 시끄러워서 잠이 깨었습니다. 밖에서 떠드는 소리가 들렸습니다. 나는 밖에 나가 봤습니다. 부인이 울고 있었습니다. *여덟 달 밖에 안 되는 애기가 없어졌습니다. 아무리 찾아도 없었습니다. 동네 사람들이 모두 애기를 찾으러 다녔습니다. 그러나 애기를 찾을 수 없었습니다. 애기의 이름을 불렀습니다. 그러나 이름을 불러도 소용이 없었습니다. 왜냐하면 애기가 어리기 때문에 말을 하지 못 했습니다. 두 시간 후에 애기를 찾았습니다. 애기가 개 집에 들어가서 자고 있었습니다.

깨다	to wake up	다니다	to go about
떠들다	to be noisy	부르다	to call
들리다	to be heard	소용이 없다	to be useless
울고 있었다	was crying	어리다	to be an infant
없어지다	to disappear	개 집	a dog house
아무리 찾아도	no matter how we looked for him	자고 있었다	was sleeping

*여덟 달 밖에 안 되는 애기 an infant who is only eight months old

BRIEFING

I came back home early today. I went to bed because I was tired. I woke up because it was noisy. I heard noises from outside. I went outside. My wife was crying. Our infant who was only eight months old had disappeared. No matter where we looked for him, we couldn't find him. All the village people went around to look for him. But we were not able to find him. We called the baby's name. Even when we called his name, it was of no use. Because the child was an infant, he couldn't speak. Finally we found him after 2 hours. The baby had gone into the dog's house and was sleeping there.

UNIT 28 천천히 갑시다. Let's Go Slowly

BASIC SENTENCES : MEMORIZE

위험하니까	because it's dangerous
천천히	slowly
조심하다	to be careful
최 인 숙	
1. 위험하니까, 천천히 갑시다. 조심하세요.	Let's go slowly, because it's dangerous. Be careful, please.
걱정하다	to worry
똑바로	straight, in a straight line
운 전 수	
2. 걱정하지 마세요. 똑바로 갈까요?	Don't worry. Shall we go straight?
왼 쪽으로	to the left
돌다	to turn
오른 쪽으로	to the right
돌아가다	to turn (and go)
최 인 숙	
3. 아니오. 왼 쪽으로 돌아갑시다. 조금 가다가 오른 쪽으로 돌아 가세요.	No, let's turn to the left. Go a little, and turn to the right.
늘	always
복잡하다	to be crowded
운 전 수	
4. 여기는 늘 복잡하지요?	This area (here) is always crowded, isn't it?
여간	some, a little
최 인 숙	
5. 예, 여간 복잡하지 않아요. 사람들이 너무 많아요.	Yes, it is extremely crowded. There are too many people.

USEFUL EXPRESSIONS : MEMORIZE

1. 몸 조심하세요. — Take care of yourself.
2. 다행입니다. — It's good luck (fortune).
3. 오늘 재수가 좋아요. — I've been lucky today.
4. 오늘 재수가 없어요. — I've been unlucky today.

NOTES ON THE BASIC SENTENCES

1. 조심하다 means 'to take care (with),' 'to be careful (about),' 'to take precautions (against).' Its synonym is 주의하다. Study the following examples:

   말을 조심하세요. — Be careful in your speech.
   음식을 주의하세요. — Be careful about what you eat.
   건강에 주의하세요. — Take care of yourself. Or : Be careful of your health.

2. 걱정하다 means 'to worry,' 'to concern oneself,' 'to be solicitous (about).' Its synonyms are 염려하다, 근심하다. Study the following examples:

   걱정하지 마세요. — Don't worry.
   걱정해 주셔서 감사합니다. — Thank you for being so concerned.
   염려할 것 없어요. — You have nothing to worry about.
   근심하지 않아도 괜찮아요. — You shouldn't worry about it.

   똑바로, depending on the context or situation, mean (1) 'straight,' in a straight line,' 'directly,' (2) 'upright,' 'honestly,' 'without concealment,' etc. Study the following examples:

   똑바로 집으로 가세요. — Please go straight home.
   똑바로 서세요. — Please stand up straight.
   똑바로 말씀하세요. — Please tell me the truth.

3. 왼 쪽으로 돌아갑시다 means 'Let's turn to the left.' 왼 'left' is a noun modifier. The vowel 외 is pronounced mostly as 왜 ; -쪽 'a direction,' 'a side,' 'a way' is a bound form, and is preceded always by a noun modifier. Study the following examples:

   이 쪽으로 갑시다. — Let's go this way.
   우리 쪽이 이겼어요. — Our side won.
   해가 동 쪽에서 떠요. — The sun rises in the east.

4. 늘 means 'always,' 'ceaselessly,' 'continuously.' Its synonyms are 항상, 언제나. Study the following examples:

그분은 늘 공부해요.	He studies ceaselessly.
나는 항상 바빠요.	I'm always busy.
그분은 언제나 나한테 친절해요.	He is always kind to me.

STRUCTURE NOTES

I. The Causal Non-Final Ending -(으)니까… : 'so,' 'since,' 'because'

We have already studied -기 때문에 and -아(-어, -여)서, which indicate reason or cause. Now let's study another causal non-final ending -(으)니까, which has the same meaning. This pattern may be used with any verb. It ends usually with a comma intonation.

Examples:

그것이 좋으니까, 삽시다.	It's good, so let's buy it. Or: Because it's good, let's buy it.
추우니까, 집에 계세요.	It's cold, so stay home. Or: Because it's cold, stay home.
재미가 없으니까, 보지 맙시다.	It's not interesting, so let's not see it. Or: Because it's not interesting, let's not see it.
지금 바쁘니까, 내일 오세요.	I'm busy now, so come tomorrow.
돈이 있으니까, 걱정하지 마세요.	Because I have money, don't worry.
그분이 한국 사람이니까, 김치를 좋아해요.	He is a Korean, so he likes kimchi.
나는 잘 모르니까, 그분한테 물어 보세요.	I don't know for certain, so ask him.
눈이 오니까, 추워요.	Because it's snowing, it's cold.
그분이 주무시니까, 떠들지 마세요.	He is sleeping, so don't make noise.

Notes:

1. When the final (main) clause is an imperative or propositive, this pattern -(으)니까 may be used; the patterns -기 때문에 and -아(-어, -여)서 CAN'T be used when the final (main) clause is an imperative or propositive. Study the following examples:

추우니까, 집에 가세요.	Because it's cold, go home.
추우니까, 집에 갑시다.	Because it's cold, let's go home.
춥기 때문에, 집에 가세요.	(not used)
추워서, 집에 가세요.	(not used)

2. When the action of the main clause takes place after the action of the

dependent clause, the past tense infix (-았-) may be used. Study the following examples:

늦었으니까, 가지 마세요.	Because it's late, don't go.
그것을 먹었으니까, 배가 아파요.	Because you ate that, you have a stomachache.
그분이 왔으니까, 주무세요.	Because he came, go to bed.

3. Sometimes, this pattern -(으)니까 can be used with the polite particle -요 as an unfinished sentence, or if the over-all meaning is clear from the context. Study the following examples:

그것이 예쁘니까요.	Because it's beautiful….
피곤하니까요.	I'm tired, so….
왜 안 사세요?	Why aren't you buying?
너무 비싸니까요.	Because it's too expensive.
왜 안 잡수세요?	Why aren't you eating?
지금 시간이 없으니까요.	I have no time now, so….

4. -니까 is used after verb stems ending in a vowel;
   -으니까 is used after verb stems ending in a consonant.

II. 여간 + V.S. + Negative… : '(it) is uncommon (unusual, extraordinary)'

The word 여간 means 'some,' 'a little,' for example, 그분이 여간 일에는 화를 내지 않아요 'He never gets angry over trifles (little things),' or 그것이 여간 일이 아닙니다 'It's no easy matter.' But 여간 + V.S. + negative indicates an uncommon (extraordinary, remarkable) state or condition.

Examples:

여간 놀라지 않았어요.	I was extremely surprised, (lit. I was not a little surprised.)
그 여자가 여간 예쁘지 않아요.	She is really beautiful.
그분이 여간 바쁘지 않아요.	He is extremely busy.
날씨가 여간 덥지 않아요.	The weather is terribly hot.
그분이 여간 뚱뚱하지 않아요.	He is really fat.
그 책이 여간 좋지 않아요.	That book is awfully good.
여간 복잡하지 않아요.	It is extremely crowded.

여간 is used mostly with description verbs, but it can also be used with action verbs. When it is used with action verbs, it is followed usually by adverbial expressions, such as 많이 'lots,' 'a great deal,' 열심히 'ardently,' 'zealously,' 멀리 'far,' 'far off (away),' etc.

그분이 여간 많이 먹지 않아요.	He really eats a lot.

그분이 여간 열심히 공부하지 않아요. He studies very hard.
그분이 여간 멀리 가지 않았어요. He went very far away.

III. The Pluralizing Suffix -들 :

In general, singular and plural are not distinguished in Korean, if the over-all meaning is clear from the context. The exceptions are 나 (내, 저, 제) 'I,' and 당신 'you (plain),' which are always singular. The plural of a noun is formed by attaching the suffix -들 to it.

Examples :

나무	tree or trees	나무들	trees
책	book or books	책들	books
연필	pencil or pencils	연필들	pencils
사람	person or people	사람들	people
여자	woman or women	여자들	women
새	bird or birds	새들	birds
개	dog or dogs	개들	dogs

The pluralizing suffix -들, besides being attached to nouns, can be attached directly to any word in a sentence ; this implies a specific plural subject. Study the following examples, and note particularly the words to which pluralizing suffix -들 is attached.

사람들이 많아요. There are many people.
저리들 가세요. Go that way, you people.
재미있게들 놀았어요. We had a good time.
빨리들 주무세요. Please go to bed quickly, all of you.
잘들 먹었어요. We (they) all ate well.
늦게들 집에 갔어요. They went home late.
많이들 잡수세요. Please eat a lot, all of you.
교실에들 들어갑시다. Let's all go into the classroom.
교실에서들 공부해요. They are studying in the classroom.
가지들 마세요. Don't go, anybody.
주무시지들 마세요. Don't go to bed, anyone.
일하러들 갑시다. Let's all go out and work.
공부하러들 왔어요. We (they) came to study.
들어들 오세요. Come in, all of you.
먹어들 봅시다. Let's all try eating it.
먹고들 왔어요. We ate and came.

일하고들 잡수세요. Please work and eat, all of you.

The following pronouns may be used either with the pluralizing suffix -들 or without it:

우리	or	우리들	we (intimate)
저희	or	저희들	we (humble)
너희	or	너희들	you (plain)
여러분	or	여러분들	you (honorific)

Notes:

여러분 'you (all)' is used frequently by a lecturer or public speaker when beginning a public talk. The English equivalent of this word is 'Ladies and Gentlemen!'.

When the demonstratives 이-, 그-, 저- (or 요-, 고-, 조-) are used with nouns denoting persons, they refer to the singular. But when they are used with nouns denoting things, they refer to both the singular and plural. Study the following examples:

이분 or 이 사람 'this person'
그분 or 그 사람 'that person'
저분 or 저 사람 'that person over there'
이것 'this' or 'these'
그것 'that' or 'those'
저것 'that over there' or 'those over there'

DRILLS

ADDITIONAL VOCABULARY

고속도로	a super-highway, a freeway	차도	a traffic lane
고가도로	elevated expressway	인도	a sidewalk
지하철	the subway	횡단보도	a crosswalk
지하도	an underpass	네거리	an intersection
육교	an overpass	교통신호	traffic signal, traffic light

A. Substitution Drill

1. 고속도로로 갑시다. Let's go by the freeway.
2. 고가도로로 갑시다. Let's go by the elevated expressway.
3. 지하철로 갑시다. Let's go by subway.
4. 지하도로 갑시다. Let's go through the underpass.

5. 육교로 갑시다. Let's take the overpass.
6. 횡단보도로 갑시다. Let's cross at the crosswalk.
7. 인도로 갑시다. Let's walk on the sidewalk.
8. 차도로 갑시다. Let's go in the lane.

B. Substitution Drill

1. 그분이 여간 예쁘지 않아요. She is really beautiful.
2. 그분이 여간 바쁘지 않아요. He is extremely busy.
3. 날씨가 여간 덥지 않아요. The weather is terribly hot.
4. 그분이 여간 뚱뚱하지 않아요. He is really fat.
5. 그분이 여간 불행하지 않아요. He is really unfortunate.
6. 이 방이 여간 어둡지 않아요. This room is terribly dark.
7. 여기가 여간 시끄럽지 않아요. This area is awfully noisy.
8. 그분이 여간 불친절하지 않아요. He is really unkind.

C. Pattern Drill

Teacher: 그분이 많이 먹어요. He eats a lot.
Student: 그분이 여간 많이 먹지 않아요. He really eats a lot.

1. 멀리 가요. 여간 멀리 가지 않아요.
2. 열심히 공부해요. 여간 열심히 공부하지 않아요.
3. 빨리 일어나요. 여간 빨리 일어나지 않아요.
4. 늦게 와요. 여간 늦게 오지 않아요.
5. 천천히 읽어요. 여간 천천히 읽지 않아요.
6. 많이 일해요. 여간 많이 일하지 않아요.
7. 싸게 팔아요. 여간 싸게 팔지 않아요.
8. 재미있게 놀아요. 여간 재미있게 놀지 않아요.

D. Pattern Drill

Teacher: 빨리 주무세요. Go to bed quickly, please.
Student: 빨리들 주무세요. Please go to bed quickly, all of you.

1. 저리 가세요. 저리들 가세요.
2. 재미있게 노세요. 재미있게들 노세요.
3. 많이 잡수세요. 많이들 잡수세요.
4. 교실에 들어갑시다. 교실에들 들어갑시다.
5. 가지 마세요. 가지들 마세요.
6. 주무시지 마세요. 주무시지들 마세요.
7. 일하러 갑시다. 일하러들 갑시다.
8. 공부하러 갑시다. 공부하러들 갑시다.

9. 들어 오세요. 들어들 오세요.
10. 먹어 봅시다. 먹어들 봅시다.

E. Pattern Drill

Teacher : 그분이 갑니다. He is going.
Student : 그분들이 갑니다. They are going.

1. 이분이 부탁했어요. 이분들이 부탁했어요.
2. 저분이 말씀하셨어요. 저분들이 말씀하셨어요.
3. 선생님이 가셨어요. 선생님들이 가셨어요.
4. 학생이 공부해요. 학생들이 공부해요.
5. 우리가 먹었어요. 우리들이 먹었어요.
6. 저희가 만들었어요. 저희들이 만들었어요.
7. 사람이 많아요. 사람들이 많아요.
8. 여자가 왔어요. 여자들이 왔어요.

F. Integration Drill

Teacher : 이것이 좋습니다. 삽시다.
It's good. Let's buy it.
Student : 이것이 좋으니까, 삽시다.
It's good, so let's buy it.

1. 비가 옵니다. 가지 맙시다.
비가 오니까, 가지 맙시다.
2. 복잡합니다. 잊어버립시다.
복잡하니까, 잊어버립시다.
3. 소용이 없읍니다. 가지고 오지 마세요.
소용이 없으니까, 가지고 오지 마세요.
4. 저는 건강합니다. 걱정하지 마세요.
저는 건강하니까, 걱정하지 마세요.
5. 위험합니다. 천천히 갑시다.
위험하니까, 천천히 갑시다.
6. 날씨가 쌀쌀합니다. 옷을 더 입으세요.
날씨가 쌀쌀하니까, 옷을 더 입으세요.
7. 여기는 물이 깊습니다. 조심하세요.
여기는 물이 깊으니까, 조심하세요.
8. 돈이 필요합니다. 빨리 가지고 오세요.
돈이 필요하니까, 빨리 가지고 오세요.

G. Integration Drill

Teacher: 그것을 잡수셨어요. 배가 아파요.
You ate that. You have a stomachache.

Student: 그것을 잡수셨으니까, 배가 아파요.
Because you ate that, you have a stomachache.

1. 늦었어요. 가지 마세요.
   늦었으니까, 가지 마세요.
2. 일을 많이 했어요. 피곤해요.
   일을 많이 했으니까, 피곤해요.
3. 그분이 왔어요. 나는 가겠어요.
   그분이 왔으니까, 나는 가겠어요.
4. 일을 다 마쳤어요. 저녁을 먹겠어요.
   일을 다 마쳤으니까, 저녁을 먹겠어요.
5. 잊어버렸어요. 가르쳐 주세요.
   잊어버렸으니까, 가르쳐 주세요.
6. 그것을 잃어버렸어요. 하나 사 주세요.
   그것을 잃어버렸으니까, 하나 사 주세요.
7. 그분한테 부탁했어요. 걱정하지 마세요.
   그분한테 부탁했으니까, 걱정하지 마세요.
8. 그분이 집에 갔어요. 내일 오세요.
   그분이 집에 갔으니까, 내일 오세요.

H. Pattern Drill

Teacher: 지금 피곤해서요.	Because I am tired now,···
Student: 지금 피곤하니까요.	Because I am tired now,···
1. 날씨가 추워서요.	날씨가 추우니까요.
2. 너무 시끄러워서요.	너무 시끄러우니까요.
3. 날씨가 무더워서요.	날씨가 무더우니까요.
4. 그분은 무서워서요.	그분은 무서우니까요.
5. 이 종이가 얇아서요.	이 종이가 얇으니까요.
6. 그분은 어려서요.	그분은 어리니까요.
7. 아주 반가워서요.	아주 반가우니까요.
8. 이것이 너무 짧아서요.	이것이 너무 짧으니까요.

SHORT STORIES

1. 오늘은 늦었으니까, 가지 맙시다.
   지금 가도 그분을 만날 수 없어요.
   내일 아침에 일찍 일어나서 갑시다.

Expansion Drill

오늘은 늦었으니까, 가지 맙시다. 지금 가도 그분을 만날 수 없으니까, 내일 아침에 일찍 일어나서 갑시다.

2. 오늘은 일을 여간 많이 하지 않았어요.
빨리들 집에 가세요.
오늘은 푹 쉬고 내일 하세요. 푹 쉬다 to get a good rest

Expansion Drill

오늘은 일을 여간 많이 하지 않았으니까, 빨리들 집에 가서 오늘은 푹 쉬고, 내일 하세요.

3. 날씨가 여간 덥지 않아요.
너무 무더우니까, 정신이 없어요. 정신이 없다 can't think straight, to be distracted
일하지들 말고 쉬세요.

READING

나는 자가용차를 가지고 있습니다. 그런데 이 차가 고장이 났습니다. 그래서 이 차를 어제 고쳤습니다. 오늘 아침에는 시내에 볼일이 있었습니다. 그런데 운전수가 나오지 않았습니다. 그래서 내가 운전했습니다. 먼저 주유소에 가서 기름을 넣었습니다. 그리고 차를 몰고, 광화문 네거리까지 갔습니다. 그런데 광화문에서 교통 신호를 위반했습니다. 교통 순경이 와서 딱지를 떼었습니다. 기분이 나빴지만 할 수 없었습니다. 차를 주차장에 세워 놓았습니다. 그리고 볼일을 보았습니다.

자가용차	private car	네거리	crossroads, intersection
가지다	to have, to own	교통 신호	traffic signal
고장이 나다	to get out of order	위반하다	to violate
고치다	to repair	교통 순경	traffic police
볼일	things to do, business	딱지를 떼다	to give a ticket
운전수	driver	할 수 없다	can't do, helplessly
운전하다	to drive, to operate	주차장	parking lot
먼저	first of all, first	세워 놓다	to park (a car)
주유소	gasoline station	볼일을 보다	to do one's business
기름	oil		
몰다	to drive		

BRIEFING

I have my own car. But The car broke down. So I had this car repaired yesterday. I had business to do downtown this morning. But the driver didn't come. So I drove. I went to the gasoline station first and filled the tank. I drove my car to the Kwanghwamun intersection. But I violated the traffic signal in Kwanghwamun. The traffic policeman came and gave me a ticket. I felt very bad. But I couldn't help it. I parked my car in the parking lot. And I did my own business.

UNIT 29 며칠입니까? What Date Is It?

BASIC SENTENCES: MEMORIZE

며칠	what date
박 성 철	
1. 오늘이 며칠입니까?	What date is it today?
시월	October
십일	tenth (day of the month)
최 인 숙	
2. 시월 십일이에요.	It is October tenth.
무슨 요일	what day of the week
박 성 철	
3. 오늘이 무슨 요일입니까?	What day of the week is it today?
화요일	Tuesday
최 인 숙	
4. 화요일이에요.	It's Tuesday
세월	time and tide
빨리	fast, quickly
벌써	already
박 성 철	
5. 참 세월이 빨리 가는데요! 한국에 온 지 벌써 석 달 되었어요.	Time goes really fast. It has already been three months since I came to Korea.
세월처럼	as (like) time
최 인 숙	
6. 벌써 그렇게 되었어요? 세월처럼 빠른 것은 없군요.	Has it been that long already? Nothing passes as fast as time.

USEFUL EXPRESSIONS: MEMORIZE

1. 상관 없어요.	It is no concern of mine.
2. 굉장해요.	It's terrible (awful).
3. 고집 부리지 마세요.	Don't be so stubborn.

NOTES ON THE BASIC SENTENCES

1. 며칠 is a contraction of 며친날 'what date.' The contracted form is used more often. It can also mean 'how many days,' 'how long,' 'a few days,' etc. Study the following examples:

며칠 전에 그분을 만났어요.	I met him a few days ago.
며칠 전부터 아파요.	I've been ill these few days.
서울에 며칠이나 계시겠어요?	How long will you stay in Seoul?
배로 불란서까지 며칠 걸립니까?	How many days does it take to go to France by ship?

2. 십일 means 'tenth (of the month).' The classifier -일 is used always with Chinese numbers to name the days of the month. See the Structure Notes of this Unit.

3. The classifier -요일 indicates the days of the week. Study the following related words:

일요일	Sunday	목요일	Thursday
월요일	Monday	금요일	Friday
화요일	Tuesday	토요일	Saturday
수요일	Wednesday	주말	weekend

When the particle -에 (indicating time at which something takes place) is used with the classifiers -일 (the days of the month) and -요일 (the days of the week), it can be replaced by the word -날, making no difference in meaning. Study the following examples:

삼일에 갑시다.	Let's go on the third (of the month).
삼일날 갑시다.	Let's go on the third (of the month).
월요일에 공부했어요.	I studied on Monday.
월요일날 공부했어요.	I studied on Monday.

5. 세월 means (1) 'time passing away (going by),' (2) '(the) times,' 'business,' 'conditions,' 'things,' Study the following examples:

세월이 빨라요.	Time goes fast.
바쁜 세월을 보냅니다.	I am busy.
세월이 좋아요.	Times are good.
세월이 나빠요.	Times are bad.
요즘 세월이 어때요?	How are things with you? Or: How goes it with you?
세월이 별로 없어요.	Business is dull. Or: Trade is bad.

STRUCTURE NOTES

I. Time Classifiers (Counters) : -초, -분, -일, -주일, -년

We have already studied some of the time classifiers, such as -시 'o'clock,' -시간 'hours,' -월 (used to name) the calendar months, -달 or -개월 'months,' (used to count the number of months), etc. Now let's study the time classifiers which are used with Chinese numbers TO COUNT and NAME :

-초 is used to count the number of seconds, and to name a second of a sixty-second minute. Study the following examples :

일 초 1 second or second 1
이 초 2 seconds or second 2
삼 초 3 seconds or second 3
사 초 4 seconds or second 4
오 초 5 seconds or second 5

몇 초 걸렸습니까?	How many seconds did it take?
오 초 걸렸습니다.	It took 5 seconds.
몇 시 몇 분 몇 초입니까?	What time is it exactly, (hour, minute, second) ?
한 시 오 분 십 초입니다.	It's 1 : 05 : 10.

-분 is used to count a number of minutes, and to name a minute of an hour. Study the following examples :

일 분 1 minute or minute 1
이 분 2 minutes or minute 2
삼 분 3 minutes or minute 3
사 분 4 minutes or minute 4
오 분 5 minutes or minute 5

몇 분 걸립니까?	How many minutes does it take?
오 분 걸립니다.	It takes five minutes.
몇 분입니까?	What minute is it?
오 분 전입니다.	It's five minutes before (the hour).

-일 is used to count a number of days, and to name the days of the month. Study the following examples :

일일 1 day or the first day of the month
이일 2 days or the second
삼일 3 days or the third
사일 4 days or the fourth

오일 5 days or the fifth

부산에 며칠 계셨어요?	How many days were you in Pusan?
부산에 삼일 있었어요.	I was in Pusan for three days.
오늘이 며칠이에요?	What date is it today?
오늘이 유월 삼일이에요.	Today is June third.

There is also a pure Korean set for counting the number of days, and naming the days of the months. Study the following examples:

하루	1 day or the first day of the month
이틀	2 days or the second
사흘	3 days or the third
나흘	4 days or the fourth
닷새	5 days or the fifth
엿새	6 days or the sixth
이레	7 days or the seventh
여드레	8 days or the eighth
아흐레	9 days or the ninth
열흘	10 days or the tenth
열 하루	11 days or the eleventh
열 이틀	12 days or the twelfth
스무날	20 days or the twentieth
스무 하루	21 days or the twenty-first
스무 이틀	22 days or the twenty-second

여기에 며칠 계시겠어요?	How many days are you going to stay here?
닷새 있겠어요.	I'm going to stay here for five days.
오늘이 며칠이에요?	What date is it today?
오늘이 닷새예요.	Today is the fifth (of the month).

Notes:

1. The Korean set is used more for counting the number of days, than naming the days of the month. The latter is done mostly by older people. Younger people use the Chinese set (일일 'the first,' 이일 'the second,' etc.) more than the Korean set (하루 'the first,' 이틀 'the second,' etc.).
2. Sometimes, the prefix 초- 'first,' 'beginning' is put before words naming the days of the month, (usually from 1 to 5). For example: 초 하루 'the first,' 초 이틀 'the second,' 초 사흘 'the third,' etc.

3. Here are some frequently used words relating to time:

초순 the first third (ten days) of a month, the beginning of a month

중순 the middle third (ten days) of a month

하순 the last third (last ten days) of a month

보름 fifteen days, or the fifteenth day

그믐 the last day of the month

-주일 is used to count the number of weeks. Study the following examples:

일 주일 1 week

이 주일 2 weeks

삼 주일 3 weeks

사 주일 4 weeks

오 주일 5 weeks

몇 주일 공부하셨어요? How many weeks did you study?

삼 주일 공부했어요. I studied for three weeks.

-년 is used to count the number of years, and to name years. Study the following examples:

일 년 1 year or the year 1

이 년 2 years or the year 2

삼 년 3 years or the year 3

사 년 4 years or the year 4

오 년 5 years or the year 5

몇 년 일하셨어요? How many years did you work?

삼 년 일했어요. I worked for three years.

몇 년도에 한국에 오셨어요? What year did you come to Korea?

1990년에 한국에 왔어요. I came to Korea in (the year) 1990.

Notes:

When giving Korean dates, the longer time period always precedes the shorter, like year-month-day. For example: 천 구백 구십년 구월 오일 'September 5, 1990.'

II. A.V.S. +-ㄴ(은) 지가 + time word + 되다…: '(the time) since'

The pattern -ㄴ(은) 지가+time word+되다 indicates an interval of time which extends from a definite past to the present. The English equvalent of this pattern is 'it's been (such-and such) a time since…,' or 'from the time when…'.

Examples:

한국에 온 지가 석 달 되었어요.	It's been three months since I came to Korea.
영화를 본 지가 다섯 달 되었어요.	It's been five months since I went to see a movie.
그분을 만난 지가 오 년 되었어요.	It's been five months since I met him.
한식을 먹어 본 지가 오래 되었습니다.	It's been five years since I met him. Korean food.
편지를 받은 지가 보름 됩니다.	It's been fifteen days since I got a letter.
그분이 그 일을 시작한 지가 사흘 되었어요.	It's been three days since he began that work.

Notes:

1. The final word 되다 may be used either with the past tense infix (-았-) or with the present tense form, making no difference in meaning. However, it is used mostly with the past tense infix (-았-).
2. The particle -가 after -지 is optional.
3. -ㄴ지 is used after verb stems ending in a vowel; -은지 is used after verb stems ending in a consonant.

III. The Particle -처럼… : '(the same) as,' 'like,' 'as…as'

The particle -처럼, preceded by a noun, reflects an identical quality or condition of the noun.

Examples:

세월처럼 빠른 것은 없어요.	Time goes really fast. Or: There is nothing so fast as time.
영어처럼 재미있는 것은 없어요.	There is no language as interesting as English.
어제 아침처럼 일찍 일어나세요.	Please get up early like you did yesterday morning.
그분이 공부하는 것처럼 공부하세요.	Please study as he is studying.
한 가족처럼 같이 살아요.	We are living together like one family.
내 집처럼 좋은 데는 없어요.	There is no good place like home.
그분이 말한 것처럼 말해 보세요.	Please try saying what he just said.

DRILLS

ADDITIONAL VOCABULARY

월요일	Monday	금요일	Friday
수요일	Wednesday	토요일	Saturday

목요일 Thursday

일요일 Sunday

받다 to receive

A. Substitution Drill

1. 시월 십일이에요.	It is October tenth.
2. 일월 십 오일이에요.	It is January fifteenth.
3. 이월 구일이에요.	It is February ninth.
4. 삼월 이십일이에요.	It is March twentieth.
5. 사월 이십 오일이에요.	It is April twenty-fifth.
6. 오월 오일이에요.	It is May fifth.
7. 유월 팔일이에요.	It is June eighth.
8. 십일월 이십 삼일이에요.	It is November twenty-third.

B. Substitution Drill

1. 오늘이 월요일입니다.	Today is Monday.
2. 오늘이 화요일입니다.	Today is Tuesday.
3. 오늘이 수요일입니다.	Today is Wednesday.
4. 오늘이 목요일입니다.	Today is Thursday.
5. 오늘이 금요일입니다.	Today is Friday.
6. 오늘이 토요일입니다.	Today is Saturday.
7. 오늘이 일요일입니다.	Today is Sunday.

C. Pattern Drill

Teacher : 부산에 삼일 있었어요.	I was in Pusan for three days.
Student : 부산에 사흘 있었어요.	I was in Pusan for three days.
1. 미국에 사일 있었어요.	미국에 나흘 있었어요.
2. 영국에 오일 있었어요.	영국에 닷새 있었어요.
3. 일본에 육일 있었어요.	일본에 엿새 있었어요.
4. 불란서에 칠일 있었어요.	불란서에 이레 있었어요.
5. 독일에 이일 있었어요.	독일에 이틀 있었어요.
6. 대만에 팔일 있었어요.	대만에 여드레 있었어요.
7. 소련에 구일 있었어요.	소련에 아흐레 있었어요.
8. 중공에 십일 있었어요.	중공에 열흘 있었어요.

D. Pattern Drill

Teacher : 석 달 전에 한국에 왔어요.
I came to Korea three months ago.

Student : 한국에 온지 석 달 되었어요.
It's been three months since I came to Korea.

1. 다섯 달 전에 영화를 보았어요.	영화를 본 지 다섯 달 되었어요.
2. 오 년 전에 그분을 만났어요.	그분을 만난 지 오 년 되었어요.
3. 이 주일 전에 목욕했어요.	목욕한 지 이 주일 되었어요.
4. 삼 주일 전에 부탁했어요.	부탁한 지 삼 주일 되었어요.
5. 한 달 전에 고쳤어요.	고친 지 한 달 되었어요.
6. 닷새 전에 고장이 났어요.	고장이 난 지 닷새 되었어요.
7. 이틀 전에 편지를 받았어요.	편지를 받은 지 이틀 되었어요.
8. 두 시간 전에 넘어졌어요.	넘어진 지 두 시간 되었어요.

E. Pattern Drill

Teacher: 세월이 빨라요.	Time goes fast.
Student: 세월처럼 빠른 것은 없어요.	There is nothing as fast as time.
1. 한국말이 재미있어요.	한국말처럼 재미있는 것은 없어요.
2. 이 종이가 두꺼워요.	이 종이처럼 두꺼운 것은 없어요.
3. 이것이 맛있어요.	이것처럼 맛있는 것은 없어요.
4. 영어가 어려워요.	영어처럼 어려운 것은 없어요.
5. 그것이 예뻐요.	그것처럼 예쁜 것은 없어요.
6. 이 문제가 복잡해요.	이 문제처럼 복잡한 것은 없어요.
7. 그 일이 힘들어요.	그 일처럼 힘든 것은 없어요.
8. 그 책이 좋아요.	그 책처럼 좋은 것은 없어요.

F. Response Drill

1. 여기서 몇 분 걸립니까?	여기서 십 분 걸립니다.
2. 오늘이 며칠입니까?	오늘이 유월 삼일이에요.
3. 미국에 며칠 계셨어요?	미국에 엿새 있었어요.
4. 몇 주일 공부하셨어요?	삼 주일 공부했어요.
5. 몇 달 일하셨어요?	다섯 달 일했어요.
6. 몇 년 가르치셨어요?	십 오 년 가르쳤어요.
7. 영화를 본 지 몇 달 되었어요?	영화를 본 지 석 달 되었어요.
8. 그분이 하는 것처럼 할까요?	예, 그분이 하는 것처럼 하세요.

G. Pattern Drill

Teacher: 월요일에 갑시다.	Let's go on Monday.
Student: 월요일날 갑시다.	Let's go on Monday.
1. 지난 일요일에 만났습니다.	지난 일요일날 만났습니다.
2. 화요일에 가지 맙시다.	화요일날 가지 맙시다.
3. 수요일에 일합니다.	수요일날 일합니다.
4. 금요일에 쉽니다.	금요일날 쉽니다.

5. 목요일에 떠납시다.	목요일날 떠납시다.
6. 토요일에 공부하지 않아요.	토요일날 공부하지 않아요.
7. 월요일에 등산합시다.	월요일날 등산합시다.
8. 화요일에 왔습니다.	화요일날 왔습니다.

H. Pattern Drill

Teacher: 유월 삼일에 왔어요.	I came June third.
Student: 유월 삼일날 왔어요.	I came June third.
1. 시월 오일에 갑니다.	시월 오일날 갑니다.
2. 오월 육일에 떠났어요.	오월 육일날 떠났어요.
3. 삼월 칠일에 도착했어요.	삼월 칠일날 도착했어요.
4. 일월 이십 오일에 샀어요.	일월 이십 오일날 샀어요.
5. 십 일월 삼일에 쉽시다.	십 일월 삼일날 쉽시다.
6. 팔월 십 구일에 놉시다.	팔월 십 구일날 놉시다.
7. 칠월 삼십일에 만났어요.	칠월 삼십일날 만났어요.
8. 십 이월 팔일에 들었어요.	십 이월 팔일날 들었어요.

I. Response Drill (Review)

Teacher: 그것을 사도 괜찮아요?	May I buy it?
Student: 아니오, 그것을 사면 안 됩니다.	No, you must not buy it.
1. 고장이 나도 괜찮아요?	아니오, 고장이 나면 안 됩니다.
2. 담배를 피워도 괜찮아요?	아니오, 담배를 피우면 안 됩니다.
3. 술을 마셔도 괜찮아요?	아니오, 술을 마시면 안 됩니다.
4. 수술해도 괜찮아요?	아니오, 수술하면 안 됩니다.
5. 술에 취해도 괜찮아요?	아니오, 술에 취하면 안 됩니다.
6. 사냥을 가도 괜찮아요?	아니오, 사냥을 가면 안 됩니다.
7. 소풍을 가도 괜찮아요?	아니오, 소풍을 가면 안 됩니다.
8. 등산을 가도 괜찮아요?	아니오, 등산을 가면 안 됩니다.

SHORT STORIES

1. 지난 팔월 초순에 한국에 왔어요.
그러니까 벌써 한국에 온 지 넉 달 되었어요.
정말 세월처럼 빠른 것은 없어요.

Expansion Drill 초순 the beginning of a month

지난 팔월 초순에 한국에 왔으니까, 벌써 한국에 온 지 넉 달 되었어요. 정말 세월처럼 빠른 것은 없어요.

2. 그분이 지난 유월 중순에 미국으로 떠났어요.

다음 달 하순에 돌아올 겁니다.
그분이 돌아오면 이 일을 시작할 겁니다.

중순 the middle third of a month　　하순 the last third of a month

Expansion Drill

그분이 지난 유월 중순에 미국으로 떠났으니까, 다음 달 하순에 돌아올 겁니다. 그분이 돌아오면 이 일을 시작할 겁니다.

3. 1987년에 한국에 왔어요.
한국에서 선교사로 일한지 삼년 되었어요.
금년 가을에 미국으로 휴가 갑니다.

선교사 a missionary　　휴가 a furlough, a vacation

Expansion Drill

1987년에 한국에 와서, 선교사로 일한 지 삼년 되었어요. 금년 가을에 미국으로 휴가 갑니다.

READING

한국에 온 지 벌써 넉 달 되었습니다. 내가 한국에 왔을 때는 여름이었습니다. 그래서 여간 무덥지 않았습니다. 그런데 벌써 겨울이 되었습니다. 한국에 오기 전에는 한국말을 조금도 몰랐습니다. 한국에 와서 한국말을 배우기 시작했습니다. 한국말처럼 재미있는 것은 없습니다. 빨리 한국 사람처럼 한국말을 잘 했으면 좋겠습니다. 그런데 공부하기가 여간 힘들지 않습니다. 어떤 때는 공부하기가 싫습니다. 그래서 가끔 숙제를 하지 않습니다. 그런데 숙제를 안 하면 선생님한테 혼납니다. 요즘 숙제가 많아서 보통 저녁 열 시쯤 숙제가 끝납니다.

조금도 even a little　　가끔 occasionally, sometimes
어떤 때는 sometimes　　보통 ordinarily, usually

BRIEFING

It has already been four months since I came to Korea. When I came to Korea it was summer. So it was extremly hot. But already it's winter. Before I came to Korea, I didn't know Korean at all. I came to Korea and started to learn Korean. There is nothing as interesting as Korean. I wish I could speak Korean as well as Korean people. But studying (Korean) is extremely difficult. Sometimes I hate to study. So, occasionally, I don't do my homework. But if I don't do my homework, I will have a hard time from my teacher. These days I have a lot of homework. Usually, I finish my homework about ten o'clock.

UNIT 30 방문 A Visit

BASIC SENTENCES: MEMORIZE

만나다 — to meet

최 인 숙

1. 어제 친구를 만나셨어요? — Did you see your friend yesterday?

찾아가다 — to visit

박 성 철

2. 어제 집으로 찾아갔는데, 안 계셨어요. — I visited his home yesterday, but he was not (at home).

만나지 못하고 — without seeing him

최 인 숙

3. 그래서 만나지 못 하고 돌아 오셨어요? — So, did you return without seeing him?

전화하니까 — when I called

마침 — at the right moment, luckily, fortunately

박 성 철

4. 아니오, 학교에 전화하니까, 마침 계셨어요. 그래서 학교에 가서 그분을 만났어요. — No, when I called his school, he happened to be there. So, I went to school and met him (there).

처음에 — in the first place

약속하다 — to promise

최 인 숙

5. 처음에는 어디에서 만나기로 약속하셨어요? — Where did you promise to meet him in the first place?

원래 — originally

박 성 철

6. 원래 집에서 만나기로 약속 했어요. — Originally I had planned to meet him at his house.

USEFUL EXPRESSIONS: MEMORIZE

1. 모르셨어요? Didn't you know it?
2. 남의 일에 간섭하지 마세요. Mind your own business.
3. 그렇게 서두르지 마세요. Don't be in such a hurry.

NOTES ON THE BASIC SENTENCES

1. 만나다: The pronunciation of 만나요 'to meet' must be distinguished from 많아요 'to be many (much).' As you have studied in the Korean sound system the sound /n/, followed by the same consonant /n/, seems to cause most foreigners trouble. Let's review this double consonant /nn/.

   만나다 , 인내, 분노, 안내하다
   건너가다, 손녀, 천년, 단념

2. 찾아가다 is a compound verb made up of 찾다 and 가다. The word 찾다, depending on the context or situation, can mean (1) 'to search for,' 'to look for,' (2) 'to find (discover),' (3) 'to pay a visit,' 'to take (get) back,' etc. Study the following examples:

   그 책을 찾았어요. I found that book.
   친구를 찾고 있어요. I'm looking for my friend.
   그 돈을 찾았어요. I got back that money.
   친구를 찾아갔어요. I visited my friend.
   내일 찾아오겠어요. I'll come and see you tomorrow.

3. 그래서, as an independent conjunctive word, occurs at the beginning of a sentence. Its meaning is '(and) so,' 'therefore,' 'for that reason,' or 'on that account.' Its synonym is 그러니까 'therefore,' 'so.'

   만나지 못하고 means 'without seeing him, (lit. you couldn't see him and…).' When the consonant ㅅ occurs as the final consonant, and is followed by the consonant ㅎ initially in the next syllable, ㅎ is pronounced as ㅌ. Therefore, 못 하고 is pronunced 못 타고.

4. 마침 means 'just in time,' 'at the right moment,' 'fortunately,' etc. Study the following examples:

   마침 잘 오셨어요. You have come at just the right moment.
   마침 그 때에 돈이 있었어요. Fortunately I had money with me at that time.

5. 처음, as a noun, means (1) 'the beginning,' 'the outset,' (2) 'first (of all),' 'the first time,' etc. Its opposite word is 끝 'the end,' 'termination,' 'a close.' Study the following examples:

처음 뵙겠어요. How do you do? (A person who gets introduced regularly uses this expression.)

처음부터 다시 하세요. Please make a new start.

처음부터 끝까지 잘 하세요. Please do it well from beginning to end.

약속하다 means 'to make a promise,' 'to make an appointment,' 'to make a date,' 'to give one's word.' Study the following examples:

약속을 지켰어요. I kept my word (promise).

약속을 어겼어요. (He) broke his promise.

약속을 잊어버렸어요. I forgot the appointment.

6. 원래 means 'originally,' 'primarily,' 'by nature,' 'essentially.' When the consonant ㄴ is followed by ㄹ, the preceding consonant ㄴ becomes a lateral sound ㄹ. Therefore, 원래 is pronounced as 월래.

STRUCTURE NOTES

I. The Introductory Non-Final Ending -ㄴ(-은, -는)데:

We have already studied the sentence-final ending -ㄴ(은, -는)데요, which indicates interest, surprise, delight, astonishment, wonder, etc., (See Unit 12, Structure Notes I.) This pattern -ㄴ(은, -는)데 is used, however, as a non-final ending as well. It is used to introduce a certain fact, occurrence, or event before the sentence which follows it. The English equivalent of this pattern is '…and,' '…but,' '…so,' etc. It is used with any verb.

Examples:

친구가 있는데, 참 부자에요.
He is a friend of mine, and he is very rich.
그분이 미국 사람인데, 한국말을 잘 해요.
He is an American, but he speaks Korean very well.
그것을 사고 싶은데, 지금 돈이 없어요.
I want to buy it, but I have no money now.
나는 한국말을 공부하는데, 그분은 영어를 공부해요.
I am studying Korean, but he is studying English.
지금 바쁜데, 내일 오시겠어요?
I'm busy now, so will you come tomorrow?

Notes:

1. The past or future tense infix (-았-, -겠) may be used in this pattern -ㄴ

(-은, -는)데. Study the following examples:
열심히 공부했는데, 잘 모르겠어요.
I studied hard, but I don't understand it very well.
한국말 책을 사야겠는데, 어디에서 살 수 있어요?
I have to buy a Korean language book, but where can I buy it?

2. -ㄴ(은)데 is attached to description verb stems in the present tense and to the verb of identification 이다 in the present tense.
3. -는데 is attached to all other cases.

II. The Non-Final Ending -(으)니까…: 'when'

We have already studied the causal non-final ending -(으)니까, which indicates cause or reason, (See Unit 17, Structure Notes I.) This pattern -(으)니까, besides being used as a causal non-final ending meaning 'because,' can also be used as a time non-final ending meaning 'when.'

Examples:

집에 가니까, 집에 아무도 없었어요.
When I went home, there was nobody there.
밖에 나가니까, 아주 추웠어요.
When I went out, it was very cold.
사무실에 들어가니까, 사람이 많았어요.
When I entered my office, there were many people.
창 밖을 내다보니까, 어두웠어요.
When I looked out of the window, it was dark.
친구한테 전화하니까, 그분이 집에 없었어요.
When I phoned my friend, he was not home.
그분을 쳐다보니까, 그분이 웃었어요.
When I looked up into his face, he laughed.
이 책을 읽어 보니까, 어렵지 않아요.
When I try reading this book, it's not difficult.

Notes:

1. This non-final ending -(으)니까, meaning 'when,' is used only with action verbs; however, the causal non-final ending -(으)니까, meaning 'because,' may be used with any verb.
2. When this pattern -(으)니까 is used with the meaning 'when,' the subjects of the dependent clause and the main clause must be different. Moreover, the main clause usually takes the past tense. When this pattern -(으)니까

is used with the meaning 'because,' it does not know these limitations.

3. The tense and/or negation is expressed regularly in the final (main) clause, not in the first (dependent) clause with -(으)니까.
4. -니까 is used after verb stems ending in a vowel;
   -으니까 is used after verb stems ending in a consonant.

III. The Sentence-Final Ending -기로 하다…: 'to decide to do (so-and-so)'

This pattern -기로 하다 is attached directly to the stem of an action verb; it indicates making a choice between alternatives, or arriving at a solution to an uncertainty or dispute. The English equivalent of this pattern is 'to decide to do (so-and-so),' 'to make up one's mind to do (so-and-so),' 'to arrange (fix) to do (so-and-so).'

Examples:

오늘 저녁에 그분을 만나기로 할까요?	Shall we decide to meet him this evening?
그분을 수술하기로 했어요.	We decided to perform a surgical operation on him.
그분이 오면, 떠나기로 합시다.	Let's decide to leave if he comes.
복습하기로 합시다.	Let's decide to review.
술을 마시지 않기로 했어요.	I made up my mind not to drink.

Notes:

1. The nominalizing suffix -기 indicates 'an act,' the particle -로 implies 'goal,' and 하다 means 'to decide on,' 'to make (it) to be.'
2. The verb 하다 in this pattern can be replaced by other verbs, such as 약속하다 'to promise,' 결정하다 'to decide,' 'to settle,' 작정하다 'to intend (to do),' 'to fix one's mind on (doing),' 결심하다 'to make up one's mind,' etc Study the following examples:

그분을 도와주기로 약속했어요.	I promised to help him.
그분을 도와주기로 결정했어요.	I decided to help him.
그분을 도와주기로 작정했어요.	I fixed my mind on helping him.
그분을 도와주기로 결심했어요.	I made up my mind to help him.

3. When this pattern -기로 하다 is preceded by a negative, its meaning is 'to decide not to do (so-and-so).' But when the negation is expressed in the final verb -하다, its meaning is 'to not decide to do (so-and-so).' Study the following examples:

가지 않기로 했어요.	I decided not to go.

가기로 하지 않았어요. I haven't decide to go.

4. The tense is expressed regularly in the final verb 하다, not in the verb with -기로. Study the following examples :

가기로 합시다.	Let's decide to go.
가기로 했습니다.	I've decided to go.
가기로 하겠어요.	I will decide to go.

DRILLS

ADDITIONAL VOCABULARY

끝	the end, termination	작정하다	to intend (to do), to fix one's mind on (doing)
결정하다	to decide, to settle		
나중에	some time later	결심하다	to make up one's mind

A. Substitution Drill

1. 그분을 만나기로 합시다.	Let's (decide to) meet him.
2. 이 일을 계속하기로 합시다.	Let's (decide to) continue this work.
3. 복습하기로 합시다.	Let's (decide to) review.
4. 예습하기로 합시다.	Let's (decide to) prepare the lessons.
5. 내일 약혼하기로 합시다.	Let's (decide to) get engaged tomorrow.
6. 그것을 고치기로 합시다.	Let's (decide to) repair that.
7. 내일 청소하기로 합시다.	Let's (decide to) clean it tomorrow.
8. 조심하기로 합시다.	Let's (decide to) be careful.

B. Substitution Drill

1. 그분을 만나기로 약속했어요.	I promised to meet him.
2. 그분을 도와주기로 약속했어요.	I promised to help him.
3. 두 시까지 끝내기로 약속했어요.	I promised to finish it by two.
4. 담배를 피우지 않기로 약속했어요.	I promised not to smoke.
5. 술을 마시지 않기로 약속했어요.	I promised not to drink.
6. 울지 않기로 약속했어요.	I promised not to cry.
7. 말하지 않기로 약속했어요.	I promised not to talk.
8. 낮잠을 자지 않기로 약속했어요.	I promised not to take a nap.

C. Substitution Drill

1. 그분을 도와주기로 결정했어요.	We decided to help him.
2. 그 일을 계속하기로 결정했어요.	We decided to continue that work.
3. 거기에 가기로 결정했어요.	We decided to go there.

4. 그것을 사기로 결정했어요. We decided to buy that.
5. 영어를 공부하기로 결정했어요. We decided to study English.
6. 그것을 만들기로 결정했어요. We decided to make it.
7. 그것을 팔기로 결정했어요. We decided to sell it.
8. 그분을 수술하기로 결정했어요. We decided to operate on him.

D. Substitution Drill

1. 그분을 도와주기로 작정했어요. I fixed my mind on helping him.
2. 그것을 하기로 작정했어요. I fixed my mind on doing that.
3. 그것을 계속하기로 작정했어요. I fixed my mind on continuing that.
4. 한국말을 공부하기로 작정했어요. I fixed my mind on studying Korean.
5. 그것을 만들기로 작정했어요. I fixed my mind on making it.
6. 담배를 피우지 않기로 작정했어요. I fixed my mind on not smoking.
7. 술을 마시지 않기로 작정했어요. I fixed my mind on not drinking.
8. 말하지 않기로 작정했어요. I fixed my mind on not talking.

E. Substitution Drill

1. 그분을 도와주기로 결심했어요. I made up my mind to help him.
2. 거기에 가기로 결심했어요. I made up my mind to go there.
3. 한국말을 공부하기로 결심했어요. I made up my mind to study Korean.
4. 그분을 만나기로 결심했어요. I made up my mind to meet him.
5. 담배를 피우지 않기로 결심했어요. I made up my mind not to smoke.
6. 술을 마시지 않기로 결심했어요. I made up my mind not to drink.
7. 말하지 않기로 결심했어요. I made up my mind not to talk.
8. 그 일을 하지 않기로 결심했어요. I made up my mind not to do that work.

F. Integration Drill

Teacher : 지금 바쁩니다. 내일 오시겠습니까?
I'm busy now. Will you come tomorrow?
Student : 지금 바쁜데, 내일 오시겠습니까?
I'm busy now, so will you come tomorrow?

1. 이것이 더럽습니다. 다른 것을 주시겠습니까?
이것이 더러운데, 다른 것을 주시겠습니까?
2. 그분이 불친절합니다. 만나시겠습니까?
그분이 불친절한데, 만나시겠습니까?
3. 그것이 비쌉니다. 사시겠습니까?
그것이 비싼데, 사시겠습니까?
4. 날씨가 춥습니다. 가시겠습니까?

날씨가 추운데, 가시겠습니까?

5. 그것이 무섭습니다. 보시겠습니까?
   그것이 무서운데, 보시겠습니까?
6. 그분이 바쁩니다. 찾아가시겠습니까?
   그분이 바쁜데, 찾아가시겠습니까?
7. 지금 시끄럽습니다. 나중에 오시겠습니까?
   지금 시끄러운데, 나중에 오시겠습니까?
8. 그것이 좋지 않습니다. 사시겠습니까?
   그것이 좋지 않은데, 사시겠습니까?

G. Integration Drill

Teacher: 나는 한국말을 공부합니다. 그분은 영어를 공부합니다.
I am studying Korean. He is studying English.

Student: 나는 한국말을 공부하는데, 그분은 영어를 공부합니다.
I am studying Korean, but he is studying English.

1. 친구가 있습니다. 아주 부자입니다.
   친구가 있는데, 아주 부자입니다.
2. 고장이 났습니다. 고치지 않았습니다.
   고장이 났는데, 고치지 않았습니다.
3. 열심히 공부했습니다. 잘 모르겠습니다.
   열심히 공부했는데, 잘 모르겠습니다.
4. 애기를 낳았습니다. 참 큽니다.
   애기를 낳았는데, 참 큽니다.
5. 태풍이 불었습니다. 그분이 갔습니다.
   태풍이 불었는데, 그분이 갔습니다.
6. 소나기가 옵니다. 어떻게 가시겠습니까?
   소나기가 오는데, 어떻게 가시겠습니까?
7. 교통 신호를 위반했습니다. 괜찮았습니다.
   교통 신호를 위반했는데, 괜찮았습니다.
8. 주차장에 세워 놓았습니다. 없어졌습니다.
   주차장에 세워 놓았는데, 없어졌습니다.

H. Integration Drill

Teacher: 집에 갔습니다. 아무도 안 계셨어요.
I went home. There was nobody there.

Student: 집에 가니까, 아무도 안 계셨어요.
When I went home, there was nobody there.

1. 밖에 나갔습니다. 아주 추웠습니다.

밖에 나가니까, 아주 추웠습니다.

2. 사무실에 들어갔습니다. 사람이 많았습니다.
   사무실에 들어가니까, 사람이 많았습니다.
3. 창 밖을 내다보았습니다. 어두웠습니다.
   창 밖을 내다보니까, 어두웠습니다.
4. 친구한테 전화했습니다. 그분이 집에 없었습니다.
   친구한테 전화하니까, 그분이 집에 없었습니다.
5. 그분을 쳐다보았습니다. 그분이 웃었습니다.
   그분을 쳐다보니까, 그분이 웃었습니다.
6. 이 책을 읽어 보았습니다. 어렵지 않습니다.
   이 책을 읽어 보니까, 어렵지 않습니다.
7. 산에 올라갔습니다. 더웠습니다.
   산에 올라가니까, 더웠습니다.
8. 방을 들여다보았습니다. 아무도 없었습니다.
   방을 들여다보니까, 아무도 없었습니다.

I. Response Drill

1. 누구를 만나기로 약속하셨어요?	친구를 만나기로 약속했어요.
2. 무엇을 사기로 결정하셨어요.?	자동차를 사기로 결정했어요.
3. 무엇을 하지 않기로 결심하셨어요?	술를 마시지 않기로 결심했어요.
4. 누구를 찾아갔는데 안 계셨어요?	선생님을 찾아갔는데, 안 계셨어요.
5. 밖에 나가니까, 어떠했어요?	밖에 나가니까, 추웠어요.
6. 집에 가니까, 그분이 계셨어요?	예, 집에 가니까, 그분이 계셨어요.
7. 한국에 온 지가 몇 달 되었어요?	한국에 온 지가 두 달 되었어요.
8. 그분이 하는 것처럼 할까요?	예, 그분이 하는 것처럼 하세요.

SHORT STORIES

1. 친구와 다방에서 만나기로 약속했어요.
   그런데 그분이 제 시간에 오지 않았어요. 제 시간에 'on time'
   집에 전화하니까, 그분이 마침 계셨어요.

   Expansion Drill

   친구와 다방에서 만나기로 약속했는데, 그분이 제 시간에 오지 않았어요. 집에 전화하니까, 그분이 마침 계셨어요.

2. 김 선생님은 약속을 잘 지켰습니다. 지키다 to keep, to observe
   그런데 내가 약속을 어겼습니다. 어기다 to break

앞으로 약속을 잘 지키겠습니다. 앞으로 in the future

Expansion Drill

김 선생님은 약속을 잘 지켰는데, 내가 약속을 어겼습니다. 앞으로 약속을 잘 지키겠습니다.

3. 술을 마시지 않기로 했습니다.
   나는 술을 마시면 머리가 아픕니다.
   술을 마시지 않는 것이 좋겠어요.

   Expansion Drill

   술을 마시지 않기로 했습니다. 나는 술을 마시면 머리가 아프기 때문에, 술을 마시지 않는 것이 좋겠어요.

READING

친구를 친구(의) 집에서 만나기로 약속했어요. 그러나 어제 집으로 찾아갔는데, 그분이 안 계셨어요. 그래서 화가 굉장히 났어요. 그런데 학교에 전화하니까, 마침 그분이 계셨어요. 그래서 학교에 가서 그분을 만났어요. 그분은 미국에서 한국에 돌아온 지 넉 달 밖에 되지 않았어요. 그분은 미국에서 박사 학위를 받고 돌아왔어요. 지금 서강 대학교에서 가르치고 있어요. 그분은 대학교 교수지만 여간 겸손하지 않아요. 그분이 나한테 저녁을 같이 먹자고 했어요. 그러나 내가 시간이 없어서 사양했어요. 다음에 다시 만나기로 했어요.

박사학위	a doctor's degree	먹자고 했어요	He said 'Let's eat'
교수	a professor	사양하다	to decline respectfully
겸손하다	to be humble		

BRIEFING

I promised to meet my friend at his house. I visited him at his house yesterday. But he was not at home. So I got very angry. When I called him at school, fortunately he was there. So I went to school and I met him. It has only been four months since he came back to Korea from America. He received a Ph.D. in America and returned to Korea. Now he is teaching at Sogang University. He is a college professor. But he is very humble. He asked me to eat dinner together. But because I had no time, I had to refuse (with thanks). We decided to meet again soon.

UNIT 31 재미있게 노세요 Have Fun

BASIC SENTENCES : MEMORIZE

최 인 숙

1. 재미있게들 노세요. 저는 지금 가 봐야겠어요. — Have fun, everybody. I have to go now.

박 성 철

2. 놀다가 같이 갑시다. — Let's play together and go.
   - 안 가면 — if I don't go
   - 안 돼요 — it won't be good

최 인 숙

3. 죄송합니다. 지금 안 가면 안 돼요. — I'm sorry. If I don't go now, it won't be good.
   - 무슨 — some kind of
   - 급한 — urgent

박 성 철

4. 무슨 급한 일이 있으세요? — Do you have some urgent work to do?
   - 다른 — another

최 인 숙

5. 예, 다른 친구를 만날 일이 있어요. — Yes, I have to meet another friend.
   - 먼저 — first, ahead
   - 곧 — soon

박 성 철

6. 그럼 먼저 가세요. 저도 곧 가려고 해요. — Then, go ahead. I'm also going to go soon.

USEFUL EXPRESSIONS : MEMORIZE

1. 담배 피우세요. — How about a cigarette?
2. 내가 한잔 내겠어요. — I'll treat you to drinks.
3. 한잔 합시다. — Let's have a drink.

NOTES ON THE BASIC SENTENCES

1. 가 봐야겠어요 is a contraction of 가 보아야 하겠어요 'I have to go, (lit. I'll have to go and see).' The contracted form is used more often.
3. 안 돼요 is a contraction of 안 되어요 'it won't be good.'
4. 무슨 급한 일이 있으세요? means 'Do you have some urgent work to do?

   무슨, in this context, means 'some kind of,' 'something,' 'anything,' etc. Study the following examples:

무슨 일로 오셨어요?	You came in regards to what matter?
무슨 일을 그렇게 천천히 하세요?	Why are you so slow with your work?
무슨 좋은 일이 있으세요?	Is there anything good?

   급하다, depending on the context or situation, means (1) 'to be urgent,' (2) 'to be impatient,' (3) 'to be critical,' 'to be an emergency,' etc. Study the following examples:

급한 일이 있어요.	I have some urgent business.
이 일이 급해요.	This matter is pressing.
그분이 성미가 급해요.	He is impatient.
급한 환자가 왔어요.	An emergency patient came.

5. 다르다, depending on the context or situation, can mean (1) 'to be different from,' (2) 'to be another,' 'to be unlike,' (3) 'to be not in accordance with,' etc. Its opposite word is 같다 'to be the same.' Study the following examples:

이 책과 그 책은 달라요.	This book and that book are different (from each other).
그분은 다른 학생이에요.	He is another student.
그분은 어렸을 때와는 달라요.	He is not what he was in his youth.
그것은 아주 다른 문제에요.	That's quite another problem.
그것은 약속과는 달라요.	It's not in keeping with the agreement.

6. 먼저 means (1) 'first,' 'ahead,' (2) 'earlier,' 'beforehand,' (3) '(sometime) ago.' 'formerly,' etc. Its opposite word is 나중에 or 뒤에. Study the following examples:

먼저 들어가세요.	Please go in first.
먼저 잡수세요.	Please eat first. Or: Please eat before the others.
내가 먼저 떠났어요.	I left earlier.
먼저 말한 것처럼 이것이 좋지 않아요.	As I told you before, this is not good.

STRUCTURE NOTES

I. The Sentence-Final Ending -ㄹ(을) 일이 있다…: 'have something to do'

The pattern -ㄹ(을) 일이 있다 means literally 'an act, work or business to be done exist.' It is used when you have some work, business or activity to do in the future, and it takes only action verbs. (The modifier suffix -ㄹ(을), used with action verbs, indicates future.

Examples:

부산에 갈 일이 있어요.	I have to go to Pusan.
친구를 만날 일이 있어요.	I have to meet my friend.
지금 볼 일이 있어요.	I have to see to some business now.
지금 볼 일이 없어요.	I have no business to see to now.
그분한테 편지를 쓸 일이 있어요.	I have to write him.
친구한테 부탁할 일이 있어요.	I have to ask my friend some favors.
친구를 찾아갈 일이 있어요.	I have to visit my friend.

Notes:

1. The tense and/or negation is expressed regularly in the final verb. Study the following examples:

지금 볼 일이 있어요.	I have something to see to now.
그 때에 볼 일이 있었어요.	I had something to see to at that time.
지금 볼 일이 없어요.	I have nothing to see to now.
그 때에 볼 일이 없었어요.	I had nothing to see to at that time.

2. -ㄹ 일이 있다(없다) is used after verb stems ending in a vowel;
   -을 일이 있다(없다) is used after verb stems ending in a consonant.

II. The Intentional -(으)려고 하다…: 'intend to do,' 'be going to do'

The sentence-final ending -(으)려고 하다 is used with action verbs, as well as with the verb 있다; it indicates a subject's intention or determination to act in a certain way. The English equivalent of this pattern is 'intend to do,' 'plan to do,' 'have it in mind to do,' 'be going to do,' etc.

Examples:

서울에 한 달쯤 있으려고 해요.	I intend to stay in Seoul about one month.
그분이 가려고 해요.	He intends to go. Or: He is going to go. Or: He plans to go.

복습하려고 해요.	I'm going to review. Or: I intend to review. Or: I plan to review.
낮잠을 자려고 해요.	I'm going to take a nap.
그분한테 부탁하려고 해요.	I'm going to ask him a favor.

The negation is expressed in the main verb with -(으)려고, not in the final verb 하다. Study the following examples:

그것을 사려고 해요.	I'm going to buy it.
그것을 사지 않으려고 해요.	I'm not going to buy it.

However, the tense is expressed in the final verb 하다, not in the main verb with -(으)려고. Study the following examples:

그것을 사려고 해요.	I am going to buy it.
그것을 사려고 했어요.	I was going to buy it.

Notes:

1. This pattern -(으)려고 하다 may be used with all persons, whereas the intentional -ㄹ(을)께요 is used only with first person statements, (cf. Unit 18, Structure Notes III), and the intentional -(을)래요 is used with first person statements and second person questions, (cf. Unit 23, Structure Notes II). Study the following examples:

나는 내일 갈께요.	I'll go tomorrow. Or: I intend to go tomorrow.
나는 내일 갈래요.	I'll go tomorrow. Or: I'm going to go tomorrow.
내일 가실래요?	Will you go tomorrow? Or: Do you intend to go tomorrow?
나는 내일 가려고 해요.	I'm going to go tomorrow.
내일 가시려고 해요?	Are you going to go tomorrow?
그분도 가려고 해요.	He too intends to go tomorrow.

2. -려고 하다 is used after verb stems ending in a vowel;
   -으려고 하다 is used after verb stems ending in a consonant.

III. The Ending -(으)려고: A.V.S. +-(으)려고…: 'in order to'

We have already studied the ending -(으)러, which indicates the purpose of an action, (See Unit 20, Structure Notes I.) This non-final ending -(으)려고 is interchangeable with -(으)러, making no major difference in meaning. However, a small difference is that the ending -(으)러 is followed always by either 가다, 오다 or their compounds, while the ending -(으)려고 can be followed by any action verb.

Examples :

아버지한테 주려고 이것을 샀어요.	I bought this for (to give to) my father.
부산에 가려고 일찍 일어났어요.	I got up early to go to Pusan.
독일에 가려고 독어를 공부해요.	I'm studying German to go to Germany.
친구를 만나려고 여기에 왔어요.	I came here to meet my friend.
차를 사려고 돈을 빌렸어요.	I borrowed money in order to buy a car.

Notes :

1. The tense and/or negation is expressed regularly in the final verb, not in the verb with -(으)려고. Study the following examples :

친구한테 주려고 그것을 삽니다.	I am buying it for (to give to) my friend.
친구한테 주려고 그것을 샀어요.	I bought it for (to give to) my friend.
친구한테 주려고 그것을 사지 않았어요.	I didn't buy it for (to give to) my friend.

2. This pattern -(으)려고 usually takes the past or present tense in the final verb, but it is never used in the future tense.
3. -려고 is used after verb stems ending in a vowel, and the consonant -ㄹ ; -으려고 is used after verb stems ending in all consonants except -ㄹ.

DRILLS

ADDITIONAL VOCABULARY

중요하다	to be important	고기	meat
칭찬하다	to praise	계란	eggs
빌리다	to borrow		

A. Substitution Drill

1. 무슨 급한 일이 있으세요?	Do you have anything urgent to do?
2. 무슨 기분 나쁜 일이 있으세요?	Do you have anything unpleasant to do?
3. 무슨 재미있는 일이 있으세요?	Do you have anything interesting to do?
4. 무슨 복잡한 일이 있으세요?	Do you have anything complicated to do?
5. 무슨 어려운 일이 있으세요?	Do you have anthing difficult to do?
6. 무슨 중요한 일이 있으세요?	Do you have anything important to do?
7. 무슨 기쁜 일이 있으세요?	Do you have anything happy to do?
8. 무슨 슬픈 일이 있으세요?	Do you have anything sorrowful to do?

B. Substitution Drill

1. 부산에 갈 일이 있어요.	I have to go to Pusan.

2. 친구를 만날 일이 있어요. — I have to meet my friend.
3. 지금 볼 일이 있어요. — I have some business to attend to now.
4. 친구한테 부탁할 일이 있어요. — I have to ask my friend some favors.
5. 그분한테 편지를 쓸 일이 있어요. — I have to write letter to him.
6. 친구를 찾아 갈 일이 있어요. — I have to visit my friend.
7. 사양할 일이 있어요. — I have to decline (it) respectfully.
8. 그분한테 전화할 일이 있어요. — I have to make a phone call to him.

C. Substitution Drill

1. 복습하려고 합니다. — I intend to review. Or : I plan to review. Or : I'm going to review.
2. 낮잠을 자려고 합니다. — I intend to take a nap.
3. 사양하려고 합니다. — I intend to decline (it) with respectfully.
4. 내가 결정하려고 합니다. — I intend to make a decision.
5. 전화하려고 합니다. — I intend to make a phone call.
6. 이 차를 운전하려고 합니다. — I intend to drive this car.
7. 그것을 고치려고 합니다. — I intend to repair it.
8. 약혼하려고 합니다. — I'm going to get engaged.

D. Pattern Drill

Teacher : 복습하려고 합니다. — I intend to review.
Student : 복습하지 않으려고 합니다. — I don't intend to review.

1. 바람이 불려고 합니다. — 바람이 불지 않으려고 합니다.
2. 번개가 치려고 합니다. — 번개가 치지 않으려고 합니다.
3. 등산을 가려고 합니다. — 등산을 가지 않으려고 합니다.
4. 사냥을 가려고 합니다. — 사냥을 가지 않으려고 합니다.
5. 사양하려고 합니다. — 사양하지 않으려고 합니다.
6. 인사하려고 합니다. — 인사하지 않으려고 합니다.
7. 칭찬하려고 합니다. — 칭찬하지 않으려고 합니다.

E. Pattern Drill

Teacher : 공부하려고 했어요. — I was going to study.
Student : 공부하지 않으려고 했어요. — I was not going to study.

1. 전화하려고 했어요. — 전화하지 않으려고 했어요.
2. 결심하려고 했어요. — 결심하지 않으려고 했어요.
3. 수술하려고 했어요. — 수술하지 않으려고 했어요.
4. 지나가려고 했어요. — 지나가지 않으려고 했어요.

5. 애기를 안으려고 했어요. 애기를 안지 않으려고 했어요.
6. 그것을 덮으려고 했어요. 그것을 덮지 않으려고 했어요.
7. 애기를 낳으려고 했어요. 애기를 낳지 않으려고 했어요.
8. 돈을 벌려고 했어요. 돈을 벌지 않으려고 했어요.

F. Integration Drill

Teacher: 독일에 가려고 합니다. 독일말을 공부합니다.
I am going to go to Germany. I'm studying German.
Student: 독일에 가려고 독일말을 공부합니다.
I'm studying German to go to Germany.

1. 친구를 만나려고 합니다. 여기에 옵니다.
친구를 만나려고, 여기에 옵니다.
2. 차를 사려고 했습니다. 돈을 빌렸습니다.
차를 사려고, 돈을 빌렸습니다.
3. 아버지한테 드리려고 했습니다. 이것을 샀습니다.
아버지한테 드리려고, 이것을 샀습니다.
4. 술을 마시려고 했습니다. 거기에 갔습니다.
술을 마시려고, 거기에 갔습니다.
5. 계란을 삶으려고 했어요. 이것을 가지고 왔어요.
계란을 삶으려고, 이것을 가지고 왔어요.
6. 고기를 구우려고 했어요. 여기에 왔어요.
고기를 구우려고, 여기에 왔어요.
7. 선교사로 일하려고 합니다. 한국말을 공부합니다.
선교사로 일하려고, 한국말을 공부합니다.
8. 그분을 도와주려고 했습니다. 거기에 들어갔습니다.
그분을 도와주려고, 거기에 들어갔습니다.

G. Response Drill (Review)

Teacher: 내일 가실래요? Will you go tomorrow?
Student: 예, 내일 갈래요. Yes, I'll go tomorrow.

1. 노래를 부르실래요? 예, 노래를 부를래요.
2. 쳐다보실래요? 예, 쳐다볼래요.
3. 내려다보실래요? 예, 내려다볼래요.
4. 내다보실래요? 예, 내다볼래요.
5. 들여다보실래요? 예, 들여다볼래요.
6. 인사하실래요? 예, 인사할래요.
7. 조심하실래요? 예, 조심할래요.
8. 약속하실래요? 예, 약속할래요.

H. Substitution Drill (Review)

1. 내가 내일 갈께요.	I'll go tomorrow.
2. 내가 사양할께요.	I'll decline respectfully.
3. 내가 결정할께요.	I'll make a decision.
4. 내가 그것을 삶을께요.	I'll boil it.
5. 내가 그것을 구울께요.	I'll roast it.
6. 내가 그것을 덮을께요.	I'll cover it.
7. 내가 그것을 계속할께요.	I'll continue it.
8. 내가 그것을 약속할께요.	I'll promise it.

SHORT STORIES

1. 그분은 몸이 아주 튼튼합니다.
그런데 나는 몸이 약합니다.
그래서 오늘부터 운동을 시작하려고 합니다.

몸	one's body
튼튼하다	to be strong
약하다	to be weak

Expansion Drill

그분은 몸이 아주 튼튼한데, 나는 몸이 약해서 오늘부터 운동을 시작하려고 합니다.

2. 차를 사려고 돈을 빌렸습니다.
한 달 후에 갚으려고 합니다.
열심히 일하면 갚을 수 있을 것 같아요.

갚다	to pay back

Expansion Drill

차를 사려고 돈을 빌렸는데, 한 달 후에 갚으려고 합니다. 열심히 일하면 갚을 수 있을 것 같아요.

3. 급한 일이 생겼습니다.
그래서 친구한테 부탁할 일이 있어서 찾아갔어요.
그런데 친구가 없어서 그냥 돌아왔어요.

생기다	to happen, to take place
그냥	in the same way as before, as it is (was)

Expansion Drill

급한 일이 생겼습니다. 친구한테 부탁할 일이 있어서 찾아갔는데, 친구가 없어서 그냥 돌아왔어요.

READING

어제는 친구의 생일이었습니다. 나는 친구한테서 초대를 받았습니다. 그래서 선물을 하나 사 가지고 갔습니다. 친구의 집에 가니까, 사람이 많이 와 있었습니다. 우리는 아주 재미있게들 놀았습니다. 나는 더 놀고 싶었습니다. 그런데 다른 친구를 만날 일이 있었습니다. 그래서 놀다가 돌아왔습니다. 나는 친구를 만나려고 다방에 갔습니다. 그런데 그 친구가 제 시간에 나오지 않았습니다. 그래서 그분이 도착할 때까지 약 십 분 기다렸습니다. 그 친구와 저녁을 같이 먹고 싶었습니다. 그런데 그 친구가 사양했습니다.

생일	a birthday	초대를 받다	to receive an invitation
초대	an invitation	선물	a gift
초대하다	to invite	와 있었다	lit. (They) came and were (there).
받다	to receive		

BRIEFING

Yesterday was my friend's birthday. He invited me to his party. So I bought a gift and went to his house. When I got to my friend's house, a lot of people were there. We had a wonderful time. I wanted to have a little more fun, but I had to meet another friend. I came back home, and then I went to the tearoom to meet my friend. But my friend didn't come on time. So I waited for him for about 10 minutes until he arrived. I wanted to eat dinner with him, but my friend refused with thanks.

UNIT 32 복습 Review

BASIC SENTENCES : MEMORIZE

최 인 숙

1. 지금 무엇을 하고 계세요? — What are you doing now?

    녹음기 — a tape-recorder

박 성 철

2. 녹음기로 복습하고 있어요. — I'm reviewing with a taperecorder.

    하루 — a day, one day

    몇 시간쯤 — about how many hours

최 인 숙

3. 하루에 몇 시간쯤 복습하세요? — About how many hours do you review a day?

    대개 — generally, mostly, nearly, about

    숙제 — homework

박 성 철

4. 대개 두 시간쯤 복습해요. 그런데 숙제가 많아서 죽겠어요. — Generally, I review about two hours. But there is so much homework that I could die.

    과로하다 — to overwork

    적당히 — reasonably, adequately

최 인 숙

5. 과로하지 말고, 적당히 공부하세요. — Don't overwork, just study reasonably.

    혼나다 — to have a hard time, to have a bitter experience

박 성 철

6. 그러나, 숙제를 안 하면, 선생님한테 혼나요. — But, if I don't do my homework, my teacher will give me a hard time.

USEFUL EXPRESSIONS : MEMORIZE

1. 섭섭합니다. — I miss you. Or : I'm sad, (disappointed).
2. 사과합니다. — I apologize to you.
3. 용서하세요. — Pardon (forgive) me, please.

NOTES ON THE BASIC SENTENCES

2. 녹음기 is a noun which means literally 'a recording machine.' Study the following words relating to (sound) recording.
   녹음하다 'to record'
   녹음실 'a recording room'
   녹음 테이프 'a recording tape'
   복습하고: When the consonant -ㅂ occurs as a final consonant, and is followed directly by the consonant ㅎ of the next syllable, ㅎ is pronounced as ㅍ. Therefore, 복습하고 is pronounced as 복습파고.
4. 대개, a noun meaning 'an outline,' 'a summary,' can also be used as an adverb meaning 'generally,' 'mostly,' 'for the most part,' 'nearly,' 'almost,' et. Study the following examples:
   대개 늦게 집에 갑니다. I usually go home late.
   일요일엔 대개 낚시질 가요. I go fishing nearly every Sunday.
   한국 사람은 대개 김치를 좋아해요. Most Koreans like kimchi.
5. 과로하다 means 'to overwork,' 'to work too hard.' 과 indicates 'excess,' 'immoderation,' or 'to pass.' Study the following words:
   과식하다 'to overeat,' 'to eat too much'
   과음하다 'to drink too much'
   과용하다 'to spend too much'
   과신하다 'to place too much confidence (in a person),' 'to be overconfident'
   적당히 is an adverb meaning 'adequately,' 'reasonably,' 'properly,' suitably.' Study the following examples:
   적당히 일하세요. Just work reasonably.
   적당히 하세요. Do as you see fit.
   적당한 값으로 사세요. Buy it at a reasonable price.
6. 혼나다, depending on the context or situation, can mean (1) 'to get frightened out of one's wits,' 'to be startled (horrified),' (2) 'to have a bitter experience,' 'to have a hard time of it.' It is used always with the particle -한테 'by,' whereas 혼내다, 'to make (a person) smart,' 'to give (a person) a hard time' is used always with the object particle -를/-을. Study the following examples, and note particularly noting the preceding particles.
   개한테 혼났어요. I got frightened by a dog.
   선생님한테 혼났어요. I was severely scolded by my teacher.
   그분을 혼내 주겠어요. I'll get him to cry for mercy.

STRUCTURE NOTES

I. The Progressive -고 있다… : '(someone) is doing (something)'

The sentence-final ending -고 있다, preceded by action verbs, indicates a kind of process or continuing action.

Examples :

친구를 기다리고 있어요.	I'm waiting for my friend.
애기가 낮잠을 자고 있어요.	The baby is taking a nap.
동생이 편지를 쓰고 있어요.	My younger brother is writing a letter.
바람이 불고 있어요.	The wind is blowing.
지금 복습하고 있어요.	I'm reviewing now.
학생이 수영하고 있어요.	The student is swimming.

The tense and/or negation is expressed regularly in the final verb 있다, not in the main verb with -고. Study the following examples:

바람이 불고 있어요.	The wind is blowing.
바람이 불고 있지 않아요.	The wind is not blowing.
바람이 불고 있었어요.	The wind was blowing.
바람이 불고 있지 않았어요.	The wind was not blowing.

The final verb 있다 can be replaced by the honorific verb 계시다, whenever one addresses or refers to person of superior social standing: older people, teachers, doctors, foreigners, and so forth. Study the following examples:

무엇을 하고 계십니까?	What are you doing now?
아버지가 주무시고 계세요.	My father is sleeping.
선생님이 점심을 잡수시고 계세요.	My teacher is eating lunch.
형님이 책을 읽고 계세요.	My older brother is reading a book.
그분이 일하고 계시지 않아요.	He is not working.

However, this pattern can have two different meanings when used with verbs dealing with items of clothing; some of these one: 입다 'to put on (clothes),' 쓰다 'to put on (a hat),' 신다 'to put on (shoes),' etc. Study the following examples:

그분이 새 옷을 입고 있어요.	She is putting on a new dress. Or : She has on a new dress.
그분이 모자를 쓰고 있었어요.	He was putting on a hat. Or : He had on a hat.
그분이 신을 신고 있어요.	He is putting on his shoes. Or : He has his shoes on.

그분이 넥타이를 매고 있었어요. He was putting on a necktie. Or : He had on a necktie.

This pattern -고 있다, when preceded by a time word+a particle, (such as -부터 'from' or -동안 'during,' 'for'), indicates an action which took place in the past, and is still going on. Study the following examples:

지난 달부터 일하고 있어요. I've been working since last month (lit. I'm working from last month.)

여기서 십 년동안 일하고 있어요. I've been working here for the past ten years.

Notes:

1. A simple verb indicates an action itself, making no reference to duration of time; however, the progressive form indicates the fact that an action lasts for a while. Study the following examples:

   한국말을 공부했어요. I studied Korea.

   한국말을 공부하고 있었어요. I was studying Korean.

2. This pattern -고 있다 cannot be used for the immediate future, like 'I'm leaving' for 'I'll leave' in English.

II. The Pattern -아(-어, -여)서 죽겠다… : 'because of (so-and-so), I could die'

This pattern -아(-어, -여)서 죽겠다 may be used with any verb, except -이다. However, it's used mostly with description verbs. When the causal non-final ending -아(-어, -여)서 is followed by 죽겠다 'will die,' it indicates extreme anxiety, pain, or anguish, caused by a certain fact or event.

Examples:

보고 싶어서 죽겠어요. I'm dying to see you.

피곤해서 죽겠어요. I'm so tired, I could die.

날씨가 추워서 죽겠어요. The weather is so cold that I could die.

그분이 자꾸 찾아와서 죽겠어요. Because he keeps coming to see me, I could die.

요즘 돈이 없어서 죽겠어요. Because I don't have any money these days, I could die.

배가 고파서 죽겠어요. I feel so hungry, I could die.

비가 너무 와서 죽겠어요. Because it's raining so much, I could die.

머리가 아파서 죽겠어요. Because of my headaches, I could die.

Notes:

1. The particle -서 after -아(-어, -여) may be dropped, making no differ-

ence in meaning. But it's better to practice it in the beginning.

2. -아서 죽겠다 is used after -아 and -오 ;
-어서 죽겠다 is used after any other vowel ;
-여서 죽겠다 is used after 하다, or the stem of the verb -하다.

III. A.V.S. +-지 말고… : 'not, (but)…'

We have already studied the pattern A.V.S. +-지 말다, which indicates prohibition or dissuasion. This pattern -지 말고 is a compound pattern : i.e., -지 말(다), plus -고 meaning 'and.' It is used when you attempt to dissuade someone from doing a certain action, in favor of another.

Examples :

일하지 말고, 쉬세요.	Don't work, (but) rest.
주무시지 말고, 일어나세요.	Don't sleep ; get up.
떠들지 말고, 조용히 하세요.	Don't make noise, (but) be quiet.
울지 말고, 웃으세요.	Don't cry ; laugh.
여기에 계시지 말고, 집에 가세요.	Don't stay here ; go home.
올라가지 말고, 내려오세요.	Don't go up ; come down.
산보하지 말고, 공부합시다.	Let's study without taking a walk.
술을 마시지 말고,. 갑시다.	Let's go without drinking.
놀지 말고, 일합시다.	Let's work without playing around.

This pattern -지 말고 is followed mostly by imperative or propositive forms, whereas -지 않고 doesn't have this limitation. Study the following examples :

아침을 먹지 않고, 왔어요.	I came without eating breakfast.
일하지 않고, 가겠어요.	I'll go without working.
싸우지 않고, 잘 놀아요.	They play well without fighting.

Notes :

1. The pattern -지 말고 may be used with action verbs, and the verb of existence 있다. However, it usually goes with action verbs.
2. When -말고 (without -지) is preceded by a noun, it is used to express rejection of one object, in fovor of another. Study the following examples :

이것 말고, 다른 것 없어요?	Don't you have something else, besides this one?
만년필 말고, 연필 주세요.	Give me a pencil, not a fountain pen.

DRILLS

ADDITIONAL VOCABULARY

모자	a hat	장갑	gloves
쓰다	to put on (hat, glasses)	끼다	to put on (gloves, ring)
신다	to put on (shoes, socks)	양말	(socks)
안경	glasses	차다	to put on (watch, sword)

A. Substitution Drill

1. 친구를 기다리고 있습니다. — I'm waiting for my friend.
2. 예습하고 있습니다. — I'm preparing the lessons.
3. 바람이 불고 있습니다. — The wind is blowing.
4. 학생이 수영하고 있습니다. — The student is swimming.
5. 창밖을 내다보고 있습니다. — I'm looking out the window.
6. 물을 끓이고 있습니다. — I'm boiling water.
7. 그 일을 계속하고 있습니다. — I'm continuing that work.
8. 계란을 삶고 있습니다. — I'm boiling eggs.

B. Substitution Drill

1. 아버지가 주무시고 계십니다. — My father is sleeping.
2. 선생님이 점심을 잡수시고 계십니다. — My teacher is eating lunch.
3. 형님이 책을 읽고 계십니다. — My older brother is reading a book.
4. 어머니가 밖에서 일하고 계십니다. — My mother is working outside.
5. 누님이 목욕하고 계십니다. — My older sister is taking a bath.
6. 그분이 면도하고 계십니다. — He is shaving (himself).
7. 할아버지가 그분을 도와주고 계십니다. — My grandfather is helping him.
8. 할머니가 편지를 쓰고 계십니다. — My grandmother is writing a letter.

C. Substitution Drill

1. 그 여자가 옷을 입고 있습니다. — She is putting on a dress. Or: She has on a dress.
2. 그분이 모자를 쓰고 있습니다. — He is putting on a hat. Or: He has a hat on.
3. 그분이 신을 신고 있습니다. — He is putting on his shoes. Or: He has his shoes on.
4. 그분이 넥타이를 매고 있습니다. — He is putting on a necktie. Or: He has on a necktie.

5. 그분이 안경을 쓰고 있습니다. — He is putting on his glasses. Or : He has his glasses on.

6. 그분이 장갑을 끼고 있습니다. — He is putting on his socks. Or : He has his socks on.

7. 그분이 양말을 신고 있습니다. — He is putting on his socks. Or : He has his socks on.

8. 그분이 시계를 차고 있습니다. — He is putting on his watch. Or : He has his watch on.

9. 그분이 옷을 벗고 있습니다. — He is taking off his clothes. Or : He has his clothes off.

D. Substitution Drill

1. 그분을 보고 싶어서 죽겠어요. — I'm dying to see him.
2. 피곤해서 죽겠어요. — I'm so tired, I could die.
3. 날씨가 추워서 죽겠어요. — The weather is so cold that I could die.
4. 그분이 자꾸 찾아와서 죽겠어요. — Because he keeps coming to see me, I could die.
5. 요즘 돈이 없어서 죽겠어요. — Because I don't have any money these days, I could die.
6. 배가 고파서 죽겠어요. — I feel so hungry, I could die.
7. 너무 비가 와서 죽겠어요. — It's raining so much that I could die.
8. 머리가 아파서 죽겠어요. — Because of my headaches, I could die.

E. Pattern Drill

Teacher : 바람이 불고 있어요. — The wind is blowing.
Student : 바람이 불고 있지 않아요. — The wind is not blowing.

1. 구경하고 있어요. — 구경하고 있지 않아요.
2. 편지를 쓰고 있어요. — 편지를 쓰고 있지 않아요.
3. 대답하고 있어요. — 대답하고 있지 않아요.
4. 생각하고 있어요. — 생각하고 있지 않아요.
5. 옷을 갈아입고 있어요. — 옷을 갈아입고 있지 않아요.
6. 장난하고 있어요. — 장난하고 있지 않아요.
7. 그것을 넣고 있어요. — 그것을 넣고 있지 않아요.
8. 그것을 꺼내고 있어요. — 그것을 꺼내고 있지 않아요.

F. Pattern Drill

Teacher : 바람이 불고 있었어요. — The wind was blowing.
Student : 바람이 불고 있지 않았어요. — The wind was not blowing.

1. 전화하고 있었어요. — 전화하고 있지 않았어요.

2. 걱정하고 있었어요.	걱정하고 있지 않았어요.
3. 수술하고 있었어요.	수술하고 있지 않았어요.
4. 애기를 안고 있었어요.	애기를 안고 있지 않았어요.
5. 돈을 벌고 있었어요.	돈을 벌고 있지 않았어요.
6. 돈을 빌리고 있었어요.	돈을 빌리고 있지 않았어요.
7. 그분을 칭찬하고 있었어요.	그분을 칭찬하고 있지 않았어요.
8. 복습하고 있었어요.	복습하고 있지 않았어요.

G. Pattern Drill

Teacher: 아버지가 주무시고 계세요.
My father is sleeping.

Student: 아버지가 주무시고 계시지 않아요.
My father is not sleeping.

1. 어머니가 잡수시고 계세요.	어머니가 잡수시고 계시지 않아요.
2. 그분이 수영하고 계세요.	그분이 수영하고 계시지 않아요.
3. 형님이 걱정하고 계세요.	형님이 걱정하고 계시지 않아요.
4. 누님이 옷을 입고 계세요.	누님이 옷을 입고 계시지 않아요.
5. 그분이 고기를 굽고 계세요.	그분이 고기를 굽고 계시지 않아요.
6. 그분이 놀고 계세요.	그분이 놀고 계시지 않아요.
7. 선생님이 가르치고 계세요.	선생님이 가르치고 계시지 않아요.
8. 신부님이 일하고 계세요.	신부님이 일하고 계시지 않아요.

H. Pattern Drill

Teacher: 아버지가 주무시고 계셨어요.
My father was sleeping.

Student: 아버지가 주무시고 계시지 않았어요.
My father was not sleeping.

1. 목사님이 웃고 계셨어요.	목사님이 웃고 계시지 않았어요.
2. 누님이 울고 계셨어요.	누님이 울고 계시지 않았어요.
3. 수녀님이 그것을 씻고 계셨어요.	수녀님이 그것을 씻고 계시지 않았어요.
4. 수사님이 물을 끓이고 계셨어요.	수사님이 물을 끓이고 계시지 않았어요.
5. 어머니가 도와주고 계셨어요.	어머니가 도와주고 계시지 않았어요.
6. 그분이 초인종을 누르고 계셨어요.	그분이 초인종을 누르고 계시지 않았어요.
7. 그분이 밖을 내다보고 계셨어요.	그분이 밖을 내다보고 계시지 않았어요.
8. 형님이 쳐다보고 계셨어요.	형님이 쳐다보고 계시지 않았어요.

I. Integration Drill

Teacher: 일하지 마세요. 쉬세요. Don't work. Rest.

Student : 일하지 말고, 쉬세요.	Don't work, (but) rest.
1. 돈을 벌지 마세요. 쓰세요.	돈을 벌지 말고, 쓰세요.
2. 울지 마세요. 웃으세요.	울지 말고, 웃으세요.
3. 돈을 빌리지 마세요. 갚으세요.	돈을 빌리지 말고, 갚으세요.
4. 약속을 어기지 마세요. 지키세요.	약속을 어기지 말고, 지키세요.
5. 넘어지지 마세요. 일어나세요.	넘어지지 말고, 일어나세요.
6. 결정하지 맙시다. 갑시다.	결정하지 말고, 갑시다.
7. 사양하지 맙시다. 받읍시다.	사양하지 말고, 받읍시다.
8. 교통 신호를 위반하지 맙시다. 지킵시다.	교통 신호를 위반하지 말고, 지킵시다.

J. Integration Drill

Teacher : 먹지 않겠어요. 가겠어요.	I won't eat. I'll go.
Student : 먹지 않고 가겠어요.	I'll go without eating.
1. 아침을 안 먹었어요. 왔어요.	아침을 안 먹고 왔어요.
2. 연습하지 않았어요. 갔어요.	연습하지 않고 갔어요.
3. 쳐다보지 않았어요. 갔어요.	쳐다보지 않고 갔어요.
4. 사양하지 않았어요. 받았어요.	사양하지 않고 받았어요.
5. 약속을 지키지 않았어요. 어겼어요.	약속을 지키지 않고 어겼어요.
6. 돈을 갚지 않았어요. 빌렸어요.	돈을 갚지 않고 빌렸어요.
7. 결정하지 않았어요. 했어요.	결정하지 않고 했어요.
8. 전화하지 않았어요. 갔어요.	전화하지 않고 갔어요.

SHORT STORIES

1. 집에서 공부하고 있었어요.
   그런데 친구가 찾아왔어요.
   그래서 공부를 그만두고 친구하고 놀았어요.

   그만두다 to stop (doing), to cease (doing)

   Expansion Drill

   집에서 공부하고 있는데, 친구가 찾아와서, 공부를 그만두고 친구하고 놀았어요.

2. 아버지를 만나러 사무실에 들어갔어요.
   그런데 아버지가 일하고 계셨어요.
   그래서 말씀드리지 않고 나왔어요.

Expansion Drill

아버지를 만나러 사무실에 들어갔는데, 아버지가 일하고 계셨기 때문에, 말씀드리지 않고 나왔어요.

3. 지금 피곤해서 죽겠어요.
그러니까 지금 이 일을 하지 말고, 내일 합시다.
과로하면 건강에 나빠요. 건강 health

Expansion Drill

지금 피곤해서 죽겠으니까, 지금 이 일을 하지 말고, 내일 합시다. 과로하면 건강에 나빠요.

READING

녹음실에서 녹음하고 있었습니다. 그런데 친한 친구가 찾아왔습니다. 그래서 나는 녹음하다가 그만두었습니다. 나는 친구하고 같이 술집에 술을 마시러 갔습니다. 밤 늦게까지 술을 마셨습니다. 술값은 친구가 내었습니다. 친구가 과용한 것 같습니다. 오늘 아침에 일어나니까, 머리가 아팠습니다. 과음하면 건강에 나쁩니다. 그런데 나는 과음했습니다. 난 이제 늙었습니다. 내가 젊었을 때는 과음해도 괜찮았습니다. 그리고 좀 과식해도 괜찮았습니다. 요즘은 과음하면 다음날 좋지 않습니다. 내가 내 건강을 너무 과신하는 것 같습니다. 건강에 주의해야겠습니다.

녹음실	a recording room	이제	now
녹음하다	to record	늙다	to grow old
술값	drinking money	젊다	to be young
내다	to pay	과식하다	to overeat
과용하다	to spend too much	과신하다	to be overconfident
과음하다	to drink too much		

BRIEFING

I was recording in the recording room. But my close friend visited me. So I stopped recording. I went to the bar with my friend to drink. We drank until midnight. My friend paid for the drinks. I think my friend spent too much money. When I got up this morning I had headache. If I drink too much it's bad for my health. But I drank too much. Now I am old. When I was young it was alright even if I drank too much. And it was alright even if I overate. These days if I drink too much I don't feel good the follwoing day. I think I'm overconfident about my health. I must be careful for my health.

UNIT 33 아이들 Children

BASIC SENTENCES : MEMORIZE

아이들 — children

모두 — altogether, in all

최 인 숙

1. 아이들이 모두 몇이나 됩니까? — (About) how many children do you have?

박 성 철

2. 모두 일곱이나 됩니다. — Altogether there are seven.

큰 애 — the oldest child

몇 살 — how old

최 인 숙

3. 제일 큰 애가 몇 살입니까? — How old is your oldest child?

열 여섯 살 — sixteen years old

고등 학교 — a high school

다니다 — to attend

박 성 철

4. 열 여섯 살이에요. 지금 고등 학교에 다니고 있어요. — He is sixteen years old. He is attending hight school now.

정신 — mind, spirit, soul

최 인 숙

5. 집에 가면 정신이 없지요? — If you go home, I bet you can't think straight, can you?

시끄럽다 — to be noisy

싸우다 — to fight

박 성 철

6. 그럼요. 여간 시끄럽지 않아요. 잘 놀기도 하고, 잘 싸우기도 해요. — Really, It is extremely noisy. They both play well and fight well.

USEFUL EXPRESSIONS : MEMORIZE

1. 화를 내지 마세요. — Don't get angry.
2. 축하합니다. — Congratulations.
3. 덕택에. — Thanks for your help, (favor, aid).

NOTES ON THE BASIC SENTENCES

1. 되다 'to become,' depending on the context or situation, can have many meanings. In the context of Sentence 1, 되다 means 'to have,' 'to exist.'
3. 제일 큰 애가 몇 살입니까? means 'How old is your oldest child?' 제일 is the superlative marker, (meaning literally 'the first,' 'number one').
   애 is a contraction of 아이 'a child,' 'a kid.' -살 'years of age' is a classifier used with Korean numbers. Study the following examples:

한 살	one year old	마흔 살	forty years old
두 살	two years old	쉰 살	fifty years old
세 살	three years old	예순 살	sixty years old
네 살	four years old	일흔 살	seventy years old
다섯 살	five years old	여든 살	eighty years old
열 살	ten years old	아흔 살	ninety years old
스무 살	twenty years old	백 살	one hundred years old
서른 살	thirty years old		

   But the classifier -세 'years of age' is used with Chinese numbers. Study the following examples:

이십 세	twenty years old	오십 세	fifty years old
삼십 세	thirty years old	육십 세	sixty years old
사십 세	forty years old	칠십 세	seventy years old

   나이 'age,' 'years' as an independent word is commonly used, whereas 연세 and 춘추 'one's honored age' are honorifics used when speaking to old people. Study the following examples:

나이가 몇입니까?	How old are you?
연세가 몇이십니까?	How old are you?(honorific)
춘추가 몇이십니까?	How old are you? (very honorific)

4. 고등 학교 means 'a (liberal) high school.' Study the following words relating to school, which make up particularly the Korean education system.
   유치원 'a kindergarten,' which is a one year course.
   국민 학교 'a primary (elementary) school,' which is a six year course.
   중 학교 'a middle school,' which is a three year course.
   고등 학교 'a high school,' which is a three year course.
   대 학교 'a college,' which is a four year course.
   대 학원 'a graduate school,' which is a two year course.
5. 정신이 없다 means literally 'I have no mind (spirit). This expression is used

(1) when you are distracted, (2) when it's so noisy that you can't think straight, (3) when you forget something completely.

STRUCTURE NOTES

I. The Particle -(이)나 :

This particle -(이)나, depending on the context or situation, can have many different meanings.

1. Noun +-(이)나… : 'or something'

The particle -(이)나, when preceded directly by a noun, indicates a selection or an option. Study the following examples:

술이나 마시겠어요.	I'll drink some wine (or something.)
한국말이나 공부합시다.	Let's study Korean (or something).
불고기나 먹겠어요.	I'll eat pulgogi (or something).
자동차나 하나 살까요?	Shall I buy a car (or something).
만년필이나 볼펜을 주세요.	Give me a fountain pen or ball pen.

2. 몇 + Noun +-(이)나… : 'about,' 'approximately'

When the particle -(이)나 is used with the word 몇- 'how many,' it indicates approximation. Study the following examples:

몇 사람이나 오셨어요?	About how many people came?
몇 권이나 사셨어요?	About how many books did you buy?
몇 번이나 읽으셨어요?	About how many times did you read it?
몇 시간이나 공부하시겠어요?	About how many hours will you study?
맥주를 몇 병이나 마셨어요?	About how many bottles of beer did you drink?

3. Number + Noun +-(이)나… : 'more than expected'

When the particle -(이)나 is used with numbers, it indicates 'much more than is expected.' Study the following examples:

맥주를 열 병이나 마셨어요.	He drank ten bottles of beer, (more than I thought).
어제 열 시간이나 공부했어요.	I studied ten hours yesterday, (much more than expected).
그 책을 다섯 번이나 읽었어요.	I read that book five times.
벌써 일곱 시나 되었어요.	It's seven o'clock already.

4. Noun + Other Particle +-나 :

The particle -나 can also be used with other particles, and indicates selection of place, time, etc. Study the following examples:

집에나 갈까요? — Shall we go home (or some place)?

저녁에나 시간이 있을 것 같아요. — I think I'll have time in the evening (or sometime).

Notes:

This particle -(이)나 can further be used with other words, such as 아무 'any (person),' or the interrogative pronouns 무엇 'what,' 누구 'who,' etc. But this will be studied later in detail.

II. The particle -도(…-도)…: 'both…and…,' '(n)either…(n)or…'

We have studied the particle -도 when it means 'also,' 'too,' 'even,' 'indeed,' etc. Now let's study this particle -도 in more detail.

1. When the particle -도 (attached to a noun or other particles) is followed by a negative predicate, it means 'either.' Study the following examples:

나도 안 먹겠어요.	I won't eat either.
책도 안 샀어요.	I did not buy a book either.
집에서도 공부하지 않아요.	I don't study at home either.
그분은 밤에도 안 자요.	He doesn't sleep at night either.
이 책도 좋지 않아요.	This book isn't good either.

2. When there are two phrases in a row, each ending in -도, it means 'both …and…,' if the predicate is affirmative. Study the following examples:

나도 그분도 한국 사람이에요.	Both he and I are Korean.
책도 사고, 연필도 샀어요.	I bought both a book and a pencil.
바람도 불고, 비도 와요.	The wind is blowing and it's raining too.

3. But,…-도 …-도 means '(n)either …(n)or …,' if the predicate is negative. Study the following examples:

나도 안 가고, 그분도 안 갔어요.	Neither I nor he went. Or: I didn't go and he didn't go either.
춥지도 않고, 덥지도 않아요.	It's neither cold nor hot.
이것도 좋지 않고, 그것도 좋지 않아요.	Neither this nor that is good. Or: This isn't good and that isn't good either.
복숭아도 좋아하지 않고, 참외도 좋아하지 않아요.	I like neither peaches nor melons.

DRILLS

ADDITIONAL VOCABULARY

유치원	kindergarten	대학원	graduate school

국민학교	primary school	회사	a company
중학교	middle school	공장	a factory
고등학교	high school		

A. Substitution Drill

1. 유치원에 다니고 있어요.	I am attending kindergarten.
2. 국민학교에 다니고 있어요.	I am attending primary school.
3. 중학교에 다니고 있어요.	I am attending middle school.
4. 고등학교에 다니고 있어요.	I am attending hight school.
5. 대학교에 다니고 있어요.	I am attending university.
6. 대학원에 다니고 있어요.	I am attending graduate school.
7. 회사에 다니고 있어요.	I am working for a company.
8. 공장에 다니고 있어요.	I am working in a factory.

B. Substitution Drill

1. 그분이 열 여섯 살이에요.	He is sixteen years old.
2. 그분이 스무 살이에요.	He is twenty years old.
3. 그분이 스물 다섯 살이에요.	He is twenty five years old.
4. 그분이 서른 살이에요.	He is thirty years old.
5. 그분이 서른 한 살이에요.	He is thirty one years old.
6. 그분이 마흔 살이에요.	He is forty years old.
7. 그분이 마흔 두 살이에요.	He is forty two years old.
8. 그분이 쉰 세 살이에요.	He is fifty three years old.
9. 그분이 예순 네 살이에요.	He is sixty four years old.
10. 그분이 일흔 여덟 살이에요.	He is seventy eight years old.

C. Pattern Drill

Teacher : 술을 마시겠어요.	I'll drink some wine.
Student : 술이나 마시겠어요.	I'll drink some wine(or something).
1. 사냥을 가겠어요.	사냥이나 가겠어요.
2. 책을 읽겠어요.	책이나 읽겠어요.
3. 등산을 가겠어요.	등산이나 가겠어요.
4. 담배를 피우겠어요.	담배나 피우겠어요.
5. 소풍을 가겠어요.	소풍이나 가겠어요.
6. 한국말을 배우겠어요.	한국말이나 배우겠어요.
7. 이 일을 계속하겠어요.	이 일이나 계속하겠어요.
8. 복습을 하겠어요.	복습이나 하겠어요.

D. Pattern Drill

Teacher : 몇 사람이 오셨어요? — How many people came?

Student : 몇 사람이나 오셨어요? — About how many people came?

1. 몇 권을 사셨어요?	몇 권이나 사셨어요?
2. 몇 번(을) 읽으셨어요?	몇 번이나 읽으셨어요?
3. 맥주를 몇 병 마셨어요?	맥주를 몇 병이나 마셨어요?
4. 집을 몇 채 사셨어요?	집을 몇 채나 사셨어요?
5. 담배를 몇 갑 드릴까요?	담배를 몇 갑이나 드릴까요?
6. 그분이 몇 살 되었어요?	그분이 몇 살이나 되었어요?
7. 몇 시간 공부하셨어요?	몇 시간이나 공부하셨어요?
8. 차가 몇 대 있어요?	차가 몇 대나 있어요?

E. Pattern Drill

Teacher : 맥주를 열 병 마셨어요. — I drank ten bottles of beer.

Student : 맥주를 열 병이나 마셨어요. — I drank ten bottles of beer, (more than I thought).

1. 열 시간 공부했어요.	열 시간이나 공부했어요.
2. 다섯 번 읽었어요.	다섯 번이나 읽었어요.
3. 담배를 두 갑 피워요.	담배를 두 갑이나 피워요.
4. 책을 열 권 샀어요.	책을 열 권이나 샀어요.
5. 종이를 천 장 샀어요.	종이를 천 장이나 샀어요.
6. 다섯 달 가르쳤어요.	다섯 달이나 가르쳤어요.
7. 다섯 분 오셨어요.	다섯 분이나 오셨어요.
8. 일본에 삼 주일 있었어요.	일본에 삼 주일이나 있었어요.

F. Pattern Drill

Teacher : 저녁에 시간이 있어요. — I'll have time in the evening.

Student : 저녁에나 시간이 있어요. — I'll have time in the evening,(or sometime).

1. 집에 갑시다.	집에나 갑시다.
2. 극장에 갑시다.	극장에나 갑시다.
3. 월요일에 만납시다.	월요일에나 만납시다.
4. 아침에 가 봅시다.	아침에나 가 봅시다.
5. 낮에 먹읍시다.	낮에나 먹읍시다.
6. 밤에 시간이 있어요.	밤에나 시간이 있어요.
7. 새벽에 와 보세요.	새벽에나 와 보세요.
8. 부산에 갑시다.	부산에나 갑시다.

G. Pattern Drill

Teacher :	나도 점심을 먹었어요.	I also ate lunch.
Student :	나도 점심을 먹지 않았어요.	I didn't eat lunch either.

1. 책도 샀어요. — 책도 사지 않았아요.
2. 나도 사양했어요. — 나도 사양하지 않았어요.
3. 계란도 삶았어요. — 계란도 삶지 않았어요.
4. 나도 그분을 칭찬했어요. — 나도 그분을 칭찬하지 않았어요.
5. 그분도 좋아했어요. — 그분도 좋아하지 않았어요.
6. 이 책도 좋아요. — 이 책도 좋지 않아요.
7. 집에서도 공부했어요. — 집에서도 공부하지 않았어요.
8. 극장에도 갔어요. — 극장에도 가지 않았어요.

H. Integration Drill

Teacher : 책도 샀어요. 연필도 샀어요.
I bought a book too. I bought a pencil too.

Student : 책도사고, 연필도 샀어요.
I bought both a book and a pencil.

1. 바람도 불어요. 비도 와요.
바람도 불고, 비도 와요.
2. 일본말도 공부해요. 독일말도 공부해요.
일본말도 공부하고, 독일말도 공부해요.
3. 과로도 했어요. 과음도 했어요.
과로도 하고, 과음도 했어요.
4. 울기도 했어요. 웃기도 했어요.
울기도 하고, 웃기도 했어요.
5. 책도 읽겠어요. 편지도 쓰겠어요.
책도 읽고, 편지도 쓰겠어요.
6. 예습도 합니다. 복습도 합니다.
예습도 하고, 복습도 합니다.
7. 번개도 칩니다. 태풍도 붑니다.
번개도 치고, 태풍도 붑니다.
8. 춥기도 합니다. 배도 고픕니다.
춥기도 하고, 배도 고픕니다.

I. Integration Drill

Teacher : 나도 안 갔어요. 그분도 안 갔어요.
I didn't go either. He didn't go either.

Student : 나도 안 가고, 그분도 안 갔어요.
Neither I nor he went.

1. 시간도 없어요. 돈도 없어요.
시간도 없고, 돈도 없어요.
2. 전화도 안 했어요. 약속도 안 했어요.
전화도 안 하고, 약속도 안 했어요.
3. 말도 안 합니다. 인사도 안 합니다.
말도 안 하고, 인사도 안 합니다.
4. 과로도 안 합니다. 과음도 안 합니다.
과로도 안 하고, 과음도 안 합니다.
5. 시간도 안 지킵니다. 약속도 안 지킵니다.
시간도 안 지키고, 약속도 안 지킵니다.
6. 술도 안 마십니다. 담배도 안 피웁니다.
술도 안 마시고, 담배도 안 피웁니다.
7. 예습도 안 합니다. 복습도 안 합니다.
예습도 안 하고, 복습도 안 합니다.
8. 웃지도 않습니다. 울지도 않습니다.
웃지도 않고, 울지도 않습니다.

SHORT STORIES

1. 어제 저녁에 친구하고 맥주를 열 병이나 마셨어요.
그래서 모두 굉장히 취했어요.
집에 돌아오니까 열 두시 였어요.

Expansion Drill

어제 저녁에 친구하고 맥주를 열 병이나 마셨기 때문에, 모두 굉장히 취했어요. 집에 돌아오니까, 열 두 시였어요.

2. 지금은 너무 바빠서 시간이 없어요.
저녁에나 시간이 있을 것 같아요.
그 때에 저녁도 먹고 영화도 봅시다.

Expansion Drill

지금은 너무 바빠서 시간이 없어요. 저녁에나 시간이 있을 것 같으니까, 그 때에 저녁도 먹고 영화도 봅시다.

3. 친구하고 만나기로 약속했어요.
여기서 그분을 두 시간이나 기다렸어요.

그분이 안 오니까, 극장에나 가겠어요.

Expansion Drill

친구하고 만나기로 약속했기 때문에, 여기서 그분을 두 시간이나 기다렸어요. 그분이 안 오니까, 극장에나 가겠어요.

READING

저는 가족이 많습니다. 가족이 모두 일곱이나 됩니다. 아들이 셋이고 딸이 둘입니다. 그러니까 모두 삼남 이녀입니다. 큰 아들 (장남)은 대학교 삼학년입니다. 둘째 아들 (차남) 은 대학교 일 학년입니다. 그리고 셋째 아들 (삼남)은 고등학교 이 학년입니다. 큰 딸 (장녀)은 중학교에 다니는데, 이제 일 학년입니다. 그리고 작은 딸 (차녀)이 막내인데 지금 국민학교 사학년입니다. 그래서 생활비도 많이 들고, 교육비도 많이 듭니다.

가족	a family	삼남	the third son
아들	a son	장녀	the eldest daughter
딸	a daughter	차녀	the second (eldest) daughter
삼남 이녀	three sons and two daughters	막내	the lastborn
		생활비	living expenses
장남	the eldest son	들다	to be needed, to cost
차남	the second son	교육비	education expenses

BRIEFING

I have a large family. We are a family of seven, in all. I have three sons and two daughters. The eldest son is a junior in college. The second son is a freshman in college. The third son is a sophomore in high school. The eldest daughter is in the first year of middle school. The second daughter is the youngest and she is in the fourth grade. Therefore, both a lot of living expenses and education expenses are needed.

UNIT 34 공부 A Study

BASIC SENTENCES : MEMORIZE

조용히	quietly, silently, calmly, peacefully
박 성 철	
1. 공부할 때가 되었어요. 모두 조용히들 합시다.	It's time to study. Let's be quiet, everybody.
자	come on!
선 생 님	
2. 자! 책을 보지 말고, 잘 들어 보세요.	Come on! Don't look at the book, but try to listen well.
발음	pronunciation
질문	question
묻다	to ask
박 성 철	
3. 선생님! 발음에 대해서 질문이 있어요. 지금 물어 봐도 괜찮아요?	Teacher! I have a question about pronunciation. May I ask you a question now?
나중에	later
방해하다	to disturb, to interfere with, to interrupt
선 생 님	
4. 질문은 나중에 하세요. 지금 하면, 다른 학생한테 방해가 돼요.	Please ask a question (sometime) later. If you ask a question now, it becomes a bother to others
수업	the class, lesson
박 성 철	
5. 그럼, 수업이 끝난 후에, 선생님한테 갈까요?	Then, shall I go to see you after the class is over?
언제라도	anytime
선 생 님	
6. 그렇게 하세요. 오후에는 언제라도 좋아요.	Do it that way. Come anytime in the afternoon.

USEFUL EXPRESSIONS : MEMORIZE

1. 참을 수 없어요. — I can't bear it.
2. 안 됩니다. — You should not do it. Or : It won't do.
3. 아이 귀찮아 ! — It's a bother !

NOTES ON THE BASIC SENTENCES

1. 조용히 is an adverb meaning 'quietly,' 'silently,' 'calmly,' etc. Study the following words relating to it.

   조용히 하다 to keep quiet, to keep still
   조용하다 to be quiet, to be silent
   떠들다 to make noise
   시끄럽다 to be noisy

조용히 하세요.	Keep quiet, please.
그분은 조용한 사람이에요.	He is a quiet (mannered) person.
떠들지 마세요.	Don't make noise.
시끄러워서 죽겠어요.	Because it's noisy, I could die.

2. 자 is an exclamatory expression used to attract someone's attention or to arouse one to action. It corresponds to the English 'Come on !,' 'Come now !,' 'Here !,' 'Here you are !,' etc.

3. 발음 'pronunciation' should not be confused with 바람 'a wind.' 질문 is a noun meaning ' a question,' 'an inquiry.' 질문하다 is a verb meaning 'to ask a question,' 'to put a question to.' Its opposite word is 대답하다 'to answer.' Study the following examples :

질문해도 좋습니까 ?	May I ask you a question ?
질문이 있습니다.	I have a question to ask you.
질문에 대답해 주세요.	Please answer me this question.

4. 방해하다 means 'to disturb (a person's sleep),' 'to obstruct or hinder (a person from doing something).' 방해(가)되다 is a passive form. Some verbs are made passive by replacing -하다 with -되다. You will study passive formations in detail, later.

STRUCTURE NOTES

I. -ㄷ Irregular Verbs:

Some verbs ending in a final consonant -ㄷ are irregular:

묻(다)	'to ask'	듣(다)	'to hear'	걷(다)	'to walk'
싣(다)	'to load'	깨닫(다)	'to perceive,' 'to apprehend'		

1. The final consonant -ㄷ of the stem changes into -ㄹ when followed by a vowel. Study the following examples:

물어 볼까요?	Shall I ask you a question?
물었읍니다.	I asked him a question.
물어도 좋습니다.	You may ask me a question.
물을 것 같아요.	It seems that he will ask me a question.
물으면 안 돼요.	You must not ask me a question.

2. But the final consonant -ㄷ of the stem is not changed when followed by a consonant. Study the following examples:

묻지 마세요.	Don't ask me a question.
묻겠습니다.	I'll ask you a question.
묻고 싶어요.	I want to ask you a question.

Note:

However, there are -ㄷ regular verbs which never change their stems. These regular verbs are: 닫다 'to close (a door),' 받다 'to receive,' 믿다 'to believe,' and others.

II. Noun +-에 대해서…: 'about,' 'toward'

The pattern -에 대해서, attached directly to nouns, corresponds to the English 'about,' 'toward,' 'concerning,' 'in relation to,' etc.

Examples:

발음에 대해서 질문이 있어요.	I have a question about pronunciation.
한국말에 대해서 묻고 싶어요.	I want to ask you about Korean.
그분에 대해서 말씀해 주세요.	Please tell me about him.
한국에 대해서 이야기 했어요.	We talked about Korea.
이 학교에 대해서 아무 것도 몰라요.	I know nothing about this school.

Note:

This pattern -에 대해서 is interchangeable with -에 대하여, making no difference in meaning. But -에 대해서 is used more often.

III. A.V.S. +-ㄴ(은) 후에… : 'after doing'

The word 후 is a noun meaning 'later'; the particle -에 'at,' 'on,' 'in' indicates a time at which something takes place. This non-final ending -ㄴ(은) 후에 is used to express: 'after something happens' or 'after something happened.'

Examples:

공부가 끝난 후에 가겠어요.	I'll go after my studies are finished.
산보한 후에 자고 싶어요.	I want to go to bed after taking a walk.
일한 후에 잡수세요.	Please eat after working.
그분을 만난 후에 집에 왔어요.	I came home after I met him.
전화한 후에 오세요.	Please come after you phone.
그것을 들은 후에 갔어요.	After I heard it, I went (there).
그 책을 산 후에 저녁을 먹읍시다.	Let's eat supper after buying that book.
그분하고 이야기한 후에 숙제를 했어요.	I did my homework after I had talked with him.

Notes:

1. The pattern -ㄴ(은) 후에 is interchangeable with -ㄴ(은) 다음에, making no difference in meaning, (See Unit 25, Structure Notes III).
2. The pattern -ㄴ(은) 후에 is used always with action verbs, and the subject of the two clauses can be the same or different.
3. The tense and/or negation is expressed in the final (main) clause, not in the dependent clause with -ㄴ(은) 후에. Study the following examples, and note particularly the tense of the verb in the final clause.

공부한 후에 쉽니다.	I rest after studying.
공부한 후에 쉬었습니다.	I rested after studying.
공부한 후에 쉬겠습니다.	I'll rest after studying.
공부한 후에 쉬지 않겠습니다.	I won't rest after studying.

4. -ㄴ 후에 is used after verb stems ending in a vowel;
   -은 후에 is used after verb stems ending in a consonant.

IV. Interrogative +-(이)라도… : '-ever it is,' 'no matter—it is'

This pattern -(이)라도, preceded by an interrogative word, (e.g. 누구, 언제, 무엇, 어디), or an interrogative phrase (e.g. 어느 것, 어느 분, 무슨 책, 무슨 연필, 몇 분, 몇 시, 어떤 책), corresponds to the English: '—ever it is,' 'no matter (what, who, when) it is,' 'any—at all.'

Examples:

누구라도 괜찮아요.	Anyone at all will be fine.
언제라도 좋아요.	Any time at all will be alright.
무엇이라도 먹겠습니다.	No matter what it is, I'll eat it.
어디라도 같이 가고 싶어요.	Wherever it is, I want to go together with you.
어느 분이라도 할 수 있어요.	No matter which person it is, he can do it.
무슨 책이라도 사겠어요.	No matter what kind of book it is, I'll buy it.
몇 개라도 괜찮아요.	No matter how many there are, it will be fine.
몇 권이라도 다 사겠어요.	No matter how many books there are, I'll buy them all.
어떤 것이라도 괜찮아요.	No matter what kind of thing it is, it will be fine.
얼마라도 좋아요.	Any amount at all will be fine.

The interrogative may be followed by any of the particles, such as -부터 'from,' -에서 'from,' -한테 'to,' -한테서 'from.' Study the following examples:

어디에서라도 사 와야 해요.	No matter where it is from, we must buy it, (and bring it here).
누구한테서라도 빌리세요.	No matter who it is from, borrow it.
몇 시부터라도 괜찮아요.	No matter what time it starts, it will be fine.
누구한테라도 물어 보세요.	No matter who it is, ask him.

The interrogative may be followed by A.V.S. + -아(-어, -여)도, i.e., INTERROGATIVE + A.V.S. + -(-어, -여)도. The sequence has a generic meaning, rather than an interrogative one. Study the following examples:

누가 와도 괜찮아요.	Whoever comes, it's alright.
무슨 일을 해도 잘 해요.	Whatever job he does, he does it well.
어디에 가도 살 수 있어요.	Wherever you go, you can buy it.
언제 도착해도 상관없어요.	It doesn't matter when(ever) he arrives.
누구를 찾아가도 마찬가지에요.	Whomever I visit, it's all the same.
무엇을 읽어도 재미없어요.	No matter what I read, it's not interesting.
어떤 책을 사도 비싸요.	Whichever book you buy, it's expensive.

DRILLS

ADDITIONAL VOCABULARY

조용히 하다	to keep quiet	걷다	to walk
조용하다	to be quiet	깨닫다	to perceive, to apprehend
싣다	to load	믿다	to believe

A. Substitution Drill

1. 공부할 때가 되었어요. — It's time to study.
2. 고기를 구울 때가 되었어요. — It's time to roast the meat.
3. 물을 끓일 때가 되었어요. — It's time to boil the water.
4. 계란을 삶을 때가 되었어요. — It's time to boil the eggs.
5. 저녁을 먹을 때가 되었어요. — It's time to eat supper.
6. 싸울 때가 되었어요. — It's time to fight.
7. 그 일을 그만둘 때가 되었어요. — It's time to stop that work.
8. 돈을 벌 때가 되었어요. — It's time to make money.

B. Substitution Drill

1. 누구라도 괜찮아요. — Anyone at all will be fine.
2. 언제라도 괜찮아요. — Any time at all will be fine.
3. 무엇이라도 괜찮아요. — Anything at all will be fine.
4. 어디라도 괜찮아요. — Any place at all will be fine.
5. 몇 시라도 괜찮아요. — Any hour at all will be fine.
6. 어떤 책이라도 괜찮아요. — Any kind of book at all will be fine.
7. 어느 분이라도 괜찮아요. — No matter which person it is, it will be fine.
8. 몇 개라도 괜찮아요. — No matter how many there are, it will be fine.

C. Substitution Drill

1. 지금 질문하면, 다른 사람한테 방해가 됩니다. — If you ask a question now, it becomes a bother to others.
2. 시끄러우면, 다른 사람한테 방해가 됩니다. — If it's noisy, it becomes a bother to others.
3. 울면, 다른 사람한테 방해가 됩니다. — If you cry, it becomes a bother to others.
4. 웃으면, 다른 사람한테 방해가 됩니다. — If you laugh, it becomes a bother to others.

5. 떠들면, 다른 사람한테 방해가 됩니다.	If you make noise, it becomes a bother to others.
6. 담배를 피우면, 다른 사람한테 방해가 됩니다.	If you smoke, it becomes a bother to others.
7. 술을 마시면 다른 사람한테 방해가 됩니다.	If you drink, it becomes a bother to others.
8. 지금 들어가면 다른 사람한테 방해가 됩니다.	If you go in now, it becomes a bother to others.

D. Pattern Drill

Teacher : 그분한테 물었어요.	I asked him.
Student : 그분한테 묻지 않았어요.	I didn't ask him.
1. 차에 실었어요.	차에 싣지 않았어요.
2. 들었어요.	듣지 않았어요.
3. 같이 걸었어요.	같이 걷지 않았어요.
4. 깨달았어요.	깨닫지 않았어요.
5. 문을 닫았어요.	문을 닫지 않았어요.
6. 돈을 받았어요.	돈을 받지 않았어요.
7. 그분을 믿었어요.	그분을 믿지 않았어요.

E. Pattern Drill

Teacher : 공부가 끝난 다음에, 가겠어요.
I'll go after my studies are finished.

Student : 공부가 끝난 후에, 가겠어요.
I'll go after my studies are finished.

1. 산보한 다음에, 자고 싶어요.
산보한 후에, 자고 싶어요.
2. 그분을 만난 다음에, 집에 갑시다.
그분을 만난 후에, 집에 갑시다.
3. 전화한 다음에, 가 봅시다.
전화한 후에, 가 봅시다.
4. 그 일을 마친 다음에, 점심을 먹었어요.
그 일을 마친 후에, 점심을 먹었어요.
5. 복습한 다음에, 주무세요.
복습한 후에, 주무세요.
6. 고친 다음에, 고장이 나지 않았어요.
고친 후에, 고장이 나지 않았어요.
7. 숙제를 끝낸 다음에, 오세요.

숙제를 끝낸 후에, 오세요.

8. 일한 다음에, 구경하러 갑시다.
   일한 후에, 구경하러 갑시다.

F. Response Drill

1. 무엇에 대해서 질문이 있으세요?　　발음에 대해서 질문이 있어요.
2. 무엇에 대해서 묻고 싶으세요?　　한국말에 대해서 묻고 싶어요.
3. 누구에 대해서 이야기하세요?　　친구에 대해서 이야기해요.
4. 누구에 대해서 물어보셨어요?　　선생님에 대해서 물어보았어요.
5. 무엇에 대해서 모르시겠어요?　　이 학교에 대해서 모르겠어요.
6. 무슨 책에 대해서 말씀하셨어요?　　독일말 책에 대해서 말했어요.
7. 어느 분에 대해서 알고 싶으세요?　　저 여자에 대해서 알고 싶어요.
8. 어떤 영화에 대해서 들으셨어요?　　한국 영화에 대해서 들었어요.

G. Response Drill

Teacher: 무엇이라도 잡수시겠어요?
Will you eat it no matter what it is?
Student: 예, 무엇이라도 먹겠어요.
Yes, I'll eat it no matter what it is.

1. 어디라도 가시겠어요?　　예, 어디라도 가겠어요.
2. 누구라도 할 수 있어요?　　예, 누구라도 할 수 있어요.
3. 무슨 책이라도 사시겠어요?　　예, 무슨 책이라도 사겠어요.
4. 어느 분이라도 만나시겠어요?　　예, 어느 분이라도 만나겠어요.
5. 몇 개라도 괜찮아요?　　예, 몇 개라도 괜찮아요.
6. 언제라도 갈 수 있으세요?　　예, 언제라도 갈 수 있어요.
7. 어떤 일이라도 하시겠어요?　　예, 어떤 일이라도 하겠어요.
8. 누구한테라도 물어 볼까요?　　예, 누구한테라도 물어보세요.

H. Response Drill

Teacher: 어디에 가면 살 수 있어요?
Where can I buy it? (lit. If I go to what place, can I buy it?)
Student: 어디에 가도 살 수 있어요.
Wherever you go, can buy it.

1. 무슨 일을 하면 잘 하세요?　　무슨 일을 해도 잘 해요.
2. 누가 오면 말씀하시겠어요?　　누가 와도 말하겠어요.
3. 무엇을 하면 재미있어요?　　무엇을 해도 재미있어요.
4. 누구를 찾아가면 만날 수 있어요?　　누구를 찾아가도 만날 수 있어요.
5. 어떤 책을 읽으면 재미있어요?　　어떤 책을 읽어도 재미있어요.

6. 무엇을 먹으면 맛있을까요? 무엇을 먹어도 맛있어요.
7. 어느 병원에 가면 쌉니까? 어느 병원에 가도 쌉니다.
8. 누구하고 공부하면 괜찮을까요? 누구하고 공부해도 괜찮아요.

I. Pattern Drill (Review)

Teacher: 그것이 좋지만, 안 사겠어요.
It is good, but I won't buy it.
Student: 그것이 좋아도, 안 사겠어요.
Even if it's good, I won't buy it.

1. 위험하지만, 가겠어요.
위험해도, 가겠어요.
2. 그분이 홀쭉하지만, 건강합니다.
그분이 홀쭉해도, 건강합니다.
3. 그분이 돈이 없지만, 행복합니다.
그분이 돈이 없어도, 행복합니다.
4. 시끄럽지만, 참아야 합니다.
시끄러워도, 참아야 합니다.
5. 그분하고 친하지만, 말하지 않겠어요.
그분하고 친해도, 말하지 않겠어요.
6. 그분이 친절하지만, 그분을 좋아하지 않아요.
그분이 친절해도, 그분을 좋아하지 않아요.
7. 이상하지만, 들어 보세요.
이상해도, 들어 보세요.
8. 사람이 많지만, 복잡하지 않아요.
사람이 많아도, 복잡하지 않아요.

SHORT STORIES

1. 나는 한국에 대해서 알고 싶어요.
그래서 친구한테 물어 보았어요.
그러나 그분이 한국에 대해서 잘 알지 못했어요.

Expansion Drill

나는 한국에 대해서 알고 싶어서, 친구한테 물어 봤지만, 그분이 한국에 대해서 잘 알지 못했어요.

2. 수업이 끝난 후에, 선생님을 찾아갔어요.
그런데 선생님이 안 계셨어요.
그래서 선생님이 돌아오실 때까지, 기다렸어요.

Expansion Drill

수업이 끝난 후에 선생님을 찾아갔는데, 선생님이 안 계셔서, 선생님이 돌아오실 때까지, 기다렸어요.

3. 그 책은 어느 서점에 가도, 살 수 있어요.
   그러니까 걱정하지 마세요.
   시간이 있으면, 서점에 가서 사세요.

   Expansion Drill

   그 책은 어느 서점에 가도 살 수 있으니까, 걱정하지 말고 시간이 있으면, 서점에 가서 사세요.

READING

오늘은 수업이 일찍 끝났어요. 그래서 나는 친구들을 초대했어요. 오늘은 내가 한턱 내기로 했어요. 오래간 만에 택시를 타고 시내에 갔어요. 우리들은 한식점에 들어갔어요. 좀 복잡했지만, 거기서 먹기로 했어요. 내가 초대한 친구들은 외국 사람들이었어요. 그러나 한식은 무엇이라도 다 좋아하기 때문에, 불고기를 시켰어요. 셋이서 불고기를 오 인분이나 먹었어요. 저녁을 먹은 후에, 극장에 갔어요. 영화가 참 재미있었어요. 집에 돌아오니까 11시였어요. 나는 피곤해서 곧 잤어요.

한턱 내다	to give (a person) a treat	외국 사람	foreigner
오래간 만에	after a long time	시키다	to order
한식점	Korean restaurant	셋이서	three of us
한식	Korean food	오 인분	five portions

BRIEFING

Today class finished early. Therefore, I invited my friends (for a treat). I took a taxi for the first time in some time and went downtown. We went into a Korean restaurant. It was a little crowded but we decided to eat there. Those friends whom I had invited were foreigners. But they liked all kinds of Korean food. We ordered pulgogi. Three of us ate five portions of pulgogi. After eating supper, we went to the theater. The movie was very interesting. When I returned home, it was 11 o'clock. I was so tired that I went to bed immediately.

UNIT 35 한식 Korean Food

BASIC SENTENCES: MEMORIZE

한식	Korean food
박 성 철	
1. 한식을 잡숴 본 일이 있으세요?	Have you eaten Korean food before?
여러 번	many times
존 슨	
2. 그럼요. 여러 번 먹어 봤어요.	Sure. I have eaten it many times.
어떤	what kind of
박 성 철	
3. 어떤 한식을 좋아하세요?	What kind of Korean food do you like?
무엇이든지	any kind of, whatever it is
존 슨	
4. 한식은 무엇이든지 다 잘 먹어요.	I eat any kind of Korean food well.
일식	Japanese food
박 성 철	
5. 그럼, 일식도 좋아하세요?	Then, do you also like Japanese food?
그렇게	so, so much, to that extent, (not) very much
가끔	sometimes
존 슨	
6. 일식은 그렇게 좋아하지 않아요. 그러나 가끔 먹으러 가는 일이 있어요.	I don't like Japanese food very well. But I sometimes (go to) eat it.

USEFUL EXPRESSIONS: MEMORIZE

1. 농담하지 마세요.	Don't joke!
2. 한번 생각해 보겠어요.	I'll think about it.
3. 덤비지 마세요.	Take your time. Or: Don't be so hasty.

NOTES ON THE BASIC SENTENCES

1. 한식 'Korean food' is a contraction of 한국 음식.
2. 여러 번 means 'many times.' 여러 is a modifier which means 'various,' 'many,' 'several,' 'diverse,' 'manifold,' etc. When the classifier -번 is used with Korean numbers, it indicates 'times.' Study the following words:

여러 가지 'all sorts of,' 'various kinds of'
여러 날 'many days,' 'several days'
여러 달 'many months,' 'several months'
여러 분 'all of you,' 'ladies and gentlemen'

한 번	one time	여섯 번	six times
두 번	two times	일곱 번	seven times
세 번	three times	여덟 번	eight times
네 번	four times	아홉 번	nine times
다섯 번	five times	열 번	ten times

4. 다 means 'all,' 'everything,' 'everybody,' 'everyone.' Its synonym is 모두. Study the following examples:

우리 셋이 다 (모두) 갔어요.	All three of us went (there).
다 (모두) 왔어요.	All (of us, of you, of them) came.
다 (모두) 같이 갑시다.	Let's go altogether.
일을 다 (모두) 했어요.	I'm all done.

6. 일식 means 'Japanese food.' After diplomatic relations between Korea and Japan were normalized in 1965, we have begun to call Japanese food 일식. Before normalization, Japanese food was called 왜식.

STRUCTURE NOTES

I. The Sentence-Final Ending -ㄴ(은) 일이 있다 (없다)…: '(someone) has ever (never) done (something)'

The sentence-final ending -ㄴ(은) 일이 있다 (없다) is used only with action verbs, and refers one's past experiences. Its literal meaning is 'the experience (the act, or fact) of having done something exists, (or doesn't exist).'

Examples:

한식을 잡숴 본 일이 있으세요?	Have you ever eaten Korean food?
예, 먹어 본 일이 있어요.	Yes, I have eaten it.

아니오, 먹어 본 일이 없어요.	No, I have never eaten it.
미국에 가 본 일이 있으세요?	Have you ever been to America?
예, 미국에 가 본 일이 있어요.	Yes, I have been to America.
아니오, 미국에 가 본 일이 없어요.	No, I have never been to America.
그분을 만난 일이 있으세요?	Have you ever met him?
예, 그분을 만난 일이 있어요.	Yes, I have met him.
아니오, 그분을 만난 일이 없어요.	No, I have never met him.

Notes:

1. The tense is expressed in the final verb 있다 (or 없다), not in the main verb with -ㄴ(은). Study the following examples:

거기서 일한 일이 있어요.	I've worked there.
거기서 일한 일이 있었어요.	I had worked there.
거기서 일한 일이 없었어요.	I had never worked there.

2. -ㄴ 일이 있다 is used after verb stems ending in a vowel;
   -은 일이 있다 is used after verb stems ending in a consonant.

II. -ㅎ Irregular Verbs:

Some description verbs ending in the final consonant -ㅎ are irregular.

빨갛(다)	to be red	이렇(다)	to be like this
하얗(다)	to be white	그렇(다)	to be like that
노랗(다)	to be yellow	저렇(다)	to be like that (over there)
까맣(다)	to be black	어떻(다)	how
파랗(다)	to be blue	말갛(다)	to be clear

1. The final consonant -ㅎ of the stem is dropped when followed by the consonants -ㄴ, -ㄹ, -ㅁ, -ㅇ. Study the following examples:

빨간	red (adjective)
빨갈 것입니다.	(It) will probably be red.
빨가면,…	If it is red,…
빨강	A red one (noun).

2. But the final consonant -ㅎ of the stem is not dropped when followed by any other consonants. Study the following examples:

빨갛습니다.	It is red.
빨갛지 않아요.	It is not red.
빨갛고 말고요.	Of course it is red.

Note:

However, there are -ㅎ regular verbs which never change their stem. These regular verbs are:

좋(다)	to be good	점잖(다)	to be gentle
많(다)	to be many	괜찮(다)	to be alright
옳(다)	to be right	싫(다)	to be disagreeable

III. Interrogative +-(이)든지)…: '—ever it is,' 'no matter—it is'

This pattern -(이)든지, preceded by an interrogative word, (e.g. 누구, 언제, 무엇, 어디), or an interrogative phrase, (e.g., 어느 것, 어느 분, 무슨 책, 무슨 연필, 몇 분, 몇 시, 어떤 책), corresponds to the English '—ever it is,' 'no matter (who, what, when) it is,' 'any—at all.' Therefore, this pattern -(이)든지 is interchangeable with the pattern -(이)라도, making no difference in meaning, (cf. Unit 34, Structure Notes IV.)

Examples:

누구든지 괜찮아요.	Anyone at all will be fine.
언제든지 좋아요.	Any time at all will be good.
무엇이든지 먹겠습니다.	No matter what it is, I'll eat it.
어디든지 같이 가고 싶어요.	Wherever it is, I want to go together with you.
어느 분이든지 할 수 있어요.	No matter which person it is, he can do it.
무슨 책이든지 사겠어요.	No matter what kind of book it is, I'll buy it.
몇 개든지 괜찮아요.	No matter how many there are, it will be fine.
몇 권이든지 다 사겠어요.	No matter how many books there are, I'll buy them all.
어떤 것이든지 괜찮아요.	No matter what kind of thing it is, it will be fine.
얼마든지 좋아요.	Any amount at all will be fine.
그분은 무엇이든지 먹어요.	He eats anything at all.
몇 시든지 좋아요.	Any hour at all will be fine.

The interrogative may be followed by A.V.S. +-든지, i.e., INTERROGATIVE + A.V.S. +-든지. The sequence has a generic meaning, rather than an interrogative one. Study the following examples:

누가 오든지 괜찮아요.	Whoever comes, it's alright.
무슨 일을 하든지 잘 해요.	Whatever job he does, he does it well.

어디에 가든지 살 수 있어요.	Wherever you go, you can buy it.
언제 도착하든지 상관 없어요.	It doesn't matter when(ever) he arrives.
누구를 찾아가든지 마찬가지에요.	Whomever I visit, it's all the same.
무엇을 읽든지 재미없어요.	No matter what I read, it's not interesting.
어떤 책을 사든지 비싸요.	Whichever book you buy, it's expensive.

IV. The Sentence-Final Ending -는 일이 있다 (없다)… : '(someone) sometimes does (or never does) something'

The pattern -는 일이 있다 (없다) is used only with action verbs, and brings out the idea that 'there are times (or there is never a time) when someone does (or doesn't do) something.' Its literal meaning is : 'the experience (act or fact) of doing something exists (or doesn't exist).'

Examples :

담배를 피우는 일이 있어요.	I sometimes smoke. (There are times when I smoke.)
담배를 피우는 일이 없어요.	I never smoke. (There is never a time when I smoke.)
술을 마시는 일이 있어요.	I sometimes drink. (There are times when I drink.)
술을 마시는 일이 없어요.	I never drink. (There is never a time when I drink.)
부산에 가는 일이 있어요.	I sometimes go to Pusan. (There are times when I go to Pusan.)
부산에 가는 일이 없어요.	I never go to Pusan. (There is never a time when I go to Pusan.)
영어를 가르치는 일이 있어요.	I sometimes teach English. (There are times when I teach English.)
영어를 가르치는 일이 없어요.	I never teach English. (There is never a time when I teach English.)

The tense is expressed in the final verb 있다 (or 없다), not in the main verb with -는. Study the following examples :

거기서 일하는 일이 있어요.	I sometimes work there.
거기서 일하는 일이 있었어요.	I sometimes worked there.
거기서 일하는 일이 없었어요.	I never worked there.

DRILLS

ADDITIONAL VOCABULARY

빨갛다	to be red	이렇다	to be like this
하얗다	to be white	그렇다	to be like that
노랗다	to be yellow	저렇다	to be like that (over there)
까맣다	to be black	옳다	to be right
파랗다	to be blue	점잖다	to be gentle

A. Substitution Drill

1. 어떤 친구를 좋아하세요? — What kind of friend do you like?
2. 어떤 영화를 좋아하세요? — What kind of movie do you like?
3. 어떤 녹음기를 좋아하세요? — What kind of tape-recorder do you like?
4. 어떤 차를 좋아하세요? — What kind of car do you like?
5. 어떤 인형을 좋아하세요? — What kind of doll do you like?
6. 어떤 책을 좋아하세요? — What kind of book do you like?
7. 어떤 장갑을 좋아하세요? — What kind of gloves do you like?
8. 어떤 안경을 좋아하세요? — What kind of glasses do you like?

B. Substitution Drill

1. 여러 번 먹어 봤어요. — I have eaten it many times.
2. 한 번 먹어 봤어요. — I have eaten it once.
3. 두 번 먹어 봤어요. — I have eaten it twice.
4. 세 번 먹어 봤어요. — I have eaten it three times.
5. 네 번 먹어 봤어요. — I have eaten it four times.
6. 여섯 번 먹어 봤어요. — I have eaten it six times.
7. 여덟 번 먹어 봤어요. — I have eaten it eight times.
8. 일곱 번 먹어 봤어요. — I have eaten it seven times.

C. Pattern Drill

Teacher: 연필이 빨갛습니다. — The pencil is red.
Student: 빨간 연필입니다. — It is a red pencil.

1. 모자가 노랗습니다. — 노란 모자입니다.
2. 안경이 까맣습니다. — 까만 안경입니다.
3. 장갑이 하얗습니다. — 하얀 장갑입니다.
4. 육교가 파랗습니다. — 파란 육교입니다.
5. 횡단보도가 이상합니다. — 이상한 횡단보도입니다.

6. 차도가 복잡합니다. 복잡한 차도입니다.
7. 지하도가 큽니다. 큰 지하도입니다.
8. 인도가 깨끗합니다. 깨끗한 인도입니다.
9. 선생님이 점잖습니다. 점잖은 선생님입니다.
10. 말씀이 옳습니다. 옳은 말씀입니다.

D. Response Drill

Teacher: 한식을 잡숴 본 일이 있으세요?
Have you ever eaten Korean food?
Student: 아니오, 한식을 먹어 본 일이 없어요.
No, I have never eaten it.

1. 영국에 가 본 일이 있으세요? 아니오, 영국에 가 본 일이 없어요.
2. 그분을 만나 본 일이 있으세요? 아니오, 그분을 만나 본 일이 없어요.
3. 그분을 방해한 일이 있으세요? 아니오, 그분을 방해한 일이 없어요.
4. 약속을 위반한 일이 있으세요? 아니오, 약속을 위반한 일이 없어요.
5. 돈을 빌린 일이 있으세요? 아니오, 돈을 빌린 일이 없어요.
6. 약속을 어긴 일이 있으세요? 아니오, 약속을 어긴 일이 없어요.
7. 과음한 일이 있으세요? 아니오, 과음한 일이 없어요.
8. 과로한 일이 있으세요? 아니오, 과로한 일이 없어요.

E. Pattern Drill

Teacher: 누구라도 괜찮아요. Anyone at all will be fine.
Student: 누구든지 괜찮아요. Anyone at all will be fine.

1. 언제라도 좋아요. 언제든지 좋아요.
2. 무엇이라도 먹겠어요. 무엇이든지 먹겠어요.
3. 어디라도 가겠어요. 어디든지 가겠어요.
4. 어느 분이라도 가야 해요. 어느 분이든지 가야 해요.
5. 무슨 책이라도 사겠어요. 무슨 책이든지 사겠어요.
6. 몇 개라도 괜찮아요. 몇 개든지 괜찮아요.
7. 얼마라도 좋아요. 얼마든지 좋아요.
8. 몇 시라도 괜찮아요. 몇 시든지 괜찮아요.

F. Pattern Drill

Teacher: 누가 와도 괜찮아요. Whoever comes, it's alright.
Student: 누가 오든지 괜찮아요. Whoever comes, it's alright.

1. 무슨 일을 해도 잘 해요. 무슨 일을 하든지 잘 해요.
2. 어디에 가도 살 수 있어요. 어디에 가든지 살 수 있어요.
3. 무엇을 읽어도 재미있어요. 무엇을 읽든지 재미있어요.

4. 어떤 책을 사도 비싸요. 어떤 책을 사든지 비싸요.
5. 무엇을 먹어도 맛있어요. 무엇을 먹든지 맛있어요.
6. 누가 운전해도 괜찮아요. 누가 운전하든지 괜찮아요.
7. 언제 가도 만날 수 있어요. 언제 가든지 만날 수 있어요.
8. 무엇을 가르쳐도 잘 가르쳐요. 무엇을 가르치든지 잘 가르쳐요.

G. Pattern Drill

Teacher : 담배를 피우는 일이 있어요.
I sometimes smoke.
Student : 담배를 피우는 일이 없어요.
I never smoke.

1. 그분하고 싸우는 일이 있어요. 그분하고 싸우는 일이 없어요.
2. 한턱 내는 일이 있어요. 한턱 내는 일이 없어요.
3. 그분을 초대하는 일이 있어요. 그분을 초대하는 일이 없어요.
4. 약속을 어기는 일이 있어요. 약속을 어기는 일이 없어요.
5. 그분을 칭찬하는 일이 있어요. 그분을 칭찬하는 일이 없어요.
6. 사람을 과신하는 일이 있어요. 사람을 과신하는 일이 없어요.
7. 그분을 방해하는 일이 있어요. 그분을 방해하는 일이 없어요.
8. 사양하는 일이 있어요. 사양하는 일이 없어요.

H. Integration Drill (Review)

Teacher : 편지를 쓰겠어요. 부치겠어요.
I'll write a letter. I'll mail it.
Student : 편지를 써서 부치겠어요.
I'll write a letter and mail it.

1. 돈을 벌겠어요. 집을 사겠어요.
돈을 벌어서 집을 사겠어요.
2. 사과를 씻겠어요. 드리겠어요.
사과를 씻어서 드리겠어요.
3. 계란을 삶겠어요. 먹겠어요.
계란을 삶아서 먹겠어요.
4. 물을 끓이겠어요. 마시겠어요.
물을 끓여서 마시겠어요.
5. 그분을 만나겠어요. 그분한테 말씀하겠어요.
그분을 만나서 그분한테 말씀하겠어요.
6. 잘 만들겠어요. 드리겠어요.
잘 만들어서 드리겠어요.
7. 고기를 굽겠어요. 가지고 오겠어요.

고기를 구워서 가지고 오겠어요.

8. 참외를 깎겠어요. 먹겠어요.
참외를 깎아서 먹겠어요.

I. Integration Drill (Review)

Teacher: 시장에 갑니다. 들르겠어요.
I am going to the market. I'll drop in (there).

Student: 시장에 가다가 들르겠어요.
I'll drop in (there) when I go to the market.

1. 술을 마셨어요. 혼났어요.	술을 마시다가 혼났어요.
2. 잘 놀았어요. 싸웠어요.	잘 놀다가 싸웠어요.
3. 노래를 불렀어요. 웃었어요.	노래를 부르다가 웃었어요.
4. 복습했어요. 그만두었어요.	복습하다가 그만두었어요.
5. 전화를 했어요. 화가 났어요.	전화를 하다가 화가 났어요.
6. 그분을 방해했어요. 혼났어요.	그분을 방해하다가 혼났어요.
7. 걸어갔어요. 넘어졌어요.	걸어가다가 넘어졌어요.
8. 애기를 낳았어요. 울었어요.	애기를 낳다가 울었어요.

SHORT STORIES

1. 누가 가든지 상관없어요.
빨리 가서 그분을 도와 주세요.
그분이 과로해서 넘어졌어요.

상관없다 (it) doesn't matter

Expansion Drill

누가 가든지 상관없으니까, 빨리 가서 그분을 도와 주세요. 그분이 과로해서 넘어졌어요.

2. 술은 마셔 본 일이 있어요.
그러나 담배는 피워 본 일이 없어요.
오늘은 담배를 한 번 피워 보고 싶어요.

Expansion Drill

술은 마셔 본 일이 있지만, 담배는 피워 본 일이 없기 때문에, 오늘은 담배를 한 번 피워 보고 싶어요.

3. 어디를 가든지 마찬가지에요.
시간이 없으니까, 빨리 삽시다.
그렇지 않으면, 수업 시간에 늦을 것 같아요.

마찬가지 the same　　그렇지 않으면 otherwise

READING

저는 한식은 무엇이든지 좋아합니다. 그러나 맵고 짠 음식은 좋아하지 않습니다. 좀 싱겁게 먹습니다. 옛날에는 달고 신 음식을 좋아했습니다. 그런데 식성이 변했습니다. 나는 겨울에 식욕이 제일 좋습니다. 그래서 요즘 식사를 잘 합니다.

맵다	to be hot (food)	시다	to be sour
짜다	to be salty	쓰다	to be bitter
음식	a food	식성	taste, likes and dislikes
싱겁다	to be insipid (bland)	변하다	to change
옛날에	in the old days	식욕	appetite
달다	to be sweet	식사	a meal

BRIEFING

I like any kind of Korean food. But I don't like hot and salty food. I eat bland food. In the old days, I liked sweet and sour food. But my tastes have changed. I have the best appetite in winter. So these days I eat very well.

UNIT 36 반말 A Plain Style Of Speech

BASIC SENTENCES: MEMORIZE

너	you
박 성 철	
1. 너 뭘 먹느냐?	What are you eating?
배가 고프다	to be hungry
밥	boiled-rice
최 인 숙	
2. 배가 고파서 밥을 먹는다. 너도 같이 먹자.	I'm eating boiled-rice because I'm hungry. Let's eat together.
벌써	already
많이	much, lots, plenty, a great deal
박 성 철	
3. 난 벌써 먹었다. 많이 먹어라.	I ate already. Help yourself.
종일	all the day, all day (long)
굶다	to go without food, to skip a meal, to fast
정신없이	absent-mindedly, frantically
최 인 숙	
4. 아주 바빠서 종일 굶었다. 그래서 지금 정신없이 먹고 있다.	I haven't eaten all day, because I was very busy. So now, I'm eating frantically.
서다	to stand
앉다	to sit down
박 성 철	
5. 서서 먹지 말고, 앉아서 먹어라.	Don't eat standing up, sit down and eat.

NOTES ON THE BASIC SENTENCES

1. 너 'you' in Sentence I, is a vocative. It is used always with the contrast particle -는, (너는). 네, (also meaning 'you'), is used always with the subject particle -가, (네 가). 너(는) and 네(가) are plain words, and are used when speaking to cloese friends or social inferiors.

   당신 'you' is a semi-polite word used (1) when speaking to persons of equal social status or inferiors; (2) when refering to superiors in the third person; (3) when the speaker expresses anger. But it is used between a husband and wife.

   뭘 is a contraction of 무엇을.

3. 난 is a contraction of 나는.

STRUCTURE NOTES

I. The Plain Style:

We have already studied the Formal-Polite Style, (See Unit 5 Structure Notes I), and the Informal-Polite Style, (See Unit 3. Structure Notes II). Now let's study the plain style, (which is also called the 'ordinary style,' or the 'familiar style'). The plain style is used among students, workmen, servicemen, waitresses, or in situations where a certain amount of friendship or fraternization is presumed. It is also used with truly close friends, or when speaking to social inferiors. The foreigner seldom has occasion to use it, except when addressing children; but he hears a great deal of it around him.

(a) Question forms:

The question form is made by attaching the ending -냐 (-으냐, -느냐) directly to the verb stem. Study the following examples:

그것이 무엇이냐?	What is that?
그 사람이 누구냐?	Who is that man?
그것이 예쁘냐?	Is that beautiful?
괜찮으냐?	Is it alright?
누가 선생이었느냐?	Who was a teacher?
누가 선생이겠느냐?	Who do you think is a teacher?
그것이 예뻤느냐?	Was it beautiful?
그것이 예쁘겠느냐?	Do you think it will be beautiful?
그 책이 어디 있느냐?	Where is that book?
그 책이 어디 있었느냐?	Where was that book?

그 책이 어디 있겠느냐?	Where do you think that book is?
몇 시에 일어나느냐?	What time do you get up?
몇 시에 일어났느냐?	What time did you get up?
몇 시에 일어나겠느냐?	What time will you get up?

Notes:

1. This question form -냐 (-으냐, -느냐) is used mostly with the indirect discourse -고 하다, rather than by itself.
2. -(으)냐 is used with description verbs in the present tense and with -이(다) in the present tense. (-냐 is used after verb stems ending in a vowel; -느냐 is used after verb stems ending in a consonant).
3. In all other cases, -느냐 is used.

(b) **Declarative forms:**

The declarative form is made by attaching the ending -ㄴ다 (-는다, -다) directly to the verb stem. Study the following examples:

눈을 뜬다.	I open my eyes.
눈을 감는다.	I close my eyes.
낮잠을 잤다.	I took a nap.
낮잠을 자겠다.	I'll take a nap.
그분이 바쁘다.	He is busy.
그분이 바빴다.	He was busy.
그분이 바쁘겠다.	I think he will be busy.
그분이 선생님이다.	He is a teacher.
그분이 선생님이었다.	He was a teacher.
그분이 선생님이겠다.	I think he is a teacher.
그것이 사무실에 있다.	It is in the office.
그것이 사무실에 있었다.	It was in the office.
그것이 사무실에 있겠다.	I think it is in the office.

Notes:

1. -ㄴ(는)다 is used with action verbs in the present tense: (-ㄴ다 is used after verb stems ending in a vowel; -는다 is used after verb stems ending in a consonant).
2. In all other cases, -다 is used.

(c) **Propositive form**:

The propositive form is made by attaching the ending -자 directly to the verb stem. Study the following examples:

지금 공부하자.	Let's study now.

일어나자.	Let's get up.
지금 떠나자.	Let's leave now.
그분을 도와주자.	Let's help him.
그것을 잊어버리자.	Let's forget it.

(d) **Imperative forms:**

: imperative form is made by attaching the ending -아(-어, -여)라 directly to the verb stem. Study the following examples:

지금 일어나라.	Get up now.
이 책을 읽어라.	Read this book.
한국말을 공부하여라.	Study Korean.

Notes:

-아라 is used after -아- and -오-;
-어라 is used after any other vowel;
-여라 is used after a 하(다) verb.

Another imperative form is made by attaching the ending -(으)라 directly to the verb stem. (This form is used mostly with the indirect discourse -고 하다.) Study the following examples:

학교에 가라.	Go to school.
지금 일하라.	Work now.
눈을 감으라.	Close your eyes.
이 음식을 먹으라.	Eat this food.

Notes:

-라 is used after verb stems ending in a vowel;
-으라 is used after verb stems ending in a consonant.

(e) **Other imperative expressions:**

We have already studied the sentence-final ending -아(-어, -여) 주다, (See Unit 17, Structure Notes II). It is used when a speaker requests something for himself, or when he does something for an inferior or an equal. For example, 도와 주세요 'Help me, please.' The plain imperative form is made by replacing the word 주세요 with 달라. Study the following examples:

문을 열어 달라.	Open the door (for me).
문을 닫아 달라.	Close the door (for me).
불을 켜 달라.	Turn on the light (for me).
불을 꺼 달라.	Turn off the light (for me).

DRILLS

ADDITIONAL VOCABULARY

불	the light	이기다	to win
켜다	to turn on	지다	to lose, to be defeated
끄다	to turn off	꼭	certainly, by all means

A. Substitution Drill (Review)

1. 너무 바빠서 정신이 없어요.	I'm so busy that I can't think straight.
2. 너무 추워서 정신이 없어요.	It's so cold that I can't think straight.
3. 너무 더워서 정신이 없어요.	It's so hot that I can't think straight.
4. 너무 시끄러워서 정신이 없어요.	It's so noisy that I can't think straight.
5. 너무 복잡해서 정신이 없어요.	It's so complicated that I can't think straight.
6. 너무 떠들어서 정신이 없어요.	They are making so much noise that I can't think straight.
7. 너무 무더워서 정신이 없어요.	It's so humid that I can't think straight.
8. 너무 힘들어서 정신이 없어요.	It's so difficult that I can't think straight.

B. Substitution Drill (Review)

1. 와 주셔서 감사합니다.	Thank you for coming.
2. 도와 주셔서 감사합니다.	Thank you for helping me.
3. 전화해 주셔서 감사합니다.	Thank you for calling.
4. 잘 가르쳐 주셔서 감사합니다.	Thank you for teaching me so well.
5. 잘 설명해 주셔서 감사합니다.	Thank you for explaining it so well.
6. 초대해 주셔서 감사합니다.	Thank you for inviting me.
7. 돈을 갚아 주셔서 감사합니다.	Thank you for paying it back.
8. 이것을 고쳐 주셔서 감사합니다.	Thank you for repairing this.

C. Level Drill

Teacher : 이것이 무엇입니까?	What is this?
Student : 이것이 무엇이냐?	What is this?
1. 저분이 누굽니까?	저분이 누구냐?
2. 여기가 어딥니까?	여기가 어디냐?
3. 저것이 어떻습니까?	저것이 어떠냐?
4. 지금 몇 십니까?	지금 몇 시냐?
5. 모두 몇 분입니까?	모두 몇 분이냐?

6. 책이 모두 몇 권입니까? — 책이 모두 몇 권이냐?
7. 오늘이 며칠입니까? — 오늘이 며칠이냐?
8. 오늘이 무슨 요일입니까? — 오늘이 무슨 요일이냐?

D. Level Drill

Teacher: 그것이 예쁩니까? — Is that beautiful?
Student: 그것이 예쁘냐? — Is that beautiful?

1. 그분이 겸손합니까? — 그분이 겸손하냐?
2. 위험합니까? — 위험하냐?
3. 그분이 튼튼합니까? — 그분이 튼튼하냐?
4. 그분의 몸이 약합니까? — 그분의 몸이 약하냐?
5. 그분이 젊습니까? — 그분이 젊으냐?
6. 그분이 건강합니까? — 그분이 건강하냐?
7. 지금 기쁩니까? — 지금 기쁘냐?
8. 왜 슬픕니까? — 왜 슬프냐?

E. Level Drill

Teacher: 학교에 갔느냐? — Did you go to school?
Student: 학교에 가지 않았느냐? — Didn't you go to school?

1. 그분을 만났느냐? — 그분을 만나지 않았느냐?
2. 잊어버렸느냐? — 잊어버리지 않았느냐?
3. 숙제를 했느냐? — 숙제를 하지 않았느냐?
4. 식성이 변했느냐? — 식성이 변하지 않았느냐?
5. 한턱 내었느냐? — 한턱 내지 않았느냐?
6. 약속하겠느냐? — 약속하지 않겠느냐?
7. 결심하겠느냐? — 결심하지 않겠느냐?
8. 방해하겠느냐? — 방해하지 않겠느냐?

F. Level Drill

Teacher: 눈을 뜹니다. — I open my eyes.
Student: 눈을 뜬다. — I open my eyes.

1. 아침을 먹습니다. — 아침을 먹는다.
2. 눈을 감습니다. — 눈을 감는다.
3. 그분을 믿습니다. — 그분을 믿는다.
4. 차가 멎습니다. — 차가 멎는다.
5. 그분이 넘어집니다. — 그분이 넘어진다.
6. 모자를 씁니다. — 모자를 쓴다.
7. 장갑을 낍니다. — 장갑을 낀다.

8. 시계를 찹니다. 시계를 찬다.

G. Pattern Drill

Teacher : 학교에 간다.	I go to school.
Student : 학교에 가지 않는다.	I don't go to school.
1. 돈을 빌린다.	돈을 빌리지 않는다.
2. 돈을 갚는다.	돈을 갚지 않는다.
3. 약속을 지킨다.	약속을 지키지 않는다.
4. 약속을 어긴다.	약속을 어기지 않는다.
5. 불을 켠다.	불을 켜지 않는다.
6. 불을 끈다.	불을 끄지 않는다.
7. 양말을 신는다.	양말을 신지 않는다.
8. 대답한다.	대답하지 않는다.

H. Pattern Drill

Teacher : 낮잠을 자겠다.	I will take a nap.
Student : 낮잠을 자지 않겠다.	I won't take a nap.
1. 약혼하겠다.	약혼하지 않겠다.
2. 시집가겠다.	시집가지 않겠다.
3. 애기를 낳겠다.	애기를 낳지 않겠다.
4. 걸어가겠다.	걸어가지 않겠다.
5. 싸우겠다.	싸우지 않겠다.
6. 딱지를 떼겠다.	딱지를 떼지 않겠다.
7. 전화하겠다.	전화하지 않겠다.
8. 조용히 하겠다.	조용히 하지 않겠다.

I. Level Drill

Teacher : 지금 공부합시다.	Let's study now.
Student : 지금 공부하자.	Let's study now.
1. 뛰어갑시다.	뛰어가자.
2. 등산갑시다.	등산가자.
3. 소풍갑시다.	소풍가자.
4. 사냥갑시다.	사냥가자.
5. 계속합시다.	계속하자.
6. 초인종을 누릅시다.	초인종을 누르자.
7. 거기에 들릅시다.	거기에 들르자.
8. 꼭 이깁시다.	꼭 이기자.

J. Pattern Drill

Teacher : 일어나자.	Let's get up.
Student : 일어나지 말자.	Let's not get up.
1. 사양하자.	사양하지 말자.
2. 계란을 삶자.	계란을 삶지 말자.
3. 고기를 굽자.	고기를 굽지 말자.
4. 사과를 깎자.	사과를 깎지 말자.
5. 물을 끓이자.	물을 끓이지 말자.
6. 옷을 갈아입자.	옷을 갈아입지 말자.
7. 넥타이를 매자.	넥타이를 매지 말자.
8. 설탕을 넣자.	설탕을 넣지 말자.

K. Level Drill

Teacher : 학교에 가세요.	Go to school, please.
Student : 학교에 가라.	Go to school.
1. 일어나세요.	일어나라.
2. 눈을 감으세요.	눈을 감으라.
3. 눈을 뜨세요.	눈을 뜨라.
4. 책을 읽으세요.	책을 읽으라.
5. 빨리 끝내세요.	빨리 끝내라.
6. 이를 닦지 마세요.	이를 닦지 말라.
7. 복습하지 마세요.	복습하지 말라.
8. 답장하지 마세요.	답장하지 말라.

L. Level Drill

Teacher : 문을 열어 주세요.	Please open the door (for me).
Student : 문을 열어 달라.	Open the door (for me).
1. 문을 닫아 주세요.	문을 닫아 달라.
2. 태워 주세요.	태워 달라.
3. 만들어 주세요.	만들어 달라.
4. 설명해 주세요.	설명해 달라.
5. 나한테 보여 주세요.	나한테 보여 달라.
6. 이것을 고쳐 주세요.	이것을 고쳐 달라.
7. 나가 주세요.	나가 달라.
8. 그것을 꺼내어 주세요.	그것을 꺼내어 달라.

SHORT STORIES

1. 어제 바빠서 가지 못했다.
   오늘 오후에 가겠다.
   옷을 준비해 달라. 준비하다 to prepare

   Expansion Drill

   어제 바빠서 가지 못 했는데, 오늘 오후에 가겠으니까, 옷을 준비해 달라.

2. 배가 고파서 죽겠다.
   저녁부터 먹자.
   그리고 이 일을 계속하자.

   Expansion Drill

   배가 고파서 죽겠으니까, 저녁부터 먹고 이 일을 계속하자.

3. 어두워서 잘 안 보인다.
   불을 켜 달라.
   그리고 추우니까 문을 닫아 달라.

   Expansion Drill

   어두워서 잘 안 보이니까, 불을 켜 달라. 그리고 추우니까, 문을 닫아 달라.

READING

사람은 머리로 생각합니다. 어떤 사람은 머리가 좋습니다. 그런데 어떤 사람은 머리가 나쁩니다. 눈으로 봅니다. 그런데 눈이 나쁜 사람은 안경을 낍니다. 귀로 듣습니다. 입으로 말하고 먹습니다. 그런데 어떤 사람은 말을 잘 하는 재주가 있습니다. 혀로 맛을 봅니다. 그리고 이로 음식을 씹어서 먹습니다. 코로 숨을 쉽니다. 그리고 냄새를 맡습니다. 손으로 만져봅니다. 그리고 손으로 일을 합니다. 손으로 못 하는 일이 없습니다. 다리로 걸어다닙니다.

머리	the head	씹다	to chew
머리가 좋다	to have brains, to be intelligent	코	a nose
		숨을 쉬다	to breathe
머리가 나쁘다	to be dull-brained, to be slow (in study)	냄새	a smell
		냄새를 맡다	to smell
눈	an eye	손	a hand
귀	an ear	만지다	to finger, to touch

이	a tooth	다리	a leg
입	a mouth	걸어다니다	to walk around
말을 잘 하다	to speak well	맛	taste
재주	talent, gifts	맛을 보다	to taste
혀	a tongue		

BRIEFING

A man thinks with his head. Some men have brains. However, some men are slow in study. We see with our eyes. But the man who has bad eyes wear glasses. We listen with our ears. We speak and eat with our mouths. Some men have gifted, glib tongues. We taste with our tongues. We chew and eat food with our teeth. We breathe with our noses. And we smell with our noses. We touch with our hands. And we work with our hands. There is nothing we can't do with our hands. We walk with our legs.

UNIT 37 며칠 How Many Days?

BASIC SENTENCES : MEMORIZE

며칠	how many days
박 성 철	
1. 며칠 만에 학교에 오셨어요?	How many days were you out before you came to school?
꼭	just
일 주일	one week
닷새	five days
결석하다	to be absent
최 인 숙	
2. 꼭 일 주일 만에 학교에 왔어요. 그러니까, 닷새 결석했어요.	I came to school exactly after one week. Therefore, I was absent for five days.
이제	now
박 성 철	
3. 이젠 괜찮아요?	Are you all right now?
거의	almost
낫다	to get well, to recover
아직	still
불편하다	to not feel well
최 인 숙	
4. 거의 다 나았어요. 그러나 아직도 좀 불편해요.	I am almost completely recovered (from the illness). But I still don't feel well.
박 성 철	
5. 그럼, 일찍 집에 가서 쉬시지요.	Then, please go home early and rest.
조퇴하다	to leave school early
최 인 숙	
6. 예, 오늘은 조퇴해야겠어요.	Yes, I must leave (school) early today.

NOTES ON THE BASIC SENTENCES

2. 꼭, depending on the context or situation, means (1) 'certainly,' 'without fail,' 'by all means,' (2) 'without discrepancy,' 'quite,' (3) 'firmly,' 'hard,' 'without giving in,' (4) 'exactly,' 'to a T.' Study the following examples:

꼭 하세요.	Do it without fail.
꼭 가겠습니다.	I'll go for sure.
꼭 같아요.	They are quite alike.
그분은 꼭 어린애 같아요.	He behaves just like a child.
꼭 쥐세요.	Please grasp it firmly.
꼭 매세요.	Please fasten it tight.
이 옷이 꼭 나한테 맞아요.	These clothes fit me perfectly.

결석하다 means 'to absent oneself (from school),' whereas 결근하다 means 'to absent oneself (from office, work).' Study the following examples:

그분은 두 달이나 결석했어요.	He was absent from school for two months.
그분은 오늘 결근했어요.	He was absent from duties today. Or: He didn't come to the office today.

3. 이젠 is a contraction or 이제는. 이제 'now,' from now on' is used mostly with the contrast particle -는, or the emphatic particle -야. Study the following examples:

이젠 그렇게 하지 않겠어요.	I won't do so in the future.
이제야 그분이 왔어요.	At long last he has come.
이제야 생각이 나요.	Now I remember.

4. 낫다 is an irregular verb. The final consonant -ㅅ of the stem is dropped when followed by a vowel, (See this Unit, Structure Notes III.) 낫다, depending on the context or situation, can mean (1) 'to be better (than),' 'to be superior to,' 'to be excellent,' (2) 'to recover (from illness),' 'to be cured (of a disease).' Study the following examples:

이것이 그것보다 훨씬 나아요.	This is much better than that.
건강이 돈보다 낫습니다.	Health is above wealth.
그분의 병이 나아 갑니다.	His illness is getting better.
이젠 나았어요.	I have quite gotten over it.

아직 means 'still,' '(not) yet.' The particle -도, when used with an adverb, indicates admiration, or places emphasis on the adverb itself, (See Unit 13, Structure Notes III.)

불편하다 means (1) 'to be uncomfortable,' 'to be feeling rather sick,' (2) 'to be inconvenient.' The opposite word of 불편하다 is 편리하다 'to be convenient.' Study the following examples:

지금 몸이 불편해요. — I'm feeling rather ill now.
교통이 불편해요. — The transportation is inconvenient.
교통이 편리해요. — Transportaion is convenient.

6. 조퇴하다 means 'to leave work or school earlier than the agreed or fixed time.' Its opposite word is 지각하다 'to come to school or work after the agreed or fixed time.'

STRUCTURE NOTES

I. Time Word +-만에…: 'after (of time)'

The pattern -만에, preceded by time words, indicates passage of time. It corresponds to the English 'after (the passage of a stretch of time).'

Examples:

오래간 만에 그분을 만났어요. — I met him after a long while.
칠 년 만에 한국에 돌아왔어요. — I came back to Korea after seven years.
한 달 만에 학교에 왔어요. — I came to school after one month.
열흘 만에 집에 돌아왔어요. — I came home after ten days.
스무 시간 만에 깨었어요. — I woke up after twenty hours.
십 년 만에 한국 음식을 먹어 봐요. — I am eating Korean food after ten years.

Notes:

1. The pattern -만, which denotes passage of time, is followed usually by the particle -에 'at,' 'on,' 'in,' indicating the time at which something takes place. But -만 can also be followed by the verb of identification -이다. Study the following examples:

   오래간 만입니다. — It's been a long time since I saw you last.
   한국에 온 지가 오 년 만입니다. — I came to Korean 5 years ago.

2. This pattern -만에 usually takes the past tense.
3. When the pattern -만에 is followed by verbs such as 찾다 'to find,' 도착하다 'to reach,' or 되다 'to become,' it indicates 'taking time to do something.' Study the following examples:

   이 책을 두 달 만에 찾았어요. — It took me two months to find this book.

열흘 만에 한국에 도착했어요.	It took him ten days to reach Korea.
오 년 만에 과장이 되었어요.	It took me five years to become head of the section.

II. 이젠, 아직도, 벌써 :

(a) 이젠 + an affirmative… : 'now'

When 이젠 is used within an affirmative context, it means 'now.' Study the following examples:

이젠 아시겠어요?	Do you understand it now?
예, 이젠 알겠어요.	Yes, I understand it now.
아니오, 아직도 모르겠어요.	No, I still don't understand it.

이젠 + a negative… : '(not) any more'

When 이젠 is used within a negative context, it means '(not) any more.' Study the following examples:

이젠 피곤하지 않아요?	Aren't you tired any more?
예, 이젠 피곤하지 않아요.	That's right. I'm not tired any more.
아니오, 아직도 피곤해요.	That's not right. I'm still tired.

Note:

The negative answer (아니오) to an 이젠 question occurs with 아직도.

(b) 아직도 + an affirmative… : 'still,' 'yet'

When 아직도 is used within an affirmative context, it means 'still,' 'yet.' Study the following examples:

아직도 잡수세요?	Are you still eating?
예, 아직도 먹어요.	Yes, I'm still eating.
아니오, 이젠 먹지 않아요.	No, I'm not eating any more.

아직도 + a negative… : 'not yet'

When 아직도 is used within a negative context, it means 'not yet.' Study the following examples:

그분이 아직도 공부하지 않아요?	Isn't he studying yet?
예, 아직도 공부하지 않아요.	That's right. He isn't studying yet.
아니오, 이젠 공부해요.	That's not right. He is studying now.

Notes:

The negative answer (아니오) to an 아직도 question occurs with 이젠, if the tense is in the present form. But if the tense is in the past form, the negative answer (아니오) to an 아직도 question occurs with 벌써 'already.' Study the following examples:

아직도 공부하지 않았어요?	Haven't you studied yet?
예, 아직도 공부하지 않았어요.	That's right. I haven't studied yet.
아니오, 벌써 공부했어요.	That's not right. I have studied already.

(c) **벌써 + an affirmative… : 'already,' 'now already'**

The word 벌써 is used always with an affirmative. It is never used with a negative. Study the following examples:

그분이 벌써 공부했어요?	Has he studied already?
예, 벌써 공부했어요.	Yes, he has studied already.
아니오, 아직도 공부하지 않았어요.	No, he hasn't studied yet.

Note:

The negative answer (아니오) to a 벌써 question occurs with 아직도.

III. -ㅅ Irregular Verbs:

Some verbs ending in a final consonant -ㅅ are irregular:

낫(다)	to recover, to get well	젓(다)	to stir, to row	긋(다)	to draw
붓(다)	to pour	짓(다)	to build	잇(다)	to unite, to connect

1. The final consonant -ㅅ of the stem is dropped when followed by a vowel. Study the following examples:

물을 그릇에 부어야 합니다.	You must pour water into a vessel.
물을 그릇에 부었어요.	I poured water into a vessel.
물을 그릇에 부어 보세요.	Try pouring water into a vessel.
물을 그릇에 부어도 괜찮아요.	You may pour water into a vessel.

2. But the final consonant -ㅅ of the stem is not dropped when followed by a consonant. Study the following examples:

물을 그릇에 붓겠어요.	I'll pour water into a vessel.
물을 그릇에 붓지 마세요.	Don't pour water into a vessel.
물을 그릇에 붓고 말고요.	Of course, I'll pour water into a vessel.

Note:

However, there are -ㅅ regular verbs which never change their stem. These regular verbs are:

벗(다)	to take off	빗(다)	to comb
웃(다)	to laugh	솟(다)	to gush out
씻(다)	to wash	빼앗(다)	to snatch (a thing) from.

DRILLS

ADDITIONAL VOCABULARY

붓다	to pour	젓다	to stir, to row
짓다	to build	씻다	to wash
잇다	to unite, to connect	빗다	to comb
긋다	to draw	빼앗다	to snatch (a thing) from

A. Substitution Drill

1. 오래간 만에 그분을 만났어요. — I met him after a long while.
2. <u>이 주일</u> 만에 그분을 만났어요. — I met him after two weeks.
3. <u>나흘</u> 만에 그분을 만났어요. — I met him after four days.
4. <u>엿새</u> 만에 그분을 만났어요. — I met him after six days.
5. <u>석 달</u> 만에 그분을 만났어요. — I met him after three months.
6. <u>넉 달</u> 만에 그분을 만났어요. — I met him after four months.
7. <u>오 년</u> 만에 그분을 만났어요. — I met him after five years.
8. <u>십 년</u> 만에 그분을 만났어요. — I met him after ten years.

B. Substitution Drill

1. 오 년 만에 박사가 되었어요. — It took me five years to achieve a doctorate.
2. <u>이십 년</u> 만에 <u>교수</u>가 되었어요. — It took me twenty years to become a professor.
3. <u>십 년</u> 만에 <u>의사</u>가 되었어요. — It took me ten years to become a medical doctor.
4. <u>십오 년</u> 만에 <u>선교사</u>가 되었어요. — It took me fifteen years to become a missionary.
5. <u>두 달</u> 만에 <u>운전수</u>가 되었어요. — It took me two months to become a driver.
6. <u>육 년</u> 만에 <u>선생</u>이 되었어요. — It took me six years to become a teacher.
7. <u>십사 년</u> 만에 <u>신부</u>가 되었어요. — It took me fourteen years to become a Catholic priest.
8. <u>십육 년</u> 만에 <u>목사</u>가 되었어요. — It took me sixteen years to become a pastor (minister).

C. Response Drill

1. 며칠 만에 학교에 오셨어요? — <u>닷새</u> 만에 학교에 왔어요.
2. 몇 달 만에 그분을 만나셨어요? — <u>석 달</u> 만에 그분을 만났어요.
3. 몇 시간 만에 찾으셨어요? — <u>네 시간</u> 만에 찾았어요.

4. 몇 주일 만에 시내에 가셨어요?	<u>삼 주일</u> 만에 시내에 갔어요.
5. 몇 년 만에 돌아오셨어요?	<u>육 년</u> 만에 돌아왔어요.
6. 며칠 만에 미국에 도착하셨어요?	<u>이틀</u> 만에 미국에 도착했어요.
7. 몇 달 만에 그것을 잡수셨어요?	<u>넉 달</u> 만에 그것을 먹었어요.
8. 몇 년 만에 운전하셨어요?	<u>오 년</u> 만에 운전했어요.

D. Response Drill

Teacher: 이젠 아시겠어요?	Do you understand it now?
Student: 아니오, 아직도 모르겠어요.	No, I still don't understand it.
1. 이젠 가시겠어요?	아니오, 아직도 가지 않겠어요.
2. 이젠 주무시겠어요?	아니오, 아직도 자지 않겠어요.
3. 이젠 잡수시겠어요?	아니오, 아직도 먹지 않겠어요.
4. 이젠 인사하시겠어요?	아니오, 아직도 인사하지 않겠어요.
5. 이젠 결정하시겠어요?	아니오, 아직도 결정하지 않겠어요.
6. 이젠 복습하시겠어요?	아니오, 아직도 복습하지 않겠어요.
7. 이젠 연습하시겠어요?	아니오, 아직도 연습하지 않겠어요.
8. 이젠 사양하시겠어요?	아니오, 아직도 사양하지 않겠어요.

E. Response Drill

Teacher: 이젠 피곤하지 않으세요?
Aren't you tired any more?
Student: 아니오, 아직도 피곤해요.
That's not right. I'm still tired.

1. 이젠 맵지 않으세요?	아니오, 아직도 매워요.
2. 이젠 시지 않으세요?	아니오, 아직도 시어요.
3. 이젠 달지 않으세요?	아니오, 아직도 달아요.
4. 이젠 싱겁지 않으세요?	아니오, 아직도 싱거워요.
5. 이젠 짜지 않으세요?	아니오, 아직도 짜요.
6. 이젠 쓰지 않으세요?	아니오, 아직도 써요.
7. 이젠 덥지 않으세요?	아니오, 아직도 더워요.
8. 이젠 춥지 않으세요?	아니오, 아직도 추워요.

F. Response Drill

Teacher: 아직도 잡수세요?	Are you still eating?
Student: 아니오, 이젠 먹지 않아요.	No, I'm not eating any more.
1. 아직도 주무세요?	아니오, 이젠 자지 않아요.
2. 아직도 싸우세요?	아니오, 이젠 싸우지 않아요.

3. 아직도 전화하세요? 아니오, 이젠 전화하지 않아요.
4. 아직도 삶으세요? 아니오, 이젠 삶지 않아요.
5. 아직도 구경하세요? 아니오, 이젠 구경하지 않아요.
6. 아직도 목욕하세요? 아니오, 이젠 목욕하지 않아요.
7. 아직도 세수하세요? 아니오, 이젠 세수하지 않아요.
8. 아직도 면도하세요? 아니오, 이젠 면도하지 않아요.

G. Response Drill

Teacher: 아직도 공부하지 않으세요?
Aren't you studying yet?
Student: 아니오, 이젠 공부해요.
That's not right. I am studying now.

1. 아직도 복습하지 않으세요? 아니오, 이젠 복습해요.
2. 아직도 주무시지 않으세요? 아니오, 이젠 자요.
3. 아직도 잡수시지 않으세요? 아니오, 이젠 먹어요.
4. 아직도 웃지 않으세요? 아니오, 이젠 웃어요.
5. 아직도 나가지 않으세요? 아니오, 이젠 나가요.
6. 아직도 일하지 않으세요? 아니오, 이젠 일해요.
7. 아직도 숙제하지 않으세요? 아니오, 이젠 숙제해요.
8. 아직도 청소하지 않으세요? 아니오, 이젠 청소해요.

H. Response Drill

Teacher: 아직도 공부하지 않으셨어요?
Haven't you studied yet?
Student: 아니오, 벌써 공부했어요.
That's not right. I have studied already.

1. 아직도 부탁하지 않으셨어요? 아니오, 벌써 부탁했어요.
2. 아직도 시키지 않으셨어요? 아니오, 벌써 시켰어요.
3. 아직도 초대하지 않으셨어요? 아니오, 벌써 초대했어요.
4. 아직도 한턱 내지 않으셨어요? 아니오, 벌써 한턱 냈어요.
5. 아직도 그만두지 않으셨어요? 아니오, 벌써 그만두었어요.
6. 아직도 신지 않으셨어요? 아니오, 벌써 실었어요.
7. 아직도 수술하지 않으셨어요? 아니오, 벌써 수술했어요.
8. 아직도 약속하지 않으셨어요? 아니오, 벌써 약속했어요.

I. Response Drill

Teacher: 벌써 공부하셨어요? Have you studied already?
Student: 아니오, 아직도 공부하지 않았어요. No, I haven't studied yet.

1. 벌써 질문하셨어요? — 아니오, 아직도 질문하지 않았어요.
2. 벌써 일어나셨어요? — 아니오, 아직도 일어나지 않았어요.
3. 벌써 돈을 갚으셨어요? — 아니오, 아직도 돈을 갚지 않았어요.
4. 벌써 고치셨어요? — 아니오, 아직도 고치지 않았어요.
5. 벌써 시키셨어요? — 아니오, 아직도 시키지 않았어요.
6. 벌써 약혼하셨어요? — 아니오, 아직도 약혼하지 않았어요.
7. 벌써 시집가셨어요? — 아니오, 아직도 시집가지 않았어요.
8. 벌써 읽으셨어요? — 아니오, 아직도 읽지 않았어요.

J. Pattern Drill

Teacher: 다 나았어요. — I have completely recovered.
Student: 다 낫지 않았어요. — I haven't completely recovered.

1. 물을 부었어요. — 물을 붓지 않았어요.
2. 집을 지었어요. — 집을 짓지 않았어요.
3. 그것을 이었어요. — 그것을 잇지 않았어요.
4. 잘 그었어요. — 잘 긋지 않았어요.
5. 잘 저었어요. — 잘 젓지 않았어요.
6. 손을 씻었어요. — 손을 씻지 않았어요.
7. 머리를 빗었어요. — 머리를 빗지 않았어요.
8. 그것을 빼앗았어요. — 그것을 빼앗지 않았어요.

SHORT STORIES

1. 오늘 한 달 만에 학교에 왔어요.
그런데 학교에 도착하니까 열 시였어요.
한 시간 지각했어요.

지각하다 to come to school or work after the agreed or fixed time

Expansion Drill

오늘 한 달 만에 학교에 왔는데, 학교에 도착하니까, 열 시였어요. 한 시간 지각했어요.

2. 몸이 아파서 이틀 결근했어요.
이틀 만에 회사에 오니까 이상했어요.
금년에 벌써 네 번 결근했어요.

결근하다 to absent oneself (from office, work)

Expansion Drill

몸이 아파서 이틀 결근했는데, 이틀 만에 회사에 오니까 이상했어요. 금년에 벌써 네 번 결근했어요.

3. 열심히 공부했는데 아직도 모르겠어요.
   이것이 복잡해서 이해하기 어려워요. 이해하다 to understand
   다시 한 번 설명해 주세요.

   Expansion Drill

   열심히 공부했는데, 아직도 잘 모르겠어요. 이것이 복잡해서 이해하기 어려우니까, 다시 한 번 설명해 주세요.

READING

몸이 아파서 닷새 결석했습니다. 꼭 일 주일 만에 학교에 왔습니다. 학교에 오니까 좀 어지러웠습니다. 거의 다 나았습니다. 그러나 아직도 좀 불편합니다. 건강에 조심해야겠습니다. 몇 년 전에는 감기에도 걸리지 않았습니다. 그런데 요즘은 자주 감기에 걸립니다. 그리고 어떤 때는 소화도 잘 되지 않습니다. 무엇보다도 과로하지 말아야겠습니다. 물론 과음도 하지 않아야겠습니다.

어지럽다	to be dizzy	소화	digestion
몇 년 전에	a few years ago	소화가 잘 되다	to digest well
감기	a cold	무엇보다도	above all
걸리다	to catch, to suffer from	물론	of course
자주	frequently		

BRIEFING

I became sick, so I was absent for five days. I came to school exactly after one week. When I came to school I felt a little bit dizzy. I'm almost completely recovered (from the illness). But I still don't feel well. I have to be careful about my health. A few years ago I didn't even catch a cold. However, these days I catch colds frequently. And sometimes I don't digest food well. Above all, I should not work too much, of course. I should not drink too much, also.

UNIT 38 문 Doors

BASIC SENTENCES : MEMORIZE

열다 — to open

박 성 철

1. 추운데 왜 문을 열어 놓았어요? — It's cold, so why did you leave the door open?

열리다 — to be opened

닫다 — to close

최 인 숙

2. 문이 열려 있었어요? 내가 문을 닫아 놓았는데요. — Was the door open? I thought I closed the door.

불 — the light

켜다 — to turn on

이상하다 — to be strange

박 성 철

3. 방에 불도 켜 있었어요. 참 이상하지요? — And the light was on in your room. It's really strange, isn't it?

아 — Oh!

아까 — some time ago

끄다 — to turn off

최 인 숙

4. 아 참! 내가 아까 불을 끄지 않고 나왔어요. — Oh! I remember. I came out some time ago without turning off the light.

꼭 — tightly

다니다 — to go about

위험하다 — to be dangerous

박 성 철

5. 문을 꼭 닫고 다니세요. 위험해요. — Please close the door tightly when you go about your business. It's dangerous.

주의하다 — to be careful

최 인 숙

6. 예, 주의할께요. — Yes, I'll be careful.

NOTES ON THE BASIC SENTENCES

1. 놓다 depending on the context or situation, can mean (1) 'to put,' 'to place,' (2) 'to leave (behind),' (3) 'to leave,' 'to let,' (4) 'to set one's mind at ease.' Study the following examples:

이것을 책상 위에 놓으세요.	Put this on the desk.
책을 어디에 놓고 왔을까?	Where did I leave my book?
그대로 놓아 두세요.	Leave it as it is.
놓아 주세요.	Let me go.
마음을 놓으세요.	Please set your mind at ease. (There is no need to worry.)

2. 열리다 'to be opened,' 'to be open,' 'to be unlocked' is used always with the subject particle -가/-이, whereas 열다 'to open' is used always with the object particle -를/-을. Study the following examples, and note particularly the preceding particles.

문이 열려 있어요.	The door is open.
문을 열었어요.	I opend the door.

3. 켜다 means 'to turn (switch) on,' 'to light (a lamp, candle),' 'to strike (a match),' etc. Its opposite word is 끄다 'to switch off (an electric light),' 'to turn off (the gas),' 'to turn out (a light, a radio).' Study the following words which relate to turning on and turning off.

   틀다 to turn on (a radio or water)

   잠그다 (1) to turn off (the water, a faucet)

   (2) to lock (a door, drawer, house, room)

4. 아 is an exclamatory expression which indicates surprise, grief, disappointment, etc. It corresponds to the English 'Ah!,' 'Oh!,' 'Alas,' 'Dear me.'

5. 다니다 means (1) 'to come and go,' 'to go about,' 'to walk around,' 'to commute,' (2) 'to attend (school, working place, office),' (3) 'to frequent.' Study the following examples:

회사에 기차로 다닙니다.	I commute to the company by train.
여기는 다니는 사람이 많아요.	Many people are coming and going here.
그분은 대학에 다녀요.	He attends college.
그분은 회사에 다닙니다.	He works for a company.
그 곳에 잘 다녔어요.	I used to frequent that place.

STRUCTURE NOTES

I. -ㅂ Irregular verbs:

Some verbs ending in a final consonant -ㅂ are irregular.

가볍(다)	to be light	더럽(다)	to be dirty
간지럽(다)	to be ticklish	돕(다)	to help
곱(다)	to be pretty	무겁(다)	to be heavy
굽(다)	to roast	아름답(다)	to be beautiful
깁(다)	to sew	어둡(다)	to be dark
눕(다)	to lie down	줍(다)	to pick up
덥(다)	to be hot	즐겁(다)	to be delightful

1. The final consonant -ㅂ of the stem, when followed by a vowel, changes into 우. Study the following examples:

추워도…	Even though it's cold…
추우면…	If it's cold…
추울 것 같아요.	It seems that it will be cold.
추워야 합니다.	It must be cold.
추웠습니다.	It was cold.

2. But the final consonant -ㅂ of the stem does not change when followed by a consonant. Study the following examples:

춥지만…	It's cold but…
춥기 때문에…	Because it's cold…
춥습니다.	It's cold.
춥겠읍니다.	It will be cold.
춥고 말고요.	Of course, it's cold.

Note:

However, there are also -ㅂ regular verbs which never change their stems.

곱(다)	to be numb (with cold)	입(다)	to put on (clothes)
뽑(다)	to pull out	잡(다)	to grasp
씹(다)	to chew	접(다)	to fold
업(다)	to carry (a person) on one's back	집(다)	to pick up

II. The Sentence-Final Ending -아(-어, -여) 놓다:

The pattern -아(-어, -여) 놓다 is used always with action verbs, and indicates an action done in preparation or anticipation of later use or benefit. The English equivalent of this pattern is 'to do something and put it aside,' 'to do something in preparation,' 'to do something in advance.'

Examples :

표를 사 놓으세요.	Buy tickets in advance.
문을 열어 놓았어요.	I opened the door (for future benefit).
편지를 써 놓았어요.	I wrote a letter and put it aside. Or : I wrote a letter in advance.
이 방을 청소해 놓았어요.	I cleaned this room in advance.
이 책을 읽어 놓으세요.	Read this book in advance.
그것을 씻어 놓았어요.	I washed that in advance. Or : I washed that and put it aside.
불을 켜 놓겠어요.	I'll turn the light on in advance.

Notes :

1. The tense and/or negation is expressed regularly in the final verb 놓다, not in the main verb with -아(-어, -여). Study the following examples :

불을 켜 놓으세요.	Turn the light on in advance.
불을 켜 놓았어요.	I turned the light on in advance.
불을 켜 놓겠어요.	I'll turn the light on in advance.
불을 켜 놓지 않았어요.	I didn't turn the light on in advance.
불을 켜 놓지 않겠어요.	I won't turn the light on in advance.

2. The pattern -아(-어, -여) 놓다 is interchangeable with -아(-어, -여) 두다, making no difference in meaning.
3. -아 놓다 is used after -아- and -오- ;
   -어 놓다 is used after any other vowel ;
   -여 놓다 is used after a 하다 verb.

III. The Sentence-Final Ending -아(-어, -여) 있다 :

The pattern -아(-어, -여) 있다 is used regularly with intransitive verbs, such as 가다 'to go,' 오다 'to come,' 서다 'to stand (up),' 앉다 'to sit (down),' 되다 'to become,' etc. These always take the subject particle -가/-이. This pattern indicates a present result of an action that has taken place in the past.

Examples :

그분이 일본에 가 있어요.	He lives in Japan, (lit. He went to Japan and is there.)

김 선생님이 여기 와 계세요.	Mr. Kim is here, (has arrived).
집에 돌아가 계십시오.	Please go back home and stay there.
그분이 아직도 돌아와 있지 않아요.	He isn't back yet.
그분이 서 있어요.	He is standing.
그분이 앉아 있어요.	He is seated.
불이 켜 있어요.	The light is on.
불이 꺼져 있어요.	The light is off.
그분이 벌써 박사가 되어 있어요.	He is (has) already become a doctor.
점심이 준비되어 있어요.	Lunch is ready now.
문이 열려 있어요.	The door is open.
문이 닫혀 있어요.	The door is closed.

Notes:

1. The tense and/or negation is expressed always in the final verb 있다, not in the main verb with -아(-어, -여). Study the following examples:

불이 켜 있어요.	The light is on.
불이 켜 있지 않아요.	The light is not on.
불이 켜 있었어요.	The light was on.
불이 켜 있지 않았어요.	The light was not on.

2. -아 있다 is used after -아- and -오-;
-어 있다 is used after any other vowel;
-여 있다 is used after a 하다 verb.

DRILLS

ADDITIONAL VOCABULARY

무겁다	to be heavy	곱다	to be pretty
가볍다	to be light	아름답다	to be beautiful
눕다	to lie down	줍다	to pick up
간지럽다	to be ticklish	깁다	to sew

A. Substitution Drill

1. 불을 끄지 않고 나왔어요.	I came out without turning off the light.
2. 문을 닫지 않고 나왔어요.	I came out without closing the door.
3. 인사하지 않고 나왔어요.	I came out (left) without saying good-bye.
4. 그림을 그리지 않고 나왔어요.	I came out without drawing a picutre.
5. 준비하지 않고 나왔어요.	I came out without preparing it.

6. 냄새를 맡지 않고 나왔어요. I came out without smelling it.
7. 그것을 만지지 않고 나왔어요. I came out without touching it.
8. 맛을 보지 않고 나왔어요. I came out without tasting it.

B. Substitution Drill

1. 문을 꼭 닫고 다니세요. Please close the door tightly and go about your business.
2. 옷을 입고 다니세요. Please put on your clothes and go about your business.
3. 모자를 쓰고 다니세요. Please put on your hat and go about your business.
4. 신을 신고 다니세요. Please put on your shoes and go about your business.
5. 시계를 차고 다니세요. Please put on your watch and go about your business.
6. 장갑을 끼고 다니세요. Please put on your gloves and go about your business.
7. 안경을 쓰고 다니세요. Please put on your glasses and go about your business.
8. 넥타이를 매고 다니세요. Please put on your tie and go about your business.

C. Pattern Drill

Teacher : 춥습니다. It is cold.
Student : 추웠습니다. It was cold.

1. 덥습니다. 더웠습니다.
2. 고기를 굽습니다. 고기를 구웠습니다.
3. 더럽습니다. 더러웠습니다.
4. 돕습니다. 도왔습니다.
5. 즐겁습니다. 즐거웠습니다.
6. 어둡습니다. 어두웠습니다.
7. 무겁습니다. 무거웠습니다.
8. 가볍습니다. 가벼웠습니다.

D. Pattern Drill

Teacher : 표를 사세요. Please buy tickets.
Student : 표를 사 놓으세요. Please buy tickets in advance.

1. 준비하세요. 준비해 놓으세요.
2. 문을 여세요. 문을 열어 놓으세요.
3. 문을 닫으세요. 문을 닫아 놓으세요.
4. 그것을 씻으세요. 그것을 씻어 놓으세요.

5. 불을 켜세요.	불을 켜 놓으세요.
6. 불을 끄세요.	불을 꺼 놓으세요.
7. 지금 청소하세요.	지금 청소해 놓으세요.
8. 편지를 쓰세요.	편지를 써 놓으세요.

E. Pattern Drill

Teacher : 그것을 씻어 놓았어요.
I washed that in advance, (for future benefit).
Student : 그것을 씻어 놓겠어요.
I'll wash that in advance, (for future benefit).

1. 그림을 그려 놓았어요.	그림을 그려 놓겠어요.
2. 음식을 시켜 놓았어요.	음식을 시켜 놓겠어요.
3. 그것을 만들어 놓았어요.	그것을 만들어 놓겠어요.
4. 전화해 놓았어요.	전화해 놓겠어요.
5. 복습해 놓았어요.	복습해 놓겠어요.
6. 약속해 놓았어요.	약속해 놓겠어요.
7. 결정해 놓았어요.	결정해 놓겠어요.
8. 실어 놓았어요.	실어 놓겠어요.

F. Pattern Drill

Teacher : 불이 꺼졌어요.	The light has gone out.
Student : 불이 꺼져 있어요.	The light is off.
1. 점심이 준비되었어요.	점심이 준비되어 있어요.
2. 문이 열렸어요.	문이 열려 있어요.
3. 문이 닫혔어요.	문이 닫혀 있어요.
4. 박사가 되었어요.	박사가 되어 있어요.
5. 그분이 앉았어요.	그분이 앉아 있어요.
6. 그분이 섰어요.	그분이 서 있어요.
7. 벌써 돌아왔어요.	벌써 돌아와 있어요.
8. 미국에 갔어요.	미국에 가 있어요.

G. Pattern Drill

Teacher : 집에 돌아가세요.	Please go (back) home.
Student : 집에 돌아가 계세요.	Please go (back) home and stay there.
1. 여기에 오세요.	여기에 와 계세요.
2. 교실에 들어가세요.	교실에 들어가 계세요.
3. 밖에 나가세요.	밖에 나가 계세요.
4. 이층에 올라가세요.	이층에 올라가 계세요.

5. 여기 앉으세요.	여기 앉아 계세요.
6. 잠깐 서세요.	잠깐 서 계세요.
7. 내려가세요.	내려가 계세요.
8. 들어오세요.	들어와 계세요.

H. Pattern Drill

Teacher : 그분이 앉아 있어요.	He is seated.
Student : 그분이 앉아 있지 않아요.	He is not seated.
1. 문이 열려 있어요.	문이 열려 있지 않아요.
2. 문이 닫혀 있어요.	문이 닫혀 있지 않아요.
3. 준비되어 있어요.	준비되어 있지 않아요.
4. 불이 꺼져 있어요.	불이 꺼져 있지 않아요.
5. 불이 켜 있어요.	불이 켜 있지 않아요.
6. 일본에 가 있어요.	일본에 가 있지 않아요.
7. 박사가 되어 있어요.	박사가 되어 있지 않아요.
8. 그분이 서 있어요.	그분이 서 있지 않아요.

I. Pattern Drill

Teacher : 그분이 서 있었어요.	He was standing.
Student : 그분이 서 있지 않았어요.	He was not standing.
1. 고장이 나 있었어요.	고장이 나 있지 않았어요.
2. 애기가 안겨 있었어요.	애기가 안겨 있지 않았어요.
3. 감기에 걸려 있었어요.	감기에 걸려 있지 않았어요.
4. 일어나 있었어요.	일어나 있지 않았어요.
5. 깨어 있었어요.	깨어 있지 않았어요.
6. 누워 있었어요.	누워 있지 않았어요.
7. 화가 나 있었어요.	화가 나 있지 않았어요.
8. 술에 취해 있었어요.	술에 취해 있지 않았어요.

J. Pattern Drill

Teacher : 무거웠어요.	It was heavy.
Student : 무겁지 않았어요.	It was not heavy.
1. 가벼웠어요.	가볍지 않았어요.
2. 누웠어요.	눕지 않았어요.
3. 간지러웠어요.	간지럽지 않았어요.
4. 고왔어요.	곱지 않았어요.
5. 아름다웠어요.	아름답지 않았어요.

6. 주웠어요. 줍지 않았어요.
7. 기웠어요. 깁지 않았어요.
8. 즐거웠어요. 즐겁지 않았어요.

SHORT STORIES

1. 나올 때 문을 잠가 놓았어요.
   그리고 불도 꺼 놓았어요.
   그런데 문이 열려 있었어요.

   잠그다 to lock

   Expansion Drill

   나올 때 문도 잠가 놓고, 불도 꺼 놓았는데, 문이 열려 있었어요.

2. 제일 친한 친구가 미국으로 떠납니다.
   그래서 여간 섭섭하지 않아요.
   오늘 저녁에 송별회가 있어요.

   섭섭하다 to be sorry, to be regrettable
   송별회 a farewell party

   Expansion Drill

   제일 친한 친구가 미국으로 떠나기 때문에, 여간 섭섭하지 않아요. 오늘 저녁에 송별회가 있어요.

3. 오늘 오후에 회의가 있어요.
   그리고 저녁에는 친구의 환영회가 있어요.
   그래서 오늘 정신없이 바쁠 것 같아요.

   회의 a meeting, a conference
   환영회 a welcoming party

   Expansion Drill

   오늘 오후에는 회의가 있고, 저녁에는 친구의 환영회가 있어서, 오늘 정신없이 바쁠 것 같아요.

READING

어제는 주말이었습니다. 나는 오래간 만에 외출을 했습니다. 방에서 나올 때 불을 끄고 나왔습니다. 그리고 문도 잠가 놓았습니다. 그런데 돌아와 보니까, 불이 켜 있었습니다. 그리고 문도 열려 있었습니다. 나는 처음에 깜짝 놀랐습니다. 이상하게 생각했습니다. 그런데 내 방에 들어가 보니까 어머니가 와 계셨습니다. 어머니는 시골에 계십니다. 그런데 어머니가 갑자기 서울에 올라 오셨습니다. 어머니는 연세가 많습니다. 지금 육십 칠 세입니다. 그러나 아주 건강하십니다. 나는 형제 자매가 많습니다. 형님이 두 분 계시고, 누님이 세 분이나 됩니다. 그런데 제가 막내아들입니다.

주말	a weekend	-세	'years of age' used with Chinese numbers.
외출하다	to go outdoors		
처음에	in the beginning	형제	brothers
시골	the country, a rural district	자매	sisters
		막내아들	the last (youngest) son
갑자기	suddenly		
연세	age		

BRIEFING

Yesterday was the weekend. I went outdoors for the first time after a long time. When I left my room, I turned off the light and came out. And I locked the door. However, when I returned, I found that the light was on. And the door was open. In the beginning I was suprised completely. I thought it was strange. But when I went into my room, I found that my mother was there. My mother is living in a rural district. But my mother came to Seoul suddenly. My mother is very old. She is sixty-seven years old now. But she is very healthy. I have many brothers and sisters. I have two older brothers and three older sisiters. I'm the last son.

UNIT 39 기다려 주세요 Please Wait

BASIC SENTENCES : MEMORIZE

잠깐	for a few minutes
최 인 숙	
1. 잠깐 드릴 말씀이 있는데요. 지금 시간이 있으신가요?	I have something to talk to you about for a few minutes. Do you have time now?
대단히	very, greatly, seriously
박 성 철	
2. 대단히 급한 일인가요?	Is it something very urgent?
최 인 숙	
3. 아니오, 그리 급하지는 않아요.	No, it's not so urgent.
식당	a dining room
마시면서	while drinking
얘기하다	to talk
박 성 철	
4. 그럼, 식당에 가서 기다려 주세요. 거기서 코피나 마시면서 얘기합시다.	Then, please go to the dining room and wait there. Let's talk while drinking some coffee there.
자꾸	constantly, always
폐를 끼치다	to cause (a person) trouble
최 인 숙	
5. 자꾸 폐를 끼쳐 미안합니다.	I'm sorry to cause you so much trouble all the time.
천만에요	that's okay
박 성 철	
6. 천만에요. 무슨 그런 말씀을 하세요?	That's okay. Why do you talk like that?

NOTES ON THE BASIC SENTENCES

2. 대단히 is an adverb which means 'very,' 'greatly,' 'seriously,' 'terribly,' 'awfully,' 'so,' 'much too,' etc. Study the following examples:

대단히 피곤해요.	I'm terribly tired.
그 여자가 대단히 예뻐요.	She is awfully beautiful.
그분이 대단히 돈이 많아요.	He has loads of money.
대단히 재미있어요.	It's extremely exciting.
그분이 대단히 아파요.	He is seriously ill.

4. 거기서 is a contraction of 거기에서.
   애기하다 is a contraction of 이야기하다 'to talk.' 'to speak,' 'to have a chat (talk).'

5. 자꾸 means (1) 'constantly,' 'incessantly,' 'continuously,' 'always,' (2) 'hard,' 'eagerly,' 'intently,' etc. Study the following examples:

자꾸 비가 와요.	It keeps on raining.
자꾸 내 얼굴을 보고 있어요.	He keeps staring right at me.
그분이 자꾸 찾아와요.	He keeps visiting me.
그분한테 자꾸 부탁했어요.	I repeatedly asked him to do me a favor.

폐를 끼치다 means 'to cause (a person) trouble.' 폐 is a noun which means 'an evil,' 'a vice,' 'a bad custom,' 'a corrupt practice.' Study the following examples:

남한테 폐를 끼치지 마세요.	Don't cause others trouble.
폐를 많이 끼쳤어요.	I caused a lot of trouble.
남한테 폐를 끼칠 것 없어요.	There is no reason to trouble others.

무슨 그런 말씀을 하세요. 'Why do you talk like that?' is used as a formal reply to an expression of thanks, respectful recognition, and apologies. It is used normally with the expression 천만에요 'You're welcome.' Sometimes, it's used when a hearer expresses an unpleasant reaction against someone's statement.

STRUCTURE NOTES

I. The Informal Polite Question Ending -ㄴ(은)가요? -는가요?:

This pattern -ㄴ(-은)가요?/-는가요? is used to ask questions, or to express doubt informally but politely. It takes any verb.

Examples :

그 책이 좋은가요?	Is that book good?
그분이 친절한가요?	Is he kind?
그분이 누구인가요?	Who is that person?
그것이 교실인가요?	Is that the classroom?
그분이 선생인가요?	Is that person a teacher?
무엇을 공부하시는가요?	What are you studying?
누가 공부했는가요?	Who studied?
어디에서 공부하시겠는가요?	Where will you study?
그것이 나빴는가요?	Was that bad?
책이 있는가요?	Do you have a book?
책이 있었는가요?	Did you have a book?
그분이 누구였는가요?	Who was that person?
누가 의사였는가요?	Who was a medical doctor?

Notes :

1. -ㄴ(-은)가요? is used with description verbs in the present tense, and with -이(다) in the present tense. -ㄴ가요? is used after verb stems ending in a vowel; -은가요? is used after verb stems ending in a consonant.
2. In all other cases, -는가요? is used.
3. The intimate style can be made by dropping the final polite particle -요. It is used with close friends or social inferiors. It is used also in a situation where a certain amount of friendship or fraternization is presumed.

II. The Non-Final Ending -(으)면서… : 'while doing something'

The pattern -으(면서) is used to indicate two simultaneous actions done by a single person. It is attached directly to the stems of action verbs. If the simultaneous actions are performed by different persons, a different pattern -는 동안에 is used; but this pattern will be studied later in detail.

Examples :

라디오를 들으면서 책을 읽었어요.	I read a book while listening to the radio. Or : While I listened to the radio, I also read a book.
산보하면서 이야기합시다.	Let's talk while taking a walk.
그분이 울면서 말했어요.	He talked and cried.
점심을 잡수시면서 읽으세요.	Please read it while eating lunch.
그분이 웃으면서 이것을 나한테 주었어요.	While laughing, he gave this to me.

담배를 피우면서 갑시다.	Let's smoke while going.
가르치면서 많이 배웠어요.	I learned a lot while teaching.
아이들이 떠들면서 놀았어요.	The children made noise as they played.

Notes :

1. In the pattern -으(면서), the final (main) clause is emphasized the most, while the first (dependent) clause with -(으)면서 is supplementary information.
2. The tense and/or negation is expressed in the final (main) clause, not in the first (dependent) clause with -(으)면서. Study the following examples:

라디오를 들으면서 책을 읽어요.	I am reading a book while listening to the radio.
라디오를 들으면서 책을 읽었어요.	I read a book while listening to the radio.
라디오를 들으면서 책을 읽지 않았어요.	I didn't read a book while listening to the radio.
라디오를 들으면서 책을 읽겠어요.	I will read a book while listening to the radio.

3. -면서 is used after verb stems ending in a vowel ;
   -으면서 is used after verb stems ending in a consonant.

DRILLS

ADDITIONAL VOCABULARY

별로	in particular, especially	축하하다	to congratulate
바꾸다	to (ex)change, to barter	방문하다	to visit
봉사하다	to serve		

A. Substitution Drill

1. 자꾸 폐를 끼쳐 미안합니다.	I'm sorry to cause you so much trouble all the time.
2. 도와주지 못 해서 미안합니다.	I'm sorry that I couldn't help you.
3. 떠들어서 미안합니다.	I'm sorry that I made noise.
4. 약속을 어겨서 미안합니다.	I'm sorry that I broke my promise.
5. 늦게 와서 미안합니다.	I'm sorry that I came late.
6. 숙제를 하지 않아서 미안합니다.	I'm sorry that I didn't do my homework.
7. 여러번 결석해서 미안합니다.	I'm sorry that I was absent from school many times.
8. 지각해서 미안합니다.	I'm sorry that I was late for school.

B. Substitution Drill

1. 별로 급하지 않아요.	It's not particularly urgent.
2. 별로 좋지 않아요.	It's not particularly good.
3. 별로 아름답지 않아요.	It's not particularly beautiful.
4. 별로 곱지 않아요.	It's not particularly pretty.
5. 별로 무겁지 않아요.	It's not particularly heavy.
6. 별로 위험하지 않아요.	It's not particularly dangerous.
7. 별로 맵지 않아요.	It's not particularly hot.
8. 별로 짜지 않아요.	It's not particularly salty.

C. Pattern Drill

Teacher: 그분이 선생님입니까?	Is he a teacher?
Student: 그분이 선생님인가요?	Is he a teacher?
1. 저것이 공장입니까?	저것이 공장인가요?
2. 이것이 주유소입니까?	이것이 주유소인가요?
3. 저것이 주차장입니까?	저것이 주차장인가요?
4. 그것이 지하철입니까?	그것이 지하철인가요?
5. 이것이 고가도로입니까?	이것이 고가도로인가요?
6. 저것이 육교입니까?	저것이 육교인가요?
7. 이것이 횡단보도입니까?	이것이 횡단보도인가요?
8. 이것이 지하도입니까?	이것이 지하도인가요?

D. Pattern Drill

Teacher: 무엇을 공부하십니까?	What are you studying?
Student: 무엇을 공부하시는가요?	What are you studying?
1. 누가 오십니까?	누가 오시는가요?
2. 누구를 방문하십니까?	누구를 방문하시는가요?
3. 그림을 그리십니까?	그림을 그리시는가요?
4. 냄새를 맡으십니까?	냄새를 맡으시는가요?
5. 숨을 쉬십니까?	숨을 쉬시는가요?
6. 맛을 보십니까?	맛을 보시는가요?
7. 무엇을 만지십니까?	무엇을 만지시는가요?
8. 한턱 내십니까?	한턱 내시는가요?

E. Integration Drill

Teacher: 산보합시다. 이야기합시다.
Let's take a walk. Let's talk.

Student: 산보하면서 이야기합시다.

Let's talk while taking a walk.

1. 떠들었어요. 놀았어요.	떠들면서 놀았어요.
2. 담배를 피웁시다. 갑시다.	담배를 피우면서 갑시다.
3. 잤어요. 꿈을 꾸었어요.	자면서 꿈을 꾸었어요.
4. 웃으세요. 말씀하세요.	웃으면서 말씀하세요.
5. 전화했어요. 울었어요.	전화하면서 울었어요.
6. 운전했어요. 장난했어요.	운전하면서 장난했어요.
7. 라디오를 들었어요. 공부했어요.	라디오를 들으면서 공부했어요.
8. 춤을 추었어요. 놀았어요.	춤을 추면서 놀았어요.

F. Level Drill (Review)

Teacher : 그것이 아름답습니까?	Is that beautiful?
Student : 그것이 아름다우냐?	Is that beautiful?
1. 어지럽습니까?	어지러우냐?
2. 이 음식이 싱겁습니까?	이 음식이 싱거우냐?
3. 그것이 맵습니까?	그것이 매우냐?
4. 섭섭합니까?	섭섭하냐?
5. 행복합니까?	행복하냐?
6. 반갑습니까?	반가우냐?
7. 그것이 가볍습니까?	그것이 가벼우냐?
8. 딸이 예쁩니까?	딸이 예쁘냐?

G. Pattern Drill (Review)

Teacher : 학교에 갔느냐?	Did you go to school?
Student : 학교에 가지 않았느냐?	Didn't you go to school?
1. 잊어버렸느냐?	잊어버리지 않았느냐?
2. 낮잠을 잤느냐?	낮잠을 자지 않았느냐?
3. 감기에 걸렸느냐?	감기에 걸리지 않았느냐?
4. 주의했느냐?	주의하지 않았느냐?
5. 문을 잠갔느냐?	문을 잠그지 않았느냐?
6. 소화가 잘 되느냐?	소화가 잘 되지 않느냐?
7. 회의를 하느냐?	회의를 하지 않느냐?
8. 외출하느냐?	외출하지 않느냐?

H. Pattern Drill (Review)

Teacher : 학교에 간다.	I go to school.
Student : 학교에 가지 않는다.	I don't go to school.
1. 그것을 깁는다.	그것을 깁지 않는다.

2. 돈을 줍는다.	돈을 줍지 않는다.
3. 문을 잠근다.	문을 잠그지 않는다.
4. 머리를 빗는다.	머리를 빗지 않는다.
5. 손을 씻는다.	손을 씻지 않는다.
6. 집을 짓는다.	집을 짓지 않는다.
7. 잘 이해한다.	잘 이해하지 않는다.
8. 조퇴한다.	조퇴하지 않는다.

I. Pattern Drill

Teacher : 그 책이 좋습니까?	Is that book good?
Student : 그 책이 좋은가요?	Is that book good?
1. 그것이 무겁습니까?	그것이 무거운가요?
2. 그것이 가볍습니까?	그것이 가벼운가요?
3. 지금 간지럽습니까?	지금 간지러운가요?
4. 그 산이 아름답습니까?	그 산이 아름다운가요?
5. 설탕이 답니까?	설탕이 단가요?
6. 그분이 점잖습니까?	그분이 점잖은가요?
7. 그분이 겸손합니까?	그분이 겸손한가요?
8. 몸이 불편합니까?	몸이 불편한가요?

J. Pattern Drill (Review)

Teacher : 일어나자.	Let's get up.
Student : 일어나지 말자.	Let's not get up.
1. 결석하자.	결석하지 말자.
2. 결근하자.	결근하지 말자.
3. 그것을 빼앗자.	그것을 빼앗지 말자.
4. 물을 붓자.	물을 붓지 말자.
5. 젓자.	젓지 말자.
6. 눕자.	눕지 말자.
7. 아침을 굶자.	아침을 굶지 말자.
8. 방해하자.	방해하지 말자.

K. Pattern Drill (Review)

Teacher : 학교에 가라.	Go to school.
Student : 학교에 가지 말라.	Don't go to school.
1. 봉사하라.	봉사하지 말라.
2. 바꾸라.	바꾸지 말라.
3. 약혼을 축하하라.	약혼을 축하하지 말라.

4. 씹어서 먹으라. 씹어서 먹지 말라.
5. 질문하라. 질문하지 말라.
6. 집을 지으라. 집을 짓지 말라.
7. 머리를 빗으라. 머리를 빗지 말라.
8. 여기에 누으라. 여기에 눕지 말라.

SHORT STORIES

1. 비를 맞았습니다.
   그래서 옷이 젖었습니다.
   나는 옷을 말렸습니다.
   옷이 잘 말랐습니다.

비를 맞다	to be exposed to the rain
젖다	to get(be) wet
말리다	to make dry
마르다	to be dry

   Expansion Drill

   비를 맞아서 옷이 젖었기 때문에, 나는 옷을 말렸습니다. 옷이 잘 말랐습니다.

2. 노래를 부르면서 춤을 추었어요.
   아주 즐겁게 놀았어요.
   그런데 너무 떠들어서 목이 아파요. 목 a throat

   Expansion Drill

   노래를 부르면서 춤을 추었어요. 아주 즐겁게 놀았는데, 너무 떠들어서 목이 아파요.

3. 어제는 주말이었습니다.
   그래서 친구를 방문했습니다.
   차를 마시면서 얘기를 많이 했습니다.

   Expansion Drill

   어제는 주말이었기 때문에, 친구를 방문했습니다. 차를 마시면서 얘기를 많이 했습니다.

READING

오래간 만에 친구를 방문했어요. 미리 전화해 놓고 갔어요. 가니까 친구가 기다리고 있었어요. 내 친구는 유명한 건축가에요. 그리고 아주 부자에요. 그래서 굉장히 큰 집에서 살고 있어요. 거실이 여간 넓지 않았어요. 나는 지금까지 그렇게 큰 거실을 본 일이 없어요. 내 친구는 얼마 전에 세계를 여행하고 돌아 왔어요. 며칠 후에 또 불란서에 가요. 그분만큼 여행을 많이 하는 분은 없어요.

미리	in advance	거실	a living room
유명하다	to be famous	세계	the world
건축가	an architect		

BRIEFING

I visited my friend for the first time after a long time. I called him in advance and went. When I got to his house, my friend was waiting for me. My friend is a famous architect. And he is very rich. So he is living in an extremely big house. The living room is extremely spacious. I've never seen such a big living room before. Some time ago my friend took a round-the-world trip and returned. In a few days he will go to France again. There is no one who likes to travel as much as he does.

UNIT 40 감기 A Cold

BASIC SENTENCES: MEMORIZE

갑자기	suddenly
감기	a cold

박 성 철

1. 날씨가 갑자기 추워 졌어요. 감기에 조심하세요. — The weather suddenly became cold. Be careful about catching a cold.

그렇지 않아도	even without your saying so
걸리다	to catch (a cold)

최 인 숙

2. 그렇지 않아도, 벌써 감기에 걸렸어요. — Even without your saying so, I caught a cold already.

그래요?	is that so?
독감	a bad cold (flu)
유행하다	to prevail, to go around

박 성 철

3. 그래요? 요즘 독감이 유행이래요. — Is that so? They say that a bad cold (flu) is going around these days.

큰 일	a serious matter, a great concern
나다	to happen
약	medicine

최 인 숙

4. 그럼, 큰 일 났는데요. 감기에 무슨 약이 좋을까요? — Then, we are really in trouble! What kind of medicine is good for a cold?

박 성 철

5. 감기엔 쉬는 것이 제일이에요. — For a cold, the best thing is to rest.

최 인 숙

6. 그럼, 일찍 집에 가서 쉬어야 겠어요. — Then, I have to go home early and rest.

NOTES ON THE BASIC SENTENCES

1. 갑자기 means (1) 'suddenly,' 'all of a sudden,' 'all at once,' 'abruptly,' 'hastily,' (2) 'unexpectedly,' 'without warning.' Its synonym is 별안간. Study the following examples:

갑자기 비가 와요.	Suddenly it is raining.
그분이 갑자기 죽었어요.	He suddenly dropped dead. Or: He suddenly died.
그분이 갑자기 돌아왔어요.	He returned unexpectedly.

2. 감기에 걸리다 'to catch a cold' is interchangeable with the phrase 감기가 들다 'to catch a cold.' Study the following examples, and note particularly the different particles after 감기.

감기에 걸렸어요.	I caught a cold.
감기가 들었어요.	I caught a cold.

걸리다, depending on the context or situation, can have many different meanings. Study the following examples:

모자가 벽에 걸려 있어요.	A hat is hanging on the wall.
한 십 분 걸려요.	It takes about ten minutes.
그분이 병에 걸렸어요.	He got sick.
전화가 안 걸렸어요.	I did not get my call through.
그것이 내 마음에 걸려요.	That weighs heavy on my mind.
내 목숨이 걸려 있어요.	My life is at stake.

3. 독감 means 'flu,' 'a bad cold.' 독 means 'a poison,' 'a poisonous substance.' Therefore, 독감 means literally 'a poisonous cold.' 유행이래요 is a contraction of 유행이라고 해요. The indirect discourse -고 하다 will be studied in this Unit, Structure Notes II.

4. 큰 일 났는데요: 큰 일 means 'a serious matter (problem),' 'a matter of great importance,' 'great trouble;' 나다 means 'to take place;' -는데요 is an exclamatory ending. Therefore, its literal meaning is 'A serious problem (matter, thing) took place.' This expression is used when you get into trouble, or when you face a matter of grave (serious) concern.

5. 감기엔 is a contraction of 감기에는.

6. 일찍 is a contraction of 일찌기 'early.'
   쉬어야겠어요 is a contraction of 쉬어야 하겠어요 'I'll have to rest.'

STRUCTURE NOTES

I. The Sentence-Final Ending -아(-어, -여) 지다… : 'become something'

The pattern -아(-어, -여)지 다 is used both with description verbs and action verbs. But it is used mostly with description verbs. This pattern indicates a change or development from a certain condition to another.

Examples :

그것이 좋아 졌어요.	It got better.
나빠 졌어요.	It got worse.
날씨가 추워 졌어요.	The weather got colder.
날씨가 따뜻해 집니다.	It's getting warmer.
나는 바빠 졌어요.	I became busier.
그분이 젊어 졌어요.	He became younger.
낮이 길어 집니다.	The days are getting longer.
그것이 비싸 졌어요.	It became expensive.
한국말이 쉬워 집니다.	Korean is getting easier.
그것이 깨 졌어요.	It got broken.
그것이 찢어 졌어요.	It got torn.

Notes :

1. The tense and/or negation is expressed regularly in the final verb -지다, not in the main verb with -아(-어, -여). Study the following examples :

그 여자가 예뻐 집니다.	She is getting more beautiful.
그 여자가 예뻐 졌습니다.	She became more beautiful.
그 여자가 예뻐지지 않았어요.	She did not become more beautiful.

2. -아 지다 is used after -아- and -오- ;
   -어 지다 is used after any other vowel ;
   -여 지다 is used after a 하다 verb.

II. The Indirect Discourse -고 하다… : '(someone) says that…'

We have already studied the Plain Style, (See Unit 36, Structure Notes I.) If you have studied it well, the formation of the indirect discourse will be easily understood. The pattern -고 하다 is attached directly to the plain style to form the indirect discourse. The tense, negation and exact words of the original speaker must be repeated or retained, when referring to someone's words.

(a) **Interrogative indirect discourse**:

The interrogative indirect discourse is made by attaching the ending -고 하다 directly to the plain question form of the verb. Study the following examples:

그것이 무엇이냐고 합니다. He asks what it is.
그분이 누구냐고 합니다. He asks who he is.
괜찮으냐고 합니다. He asks if it is alright.
누가 가느냐고 합니다. He asks who is going (there).
누가 갔느냐고 합니다. He asks who went (there).
누가 가겠느냐고 합니다. He asks who will go (there).
돈이 있느냐고 합니다. He asks if you (he, she) have money.
돈이 있었느냐고 합니다. He asks if you (he, she) had money.
그것이 예쁘냐고 합니다. He asks if that is beautiful.
그것이 예뻤느냐고 합니다. He asks if that was beautiful.
그것이 예쁘겠느냐고 합니다. He asks if that will be beautiful.

(b) **Declarative indirect discourse**:

The declarative indirect discourse is made by attaching the ending -고 하다 directly to the plain declarative form of the verb, except the verb of identification -이(다) in the present tense. Study the following examples:

그분이 공부한다고 합니다. He says he is studying.
그분이 공부하지 않는다고 합니다. He says he is not studying.
그분이 공부했다고 합니다. He says he studied.
그분이 공부하지 않았다고 합니다. He says he did not study.
그분이 공부하겠다고 합니다. He says he will study.
그분이 공부하지 않겠다고 합니다. He says he won't study.
그분이 바쁘다고 합니다. He says he is busy.
그분이 바쁘지 않다고 합니다. He says he is not busy.
그분이 바빴다고 합니다. He says he was busy.
그분이 바쁘지 않았다고 합니다. He says he was not busy.
그분이 바쁘겠다고 합니다. He says he will be busy.
그분이 바쁘지 않겠다고 합니다. He says he won't be busy.
그분이 돈이 있다고 합니다. He says he has money.
그분이 돈이 없다고 합니다. He says he has no money.
그분이 돈이 있었다고 합니다. He says he had money.
그분이 돈이 없었다고 합니다. He says he had no money.
그분이 선생이었다고 합니다. He says he was a teacher.

Note:
When the verb of identification -이(다) is in the present tense, -(이)라고 하다 is attached directly to the nouns. Study the following examples:

그분이 선생이라고 합니다. He says he is a teacher.
그것이 책이라고 합니다. He says it is a book.
그것이 복숭아라고 합니다. He says it is a peach.
그것이 지우개라고 합니다. He says it is an eraser.

(c) **Propositive indirect discourse**:

The propositive indirect discourse is made by attaching the ending -고 하다 directly to the plain propositive form of the verb. Study the following examples:

그분이 빨리 먹자고 합니다. He says, 'Let's eat quickly.'
지금 공부하자고 합니다. He says, 'Let's study now.'
그분을 도와주자고 합니다. He says, 'Let's help him.'
수영하자고 합니다. He says, 'Let's swim.'
복습하자고 합니다. He says, 'Let's review.'
연습하자고 합니다. He says, 'Let's practice.'
가지 말자고 합니다. He says, 'Let's not go.'

(d) **Imperative indirect discourse:**

When we studied the imperative forms of the plain style, there were two of them, i.e., -아(-어, -여)라 and -(으)라. The latter is used with the indirect discourse -고 하다. Study the following examples:

학교에 가라고 합니다. He says, 'Go to school.'
지금 일하라고 합니다. He says, 'Work now.'
눈을 감으라고 합니다. He says, 'Close your eyes.'
이 음식을 먹으라고 합니다. He says, 'Eat this food.'
가지 말라고 합니다. He says, 'Don't go.'

(e) **Polite imperative indirect discourse:**

The polite imperative indirect discourse is made by attaching the ending -고 하다 directly to the plain imperative form of the verb 달라다 (which means 'to ask (for),' 'to appeal,' 'to request,' etc.) Study the following examples:

불을 켜 달라고 합니다. He says, 'Turn on the light, please.'
집에 와 달라고 합니다. He says, 'Come home, please.'
문을 열어 달라고 합니다. He says, 'Open the door, please.'

Notes:

The tense and/or negation is expressed regularly in the final verb -하다.

Study the following examples:

그분이 가르친다고 합니다.	He says he is teaching.
그분이 가르친다고 했어요.	He said he is teaching.
그분이 가르친다고 하지 않았어요.	He did not say he is teaching.

III. A.V.S. +-는 것:

We have already studied verbal nouns made with the suffix -기, which indicate activity, quality, quantity, extent, or state of being, concretely (See Unit 20, Structure Notes II.) But this pattern -는 것, preceded directly by an action verb stem, indicates 'the act, (the fact, manner) of doing something.' The English equivalent of this pattern is '…ing,' the infinitive 'to (do),' or 'the thing that someone is doing.'

Examples:

쉬는 것이 제일입니다.	It's best to take a rest.
그분을 도와주는 것이 좋겠어요.	I think it's better to help him.
빨리 먹는 것이 나빠요.	It's bad to eat quickly.
여행하는 것이 어때요?	How about traveling?
저기 있는 것이 책이에요.	That over there is a book.
그분은 떠드는 것을 싫어해요.	He hates people who make noise.
공부하지 않는 것이 좋겠어요.	I think it's better not to study.
그분은 가르치는 것을 좋아해요.	He likes to teach.

Notes:

1. When the verbal noun made with -는 것 is used as a subject, it takes the particle -가/-이. But when it is used as an object, it takes the particle -를/-을.
2. This pattern can be used with the verb of existence 있다 or 없다. But it is used mostly with action verbs.

DRILLS

ADDITIONAL VOCABULARY

거절하다	to refuse, to reject	서두르다	to make haste with, to hasten
수출하다	to export		
수입하다	to import	자랑하다	to boast (of), to be proud of
소개하다	to introduce		

A. Substitution Drill

1. 그분을 도와주는 것이 좋겠어요. I think it's better to help him.
2. 그분을 방문하는 것이 좋겠어요. I think it's better to visit him.
3. 외출하는 것이 좋겠어요. I think it's better to go outdoors.
4. 그것을 빼앗는 것이 좋겠어요. I think it's better to take that away from him.
5. 그것을 잘 젓는 것이 좋겠어요. I think it's better to stir it well.
6. 그것을 붓는 것이 좋겠어요. I think it's better to pour it.
7. 그것을 잇는 것이 좋겠어요. I think it's better to connect it.
8. 주의하는 것이 좋겠어요. I think it's better to be careful.

B. Substitution Drill

1. 여행하는 것이 어때요? How about traveling?
2. 결석하는 것이 어때요? How about skipping school?
3. 결근하는 것이 어때요? How about skipping work?
4. 지각하는 것이 어때요? How about coming to school late?
5, 조퇴하는 것이 어때요? How about leaving early?
6. 문을 잠그는 것이 어때요? How about locking the door?
7. 그것을 바꾸는 것이 어때요? How about (ex)changing it?
8. 그것을 말리는 것이 어때요? How about drying it?

C. Substitution Drill

1. 쉬는 것이 제일입니다. It's best to take a rest.
2. 굶는 것이 제일입니다. It's best to go without eating.
3. 칭찬하는 것이 제일입니다. It's best to praise (him).
4. 수술하는 것이 제일입니다. It's best to operate on him.
5. 돈을 버는 것이 제일입니다. It's best to make money.
6. 돈을 갚는 것이 제일입니다. It's best to pay back the money.
7. 주의하는 것이 제일입니다. It's best to be careful
8. 거절하는 것이 제일입니다. It's best to refuse.

D. Pattern Drill

Teacher: 따뜻해요. It's warm.
Student: 따뜻해 집니다. It's getting warmer.

1. 어지러워요. 어지러워 집니다.
2. 더러워요. 더러워 집니다.
3. 시원해요. 시원해 집니다.
4. 쌀쌀해요. 쌀쌀해 집니다.
5. 길어요. 길어 집니다.

6. 넓어요.	넓어 집니다.
7. 뚱뚱해요.	뚱뚱해 집니다.
8. 홀쭉해요.	홀쭉해 집니다.

E. Pattern Drill

Teacher:	그 여자가 예뻐 졌어요.	She became beautiful.
Student:	그 여자가 예뻐 지지 않았어요.	She did not become beautiful.

1. 빨개 졌어요.	빨개 지지 않았어요.
2. 하얘 졌어요.	하얘 지지 않았어요.
3. 노래 졌어요.	노래 지지 않았어요.
4. 까매 졌어요.	까매 지지 않았어요.
5. 파래 졌어요.	파래 지지 않았어요.
6. 높아 졌어요.	높아 지지 않았어요.
7. 낮아 졌어요.	낮아 지지 않았어요.
8. 젊어 졌어요.	젊어 지지 않았어요.

F. Pattern Drill

Teacher:	그것이 무엇이냐?	What's that?
Student:	그것이 무엇이냐고 합니다.	He asks what that is.

1. 그분이 늙었으냐?	그분이 늙었느냐고 합니다.
2. 섭섭하냐?	섭섭하냐고 합니다.
3. 그분은 점잖으냐?	그분은 점잖으냐고 합니다.
4. 그분한테 부탁했느냐?	그분한테 부탁했느냐고 합니다.
5. 대답했느냐?	대답했느냐고 합니다.
6. 맛을 보겠느냐?	맛을 보겠느냐고 합니다.
7. 냄새를 맡겠느냐?	냄새를 맡겠느냐고 합니다.
8. 준비하겠느냐?	준비하겠느냐고 합니다.

G. Pattern Drill

Teacher:	그분이 공부한다.	He is studying.
Student:	그분이 공부한다고 합니다.	He says he is studying.

1. 교통 신호를 위반했다.	교통 신호를 위반했다고 합니다.
2. 거절했다.	거절했다고 합니다.
3. 많이 수출한다.	많이 수출한다고 합니다.
4. 수입하지 않는다.	수입하지 않는다고 합니다.
5. 점심을 먹는다.	점심을 먹는다고 합니다.

6. 감기에 걸렸다. 감기에 걸렸다고 합니다.
7. 소화가 잘 된다. 소화가 잘 된다고 합니다.
8. 폐를 끼쳤다. 폐를 끼쳤다고 합니다.

H. Pattern Drill

Teacher: 그분이 선생이다. He is a teacher.
Student: 그분이 선생이라고 합니다. He says he is a teacher.

1. 그분이 박사다. 그분이 박사라고 합니다.
2. 그분이 대학 교수다. 그분이 대학 교수라고 합니다.
3. 저것이 주유소다. 저것이 주유소라고 합니다.
4. 이것이 횡단보도다. 이것이 횡단보도라고 합니다.
5. 저것이 육교다. 저것이 육교라고 합니다.
6. 이것이 지하도다. 이것이 지하도라고 합니다.
7. 이것이 지하철이다. 이것이 지하철이라고 합니다.
8. 이것이 고가도로다. 이것이 고가도로라고 합니다.

I. Pattern Drill

Teacher: 연습하자. Let's practice.
Student: 연습하자고 합니다. He says, 'Let's practice.'

1. 머리를 빗자 머리를 빗자고 합니다.
2. 이것을 깁자. 이것을 깁자고 합니다.
3. 축하하자. 축하하자고 합니다.
4. 그분을 방문하자. 그분을 방문하자고 합니다.
5. 걸어 다니자. 걸어 다니자고 합니다.
6. 불을 끄자. 불을 끄자고 합니다.
7. 불을 켜자. 불을 켜자고 합니다.
8. 춤을 추자. 춤을 추자고 합니다.

J. Pattern Drill

Teacher: 불을 켜 달라. Turn on the light (for me).
Student: 불을 켜 달라고 합니다. He says, 'Turn on the light.'

1. 문을 열어 달라. 문을 열어 달라고 합니다.
2. 문을 닫아 달라. 문을 닫아 달라고 합니다.
3. 불을 꺼 달라. 불을 꺼 달라고 합니다.
4. 빨리 준비해 달라. 빨리 준비해 달라고 합니다.
5. 고쳐 달라. 고쳐 달라고 합니다.
6. 전화해 달라. 전화해 달라고 합니다.
7. 비행기에 태워 달라. 비행기에 태워 달라고 합니다.

8. 대답해 달라. 대답해 달라고 합니다.

K. Pattern Drill

Teacher : 학교에 가라. Go to school.

Student : 학교에 가라고 합니다. He says, 'Go to school.'

1. 숨을 쉬라. 숨을 쉬라고 합니다.
2. 조용히 하라. 조용히 하라고 합니다.
3. 과로하지 말라. 과로하지 말라고 합니다.
4. 과식하지 말라. 과식하지 말라고 합니다.
5. 과음하지 말라. 과음하지 말라고 합니다.
6. 신을 신으라. 신을 신으라고 합니다.
7. 장갑을 끼라. 장갑을 끼라고 합니다.
8. 조심하라. 조심하라고 합니다.

SHORT STORIES

1. 나는 사람들이 떠드는 것을 싫어해요
그런데 아이들이 떠들었어요.
그래서 조용히 하라고 했어요.

Expansion Drill

나는 사람들이 떠드는 것을 싫어하는데, 아이들이 떠들어서 조용히 하라고 했어요.

2. 갑자기 날씨가 추워 졌어요.
그래서 감기에 걸린 환자가 많아요. 환자 a patient
무엇보다도 건강에 조심하세요.

Expansion Drill

갑자기 날씨가 추워 져서 감기에 걸린 환자가 많으니까, 무엇보다도 건강에 조심하세요.

3. 그분이 누구냐고 하니까 학생이라고 했어요.
요즘 한국말을 공부한다고 했어요.
그래서 열심히 공부하라고 했어요.

Expansion Drill

그분이 누구냐고 하니까 한국말을 공부하는 학생이라고 했어요.
그래서 열심히 공부하라고 했어요.

READING

옛날에는 서당에서 한자를 가르쳤습니다. 아이들이 보통 다섯 살이 되면 한자를 배우기 시작했습니다. 하루는 어떤 학생이 자꾸 졸았습니다. 졸다가 나중에 잠이 들었습니다. 이것을 본 선생님이 그 학생을 깨우라고 했습니다. 그래서 다른 학생이 자고 있는 학생을 깨웠습니다. 선생님이 잠을 잔 학생을 야단쳤습니다. 한 번만 더 자면 혼내주겠다고 했습니다. 그런데 다음 날 선생님 자신이 피곤해서 잠이 들었습니다. 이것을 본 학생들이 막 웃었습니다. 선생님이 학생들한테 변명했습니다. 학생들을 잘 가르치기 위해서 공자님을 만나러 갔다고 했습니다. (계속)

서당	a village schoolhouse	혼내주다	to give (someone) a hard time
한자	Chinese characters		
하루는	one day	자신	one's self, oneself
자꾸	constantly, continuously	막	carelessly, at random
졸다	to doze	변명하다	to defend oneself from (an accusation)
잠이 들다	to fall asleep		
깨우다	to awaken, to wake (someone) up	-기 위해서	in order to, with the intention of
야단치다	to give (someone) a scolding	공자	Confucius

BRIEFING

In the old days we taught Chinese characters at the village schoolhouse. Usually, when children became five years old, they started to learn Chinese characters. One day a certain student kept dozing. He finally fell asleep. The teacher who saw it said, 'Wake him up.' So another student woke him up. The teacher scolded the student who had slept. The teacher said he would give him a hard time if he fell asleep once more. However, the following day the teacher himself was so tired that he fell asleep. The students who saw it laughed. The teacher made an excuse to the students. He said that he had gone to see Confucius in order to teach them better.

UNIT 41 교통사고 A Traffic Accident

BASIC SENTENCES: MEMORIZE

교통사고	a traffic accident
나다	to occur
하마터면	a close shave, by a hair's breadth

최 인 숙

1. 어제 교통 사고가 났어요. 하마터면 죽을 뻔했어요.	A traffic accident occurred yesterday. I nearly died.
다치다	to get hurt

박 성 철

2. 큰 일 날 뻔했군요! 누가 많이 다치지는 않았어요?	Something terrible nearly happened. Nobody got hurt seriously, did they?
다행히	fortunately
운전기사	a driver

최 인 숙

3. 다행히 나는 많이 다치지 않았어요. 그런데 운전기사가 많이 다쳤어요.	Fortunately, I didn't get hurt seriously. But the driver did.
병원	a hospital

박 성 철

4. 기사는 지금 병원에 있어요?	Is the driver in the hospital now?

최 인 숙

5. 예, 그래요. 그런데 그분이 어떻게 되었는지 모르겠어요.	Yes, that's right. But I don't know what happened to him.

박 성 철

6. 교통 사고 때문에 정말 큰 일 났어요.	We really are in trouble because of traffic accidents.

NOTES ON THE BASIC SENTENCES

1. 나다, depending on the context or situation, can have many different meanings. It is an intransitive verb which always takes the subject particle -가/-이. Study the following examples:

교통 사고가 났어요.	A traffic accident happened.
불이 났어요.	A fire broke out.
좋은 냄새가 났어요.	It smelled good.
소문이 났어요.	A rumor got abroad.
병이 났어요.	He got sick.
기침이 났어요.	He had a cough.
화가 났어요.	I was angry.
생각이 났어요.	The thought occurred to me.

하마터면 means 'by a close shave,' 'by the skin of one's teeth,' 'on the verge (brink) of.' It is used normally with the pattern -ㄹ(을) 뻔했다, (See this Unit, Structure Notes I.)

2. 누가 is an indefinite pronoun meaning 'somebody,' (See Unit 8, Notes 2 on the Basic Sentences).

다치다 means 'to get hurt,' 'to be injured,' 'to be wounded,' 'to receive an injury,' etc. Study the following examples:

그분이 많이 다쳤어요.	He was badly wounded. Or: He was seriously injured.
다리를 다쳤어요.	I hurt my leg.
다치지 않도록 조심하세요.	Be careful not to get hurt.

3. 운전기사 is a modern word meaning 'a driver (of a car, taxi, bus),' whereas 기관사 means 'an engineer (of a train),' 'an operator (of a machine).' Old words are 운전사 or 운전수. But 운전기사 is used more often than 운전사 or 운전수.

STRUCTURE NOTES

I. The Sentence-Final Ending -ㄹ(을) 뻔했다… : 'almost (did)'

The pattern -ㄹ(을) 뻔했다 is used to indicate that an action or event had almost occurred. The English equivalent of this pattern is '(someone or it) nearly (did so-and-so),' '…barely missed (doing so-and-so),' '…just barely escaped (doing so-and-so),' '…came close to (doing so-and-so).'

Examples :

큰 일 날 뻔했어요.	Something serious almost happened.
죽을 뻔했어요.	I nearly died.
이 책을 잃어 버릴 뻔했어요.	I almost lost this book.
그것을 잊어 버릴 뻔했어요.	I almost forgot about it.
독일에 갈 뻔했어요.	I almost went to Germany.
독일에 못 갈 뻔했어요.	I nearly didn't get to go to Germany.
그 여자와 결혼할 뻔했어요.	I came very close to marrying her. Or : I almost married her.
그분을 못 볼 뻔했어요.	I nearly missed him.
혼날 뻔했어요.	I nearly had a hard time.
내가 이길 뻔했어요.	I almost won (a game). Or : I came close to winning.
그분하고 싸울 뻔했어요.	I came close to fighting with him.

Notes :

1. This pattern is used always in the past tense. It goes well with the word 하마터면 'by the skin of one's teeth,' 'by a hair's breadth.'
2. The pattern is used mostly with action verbs. However, some exceptions take description verbs. Here are some examples :

늦을 뻔했어요.	I was almost late.
좋을 뻔했어요.	It might have been good.
위험할 뻔했어요.	It was almost dangerous.
귀찮을 뻔했어요.	It came close to being troublesome.

3. -ㄹ 뻔했다 is used after verb stems ending in a vowel ;
   -을 뻔했다 is used after verb stems ending in a consonant.

II. The Indirect Question Ending -지/-가 :

The ending -지 (or -가) is preceded always by a modifier suffix : -ㄴ (은), -는, or -ㄹ (을). It indicates an uncertain fact or occurrence. This pattern -지 (or -가), when used with a modifier suffix, is followed usually by verbs such as 알다 'to know,' 모르다 'to not know,' 말하다 'to tell,' 묻다 'to ask,' 잊다 'to forget,' 생각나다 'to remember,' 기억하다' to remember,' etc.

Examples :

그것이 무엇인지 모르겠어요.	I don't know what it is.
그분이 누구인지 아시겠어요?	Do you know who he is?
그분이 학생인지 물어 보세요.	Please ask him if he is a student.

그 곳이 어디인지 말씀해 주세요.	Please tell me where that place is.
그것이 비싼지 싼지 모르겠어요.	I don't know whether it's expensive or cheap.
그것이 큰지 작은지 몰라요.	I don't know whether it's big or small.
어느 것이 좋은지 물어 보세요.	Please ask him which one is better.
그것이 얼마인지 잊어 버렸어요.	I forgot how much it is.
그분이 어떻게 되었는지 몰라요.	I don't know what happened to him.
누가 왔는지 생각나지 않아요.	I don't remember who came.
그분이 학교에 갔는지 물어 보세요.	Please ask him if he went to school.
그분이 학교에 가겠는지 물어 보세요.	Please ask him if he will go to school.
그분이 그것을 할지 안 할지 모르겠어요.	I don't know whether he will do it or not.
그 일이 어떻게 될지 아십니까?	Do you know how that work will turn out?
어느 것이 좋을지 모르겠어요.	I don't know which one will be better.

Notes:

1. -ㄴ(은)지 is used with description verbs in the present tense, and with -이(다) in the present tense. (-ㄴ지 is used after verb stems ending in a vowel; -은지 is used after verb stems ending in a consonant).
2. In all other cases, -는지 is used.
3. -ㄹ(을) is used either with action verbs or description verbs. (-ㄹ지 is used after verb stems ending in a vowel; -을지 is used after verb stems ending in a consonant).
4. -겠는지 is interchangeable with -ㄹ(을)지, making no difference in meaning. Study the following examples:

   그분이 가겠는지 모르겠어요.
   그분이 갈지 모르겠어요. — I don't know if he will go.

5. The ending -지 is used more frequently than -가 in colloquial speech. It can be followed directly by particles such as -를/-을, -는/-은, or -도. Study the following examples:

   어느 것이 좋은지를 물어 보세요. — Please ask him which is better.
   누가 왔는지는 모르겠어요. — I don't know who came.

DRILLS

ADDITIONAL VOCABULARY

결혼하다 to marry — 필요하다 to be necessary

노력하다	to make an effort	받아쓰다	to write down, to take dictation
붙잡다	to seize, to grasp, to clasp	지나가다	to pass by, to go past
		옳다	to be right, to be correct

A. Substitution Drill

1. 큰 일 날 뻔했어요. — A terrible thing almost happened.
2. 죽을 뻔했어요. — I nearly died.
3. 이 책을 잃어버릴 뻔했어요. — I almost lost this book.
4. 독일에 못 갈 뻔했어요. — I almost didn't get to go to Germany.
5. 그 여자와 결혼할 뻔했어요. — I came close to marrying her. Or: I almost married her.
6. 그분을 못 볼 뻔했어요. — I almost couldn't see him.
7. 혼날 뻔했어요. — I almost had a hard time.
8. 내가 이길 뻔했어요. — I almost won (a game). Or: I came close to winning.
9. 그분하고 싸울 뻔했어요. — I came close to fighting with him.
10. 내가 질 뻔했어요. — I almost lost (a game).

B. Substitution Drill

1. 선생인지 학생인지 모르겠어요. — I don't know whether he is a teacher or a student.
2. 송별회인지 환영회인지 모르겠어요. — I don't know whether it's a farewell party or a welcoming party.
3. 의사인지 교수인지 모르겠어요. — I don't know whether he's a medical doctor or a professor.
4. 참말인지 거짓말인지 모르겠어요. — I don't know whether it's true or false.
5. 약방인지 책방인지 모르겠어요. — I don't know whether it's a drugstore or a bookstore.
6. 공장인지 회사인지 모르겠어요. — I don't know whether it's a factory or a company.
7. 월요일인지 화요일인지 모르겠어요. — I don't know whether it's Monday or Tuesday.
8. 중학교인지 고등학교인지 모르겠어요. — I don't know whether it's a middle school or a high school.

C. Substitution Drill

1. 무거운지 가벼운지 모르겠어요. — I don't know whether it's heavy or light.
2. 짠지 싱거운지 모르겠어요. — I don't know whether it's salty or insipid.
3. 깊은지 얕은지 모르겠어요. — I don't know whether it's deep or shallow.

4. 두꺼운지 얇은지 모르겠어요.	I don't know whether it's thick or thin (paper).
5. 긴지 짧은지 모르겠어요.	I don't know whether it's long or short.
6. 깨끗한지 더러운지 모르겠어요.	I don't know whether it's clean or dirty.
7. 넓은지 좁은지 모르겠어요.	I don't know whether it's wide or narrow.
8. 밝은지 어두운지 모르겠어요.	I don't know whether it's bright or dark.

D. Pattern Drill

Teacher : 어느 것이 좋습니까?	Which one is better?
Student : 어느 것이 좋은지 물어 보세요.	Please ask him which one is better.
1. 누가 왔습니까?	누가 왔는지 물어 보세요.
2. 누가 옳습니까?	누가 옳은지 물어 보세요.
3. 그분이 누구입니까?	그분이 누구인지 물어 보세요.
4. 오늘이 며칠입니까?	오늘이 며칠인지 물어 보세요.
5. 오늘이 무슨 요일입니까?	오늘이 무슨 요일인지 물어 보세요.
6. 시끄럽습니까?	시끄러운지 물어 보세요.
7. 어디에 가시겠습니까?	어디에 가시겠는지 물어 보세요.
8. 무엇을 잡수셨습니까?	무엇을 잡수셨는지 물어 보세요.

E. Pattern Drill

Teacher : 누가 왔습니까?	Who came?
Student : 누가 왔는지 생각나지 않아요.	I don't remember who came.
1. 무엇을 읽었습니까?	무엇을 읽었는지 생각나지 않아요.
2. 어떻게 되었습니까?	어떻게 되었는지 생각나지 않아요.
3. 몇 시간 놀았습니까?	몇 시간 놀았는지 생각나지 않아요.
4. 불을 껐습니까?	불을 껐는지 생각나지 않아요.
5. 언제 전화했습니까?	언제 전화했는지 생각나지 않아요.
6. 누구를 만났습니까?	누구를 만났는지 생각나지 않아요.
7. 무슨 꿈을 꾸었습니까?	무슨 꿈을 꾸었는지 생각나지 않아요.
8. 누가 회의를 했습니까?	누가 회의를 했는지 생각나지 않아요.

F. Pattern Drill

Teacher : 그분이 가겠는지 모르겠어요.
I don't know if he will go.
Student : 그분이 갈지 모르겠어요.
I don't know if he will go.

1. 소화가 잘 되겠는지 모르겠어요. 소화가 잘 될지 모르겠어요.
2. 회의를 하겠는지 모르겠어요. 회의를 할지 모르겠어요.
3. 그분이 방문하겠는지 모르겠어요. 그분이 방문할지 모르겠어요.
4. 집을 짓겠는지 모르겠어요. 집을 지을지 모르겠어요.
5. 머리를 빗겠는지 모르겠어요. 머리를 빗을지 모르겠어요.
6. 그분이 이해하겠는지 모르겠어요. 그분이 이해할지 모르겠어요.
7. 돈을 빌려주겠는지 모르겠어요. 돈을 빌려줄지 모르겠어요.
8. 그분이 운전하겠는지 모르겠어요. 그분이 운전할지 모르겠어요.

G. Pattern Drill

Teacher : 어느 것이 좋은지 모르겠어요.
I don't know which is better.
Student : 어느 것이 좋을지 모르겠어요.
I don't know which will be better.

1. 그분이 행복한지 모르겠어요. 그분이 행복할지 모르겠어요.
2. 그분이 친절한지 모르겠어요. 그분이 친절할지 모르겠어요.
3. 그것이 튼튼한지 모르겠어요. 그것이 튼튼할지 모르겠어요.
4. 그분이 겸손한지 모르겠어요. 그분이 겸손할지 모르겠어요.
5. 그분이 가는지 모르겠어요. 그분이 갈지 모르겠어요.
6. 몇 시에 도착하는지 모르겠어요. 몇 시에 도착할지 모르겠어요.
7. 누가 방해하는지 모르겠어요. 누가 방해할지 모르겠어요.
8. 누가 춤을 추는지 모르겠어요. 누가 춤을 출지 모르겠어요.

H. Pattern Drill

Teacher : 그것이 얼마인지 말씀해 주세요.
Please tell me how much it is.
Student : 그것이 얼마인지 잊어버렸어요.
I forgot how much it is.

1. 어떻게 썼는지 말씀해 주세요. 어떻게 썼는지 잊어버렸어요.
2. 누가 약혼했는지 말씀해 주세요. 누가 약혼했는지 잊어버렸어요.
3. 누가 결혼했는지 말씀해 주세요. 누가 결혼했는지 잊어버렸어요.
4. 어디가 고장이 났는지 말씀해 주세요. 어디가 고장이 났는지 잊어버렸어요.

5. 무엇을 구웠는지 말씀해 주세요.　　무엇을 구웠는지 잊어버렸어요.
6. 무엇을 삶았는지 말씀해 주세요.　　무엇을 삶았는지 잊어버렸어요.
7. 누구를 초대했는지 말씀해 주세요. 누구를 초대했는지 잊어버렸어요.
8. 누구를 칭찬했는지 말씀해 주세요. 누구를 칭찬했는지 잊어버렸어요.

SHORT STORIES

1. 어제 교통 사고가 났어요.
   큰 일 날 뻔했어요.
   다행히 아무도 다치지 않았어요.

   Expansion Drill

   어제 교통 사고가 나서 큰 일 날 뻔했는데, 다행히 아무도 다치지 않았어요.

2. 내 시계가 고장이 났어요.　　　　시계　a watch
   지금 몇 시인지 그분한테 물어 보세요.
   시계가 없으니까, 참 불편해요.

   Expansion Drill

   내 시계가 고장이 났으니까 지금 몇 시인지 그분한테 물어 보세요. 시계가 없으니까, 참 불편해요.

3. 그분이 두 시에 오겠다고 했어요.
   그러나 제 시간에 올지 모르겠어요.
   왜냐하면 지금 교통이 여간 복잡하지 않아요.

   Expansion Drill

   그분이 두 시에 오겠다고 했지만, 제 시간에 올지 모르겠어요. 왜냐하면 지금 교통이 여간 복잡하지 않아요.

READING

그 후 며칠이 지났습니다. 며칠 전에 선생님한테 혼난 그 학생이 또 잤습니다. 그래서 선생님이 그 학생을 다시 야단쳤습니다. 선생님이 학생한테 왜 교실에서 자느냐고 했습니다. 그러니까 자기도 공자님을 만나기 위해서 잤다고 했습니다. 선생님이 기가 막혔습니다. 그래서 공자님을 만났느냐고 물었습니다. 학생이 공자님을 만났다고 대답했습니다. 그래서 선생님이 공자님하고 무슨 이야기를 했느냐고 물었습니다. 학생이 이렇게 대답했습니다. 제가 공자님한테 우리 선생님을 만난 일이 있느냐고 물었습니다. 그랬더니 공자님이 한 번도 만난 일이 없다고 하셨어요.

그 후	after that, thereafter	자기	self, oneself
지나다	to go by, to pass	기가 막히다	to be stifled, to be at a loss (for words)
그러니까	therefore, so		
		그랬더니	when I asked (him)

BRIEFING

After that, a few days passed. The student who had previously had a hard time from the teacher slept again. So, the teacher scolded him again. The teacher asked him why he was sleeping in the classroom. The student said that he had also gone to see Confucius. The teacher was at a loss for words. So, the teacher asked him if he had met Confucius. The student answered that he had met Confucius. So the teacher asked him what he had talked about with Confucius. The student answered that he had asked Confucious, "Have you ever met my teacher?" But Confucius said, 'I've never met your teacher, even once.'

UNIT 42 예습 Preparation

BASIC SENTENCES: MEMORIZE

요즘	these days
어떻게	how
최 인 숙	
1. 요즘 집에서 어떻게 공부하세요?	How do you study at home these days?
주로	mainly
예습하다	to prepare (one's lesson)
박 성 철	
2. 주로 예습을 많이 해요.	Generally, I do a lot of prepeation work.
중요하다	to be important
잊어 버리지 않도록	so that you won't forget
복습하다	to review
최 인 숙	
3. 예습도 중요합니다. 그러나 잊어 버리지 않도록 복습을 많이 하세요.	Preparation is important. But please review a lot so that you won't forget the lessons.
단어	vocabulary
외우다	to memorize
힘들다	to be difficult. to be tough
박 성 철	
4. 복습도 합니다. 그런데 난 단어를 외우기가 제일 힘들어요.	I review too. But it's most difficult to memorize the vocabulary.
연습하다	to practice
읽는 연습	reading practice
최 인 숙	
5. 읽는 연습도 하십니까?	Do you also practice reading?
박 성 철	
6. 그럼요. 그런데 아직 잘 읽을 줄 몰라요.	Sure! But I still don't know how to read well.

NOTES ON THE BASIC SENTENCES

2. 주로 means (1) 'mainly,' 'chiefly,' 'primarily,' (2) 'mostly,' 'for the most part,' 'generally,' etc. Study the following examples:

한국 사람은 주로 밥을 먹어요.	Koreans mainly eat boiled rice.
집에서는 주로 영어를 공부해요.	I study mainly English at home.
학생은 주로 미국 사람들이에요.	The students, for the most part, are Americans.

예습하다 means 'to prepare one's lesson.' 예 means 'beforehand,' 'to prepare,' 'to make ready.' Study the following words:

예상하다 'to anticipate,' 'to presume,' 'to estimate'

예약하다 'to book in advance,' 'to make a reservation'

예언하다 'to predict,' 'to prophesy,' 'to foretell'

예정하다 'to arrange beforehand,' 'to plan'

예측하다 'to presuppose,' 'to make an estimate of'

3. 복습하다 means 'to review (one's lessons),' 'to go over (through).'
복 means 'to repeat,' 'to come back.' Study the following words:

복구하다 'to return (to a former condition),' 'to be restored (to an original state)'

복사하다 'to reproduce,' 'to duplicate'

복직하다 'to resume office,' to be reinstated to one's former position'

4. 외우다 'to memorize' is a dialect which is used in kyəngki, kangwən, Ch'ungch'əng and Kyəngsang provinces. 외다 'to memorize' is a standard language. However, 외우다 is used more often than 외다 in colloquial speech.

힘들다 means (1) 'to be laborious (strenuous, toilsome, troublesome, tough),' (2) 'to be hard (difficult).' Study the following examples:

살기 힘들어요.	I find it hard to live.
일하기 힘들어요.	It's hard to work.
그 일은 별로 힘들지 않아요.	That work is not particularly difficult.
그분은 힘든 일을 하고 있어요.	He is doing a tough job.

5. 연습하다 means 'to practice,' 'to drill,' 'to train,' 'to rehearse (a play).' Study the following examples:

연습을 시작했어요.	We began training.
피아노를 연습하고 있어요.	She is practicing piano.
연습하면 잘 될 거에요.	You will improve by practice.
연습이 부족해요.	You lack training (practice).

STRUCTURE NOTES

I. The Sentence-Final Ending -아(-어, -여) 버리다… : 'finish up doing'

The verb 버리다 means (1) 'to finish up,' 'to get through,' 'to get (it) done,' (2) 'to throw away,' 'to cast away.' The pattern -아(-어, -여) 버리다 is attached directly to the stems of action verbs, and indicates completion or thoroughness. The English equivalent of this pattern is 'finish up doing,' 'do completely (thoroughly).'

Examples:

이 음식을 먹어 버리겠어요.	I will finish eating this food.
돈을 다 써 버렸어요.	I used up all the money.
이 책을 다 읽어 버리겠어요.	I'll read this book completely.
빨리 해 버리세요.	Please finish (up) quickly.
한 시에 끝내 버렸어요.	I finished at one o'clock.
편지를 빨리 써 버리세요.	Please finish (writing) the letter quickly.
나무가 넘어져서 죽어 버렸어요.	The tree fell and died (completely).
그 책을 잃어 버렸어요.	I lost that book.
그것을 잊어 버렸어요.	I completely forgot about it.

Notes:

1. The tense and/or negation is expressed regularly in the final verb 버리다, not in the main verb with -아(-어, -여). Study the following examples:

다 씻어 버리세요.	Please finish up washing all of them.
다 씻어 버렸어요.	I finished up washing all of them.
다 씻어 버리겠어요.	I'll finish up washing all of them.
다 씻어 버리지 않았어요.	I didn't finish up washing all of them.
다 씻어 버리지 않겠어요.	I won't finish up washing all of them.

2. -아 버리다 is used after -아- and -오-;
   -어 버리다 is used after any other vowel;
   -여 버리다 is used after a 하다 verb.

II. The Non-Final Ending -도록… : 'so that…'

The pattern -도록, depending on the context or situation, can have several different meanings. First of all, let's study this pattern -도록 when it indicates 'purpose,' or 'aim.' The English equivalent is 'so that…,' 'in order to …,' 'in such a way that….'

잊어 버리지 않도록 많이 복습하세요.	Please review a lot so that you won't forget (the lessons).
내가 볼 수 있도록 이리로 가지고 오세요.	Bring that here so that I can see it.
늦지 않도록 빨리 가세요.	Please go quickly so that you won't be late.
그분이 주무시도록 조용히 하세요.	Please be quiet so that he can sleep.
내가 들을 수 있도록 크게 말씀해 주세요.	Please talk in a loud voice so that I can hear you.
그런 일이 일어나지 않도록 조심하겠어요.	I'll be careful so that such a thing won't happen.
잊어 버리지 않도록 가방에 넣으세요.	Please pack these in the suitcase so that we won't forget.
그분이 들어올 수 있도록 문을 열어 놓으세요.	Please open the door so that he can come in.

Note :

This pattern may be used with any verb, except -이(다).

III. The Sentence-Final Ending -ㄹ(을)줄 알다/모르다… : '(someone) knows (doesn't know) how to do'

We have already studied the sentence-final ending -ㄹ(을) 수 있다, which indicates ability, capability, or possibility, (See Unit 18. Structure Notes II.) This pattern -ㄹ(을)줄 알다/모르다 is used to indicate knowledge and/or lack of knowledge of a technique, or process for doing some activity.

Examples :

그분이 수영할 줄 몰라요.	He doesn't know how to swim.
한국말을 할 줄 아십니까?	Do you know how to speak Korean?
한국말을 할 줄 몰라요.	I don't know how to speak Korean.
한국 노래를 부를 줄 알아요.	I know how to sing Korean songs.
그분이 가르칠 줄 몰라요.	He doesn't know how to teach.
자동차를 고칠 줄 아십니까?	Do you know how to repair a car?
담배를 피울 줄 몰라요.	I don't know how to smoke.
춤을 출 줄 몰랐어요.	I didn't know how to dance.
타자를 칠 줄 모릅니다.	I don't know how to type.
이 문을 열 줄 몰라요.	I don't know how to open this door.

Notes :

1. The tense is expressed regularly in the final verb 알다/모르다, not in the

main verb with -ㄹ(을) 줄. Study the following examples:

한국말을 할 줄 알아요. I know how to speak Korean.
한국말을 할 줄 알았어요. I knew how to speak Korean.
한국말을 할 줄 몰라요. I don't know how to speak Korean.
한국말을 할 줄 몰랐어요. I didn't know how to speak Korean.

2. -ㄹ 줄 알다 is used after verb stems ending in a vowel; -을 줄 알다 is used after verb stems ending in a consonant.

IV. -르 Irregular Verbs:

Most verbs which have a -르 as the final syllable of the stem should not be confused with irregular verbs which end with the fianl consonant -ㄹ of the stem, (See Unit 19, Structure Notes I.)

1. The final syllable -르 of the stem, when followed by the vowel -어 and preceded by the vowels -아- or -오-, is changed into 라. Then the consonant -ㄹ is added to the preceding syllable. Study the following examples:

나르다 'to carry,' 'to transport'

이 짐을 날라야 합니다. You must carry this luggage.
이 짐을 날랐습니다. I carried this luggage.
이 짐을 날라 보세요. Try to carry this luggage

모르다 'to be unaware of'

그것을 몰라야 합니다. You shouldn't know it.
그것을 몰랐습니다. I didn't know it.
그것을 몰라도 좋아요. It's alright even if you don't know it.

-르 irregular verbs preceded by the vowel -아- or -오-:

가르(다)	to divide	바르(다)	to stick, to paste
고르(다)	to choose	오르(다)	to rise, to go up
나르(다)	to carry	자르(다)	to cut (off)
마르(다)	to be thirsty, to get dry	다르(다)	to be different
		빠르(다)	to be fast
모르(다)	to be unaware of		

2. The final syllable -르 of the stem, when followed by the vowel -어 and preceded by any other vowel than -아- or -오-, is changed into -러. Then the consonant -ㄹ is added to the preceding syllable. Study the following examples:

기르다 'to bring up,' 'to foster'

아이를 길러 보세요. Please try bringing up a child.

아이를 길렀습니다. I brought up a child.
아이를 길러야 합니다. You must bring up a child.
아이를 길러도 좋아요. You may bring up a child.

-르 irregular verbs preceded by any other vowel than -아- or -오- :

구르(다)	to roll (over)	이르(다)	to reach
기르(다)	to bring up	저지르(다)	to commit (an error)
누르(다)	to oppress	주무르(다)	to fumble with
두르(다)	to surround	찌르(다)	to pierce
부르(다)	to call, to sing	흐르(다)	to flow

DRILLS

ADDITIONAL VOCABULARY

빠르다	to be fast	흐르다	to flow
느리다	to be slow	기르다	to bring up
나르다	to carry	가르다	to divide

A. Substitution Drill

1. 저는 수영할 줄 몰라요. I don't know how to swim.
2. 그것을 붙잡을 줄 몰라요. I don't know how to seize it.
3. 저는 거절할 줄 몰라요. I don't know how to refuse.
4. 저는 소개할 줄 몰라요. I don't know how to introduce (him).
5. 저는 자랑할 줄 몰라요. I don't know how to boast.
6. 저는 봉사할 줄 몰라요. I don't know how to serve.
7. 저는 담배를 피울 줄 몰라요. I don't know how to smoke.
8. 저는 춤을 출 줄 몰라요. I don't know how to dance.

B. Substitution Drill

1. 이 음식을 먹어 버리겠어요. I'll finish this food.
2. 돈을 다 써 버리겠어요. I'll use up all the money.
3. 이 책을 다 읽어 버리겠어요. I'll read this book all the way through.
4. 빨리 해 버리겠어요. I'll finish it (up) quickly.
5. 한 시에 끝내 버리겠어요. I'll finish at one o'clock.
6. 편지를 빨리 써 버리겠어요. I'll finish (writing) the letter quickly.
7. 다 씻어 버리겠어요. I'll finish up washing all of them.
8. 그것을 잊어 버리겠어요. I'll forget about it completely.

C. Response Drill

Teacher : 자동차를 고칠 줄 아세요?
Do you know how to repair a car?
Student : 아니오, 자동차를 고칠 줄 몰라요.
No, I don't know how to repair a car.

1. 문을 잠글 줄 아세요? 아니오, 문을 잠글 줄 몰라요.
2. 불을 켤 줄 아세요? 아니오, 불을 켤 줄 몰라요.
3. 불을 끌 줄 아세요? 아니오, 불을 끌 줄 몰라요.
4. 고기를 구울 줄 아세요? 아니오, 고기를 구울 줄 몰라요.
5. 계란을 삶을 줄 아세요? 아니오, 계란을 삶을 줄 몰라요.
6. 사과를 깎을 줄 아세요? 아니오, 사과를 깎을 줄 몰라요.
7. 운전할 줄 아세요? 아니오, 운전할 줄 몰라요.
8. 물을 끓일 줄 아세요? 아니오, 물을 끓일 줄 몰라요.

D. Pattern Drill

Teacher : 복습하면 잊어 버리지 않아요.
You don't forget if you review the lessons.
Student : 잊어 버리지 않도록 복습하세요.
Please review so that you don't forget (the lessons).

1. 빨리 가면 늦지 않아요. 늦지 않도록 빨리 가세요.
2. 깨우면 일어나요. 일어나도록 깨우세요.
3. 조용히 하면 공부할 수 있어요. 공부할 수 있도록 조용히 하세요.
4. 노력하면 잘 할 수 있어요. 잘 할 수 있도록 노력하세요.
5. 들어오면 비를 맞지 않아요. 비를 맞지 않도록 들어오세요.
6. 씻으면 먹을 수 있어요. 먹을 수 있도록 씻으세요.
7. 돈을 벌면 갚을 수 있어요. 갚을 수 있도록 돈을 버세요.
8. 많이 만들면 수출할 수 있어요. 수출할 수 있도록 많이 만드세요.

E. Pattern Drill

Teacher : 아이를 기릅니다. I'm raising a child.
Student : 아이를 길렀습니다. I brought up a child.

1. 노래를 부릅니다. 노래를 불렀습니다.
2. 비행기가 빠릅니다. 비행기가 빨랐습니다.
3. 그것을 모릅니다. 그것을 몰랐습니다.
4. 초인종을 누릅니다. 초인종을 눌렀습니다.
5. 잘 마릅니다. 잘 말랐습니다.
6. 그것이 다릅니다. 그것이 달랐습니다.

7. 물이 흐릅니다. 물이 흘렀습니다.
8. 그것을 가릅니다. 그것을 갈랐습니다.

F. Integration Drill (Review)

Teacher: 그분이 옵니다. 기다리세요.
He is coming. Wait.

Student: 그분이 올 때까지 기다리세요.
Wait until he comes.

1. 이 일을 마칩니다. 앉아 계세요. 이 일을 마칠 때까지 앉아 계세요.
2. 그분이 돌아옵니다. 노세요. 그분이 돌아올 때까지 노세요.
3. 그분이 잠이 듭니다. 기다리세요. 그분이 잠이 들 때까지 기다리세요.
4. 회의가 끝납니다. 책을 읽으세요. 회의가 끝날 때까지 책을 읽으세요.
5. 그분이 도착합니다. 일하세요. 그분이 도착할 때까지 일하세요.
6. 그분이 깨웁니다. 주무세요. 그분이 깨울 때까지 주무세요.
7. 제가 전화합니다. 기다리세요. 제가 전화할 때까지 기다리세요.
8. 잘 할 수 있습니다. 연습하세요. 잘 할 수 있을 때까지 연습하세요.

G. Integration Drill (Review)

Teacher: 한국에 옵니다. 그분을 만납니다.
I come to Korea. I see him.

Student: 한국에 올 때마다 그분을 만납니다.
Every time I come to Korea, I see him.

1. 꿈을 꿉니다. 아주 이상합니다. 꿈을 꿀 때마다 아주 이상합니다.
2. 춤을 춥니다. 기분이 좋습니다. 춤을 출 때마다 기분이 좋습니다.
3. 전화합니다. 집에 안 계십니다. 전화할 때마다 집에 안 계십니다.
4. 회의를 합니다. 시끄럽습니다. 회의를 할 때마다 시끄럽습니다.
5. 여기에 옵니다. 복잡합니다. 여기에 올 때마다 복잡합니다.
6. 지각합니다. 야단칩니다. 지각할 때마다 야단칩니다.
7. 아픕니다. 결석합니다. 아플 때마다 결석합니다.
8. 조퇴합니다. 변명합니다. 조퇴할 때마다 변명합니다.

H. Integration Drill (Review)

Teacher: 이 일을 시작했습니다. 기분이 나빴습니다.
I began this work. I felt bad.

Student: 이 일을 시작할 때부터 기분이 나빴습니다.
From the time that I began this work, I felt bad.

1. 집을 지었습니다. 이상했습니다.
집을 지을 때부터 이상했습니다.

2. 점심을 먹었습니다. 배가 아팠습니다.
   점심을 먹을 때부터 배가 아팠습니다.
3. 일을 시작했습니다. 싸웠습니다.
   일을 시작할 때부터 싸웠습니다.
4. 교실에 들어왔습니다. 시끄러웠습니다.
   교실에 들어올 때부터 시끄러웠습니다.
5. 그분이 왔습니다. 화가 났습니다.
   그분이 올 때부터 화가 났습니다.
6. 공부를 시작했습니다. 배가 고팠습니다.
   공부를 시작할 때부터 배가 고팠습니다.
7. 그분이 떠났습니다. 울기 시작했습니다.
   그분이 떠날 때부터 울기 시작했습니다.
8. 회의를 시작했습니다. 재미있었습니다.
   회의를 시작할 때부터 재미있었습니다.

I. Pattern Drill (Review)

Teacher: 이것이 그것만큼 어려워요.
This is as difficult as that.
Student: 이것이 그것보다 어려워요.
This is more difficult than that.

1. 여기가 거기만큼 멀어요.	여기가 거기보다 멀어요.
2. 이 일이 그 일만큼 위험해요.	이 일이 그 일보다 위험해요.
3. 이 방이 그 방만큼 넓어요.	이 방이 그 방보다 넓어요.
4. 이분이 그분만큼 유명해요.	이분이 그분보다 유명해요.
5. 여기가 거기만큼 조용해요.	여기가 거기보다 조용해요.
6. 오늘이 어제만큼 추워요.	오늘이 어제보다 추워요.
7. 이분이 그분만큼 점잖아요.	이분이 그분보다 점잖아요.
8. 이것이 그것만큼 중요해요.	이것이 그것보다 중요해요.

SHORT STORIES

1. 친구하고 경주로 여행갔습니다.
   갈 때 돈을 충분히 가지고 갔습니다.
   그런데 돈을 다 써 버렸습니다.

   충분히 sufficiently, fully, satisfactorily

Expansion Drill

친구하고 경주로 여행갈 때, 돈을 충분히 가지고 갔는데, 돈을 다 써 버렸습니다.

2. 요즘 날씨가 여간 나쁘지 않아요.
감기에 걸려 있는 사람들이 많아요.
감기에 걸리지 않도록 조심하세요.

Expansion Drill

요즘 날씨가 여간 나쁘지 않아서, 감기에 걸려 있는 사람들이 많으니까, 감기에 걸리지 않도록 조심하세요.

3. 그분이 아직도 영어를 잘 할 줄 모릅니다.
무엇보다도 더 노력해야 합니다.
어떤 일이라도 노력하면 됩니다.

Expansion Drill

그분이 아직도 영어를 잘 할 줄 모르니까, 무엇보다도 더 노력해야 합니다. 어떤 일이라도 노력하면 됩니다.

READING

한국말을 공부한 지 석 달쯤 되었습니다. 처음에는 발음과 억양을 공부했습니다. 그 다음에 문형을 배우기 시작했습니다. 저는 학교에 가기 전에 예습합니다. 그리고 집에 돌아와서는 복습을 합니다. 저는 선생님과 공부할 때는 자신이 있습니다. 그런데 한국 사람을 만나면 말이 잘 나오지 않습니다. 답답해서 죽겠습니다. 읽는 연습도 가끔 합니다. 그런데 더듬더듬 읽습니다. 받아쓰기도 합니다. 그러나 저는 맞춤법을 잘 모릅니다. 그래서 받아쓰기를 하면 엉망입니다. 날마다 숙제도 여간 많지 않습니다. 숙제 중에서 제일 힘든 것은 글짓기 (작문) 입니다.

억양	intonation	받아쓰기	dictation
문형	pattern	맞춤법	rules of spelling
자신	(self-)confidence	엉망	a mess, (in) bad shape, a ruin, a wreck
답답하다	to be stifled to be choked up	중에서	among, between
더듬더듬 읽다	to falter over (a passage)	글짓기	composition
		작문	composition

BRIEFING

It has been about 3 months since I began to study Korean. In the beginning, I studied pronunciation and intonation. After that, I began to study patterns.

Before I go to school I prepare for class. After I come back home, I review. When I study with my teacher, I am confident. However, when I meet Korean people, I can't speak well. I'm so frustrated that I could die. Sometimes I do reading practice, also. But I falter. I do dictation, also. But I don't know the rules of spelling well. So, if I do dictation, it's terrible. I have a lot of homework everyday. Of all the homework, the most difficult is composition.

UNIT 43 피곤해 보여요 You Look Tired

BASIC SENTENCES: MEMORIZE

좀	a little
피곤하다	to be tired
보이다	to be seen, to be visible
지난 밤에	last night

최 인 숙

1. 좀 피곤해 보여요. 지난 밤에 늦게 주무셨어요? — You look a little tired. Did you go to bed late last night?

박 성 철

2. 예, 늦게 잤더니, 오늘 아주 피곤해요. — Yes. I went to bed late, so I'm very tired today.

최 인 숙

3. 무엇을 하시느라고, 늦게 주무셨어요? — What were you doing that you went to bed late?

친구하고	with my friend
얘기하느라고	because I was talking

박 성 철

4. 친구하고 얘기하느라고, 늦게 잤어요. — Because I was talking with my friend, I went to bed late.

피곤해서	because you are tired

최 인 숙

5. 오늘 피곤해서, 공부할 수 있겠어요? — Do you think you can study today although (because) you are tired?

피곤하지만	I'm tired, but

박 성 철

6. 피곤하지만, 공부하겠어요. — I'm tired, but I'll study.

NOTES ON THE BASIC SENTENCES

1. <u>피곤하다</u> means 'to be tired,' 'to be fatigued,' 'to be exhausted.' Its synonyms are <u>피로하다</u> and <u>고단하다</u>. Study the following examples:

피곤해서 죽겠어요.	I'm tired to death. Or : I'm so tired that I could die.
피로해서 못 먹겠어요.	I'm too tired to eat.
고단해 보입니다.	You look tired.

<u>보이다</u> : When it's used as an intransitive verb meaning 'to be seen,' 'to be visible,' 'to come in sight,' it takes the subject particle <u>-가/-이</u>. But when it is used as a transitive verb meaning 'to show,' 'to let (someone) see,' it takes the object particle <u>-를/-을</u>. Study the following examples:

여기서 학교가 잘 보여요.	The school can be seen very well from here.
한강이 보이는 곳에 살았어요.	I lived in sight of the Han River.
요즘 그분이 보이지 않아요.	He is out of sight these days.
그것을 저한테 보여 주세요.	Please show me that.
이것을 다른 사람한테 보이면 안 됩니다.	You should not show this to others.

STRUCTURE NOTES

I. The Sentence-Final Ending -아(-어, -여) 보이다… : 'someone (or something) looks (appears, seems)'

The pattern <u>-아(-어, -여) 보이다</u> is attached directly to the stems of description verbs, and indicates likeness, resemblance, or similarity. This pattern is never preceded by the object particle <u>-를 -을</u>. Instead, it takes the subject particle <u>-가/-이</u>, the contrast particle <u>-는/-은</u>, or <u>-도</u> 'also,' depending on the context.

Examples :

그분이 친절해 보여요.	He looks like a kind man.
그분이 뚱뚱해 보여요.	He looks fat.
그분이 건강해 보여요.	He looks healthy.
그분이 행복해 보여요.	He looks happy.
이 방이 커 보입니다.	This room seems to be big.
추워 보입니다.	You look cold.

그분이 젊어 보이지 않아요. He doesn't look young.
그것이 맛있어 보여요. That seems to be delicious.

Notes:

1. The tense and/or negation is expressed regularly in the final verb 보이다, not in the main verb with -아(-어, -여). Study the following examples:

건강해 보여요.	You look healthy.
건강해 보이지 않아요.	You don't look healthy.
건강해 보였어요.	You looked healthy.
건강해 보이지 않았어요.	You didn't look healthy.

2. -아 보이다 is after -아- and -오-;
-어 보이다 is used after any other vowel;
-여 보이다 is used after a 하(다) verb.

II. The Non-Final Ending -더니:

The pattern -더니 is used when a speaker recalls (or recollects) past facts, occurrences, or experiences. The final (main) clause, preceded by the -더니 clause, describes an immediate consequence or discovery resulting from an action. The English equivalent of this pattern is 'so …,' 'when …,' 'but …,' etc.

1. The pattern -더니, when used with the past tense infix, refers only to the first person in the dependent clause. Study the following examples:

지난 밤에 늦게까지 공부했더니, 피곤해요.	(I recall that) because I studied until late last night, I feel tired.
술을 너무 많이 마셨더니, 머리가 아파요.	(I recall that) I drank too much, so I've got a headache.
학교에 갔더니, 아무도 없었어요.	(I recall that) I went to school, but no one was there.
내가 춤을 추었더니, 모두 웃었어요.	(I recall that) I danced, so everybody laughed.
잘 쉬었더니, 기분이 좋아요.	Since I've had a nice rest, I feel good.
예습을 안 했더니, 잘 모르겠어요.	(I recall that) I didn't prepare the lessons, so I don't know well.

2. But the pattern -더니, when used in the present tense, refers to the second or third person. Study the following examples:

주무시더니, 지금 공부해요.	(I saw) he was sleeping, but now he is studying.
눈이 오더니, 따뜻해 졌어요.	(I saw) it was snowing and now it's turned warmer.

독어를 공부하더니, 지금 영어를 공부해요.	(I recall that) he (you) studied German, but now he studies English.
많이 먹더니, 배가 아파요.	(I recall that) he (you) ate too much, so his stomach is aching.
열심히 일하더니, 요즘은 일하지 않아요.	(I recall that) he (you) worked hard, but he doesn't work these days.

III. The Non-Final Ending -느라고… : 'because of doing'

The pattern -느라고 is used only with action verbs, and indicates cause or reason: excusing or explaining one's action. This pattern -느라고 is used to indicate two actions, (of the dependent clause and the main clause), done by a single person. The English equivalent of this pattern is 'because of doing,' 'as a result of doing,' etc.

Examples :

술을 마시느라고, 숙제를 하지 않았어요.	I did not do my homework because I was drinking.
한국말을 공부하느라고, 신문도 읽지 못했어요.	I couldn't even read the newspaper because I was studying Korean.
점심을 먹느라고, 늦었어요.	I was late because I was eating lunch.
편지를 쓰느라고, 늦게 잤어요.	I went to bed late because I was writing a letter.
일을 하느라고, 거기에 갈 시간이 없어요.	Because I'm working, I have no time to go there.
그분이 목욕하느라고, 오지 않아요.	He doesn't come because he is taking a bath now.
나는 복습하느라고, 정신이 없어요.	I can't think straight because I'm reviewing.

Notes :

The tense and/or negation is expressed regularly in the final (main) clause, not in the first clause with -느라고. This pattern is not used normally with the main clause in the future tense.

DRILLS

A. Substitution Drill

1. 그분이 친절해 보여요.	He looks like a kind man.
2. 그분이 건강해 보여요.	He looks healthy.
3. 그분이 행복해 보여요.	He looks happy.

4. 그분이 늙어 보여요.	He looks old.
5. 그분이 젊어 보여요.	He looks young.
6. 이 종이가 얇아 보여요.	This paper seems to be (too) thin.
7. 이 종이가 두꺼워 보여요.	This paper seems to be (too) thick.
8. 그것이 맛있어 보여요.	That seems to be delicious.

B. Substitution Drill

1. 친구하고 얘기하느라고 늦게 잤어요.	Because I was talking with my friend, I went to bed late.
2. 술을 마시느라고 늦게 잤어요.	Because I was drinking, I went to bed late.
3. 편지를 쓰느라고 늦게 잤어요.	Because I was writing a letter, I went to bed late.
4. 그분을 도와주느라고 늦게 잤어요.	Because I was helping him, I went to bed late.
5. 숙제를 하느라고 늦게 잤어요.	Because I was doing my homework, I went to bed late.
6. 목욕하느라고 늦게 잤어요.	Because I was taking a bath, I went to bed late.
7. 그림을 그리느라고 늦게 잤어요.	Because I was drawing a picture, I went to bed late.
8. 돈을 버느라고 늦게 잤어요.	Because I was making money, I went to bed late.

C. Pattern Drill

Teacher : 건강해 보입니다.	You look healthy.
Student : 건강해 보이지 않아요.	You don't look healthy.
1. 빨라 보입니다.	빨라 보이지 않아요.
2. 느려 보입니다.	느려 보이지 않아요.
3. 답답해 보입니다.	답답해 보이지 않아요.
4. 무거워 보입니다.	무거워 보이지 않아요.
5. 가벼워 보입니다.	가벼워 보이지 않아요.
6. 위험해 보입니다.	위험해 보이지 않아요.
7. 불편해 보입니다.	불편해 보이지 않아요.
8. 점잖아 보입니다.	점잖아 보이지 않아요.

D. Pattern Drill

Teacher : 건강해 보였어요.	You looked healthy.
Student : 건강해 보이지 않았어요.	You didn't look healthy.
1. 힘들어 보였어요.	힘들어 보이지 않았어요.

2. 추워 보였어요.	추워 보이지 않았어요.
3. 더워 보였어요.	더워 보이지 않았어요.
4. 피곤해 보였어요.	피곤해 보이지 않았어요.
5. 넓어 보였어요.	넓어 보이지 않았어요.
6. 좁아 보였어요.	좁아 보이지 않았어요.
7. 귀여워 보였어요.	귀여워 보이지 않았어요.
8. 튼튼해 보였어요.	튼튼해 보이지 않았어요.

E. Integration Drill

Teacher: 술을 너무 많이 마셨어요. 머리가 아파요.
I drank too much. I've got a headache.

Student: 술을 너무 많이 마셨더니, 머리가 아파요.
(I recall that) I drank too much, so I've got a headache.

1. 과식했어요. 배가 아파요.
   과식했더니, 배가 아파요.
2. 과로했어요. 굉장히 피곤해요.
   과로했더니, 굉장히 피곤해요.
3. 그분을 깨웠어요. 곧 일어났어요.
   그분을 깨웠더니, 곧 일어났어요.
4. 학생을 야단쳤어요. 울었어요.
   학생을 야단쳤더니, 울었어요.
5. 축하했어요. 고맙다고 했어요.
   축하했더니, 고맙다고 했어요.
6. 혼내주었어요. 주의했어요.
   혼내주었더니 주의했어요.
7. 방에 들어갔어요. 아무도 없었어요.
   방에 들어갔더니, 아무도 없었어요.
8. 더듬더듬 읽었어요. 모두 웃었어요.
   더듬더듬 읽었더니, 모두 웃었어요.

F. Integration Drill

Teacher: 눈이 왔어요. 따뜻해 졌어요.
It was snowing. It's turned warmer.

Student: 눈이 오더니, 따뜻해 졌어요.
(I saw) it was snowing, but now it's turned warmer.

1. 그분이 주무셨어요. 깨었어요.
   그분이 주무시더니, 깨었어요.
2. 처음에는 수출했어요. 지금은 수입해요.

처음에는 수출하더니, 지금은 수입해요.

3. 과음했어요. 병이 났어요.
   과음하더니, 병이 났어요.
4. 독어를 공부했어요. 지금 영어를 공부해요.
   독어를 공부하더니, 지금 영어를 공부해요.
5. 울었어요. 잠이 들었어요.
   울더니, 잠이 들었어요.
6. 번개가 쳤어요. 소나기가 옵니다.
   번개가 치더니, 소나기가 옵니다.
7. 시집갔어요. 애기를 낳았어요.
   시집가더니, 애기를 낳았어요.
8. 떠들었어요. 지금은 조용해요.
   떠들더니, 지금은 조용해요.

G. Integration Drill

Teacher: 술을 마셨어요. 숙제를 하지 않았어요.
I was drinking. I did not do my homework.

Student: 술을 마시느라고, 숙제를 하지 않았어요.
I didn't do my homework because I was drinking.

1. 점심을 먹었어요. 늦었어요.
   점심을 먹느라고, 늦었어요.
2. 복습했어요. 정신이 없어요.
   복습하느라고, 정신이 없어요.
3. 숙제를 했어요. 늦게 잤어요.
   숙제를 하느라고, 늦게 잤어요.
4. 회의를 했어요. 그 일을 못 했어요.
   회의를 하느라고, 그 일을 못 했어요.
5. 공부를 했어요. 늦게 결혼했어요.
   공부를 하느라고, 늦게 결혼했어요.
6. 저녁을 준비했어요. 바빴어요.
   저녁을 준비하느라고, 바빴어요.
7. 예습했어요. 약속을 지키지 못했어요.
   예습하느라고, 약속을 지키지 못했어요.
8. 춤을 추었어요. 잊어 버렸어요.
   춤을 추느라고, 잊어 버렸어요.

H. Pattern Drill (Review)

Teacher : 사람들이 갔다 왔다 해요.
People keep coming and going.

Student : 사람들이 갔다 왔다 했어요.
People kept coming and going.

1. 불을 켰다 껐다 해요. 불을 켰다 껐다 했어요.
2. 그분이 웃었다 울었다 해요. 그분이 웃었다 울었다 했어요.
3. 눈을 떴다 감았다 해요. 눈을 떴다 감았다 했어요.
4. 옷을 입었다 벗었다 해요. 옷을 입었다 벗었다 했어요.
5. 들어갔다 나왔다 해요. 들어갔다 나왔다 했어요.
6. 문을 열었다 닫았다 해요. 문을 열었다 닫았다 했어요.
7. 그분이 섰다 앉았다 해요. 그분이 섰다 앉았다 했어요.
8. 집을 샀다 팔았다 해요. 집을 샀다 팔았다 했어요.

I. Response Drill (Review)

Teacher : 여기서 담배를 피워도 괜찮아요?
May I smoke here?

Student : 아니오, 여기서 담배를 피우면 안 됩니다.
No, you should not smoke here.

1. 수출해도 괜찮아요? 아니오, 수출하면 안 됩니다.
2. 수입해도 괜찮아요? 아니오, 수입하면 안 됩니다.
3. 서둘러도 괜찮아요? 아니오, 서두르면 안 됩니다.
4. 자랑해도 괜찮아요? 아니오, 자랑하면 안 됩니다.
5. 소개해도 괜찮아요? 아니오, 소개하면 안 됩니다.
6. 야단쳐도 괜찮아요? 아니오, 야단치면 안 됩니다.
7. 혼내주어도 괜찮아요? 아니오, 혼내주면 안 됩니다.
8. 변명해도 괜찮아요? 아니오, 변명하면 안 됩니다.

J. Pattern Drill (Review)

Teacher : 한식을 먹었어요. I ate Korean food.

Student : 한식을 먹어 봤어요. I tried eating Korean food.

1. 그것을 만들었어요. 그것을 만들어 봤어요.
2. 그분한테 부탁했어요. 그분한테 부탁해 봤어요.
3. 춤을 추었어요. 춤을 추어 봤어요.
4. 점심을 굶었어요. 점심을 굶어 봤어요.
5. 집을 지었어요. 집을 지어 봤어요.
6. 회의를 했어요. 회의를 해 봤어요.
7. 그것을 빼앗았어요. 그것을 빼앗아 봤어요.

8. 방에 누웠어요. 방에 누워 봤어요.

SHORT STORIES

1. 그분이 어제 일을 많이 하시더니, 늦게 일어났어요.
   학교에 왔는데, 아주 피곤해 보였어요.
   그래서 그분한테 과로하지 말라고 했어요.

   Expansion Drill

   그분이 어제 일을 많이 하시더니, 늦게 일어났어요. 학교에 왔는데, 아주 피곤해 보여서 그분한테 과로하지 말라고 했어요.

2. 어제 일을 하느라고, 집에 늦게 갔어요.
   집에 갔더니, 모두 기다리고 있었어요.
   그래서 미안하다고 사과했어요. 사과하다 to apologize

   Expansion Drill

   어제 일을 하느라고, 집에 늦게 갔더니, 모두 기다리고 있어서, 미안하다고 사과했어요.

3. 그분이 홀쭉하더니, 요즘 뚱뚱해 졌어요.
   그래서 아침도 먹지 않고, 점심도 먹지 않아요.
   그러나 저녁 식사는 아주 많이 먹어요.

   Expansion Drill

   그분이 홀쭉하더니, 요즘 뚱뚱해 져서, 아침도 먹지 않고 점심도 먹지 않지만, 저녁 식사는 아주 많이 먹어요.

READING

며칠 전에 학기말 시험을 치느라고 아주 혼났어요. 시험이 아주 어려웠어요. 받아쓰기는 잘 한 것 같아요. 그런데 문형 시험과 작문은 엉망이 되었어요. 선생님께서 좀 더 노력하라고 하셨어요. 어쨌든 일학기는 끝났어요. 해방이 된 것 같아요. 앞으로 이 주일 동안 겨울방학이에요. 방학 동안에 푹 쉬고 싶어요. 그런데 며칠 있으면 성탄절이에요. 성탄절이 되면 바쁠 것 같아요. 여러가지 모임이 많을 것 같아요. 망년회도 있고 신년회도 있을 거에요.

학기말	the end of the school term
학기말 시험	a final exam
시험을 치다	to take an exam
어쨌든	anyhow, anyway
일 학기	the first term
해방	liberation
-동안	during, for
방학	vacation
성탄절	Christmas
여러가지	all sorts (of), various kinds (of)
모임	a gathering, a party
망년회	a year-end party
신년회	a New Year's Party

BRIEFING

A few days ago, I had a hard time when taking a final exam. The exam was very difficult. I think I did well on the dictation. However, I did poorly on the pattern exam and composition. The teacher told me to make a greater effort. Anyway, the first term was finished. It seems that I'm liberated. Now we will have two weeks' vacation. I want to have a good rest during the vacation. But in a few days, it will be Christmas. On Christmas, I think I will be busy. I think there will be various kinds of gatherings. There will be a year-end party and a new year's party.

UNIT 44 친구 A Friend

BASIC SENTENCES: MEMORIZE

정말 — truly, really

이런 데서 — in a place like this

박 성 철

1. 참 오래간 만입니다. 정말 이런 데서 만날 줄은 몰랐어요. — It's really been a long time since we've met. I never expected to meet you in a place like this.

반갑다 — to be glad, to be joyful

소식 — news, report, information

최 인 숙

2. 정말 반갑습니다. 어떻게 그렇게 소식이 없었어요? — I'm really glad to see you. How is it that there's been no news from you?

지금까지 — until now

쭉 — all during, throughout, straight (through)

박 성 철

3. 지금까지 쭉 미국에 있었어요. 한국에 돌아온 지 이틀 되었어요. — I have been in America until now. It has been just two days since I came back to Korea.

대포 — whiskey, drink

최 인 숙

4. 그래요? 자 우리 대포라도 한 잔 할까요? — Is that so? Shall we have a drink?

다른 친구 — another friend

만나야 돼요 — I have to meet

박 성 철

5. 지금은 다른 친구를 만나야 돼요. 내일 다시 만나는 것이 어때요? — I have to meet another friend now. How about meeting again tomorrow?

최 인 숙

6. 지금 바쁘시면, 내일 만납시다. — If you are busy now, let's meet tomorrow.

NOTES ON THE BASIC SENTENCES

1. 이런 데서 'in a place like this' is a contraction of 이런 데에서. -데 'place' is a dependent noun preceded always by words such as demonstratives or modifiers. Study the following examples:

위험한 데에 가지 마세요.	Don't go to a dangerous place.
표 파는 데가 어딥니까?	Where is the place that sells tickets?
좋은 데로 갑시다.	Let's go to a good place.

2. 반갑습니다 means 'I am glad (to meet you).' This expression is used (1) when you give someone a joyful welcome, (2) when you meet an old friend on the street, (3) when you hear good news.

3. 쭉 is an emphatic expression of 죽, which is less common. It can have many different meanings, depending on the context. Study the following examples:

지금까지 쭉 기다렸읍니다.	I've been waiting for you all this while.
집에서 학교까지 쭉 걸어왔어요.	I've walked all the way to school from my house.
아침부터 쭉 공부했어요.	I studied all through the morning.
사람들이 쭉 서 있어요.	People are standing in a row.
기운이 쭉 빠졌어요.	I'm utterly exhausted.

4. 대포 means to drink wine, beer or whiskey in a bar or tavern. Study the following examples:

대포 한잔 합시다.	Let's have a quick one.
대포집에 갑시다.	Let's go to a bar.

5. 만나야 돼요 is a contraction of 만나야 되어요. It is interchangeable with 만나야 해요, making no difference in meaning, (See Unit 25, Structure Notes II).

STRUCTURE NOTES

I. The Sentence-Final Ending -줄 알다/모르다:

We have already studied the pattern -ㄹ(을) 줄 알다/모르다, when it indicates knowledge and/or lack of knowledge of a technique or process for doing some activity, (See Unit 42, Structure Notes III.) This pattern -줄 알다/모르다, depending on the context, may also indicate an assumed fact, expectation, or likelihood. It may be preceded by any modifier suffix, such as -ㄴ(은), -는, -ㄹ(을). The final verb 알다/모르다 can be replaced by other verbs as well, such as 믿다 'to believe,' 생각하다 'to think.' etc.

Examples :

그분이 공부한 줄 알았어요. I thought he had studied.
그분이 공부하는 줄 알았어요. I thought he was studying.
그분이 공부할 줄 알았어요. I thought he would study.
그분이 뚱뚱한 줄 몰랐어요. I didn't know he was fat.
그분이 뚱뚱할 줄 몰랐어요. I didn't know he would be fat.
그분이 선생님인 줄 몰랐어요. I didn't know he was a teacher.
그분이 학교에 있는 줄 알았어요. I supposed that he was at school.
그분이 올 줄 믿어요. I believe he will come.
그분이 미국에 갈 줄 생각했어요. I thought he would go to America.
여기서 만날 줄 꿈에도 몰랐어요. I never dreamed I'd meet you here.
그분이 그럴 줄 몰랐어요. I had no idea he would be that way.

Notes :

1. When -줄 is followed by 알고 있다, it indicates knowledge of a fact or event. Study the following examples :
   그분이 미국에 간 줄 알고 있어요. I know he went to America.
   그분이 수영하는 줄 알고 있어요. I know he is swimming.
   그분이 여기에 올 줄 알고 있었어요. I knew he would come here.
2. This pattern can be used with any verb ; -줄 may be followed directly by particles, such as -로 (for supposition) -을 (for knowledge), for the purpose of emphasis. Study the following examples :
   그분이 여기에 올 줄로 알았어요. I thought he would come here.
   그분이 여기에 올 줄을 알고 있었어요. I knew he would come here.

II. The Particle -(이)라도… : 'even if (it be)'

We have already studied the INTERROGATIVE + -(이)라도, which means '…ever it is,' 'no matter (what, who, when, where) it is,' 'any…at all.' But here, this particle -(이)라도 is attached directly to nouns, or to nouns plus other particles. This pattern indicates a lack of enthusiasm about one's choice. Its literal meaning is 'even if (it be).'

Examples :

버스라도 타고 갑시다. Let's settle on riding a bus. (lit. Even if it's a bus, let's ride it and go.)

이것이라도 삽시다. Let's settle on buying this.

우유라도 마시겠어요. I'll settle on drinking milk.
극장에라도 갑시다. Let's settle on going to the theater.
이 방에서라도 공부합시다. Let's settle on studying in this room.

Notes:

1. The particle -(이)라도, preceded by nouns or nouns plus particles, can mean 'even as well.' Study the following examples:

   여자라도 움직일 수 있어요. Even a woman can move it.
   남자라도 할 수 없어요. Even a man can't do that.
   꿈에라도 보고 싶어요. I wish I could see you even in my dreams.

2. -라도 is used after nouns ending in a vowel;
3. -이라도 is used after nouns ending in a consonant.

III. The Obligatory Ending -아(-어, -여)야 되다…: 'must,' 'have to'

The pattern -아(-어, -여)야 되다 may be used with any verb; it indicates obligation or necessity. -아(-어, -여)야 되다 is interchangeable with -아(-어, -여)야 하다 making no difference in meaning, (See Unit 25, Structure Notes II.)

Examples:

그분을 만나야 됩니다. I have to meet him.
빨리 가야 됩니다. I must go (there) quickly.
돈이 있어야 됩니다. You must have money.
그것이 좋아야 됩니다. It has got to be good.
그것이 깨끗해야 됩니다. It has got to be clean.
그것이 책이어야 됩니다. It has to be a book.

Notes:

1. This pattern -아(-어, -여)야 되다 is never used in the past tense. It is used mostly in the present and future tenses. The tense is expressed regularly in the final verb -되다. Study the following examples:

   집에 가야 됩니다. I must go home.
   집에 가야 되겠습니다. I'll have to go home.
   집에 가야 되었습니다. (never used)

2. The negation of this pattern is -(으)면 안 되다 'someone must not do something,' (lit. 'If someone does something, it won't do'). Study the following examples:

   가면 안 됩니다. You must not go.

공부하면 안 됩니다. You must not study.

3. -아야 되다 is used after -아- and -오- ;
-어야 되다 is used after any other vowel ;
-여야 되다 is used after a 하다 verb.

DRILLS

A. Substitution Drill

1. 그분이 여기에 올 줄 알았어요. I thought he would come here.
2. 그분이 거절할 줄 알았어요. I thought he would refuse.
3. 그분이 야단칠 줄 알았어요. I thought he would give me a good scolding.
4. 그분이 변명할 줄 알았어요. I thought he would defend himself.
5. 그분이 나를 깨울 줄 알았어요. I thought he would wake me up.
6. 그분이 결혼할 줄 알았어요. I thought he would marry.
7. 그분이 소개할 줄 알았어요. I thought he would introduce (him).
8. 그분이 나를 방문할 줄 알았어요. I thought he would visit me.

B. Substitution Drill

1. 그분을 만나야 됩니다. You have to meet him.
2. 노력해야 됩니다. You have to make an effort.
3. 그분을 야단쳐야 됩니다. You have to scold him.
4. 그것을 씻어야 됩니다. You have to wash it.
5. 거절해야 됩니다. You have to refuse.
6. 그것을 이해해야 됩니다. You have to understand it.
7. 서둘러야 됩니다. You have to hurry.
8. 맛을 보아야 됩니다. You have to taste it.

C. Substitution Drill

1. 그분이 선생님인 줄 몰랐어요. I didn't know he was a teacher.
2. 그분이 교수인 줄 몰랐어요. I didn't know he was a professor.
3. 그분이 선교사인 줄 몰랐어요. I didn't know he was a missionary.
4. 그분이 의사인 줄 몰랐어요. I didn't know he was a medical doctor.
5. 그분이 건축가인 줄 몰랐어요. I didn't know he was an architect.
6. 그분이 운전기사인 줄 몰랐어요. I didn't know he was a driver.
7. 그분이 환자인 줄 몰랐어요. I didn't know he was a patient.
8. 그분이 외국 사람인 줄 몰랐어요. I didn't know he was a foreigner.

D. Pattern Drill

Teacher: 그분이 뚱뚱한 줄 몰랐어요.
I didn't know he was fat.
Student: 그분이 뚱뚱할 줄 몰랐어요.
I didn't know he would be fat.

1. 그것이 무거운 줄 몰랐어요. 그것이 무거울 줄 몰랐어요.
2. 교통이 불편한 줄 몰랐어요. 교통이 불편할 줄 몰랐어요.
3. 그분이 행복한 줄 몰랐어요. 그분이 행복할 줄 몰랐어요.
4. 그분이 겸손한 줄 몰랐어요. 그분이 겸손할 줄 몰랐어요.
5. 날씨가 추운 줄 몰랐어요. 날씨가 추울 줄 몰랐어요.
6. 그 일이 위험한 줄 몰랐어요. 그 일이 위험할 줄 몰랐어요.
7. 돈이 필요한 줄 몰랐어요. 돈이 필요할 줄 몰랐어요.
8. 그것이 빠른 줄 몰랐어요. 그것이 빠를 줄 몰랐어요.

E. Pattern Drill

Teacher: 그분이 공부한 줄 알았어요.
I thought he had studied.
Student: 그분이 공부하는 줄 알았어요.
I thought he was studying.

1. 맛을 본 줄 알았어요. 맛을 보는 줄 알았어요.
2. 불을 켠 줄 알았어요. 불을 켜는 줄 알았어요.
3. 불을 끈 줄 알았어요. 불을 끄는 줄 알았어요.
4. 한턱 낸 줄 알았어요. 한턱 내는 줄 알았어요.
5. 결정한 줄 알았어요. 결정하는 줄 알았어요.
6. 담배를 피운 줄 알았어요. 담배를 피우는 줄 알았어요.
7. 굶은 줄 알았어요. 굶는 줄 알았어요.
8. 수출한 줄 알았어요. 수출하는 줄 알았어요.

F. Pattern Drill

Teacher: 이것을 삽시다. Let's buy this.
Student: 이것이라도 삽시다. Let's settle on buying this, (lit. Even if it is this, let's buy it).

1. 우유를 마시겠어요. 우유라도 마시겠어요.
2. 버스를 타고 갑시다. 버스라도 타고 갑시다.
3. 책을 읽겠어요. 책이라도 읽겠어요.
4. 사과를 먹겠어요. 사과라도 먹겠어요.
5. 영화를 보겠어요. 영화라도 보겠어요.
6. 송별회를 합시다. 송별회라도 합시다.
7. 환영회를 합시다. 환영회라도 합시다.

8. 망년회를 합시다. 망년회라도 합시다.

G. Pattern Drill

Teacher: 극장에 갑시다. Let's go to the theater.

Student: 극장에라도 갑시다. Let's settle on going to the theater, (lit. Even if it's the theater, let's go).

1. 방에서 공부합시다. 방에서라도 공부합시다.
2. 교실에서 잡시다. 교실에서라도 잡시다.
3. 여기서 목욕합시다. 여기서라도 목욕합시다.
4. 학생한테 물어 봅시다. 학생한테라도 물어 봅시다.
5. 공장에서 일합시다. 공장에서라도 일합시다.
6. 병원에서 눕시다. 병원에서라도 눕시다.
7. 마당에 세워 놓읍시다. 마당에라도 세워 놓읍시다.
8. 휴게실에서 회의를 합시다. 휴게실에서라도 회의를 합시다.

H. Pattern Drill

Teacher: 가야 됩니다. You have to go.

Student: 가면 안 됩니다. You must not go.

1. 개를 길러야 됩니다. 개를 기르면 안 됩니다.
2. 그것을 갈라야 됩니다. 그것을 가르면 안 됩니다.
3. 그것을 외워야 됩니다. 그것을 외우면 안 됩니다.
4. 거기를 지나가야 됩니다. 거기를 지나가면 안 됩니다.
5. 그것을 붙잡아야 됩니다. 그것을 붙잡으면 안 됩니다.
6. 봉사해야 됩니다. 봉사하면 안 됩니다.
7. 축하해야 됩니다. 축하하면 안 됩니다.
8. 그분을 방문해야 됩니다. 그분을 방문하면 안 됩니다.

I. Response Drill (Review)

Teacher: 사람이 몇분이나 오셨어요?
About how many people came?

Student: 사람이 열 분이나 왔어요.
Ten people came, (more than I expected).

1. 몇 번이나 보셨어요? <u>다섯 번</u>이나 보았어요.
2. 몇 권이나 읽으셨어요? <u>서른 권</u>이나 읽었어요.
3. 몇 년이나 계셨어요? <u>십 년</u>이나 있었어요.
4. 몇 병이나 마셨어요? <u>열 병</u>이나 마셨어요.
5. 몇 갑이나 피우셨어요? <u>세 갑</u>이나 피웠어요.
6. 몇 달이나 계셨어요? <u>넉 달</u>이나 있었어요.
7. 차가 몇 대나 있어요? 차가 <u>스무 대</u>나 있어요.

8. 그분이 몇 살이나 되었어요? 그분이 마흔 살이나 되었어요.

J. Pattern Drill (Review)

Teacher: 저녁에 시간이 있어요.	I'll have time this evening.
Student: 저녁에나 시간이 있어요.	I'll have time this evening (sometime).
1. 휴게실에 갑시다.	휴게실에나 갑시다.
2. 화요일에 만납시다.	화요일에나 만납시다.
3. 내년에 시작합시다.	내년에나 시작합시다.
4. 다음 달에 와 보세요.	다음 달에나 와 보세요.
5. 유월 초순에 가 보세요.	유월 초순에나 가 보세요.
6. 시월 중순에 결정합시다.	시월 중순에나 결정합시다.
7. 연말에 드리겠어요.	연말에나 드리겠어요.
8. 주말에 될 것 같아요.	주말에나 될 것 같아요.

SHORT STORIES

1. 그 영화가 시시한 줄 알았어요.
그런데 가 보니까 여간 재미있지 않아요.
기회가 있으면 한 번 더 보고 싶어요.

시시하다	to be worthless, to be dull and flat	기회	a chance, an opportunity

Expansion Drill

그 영화가 시시한 줄 알았는데, 가 보니까 여간 재미있지 않아요.
기회가 있으면 한 번 더 보고 싶어요.

2. 택시를 타려고 했어요.
그런데 택시가 없으니까 버스라도 타고 갑시다.
늦게 가면 그분을 만나지 못해요.

Expansion Drill

택시를 타려고 했는데, 택시가 없으니까, 버스라도 타고 갑시다.
늦게 가면 그분을 만나지 못해요.

3. 그분이 과로해서 병이 났습니다.
그런데 병이 점점 심해 집니다.
빨리 입원해야 됩니다.

병이 나다	to get sick
점점	gradually, little by little
심하다	to be serious
입원하다	to be hospitalized

Expansion Drill

그분이 과로해서 병이 났는데, 병이 점점 심해 지니까, 빨리 입원 해야 됩니다.

READING

학교에 가다가 우연히 옛날 친구를 만났습니다. 그분은 고등학교 동창생이었습니다. 그분을 25년 만에 만났습니다. 그래서 여간 반갑지 않았습니다. 너무 반가워서 말이 나오지 않았습니다. 그 친구가 자기 집에 가자고 했습니다. 그래서 친구 집에 택시를 타고 갔습니다. 집에 도착할 때까지 친구는 아무 말도 하지 않았습니다. 집에 가니까 부인이 나왔습니다. 나는 부인을 만났을 때 깜짝 놀랐습니다. 그 여자는 내 누이동생이었습니다. 나는 6·25 동란 때 누이동생과 헤어졌습니다. 그 후에 누이동생을 굉장히 찾았습니다. 그러나 찾을 수 없었습니다. 그래서 누이동생이 죽은 줄 알았습니다. 정말 누이동생을 만날 줄 꿈에도 몰랐습니다.

우연히	accidently	누이동생	one's younger sister
동창생	a classmate	6·25 동란	the Korean War
자기	one's own, oneself	헤어지다	to separate, to part from (with)
아무	any		
		찾다	to look for

BRIEFING

On the way to school by accident I met my old friend. He was my high school classmate. I met him for the first time in 25 years. So I was glad to see him. I was so happy that I could not speak. My friend asked me to go to his house. So we went to my friend's house by taxi. My friend didn't say anything until we arrived at his house. When we got to his house, his wife came out. When I saw his wife, I was totally suprised. She was my younger sister. During the Korean War, I parted from my sister. After that, I looked very hard for my sister. But I couldn't find her. So I thought my younger sister had died. Really I never expected to see my sister, even in a dream.

UNIT 45 연하장 New Year's Card

BASIC SENTENCES: MEMORIZE

어젯밤에	last night
늦게까지	until late
불	the light

박 성 철

1. 어젯밤에 늦게까지 불이 켜 있던데요! 늦도록 무엇을 하셨어요? — (As I recall), the light was on (in your room) until late last night. What did you do until so late?

연하장	a New Year's card

최 인 숙

2. 연하장을 썼어요. — I wrote New Year's cards.

몇 장이나	about how many cards

박 성 철

3. 몇 장이나 쓰셨어요? — About how many cards did you write?

백 장이나	one hundred cards (more than one thought)

최 인 숙

4. 놀라지 마세요. 100 장이나 썼어요. — Don't be surprised. I wrote one hundred cards.

다	all

박 성 철

5. 이젠 다 쓰셨어요? — Did you finish writing them all?

최 인 숙

6. 아니오, 아직도 200 장쯤 더 써야 해요. — No, I still have to write about two hundred more.

아이구	Good Heavens!

박 성 철

7. 아이구! 그걸 다 쓰다가는 혼나시겠어요. — Good Heavens! You'll have a hard time trying to write them all.

NOTES ON THE BASIC SENTENCES

1. 어젯밤 means 'yesterday evening,' 'last night.' When the possessive particle -의 occurs between two words, it can be contracted into a -ㅅ. If the first word ends in a vowel, -ㅅ instead of -의 is attached to the first word, and the following consonant (of the second word) becomes glottalized in pronunciation.

어젯밤 (어제의 밤)	yesterday evening
냇가 (내의 가)	a riverside, riverbank
콧등 (코의 등)	the ridge of the nose
촛불 (초의 불)	candlelight
깃발 (기의 발)	flag
빗소리 (비의 소리)	the sound of rain
찻잔 (차의 잔)	a teacup
뒷방 (뒤의 방)	a back room

4. 놀라지 마세요 means 'Don't be surprised.' 놀라다 'to be surprised,' 'to be startled' is used regularly with the subject particle -가/-이, whereas 놀래다 (놀라게 하다) 'to surprise,' 'to startle,' 'to astonish' is used always with the object particle -를/-을. Study the following examples:

그분이 깜짝 놀랐어요.	He was surprised (taken aback.)
학생들을 놀래 줄 일이 있어요.	I have a surprise in store for the students.

5. 이젠 is a contraction of 이제는.
7. 그걸 is a contraction of 그것을. Study the following examples:

이걸=이것을
그걸=그것을
저걸=저것을
무얼=무엇을

이걸 잡수세요.	Please eat this.
그걸 주세요.	Please give me that.
저걸 보세요.	Please look at that over there.
무얼 하셨어요?	What did you do?

STRUCTURE NOTES

I. The Retrospective Infix -더- :

We have already studied the non-final ending -더니, used when a speaker recalls (or recollects) past facts, occurrences, or experiences, (See Unit 43, Strucure Notes II). This infix -더- is also used when a speaker looks back on past facts, occurrences, or experiences. However, this infix -더-, when used as a sentence-final ending, is followed normally by the exclamatory ending, such as -군요 or -ㄴ데요. The English equivalent of this pattern is 'as I recall,' 'as I remember,' 'looking back,' etc.

Examples :

그분이 좋더군요. 그분이 좋던데요.	(I recall that) he was good.
그분이 아주 잘 가르치더군요. 그분이 아주 잘 가르치던데요.	(I recall that) he taught very well.
그분이 일하더군요. 그분이 일하던데요.	(I recall that) he was working. Or : I remember seeing him work.
그분이 주무시더군요. 그분이 주무시던데요.	(I saw) he was sleeping.
교실에 학생이 많더군요. 교실에 학생이 많던데요.	(I remember that) there were many students in the classroom.
그분이 의사더군요. 그분이 의사던데요.	(I remember that) he was a medical doctor.

Notes :

1. When this infix -더- is used as a sentence-final ending with the exclamatory endings -군요 or -ㄴ데요, the subject is usually in the third person. When the verb is a description verb, it can be used with the first person. But it's seldom used.
2. This infix -더- is inserted between the verb stem, (or the verb stem plus the infixes -시-, -았- or -겠-, etc.), and the exclamatory ending. Study the following examples :

그분이 공부하더군요. 그분이 공부하던데요.	(I recall that) he was studying.
그분이 공부하시더군요. 그분이 공부하시던데요.	(I recall that) he was studying.

그분이 공부했더군요. (I recall that at the time I met him) he had studied.

그분이 공부하겠더군요. (I recall that at the time I met him)
그분이 공부하겠던데요. I thought that he was going to study.

3. This infix -더- also occurs with other endings, besides exclamatory ones. But this will be studied latter in detail.

II. The Non-Final Ending -도록… : 'until'

We have already studied this pattern -도록, when it indicates 'purpose' or 'aim,' (See Unit 42, Structure Notes II). This pattern -도록, depending on the context or situation, can also indicate continuance of an action or condition to a specified time. The English equivalent of this is 'until.'

Examples :

어젯밤에 늦도록 공부했어요.	I studied until late last night.
해가 뜨도록 잤어요.	I slept until sunrise.
열 두 시가 되도록 술을 마셨어요.	We drank until twelve o'clock.
아홉 시가 되도록 기다렸어요.	I waited until nine o'clock.
밤이 되도록 일했어요.	I worked until night.

When this pattern -도록 (directly attached to an action verb stem) is followed by -되다, however, it indicates the idea that the situation has been developed on its own. The Englsh equivalent of this pattern is 'to reach the point where….'

A.V.S. + -도록 되다… : 'to reach the point where…'

Examples :

한국말을 가르치도록 되었어요.	I've reached the point where I teach Korean.
담배를 수출할 수 있도록 되었어요.	We've reached the point where we can export cigarettes.
이 회사에서 일할 수 있도록 되었어요.	I've reached the point where I can work in this company.

III. -으 Irregular Verbs :

Most verbs ending in a final vowel -으 of the stem are irregular.

1. The final vowel -으 of the stem, when followed by the vowel -어 and preceded by the vowels -아- or -오-, is changed into -아-. Study the following examples :

바쁘(다) 'to be busy,' 'to be occupied'

오늘 아침에 바빴습니다.	I was busy this morning.
바빠야 합니다.	You should be busy.
바빠서 못 갔어요.	Because I was busy, I couldn't go.
바빠도 괜찮아요.	It's alright even if I'm busy.

배가 고프(다) 'to be hungry,' 'to feel hungry'

배가 고파요.	I'm hungry.
배가 고파야 합니다.	You should be hungry.
배가 고파서 죽겠어요.	I'm so hungry that I could die.
배가 고파도 괜찮아요.	It's alright even if I'm hungry.

-으 irregular verbs preceded by the vowel -아- or -오-:

바쁘(다)	to be busy	배가 고프(다)	to be hungry
나쁘(다)	to be bad	잠그(다)	to lock
아프(다)	to be painful		

2. The final vowel -으 of the stem, when followed by the vowel -어 and preceded by vowels other than -아- or -오-, is completely dropped. Study the following examples:

쓰(다) 'to write,' 'to use,' 'to be bitter,' 'to put on (a hat)'

편지를 썼어요.	I wrote a letter.
편지를 써야 합니다.	I have to write a letter.
편지를 써서 부쳤어요.	I wrote a letter and mailed it.
편지를 써도 괜찮아요.	You may write a letter.

-으 irregular verbs preceded by vowels other than -아- or -오-:

예쁘(다)	to be beautiful	크(다)	to be big
기쁘(다)	to be happy	뜨(다)	to rise
슬프(다)	to be sad	끄(다)	to turn off

IV. The Non-Final Ending -다가는…: 'if'

We have already studied the conditional non-final ending -(으)면, which indicates condition or stipulation, (See Unit 19, Structure Notes III.) This pattern -다가는 always refers to a condition that has an unpleasant result, or a negative or bad effect. The best way to understand -다가는 is to see it as a participle: i.e., 'Sleeping like that could make you lazy;' 'Working too hard could cause all kinds of sickness, etc.' This pattern -다가는 is used always with action verbs.

Examples :

여기서 자다가는 감기에 걸릴 것 같아요.	If you sleep here, you'll catch a cold.
그분을 기다리다가는 늦을 것 같아요.	If you wait for him, I think you'll be late.
술만 마시다가는 아무 것도 못 하시겠어요.	Should you only drink, you won't be able to do anything.
그렇게 놀다가는 언제 숙제를 하시겠습니까?	If you play like that, when will you do your homework?
이 물을 마시다가는 병에 걸리겠어요.	If you drink this water, you'll get sick.
한국말만 공부하다가는 큰 일 나겠어요.	If you only study Korean, you'll be in a fix.
이 일을 계속하다가는 다른 일을 못 하겠어요.	If you continue this work, you won't be able to do other work.
그분하고 이야기하다가는 늦겠어요.	If you continue to talk with him, you'll be late.
옷을 갈아입다가는 지각할 거에요.	If you change your clothes, you'll be late for school.

Notes :

1. This pattern -다가는 is followed always by patterns which indicate future, supposition, presumption, similarity, or probability.
2. The past tense can't be used in the main clause, preceded by the -다가는 clause. However, if the pattern of the main clause is -ㄹ(을) 것 같다, the past tense can be used in the main clause. Study the following examples:

그분하고 얘기하다가는 늦을 것 같았어요.	If I continued to talk with him, I thought I'd be late.
여기서 자다가는 감기에 걸릴 것 같았어요.	If you were to sleep here, I thought you'd catch a cold.

DRILLS

ADDITIONAL VOCABULARY

해	the sun	병에 걸리다	to get sick
뜨다	to rise	창피하다	to be shameful
지다	to set (go down)		

A. Substitution Drill

1. 담배를 수출할 수 있도록 되었어요. — We've reached the point where we can export cigarettes.
2. 기름을 수입할 수 있도록 되었어요. — We've reached the point where I can import oil.

3. 이 회사에서 일할 수 있도록 되었어요.	I've reached the point where I can work in this company.
4. 그분을 만날 수 있도록 되었어요.	I've reached the point where I can meet him.
5. 그 여자와 결혼할 수 있도록 되었어요.	I've reached the point where I can marry her.
6. 그것을 이해할 수 있도록 되었어요.	I've reached the point where I can understand it.
7. 그분을 도와줄 수 있도록 되었어요.	I've reached the point where I can help him.
8. 그분을 초대할 수 있도록 되었어요.	I've reached the point where I can invite him.

B. Substitution Drill

1. 그걸 다 쓰다가는 큰 일 나겠어요.	If you write them all, you'll get into trouble.
2. 여기서 일하다가는 큰 일 나겠어요.	If you work here, you'll get into trouble.
3. 그 여자와 결혼하다가는 큰 일 나겠어요.	If you marry her, you'll get into trouble.
4. 변명하다가는 큰 일 나겠어요.	If you defend yourself, you'll get into trouble.
5. 여기서 자다가는 큰 일 나겠어요.	If you sleep here, you'll get into trouble.
6. 외출하다가는 큰 일 나겠어요.	If you go outdoors, you'll get into trouble.
7. 결근하다가는 큰 일 나겠어요.	If you skip work, you'll get into trouble.
8. 결석하다가는 큰 일 나겠어요.	If you skip school, you'll get into trouble.

C. Pattern Drill

Teacher : 그분이 좋더군요.	(I recall that) he was good.
Student : 그분이 좋던데요.	(I recall that) he was good.
1. 그분이 행복하더군요.	그분이 행복하던데요.
2. 그분이 건강하더군요.	그분이 건강하던데요.
3. 그분이 점잖더군요.	그분이 점잖던데요.
4. 그분이 튼튼하더군요.	그분이 튼튼하던데요.
5. 그분이 무섭더군요.	그분이 무섭던데요.
6. 김치가 맵더군요.	김치가 맵던데요.
7. 음식이 싱겁더군요.	음식이 싱겁던데요.
8. 날씨가 쌀쌀하더군요.	날씨가 쌀쌀하던데요.

D. Pattern Drill

Teacher :	그분이 공부하더군요.	(I recall that) he was studying.
Student :	그분이 공부했더군요.	(I recall that at the time I met him) he had studied.
1.	그분이 잘못하더군요.	그분이 잘못했더군요.
2.	그분이 입원하더군요.	그분이 입원했더군요.
3.	그분이 졸더군요.	그분이 졸았더군요.
4.	문을 잠그더군요.	문을 잠갔더군요.
5.	회의를 하더군요.	회의를 했더군요.
6.	시험을 치더군요.	시험을 쳤더군요.
7.	더듬더듬 읽더군요.	더듬더듬 읽었더군요.
8.	그분이 서두르더군요.	그분이 서둘렀더군요.

E. Pattern Drill

Teacher :	두 시까지 기다렸어요.	I waited it became two o'clock.
Student :	두 시가 되도록 기다렸어요.	I waited until it became two o'clock.
1.	한 시까지 술을 마셨어요.	한 시가 되도록 술을 마셨어요.
2.	밤까지 일했어요.	밤이 되도록 일했어요.
3.	세 시까지 떠들었어요.	세 시가 되도록 떠들었어요.
4.	네 시까지 회의를 했어요.	네 시가 되도록 회의를 했어요.
5.	다섯 시까지 준비했어요.	다섯 시가 되도록 준비했어요.
6.	늦게까지 구경했어요.	늦도록 구경했어요.
7.	해가 뜰 때까지 잤어요.	해가 뜨도록 잤어요.
8.	해가 질 때까지 울었어요.	해가 지도록 울었어요.

F. Pattern Drill

Teacher :	바쁩니다.	I am busy.
Student :	바빴습니다.	I was busy.
1.	그것이 나쁩니다.	그것이 나빴습니다.
2.	머리가 아픕니다.	머리가 아팠습니다.
3.	배가 고픕니다.	배가 고팠습니다.
4.	문을 잠급니다.	문을 잠갔습니다.
5.	편지를 씁니다.	편지를 썼습니다.
6.	해가 뜹니다.	해가 떴습니다.
7.	불을 끕니다.	불을 껐습니다.
8.	참 기쁩니다.	참 기뻤습니다.

G. Pattern Drill

Teacher : 여기서 자면, 감기에 걸리겠어요.
If you sleep here, you'll catch a cold.

Student : 여기서 자다가는, 감기에 걸리겠어요.
If you sleep here, you'll catch a cold.

1. 그분을 기다리면, 늦겠어요.
그분을 기다리다가는, 늦겠어요.
2. 술만 마시면, 집에 못 가겠어요.
술만 마시다가는, 집에 못 가겠어요.
3. 이 물을 마시면, 병에 걸리겠어요.
이 물을 마시다가는, 병에 걸리겠어요.
4. 이 일을 계속하면, 지각하겠어요.
이 일을 계속하다가는, 지각하겠어요.
5. 그 여자와 결혼하면, 큰 일 나겠어요.
그 여자와 결혼하다가는, 큰 일 나겠어요.
6. 늦게 가면, 비를 맞을 것 같아요.
늦게 가다가는, 비를 맞을 것 같아요.
7. 변명하면, 혼날 것 같아요.
변명하다가는, 혼날 것 같아요.
8. 야단치면, 울 것 같아요.
야단치다가는, 울 것 같아요.

H. Pattern Drill

Teacher : 그분하고 얘기하다가는, 늦겠어요.
If I continue to talk with him, I'll be late.

Student : 그분하고 얘기하다가는, 늦을 것 같았어요.
If I were to continue talking with him, I thought I'd be late.

1. 여기서 자다가는, 감기에 걸리겠어요.
여기서 자다가는, 감기에 걸릴 것 같았어요.
2. 낮잠을 자다가는, 못 가겠어요.
낮잠을 자다가는, 못 갈 것 같았어요.
3. 늦게 가다가는, 시험을 못 치겠어요.
늦게 가다가는, 시험을 못 칠 것 같았어요.
4. 그분을 야단치다가는, 내가 혼나겠어요.
그분을 야단치다가는, 내가 혼날 것 같았어요.
5. 그분을 도와주다가는, 지각하겠어요.
그분을 도와주다가는, 지각할 것 같았어요.

6. 집을 짓다가는, 큰 일 나겠어요.
   집을 짓다가는, 큰 일 날 것 같았어요.
7. 과로하다가는, 병이 나겠어요.
   과로하다가는, 병이 날 것 같았어요.
8. 과음하다가는, 집에 못 가겠어요.
   과음하다가는, 집에 못 갈 것 같았어요.

I. Response Drill (Review)

Teacher : 아직도 잡수세요?	Are you still eating?
Student : 아니오, 이젠 먹지 않아요.	No, I'm not eating any more.
1. 아직도 주무세요?	아니오, 이젠 자지 않아요.
2. 아직도 씻으세요?	아니오, 이젠 씻지 않아요.
3. 아직도 머리를 빗으세요?	아니오, 이젠 머리를 빗지 않아요.
4. 아직도 집을 지으세요?	아니오, 이젠 집을 짓지 않아요.
5. 아직도 회의를 하세요?	아니오, 이젠 회의를 하지 않아요.
6. 아직도 준비하세요?	아니오, 이젠 준비하지 않아요.
7. 아직도 복습하세요?	아니오, 이젠 복습하지 않아요.
8. 아직도 창피하세요?	아니오, 이젠 창피하지 않아요.

SHORT STORIES

1. 어젯밤에 늦도록 일을 했어요.
   그래서 오늘 아침에 열 시가 되도록 잤어요.
   과로하면 항상 그 다음 날 피곤해요.

   Expansion Drill

   어젯밤에 늦도록 일을 했기 때문에, 오늘 아침에 열 시가 되도록 잤어요. 과로하면 항상 그 다음 날 피곤해요.

2. 친구를 찾아가니까, 그분이 자더군요.
   그래서 그분이 깰 때까지 기다렸어요.
   그런데 한 시간을 기다려도 일어나지 않았어요.

   Expansion Drill

   친구를 찾아가니까, 그분이 자더군요. 그래서 그분이 깰 때까지 기다렸는데, 한 시간을 기다려도 일어나지 않았어요.

3. 친구가 도와 달라고 했어요.
   그런데 친구를 도와주다가는 지각할 것 같았어요.
   그래서 도와주지 않고 학교에 왔어요.

Expansion Drill

친구가 도와 달라고 했는데, 친구를 도와주다가는 지각할 것 같아서, 도와 주지 않고 학교에 왔어요.

READING

어제는 친구의 생일(날)이었습니다. 나도 친구한테서 초대를 받았습니다. 나는 다섯시쯤 우리집 앞에서 버스를 탔습니다. 왜냐하면 바로 우리집 앞이 종점입니다. 버스 안에 들어가니까 별로 복잡하지 않았습니다. 버스요금을 내려고 잔돈을 찾았습니다. 그런데 잔돈이 없었습니다. 그래서 지갑 속에 있는 천원짜리를 꺼냈습니다. 그것을 운전기사한테 주었습니다. 마침 뒤에 자리가 있었습니다. 가운데 자리가 비어 있었습니다. 그래서 뒤에가서 앉았습니다. 내 옆에는 대학생이 앉아 있었습니다. 나는 국립박물관 앞에서 내려야 했습니다. 버스에서 내려서 한국일보사 앞까지 걸어갔습니다. 친구의 집은 한국일보사 부근에 있다고 했습니다. 마침 한국일보사 맞은 편에 공중전화 가 있었습니다. 전화를 걸었더니 친구가 전화를 받았습니다. 친구의 집은 이층집이었습니다. 큰 건물 사이에 있었습니다. 내가 방에 들어가니까 모두 기다리고 있었습니다.

생일 a birthday
앞 before, in front of
바로 just, exactly, immediately
종점 the last stop, the terminal
안 inside (something spacious)
버스요금 bus fare
잔돈 small change, loose money
지갑 a wallet
뒤 behind, back
자리 a seat
가운데 center, between, middle
비다 to be empty
옆 beside, on the side of
대학생 a college student

국립박물관 National Museum
내리다 to get off
속 inside (something small or full)
운전기사 a bus driver
한국일보사 the Han-kuk Daily Newspaper building
부근에 in the vicinity of the opposite side,
맞은편 the other side
공중전화 a telephone booth
이층집 a two-story house
건물 a building
사이 between
아래 below, underneath

These words 앞 'in front of' and 안 'inside', etc., are nouns, so they occur with particles such as -가/-이, -를/-을, -에, -에서, -까지, -으로, etc.

BRIEFING

Yesterday was my friend's birthday. I was invited by my friend. About 5 o'clock I caught a bus in front of my house, because the bus stop is located there. When I got into the bus, it was not crowded. I was looking for small change in order to pay the bus fare. But I didn't have any small change with me. I took out a one thousand bill from my wallet and gave it to the driver. The driver didn't like it. Fortunately, there was a seat in the back. The middle seat (in the back) was empty. So I went to the back and sat down. A college student was sitting beside me. I had to get off in front of the National Musem. I got off the bus and walked to the front of the Hankuk Daily Newspaper Building. My friend said that his house was in the vicinity of the Hankuk Daily Newspaper Building. Fortunately, on the opposite side of the Hankuk Daily Newspaper Building, there was a telephone booth. When I made a phone call, my friend answered. My friend's house was a two-storey house located between two big buildings. When I went into the room, everybody was waiting for me.

UNIT 46 독일어 German

BASIC SENTENCES: MEMORIZE

독일어	German language
최 인 숙	
1. 왜 독일어를 공부하세요?	Why do you study German?
박 성 철	
2. 독일에 가려고 독어를 공부해요.	I'm studying German in order to go to Germany.
최 인 숙	
3. 언제쯤 가시게 됩니까?	About when are you scheduled to go there?
아직	still, yet
대학	a college
졸업하다	to graduate from
박 성 철	
4. 아직 잘 모르겠어요. 대학을 졸업해야 알 수 있을 것 같아요.	I don't know yet. Once I graduate from college, I think I'll be able to know.
몇 년	how many years
예정	a schedule, a program, a plan, prearrangement
최 인 숙	
5. 몇 년동안 독일에 계실 예정입니까?	How many years do you plan to stay in Germany?
확실히	for certain
될 수 있으면	if possible
박 성 철	
6. 확실히 잘 모르겠어요. 될 수 있으면 빨리 돌아올 예정이에요.	I don't know for certain. If possible, I plan to return quickly.

NOTES ON THE BASIC SENTENCES

1. 독일어 means 'the German Language.' It is interchangeable with 독일말, making no difference in meaning. However, (독 일)말 is refers to the colloquial language. Study the following additional words which refer to languages only.

한국말(or 한국어)	Korean
영어	English
불란서말 (or 불란서어 or 불어)	French
독일말 (or 독일어 or 독어)	German
이태리말 (or 이태리어)	Italian
중국말 (or 중국어 or 중어)	Chinese
일본말 (or 일본어 or 일어)	Japanese
서반아말 (or 서반아어)	Spanish
인도말 (or 인도어)	Hindustani
소련말 (or 노어)	Russian

2. 독어 also means 'the German language.' 독일어 occurs in the abbreviated form 독어. Study the above words well.
대학 usually means 'a college,' which must be distinguished from 대학교 'a university.'
졸업하다 means 'to graduate (from).' In English, the verb 'to graduate' takes the preposition 'from,' but in Korean, 졸업하다 always takes the object particle -를/-을. Study the following examples:

고등학교를 졸업했어요.	I graduated (from) high school.
대학을 졸업하고 미국에 가겠어요.	I'll graduate (from) college and go to America.

STRUCTURE NOTES

I. The Sentence-Final Ending -게 되다… : '(it) just so happens that'

The pattern -게 되다 is used to indicate the idea that the situation has been arranged by certain environmental factors or condition. The English equivalent of this pattern is '(it) turns out that,' '(it) is arranged that,' '(it) just so happened that,' etc. It's used with action verbs.

Examples:

이 학교에서 공부하게 되었어요.	It's arranged that I can study in this school.
나는 독일에 못 가게 되었어요.	It just so happened that I couldn't go to Germany.
다시 그분을 못 보게 될 것 같아요.	I think that we won't get to see him anymore.
내년에는 한국말을 잘 하게 됩니다.	You'll be able to speak Korean very well next year.
언제 미국에 가시게 됩니까?	When are you scheduled to go to America?
어떻게 그분을 만나게 되었어요?	How did it happen that you saw him?
우연히 그분을 만나게 되었어요.	I happened to meet him by accident.
할 수 없이 같이 가게 되었어요.	It happened that I had no choice but to go along.
어른이 되면 이해하게 됩니다.	When you've grown up, you'll understand it.

This pattern -게 되다, besides being used with action verbs, can be used also with description verbs. We have already studied that most description verbs can be changed into adverbs by attaching the suffix -게 to the verb stems: e.g., 예쁘게 'beautifully,' 싸게 'cheaply,' etc., (See Unit 13, Structure Notes IV). The verb 되다 means 'to become,' 'to get to be,' 'to turn (change, pass) into,' 'to turn out,' 'to grow to be,' etc. Therefore, when the pattern -게 되다 is used with description verbs, it corresponds to the English '(it) happens to become such-and-such,' '(it) turns (out) such-and-such.' Study the following examples:

그것이 예쁘게 되었어요.	It became beautiful.
그분의 얼굴이 하얗게 되었어요.	His face happened to turn white.
너무 크게 되었어요.	It happened to become too big.

II. The Provisional Non-Final Ending -아(-어, -여)야…: 'provided'

The pattern -아(-어, -여)야 is used to express 'if something takes place (now or in the future),' or 'provided something takes place or is ture.' This pattern can be used with any verb, except -이(다).

Examples:

그 책이 좋아야, 읽겠어요.	Provided (if) that book is good, I'll read it.
그것이 싸야, 사겠어요.	Provided (if) it is cheap, I'll buy it.

돈이 있어야, 여기서 공부할 수 있어요.	Provided (if) you have money, you can study here.
연습을 해야, 잘 할 수 있어요.	Provided (if) you practice, you can do it well.
그분이 초대해야, 가겠어요.	Provided (if) he invites me, I'll go.
울지 않아야, 돈을 주겠어요.	If (provided) you don't cry, I'll give you money.
비가 오지 않아야, 거기에 가겠어요.	If (provided) it doesn't rain, I'll go there.
그것이 쓰지 않아야, 먹겠어요.	If (provided) it is not bitter, I'll eat it.

Notes:

1. This pattern -아(-어, -여)야 is followed normally by patterns which indicate future, possibility, or a speaker's intention.
2. The tense is expressed in the final (main) clause, not in the first (dependent) clause with -아(-어, -여)야.
3. This provisional -아(-어, -여)야 is interchangeable with the conditional -(으)면, making no difference in meaning. But the provisional is never used with the imperative and propositive forms. It is used only with interrogative and declarative forms, whereas the conditional -으면 does not know these limitations. Study the following examples:

그분이 가면, 가세요.	If he goes, please go. (imperative)
그분이 가야, 가세요.	(never used)
날씨가 좋으면, 사냥갑시다.	If the weather is good, let's go hunting. (propositive)
날씨가 좋아야, 사냥갑시다.	(never used)
그분이 가야, 가시겠어요?	If (provided) he goes, will you go? (interrogative)
예, 그분이 가야 가겠어요.	Yes, if (provided) he goes, I'll go. (declarative)

4. -아야 is used after -아- or -오-;
   -어야 is used after any other vowel;
   -여야 is used after 하다 verb.

III. The Sentence-Final Ending -ㄹ(을) 예정이다… : '(one) plans to do'

The pattern -ㄹ(을) 예정이다 indicates a speaker's schedule, plan or intention. The suffix -ㄹ(을), when used with action verbs or description verbs, indicates the future tense. The noun 예정 means 'prearrangement,' 'a plan,' 'a schedule.'

Examples:

내일 사냥갈 예정입니다.	I plan to go hunting tomorrow.
그분을 방문할 예정입니다.	I'm scheduled to visit him.
그분을 야단칠 예정입니다.	I plan to give him a good scolding.
모레 회의를 할 예정이에요.	We plan to hold a conference the day after tomorrow.
담배를 수출할 예정이에요.	We plan to export cigarettes.
무엇을 수입할 예정이에요?	What do you plan to import?
어디서 결혼할 예정이에요?	Where do you plan to marry?
누구를 도와줄 예정이에요?	Whom do you plan to help?

Notes:

1. The tense is expressed regularly in the final verb -이다, not in the main verb with -ㄹ(을). Study the following examples:

그분을 만날 예정입니다.	I plan to meet him. Or: I'm going to meet him.
그분을 만날 예정이었습니다.	I planned to meet him. Or: I was going to meet him.

2. The negation is expressed, however, normally in the main verb, not in the final verb with -이다. Study the following examples.

그분을 만나지 않을 예정이에요	I plan not to meet him. Or: I'm not going to meet him.
그분을 만나지 않을 예정이었어요.	I planned not to meet him. Or: I was not going to meet him.

3. -ㄹ 예정이다 is used after verb stems ending in a vowel;
-을 예정이다 is used verb stems ending in a consonant.

DRILLS

ADDITIONAL VOCABULARY

불편하다	to be inconvenient	중어	Chinese
편리하다	to be convenient	일어	Japanese
한국어	Korean	서반아어	Spanish
불어	French	노어	Russian
인도어	Hindustani		

A. Substitution Drill

1. 그것이 예쁘게 되었어요.	It happened to become beautiful.
2. 얼굴이 하얗게 되었어요.	His face happened to turn white.

3. 너무 크게 되었어요. It happened to become too big.
4. 유명하게 되었어요. It happened to become famous.
5. 그 일이 어렵게 되었어요. That work happened to become difficult.
6. 교통이 불편하게 되었어요. The traffic happened to get worse (these days).
7. 교통이 편리하게 되었어요. Transportation happens to be easier (these days).
8. 그것이 빨갛게 되었어요. It happened to turn red.

B. Substitution Drill

1. 유치원을 졸업했어요. I graduated (from) kindergarten.
2. 국민학교를 졸업했어요. I graduated (from) primary school.
3. 중학교를 졸업했어요. I graduated (from) middle school.
4. 고등학교를 졸업했어요. I graduated (from) high school.
5. 대학교를 졸업했어요. I graduated (from) the university.
6. 대학원를 졸업했어요. I graduated (from) graduate school.
7. 한국어학교를 졸업했어요. I graduated (from) the Korean language school.

C. Substitution Drill

1. 내일 사냥갈 예정입니다. I plan to go hunting tomorrow.
2. 그분을 방문할 예정입니다. I'm scheduled to visit him.
3. 지금 회의를 할 예정입니다. I plan to hold a conference now.
4. 거기서 결혼할 예정입니다. I plan to marry there.
5. 입원할 예정입니다. I plan to be hospitalized.
6. 그것을 거절할 예정입니다. I plan to refuse it.
7. 집을 지을 예정입니다. I plan to build a house.
8. 변명할 예정입니다. I plan to defend myself.

D. Pattern Drill

Teacher: 그분을 만날 예정입니다.
I plan to meet him.
Student: 그분을 만나지 않을 예정입니다.
I plan not to meet him.

1. 헤어질 예정입니다. 헤어지지 않을 예정입니다.
2. 자랑할 예정입니다. 자랑하지 않을 예정입니다.
3. 그분을 소개할 예정입니다. 그분을 소개하지 않을 예정입니다.
4. 시험을 칠 예정입니다. 시험을 치지 않을 예정입니다.
5. 한턱 낼 예정입니다. 한턱 내지 않을 예정입니다.

6. 돈을 빌릴 예정입니다. 돈을 빌리지 않을 예정입니다.
7. 돈을 갚을 예정입니다. 돈을 갚지 않을 예정입니다.
8. 그분을 칭찬할 예정입니다. 그분을 칭찬하지 않을 예정입니다.

E. Pattern Drill

Teacher : 한국말을 공부합시다. Let's study Korean.
Student : 한국어를 공부합시다. Let's study Korean.

1. 불란서말을 배웠어요. 불어를 배웠어요.
2. 독일말을 가르칩니다. 독어를 가르칩니다.
3. 중국말을 공부했어요. 중어를 공부했어요.
4. 일본말을 잘 합니다. 일어를 잘 합니다.
5. 서반아말이 재미있어요. 서반아어가 재미있어요.
6. 인도말이 복잡해요. 인도어가 복잡해요.
7. 소련말이 어려워요. 노어가 어려워요.
8. 이태리말을 공부해요. 이태리어를 공부해요.

F. Pattern Drill

Teacher : 여기서 일하도록 되었어요.
I've reached the point where I can work here.
Student : 여기서 일하게 되었어요.
It's arranged that I can work here.

1. 그 일을 하도록 되었어요. 그 일을 하게 되었어요.
2. 회의를 하도록 되었어요. 회의를 하게 되었어요.
3. 폐를 끼치도록 되었어요. 폐를 끼치게 되었어요.
4. 그분을 깨우도록 되었어요. 그분을 깨우게 되었어요.
5. 결혼하도록 되었어요. 결혼하게 되었어요.
6. 입원하도록 되었어요. 입원하게 되었어요.
7. 시험을 치도록 되었어요. 시험을 치게 되었어요.
8. 자랑하도록 되었어요. 자랑하게 되었어요.

G. Pattern Drill

Teacher : 그분을 만날 예정이었어요.
I planned to meet him.
Student : 그분을 만나지 않을 예정이었어요.
I planned not to meet him.

1. 혼내줄 예정이었어요. 혼내주지 않을 예정이었어요.
2. 헤어질 예정이었어요. 헤어지지 않을 예정이었어요.
3. 입원할 예정이었어요. 입원하지 않을 예정이었어요.

4. 야단칠 예정이었어요. 야단치지 않을 예정이었어요.
5. 받아쓸 예정이었어요. 받아쓰지 않을 예정이었어요.
6. 외울 예정이었어요. 외우지 않을 예정이었어요.
7. 붙잡을 예정이었어요. 붙잡지 않을 예정이었어요.
8. 축하할 예정이었어요 축하하지 않을 예정이었어요.

H. Pattern Drill

Teacher: 그 책이 좋으면, 읽겠어요.
If that book is good, I'll read it.
Student: 그 책이 좋아야, 읽겠어요.
Provided that book is good, I'll read it.

1. 그분이 결석하면, 나도 결석하겠어요.
   그분이 결석해야, 나도 결석하겠어요.
2. 그분이 가르치면, 공부하겠어요.
   그분이 가르쳐야, 공부하겠어요.
3. 비가 오지 않으면, 등산가겠어요.
   비가 오지 않아야, 등산가겠어요.
4. 그것이 쓰지 않으면, 먹겠어요.
   그것이 쓰지 않아야, 먹겠어요.
5. 그분이 겸손하면, 만나겠어요.
   그분이 겸손해야, 만나겠어요.
6. 그 방이 깨끗하면, 들어가겠어요.
   그 방이 깨끗해야, 들어가겠어요.
7. 그분이 오면, 회의를 하겠어요.
   그분이 와야, 회의를 하겠어요.
8. 그분이 깨우면, 일어나겠어요.
   그분이 깨워야, 일어나겠어요.

I. Pattern Drill

Teacher: 그분이 초대해야, 가겠어요.
Provided (if) he invites me, I'll go.
Student: 그분이 초대해야, 갈 수 있어요.
Provided (if) he invites me, I can go.

1. 입원해야, 낫겠어요.
   입원해야 나을 수 있어요.
2. 해가 떠야, 가겠어요.
   해가 떠야, 갈 수 있어요.
3. 차를 고쳐야, 떠나겠어요.

차를 고쳐야, 떠날 수 있어요.
4. 나를 도와줘야, 한턱 내겠어요.
나를 도와줘야, 한턱 낼 수 있어요.
5. 돈을 갚아야, 이걸 드리겠어요.
돈을 갚아야, 이걸 드릴 수 있어요.
6. 약속을 지켜야, 도와주겠어요.
약속을 지켜야, 도와줄 수 있어요.
7. 춤을 춰야, 노래를 부르겠어요.
춤을 춰야, 노래를 부를 수 있어요.
8. 그것이 맵지 않아야, 먹겠어요.
그것이 맵지 않아야, 먹을 수 있어요.

SHORT STORIES

1. 금년 봄에 대학교를 졸업했어요.
불어를 전공했어요. 전공하다 to major in
다음 달에 불란서에 가게 될 것 같아요.

Expansion Drill

금년 봄에 대학교를 졸업했는데, 불어를 전공했어요. 다음 달에 불란서에 가게 될 것 같아요.

2. 미국으로 유학갈 예정입니다. 유학가다 to go abroad for study
그러나 영어를 잘 해야, 유학갈 수 있어요.
그래서 아무 것도 하지 않고 영어만 공부해요.

Expansion Drill

미국으로 유학갈 예정이지만, 영어를 잘 해야 유학갈 수 있기 때문에, 아무 것도 하지 않고 영어만 공부해요.

3. 일이 잘 되지 않아서 속상해 죽겠어요.
신경을 썼더니, 아주 피곤해요.
오늘은 아무 것도 하지 않을 예정이에요.

속상하다 to be distressing, to be worrisome, 신경을 쓰다 to worry about, to strain one's nerves

Expansion Drill

일이 잘 되지 않아서 속상해 죽겠어요. 신경을 썼더니, 아주 피곤해서, 오늘은 아무 것도 하지 않을 예정이에요.

READING

공자님이 마차를 타고 여행을 하고 있었습니다. 그런데 길에서 아이들이 놀고 있었습니다. 아이들이 길 한복판에 흙으로 성을 만들어 놓았습니다. 공자님은 아이들한테 길을 비키라고 했습니다. 그런데 아이들이 말을 듣지 않았습니다. 한 아이가 나타나더니, 어떻게 성이 마차를 비키느냐고 했습니다. 마차가 성을 둘러가야 한다고 했습니다. 그래서 공자님은 그 아이한테 물었습니다. 네가 어린애인데 어떻게 그런 이치를 아느냐고 물었습니다. 그랬더니 그 아이가 이런 것쯤은 문제 없다고 했습니다. 그래서 공자님은 다시 그 아이한테 물었습니다. 네가 앞일도 알 수 있느냐고 했습니다. 그랬더니 그 아이가 사람이 눈 앞 일도 모르는데, 어떻게 앞일을 알 수 있느냐고 했습니다. 그러면서 공자님한테 선생님은 앞일을 아시느냐고 했습니다. 그래서 공자님은 눈 앞에 일어나는 일은 조금 안다고 했습니다. 그랬더니 그 아이가 공자한테 선생님의 속눈썹이 몇 개냐고 물었습니다.

마차	a carriage, a coach
길	a road, a street
한복판에	(right) in the middle of
흙	soil, mud, clay
성	a castle
비키다	to get out of the way, to step aside
나타나다	to appear, to come out
둘러가다	to go around
어린애	a child, an infant
이치	(good) reason, principle
문제 없다	no problem
앞일	things to come, the future
그러면서	saying that
속눈썹	eyelashes

BRIEFING

Confucius was travelling by coach. But, children were playing in the road. The children had made a castle with clay in the middle of the road. Confucius asked the children to get out of the way. However, the children didn't obey. One of the children came out and asked how the castle could step aside for the coach. He said that the coach must go around the castle. So Confucius asked him, how, being a child, he could know such a principle. The child answered that this kind of thing was no problem at all. So Confucius asked the child again if he could know things to come. The child said that if a man could not know an occurrence before his eyes, how could he know things to come. The child asked Confucius if he knew things to come. So Confucius said that he sometimes knew an occurrence taking place before his eyes. The child asked Confucius how many eyelashes Confucius had.

VOCABULARY

(ㄱ)

가늘다	to be thin (tree)
가다	to go
가르다	to divide
가르치다	to teach
가물다	to be dry, to be parched
가볍다	to be light
가운데	center, between, middle
가을	fall, autumn
가족	family
가지다	to have, to possess
가지고 가다	to take or bring (something somewhere)
가지고 오다	to bring (something somewhere)
가깝다	to be near, to be close
가끔	occasionally
각	each
간섭하다	to interfere (in a matter) with (one)
간지럽다	to be ticklish
갈아입다	to change (clothes)
감기	a cold
감다	to close (eyes)
감사합니다	Thank you!
감싸다	to shield
갑자기	suddenly
갓난 애기	newborn baby
갖은	all sorts of
같다	to be the same
같이	together
갚다	to pay back
개	dog
개다	to clear up
개집	dog house
길다	to be long
거실	living-room
거의	almost
거절하다	to refuse
거짓	false
거짓말	lie
거짓말하다	to tell a lie
걱정하다	to worry about
건강	health
건강하게	healthily
건물	building
건축가	architect
걷다	to walk
걸리다	to take (time), to catch (a cold), to suffer from
걸어가다	to go on foot, to walk
걸어다니다	to walk around
걸어서	on foot
겨우	barely
겨울	winter
결근하다	to absent oneself (from office or work)
결석하다	to be absent (from school)
결심하다	to make up one's mind
결정하다	to decide
결혼하다	to marry
겸손하다	to be humble
계란	eggs
계속해서	continuously

계시다	to be, to exist (honorific)
고가도로	elevated expressway
고기	meat
고단하다	to be tired
고등학교	high school
-고 말고요	of course
고속도로	super-highway
고속버스	highway-bus
고장이 나다	to get out of order
고집부리다	to be stubborn
고치다	to repair
곧	soon, immediately
곱다	to be pretty
공부	study
공부하다	to study
공자	Confucius
공장	factory
공중전화	telephone booth
공책	notebook
과로하다	to overwork
과용하다	to spend too much
과음하다	to drink too much
과식하다	to overeat
과신하다	to be overconfident
관심	concern, interest
관심이 없다	to be not interested in
관심이 있다	to be interested in
괜찮다	to be alright
굉장하다	to be terrible
굉장히	magnificently, awfully
교수	professor
교실	classroom
교육비	educational expenses
교통사고	traffic accident
교통순경	traffic police
교통신호	traffic signal
구경하다	to watch (with interest), to sight-see
구름	cloud
국민학교	primary school
굵다	to be thick (tree)
굶다	to go without food, to skip a meal, to starve
굽다	to roast
-권	volume
귀	ear
귀엽다	to be lovable, to be cute
귀찮다	to be bothersome, annoying
그것	that thing
그냥	in the same way, as before, as it is
그냥 두다	to leave (a thing) as it is
그다지	so, too, that extent (degree)
그때(에)	(at) that time
그때부터	from that time on
그래서	therefore, so
그래요?	Is that so?
그랬더니	when I asked (did)
그러나	but
그러니까	therefore
그러면서	saying that
그런 것 같다	to think so
그런데	but, and (yet)
그럼	well!, then!
그렇게	such
그렇다	to be like that
그렇지 않아도	even without your saying so
그렇지 않으면	otherwise
그리	(not) very, (not) too
그리(로)	to that place, to that direction

그리고	and
그만두다	to stop (doing)
그분	that person
그분한테	to him
그저 그래요	just so-so
그저께	the day before yesterday
그후	after that
극장	theater
근심하다	to worry about
글쎄요	Well!, Let me see!
글짓기	composition
금요일	Friday
급한	urgent
긋다	to draw
기가 막히다	to be stifled
기다리다	to wait
기르다	to bring up
기름	oil
기분	feelings, mood
기쁘다	to be glad, to be happy
-기 위해서	in order to
기차	train
기침	cough
기회	chance, opportunity
길	road, street
김포공항	Kimpo Airport
깁다	to sew
깊다	to be deep
까맣다	to be black
-까지	until, to
깎다	to lower, to peel
깜빡	completely, entirely
깜짝	with a start, suddenly
깨끗이	cleanly
깨끗하다	to be clean
깨다	to wake up
깨닫다	to perceive, to apprehend
깨우다	to awaken, to wake (someone) up
꺼내다	to take, (bring, pull) out
꽤	quite
끄다	to turn off
끓이다	to boil (water)
끓인 물	boiled water
끝	end
끝나다	to finish, to end
끼다	to cloud up

(ㄴ)

나가다	to go out
나다	to happen, to break out
나르다	to carry
나쁘다	to be bad
나중에	later
나타나다	to appear, to come out
낚시질가다	to go fishing
날	day
날씨	the weather
남	other persons
남대문	the Great South Gate
남동생	younger brother
남자	man, male
남편	husband
낫다	to get well, to recover
낮다	to be low
낮잠을 자다	to take a nap
낳다	to give birth to
내	I, my
내다	to pay
내다보다	to look out
내려가다	to go down
내려다 보다	to look down
내려오다	to come down

내리다	to get off
내일	tomorrow
냄새	smell
냄새를 맡다	to smell
냉차	iced tea
너	you
너무	too (much)
넓다	to be wide
넘어지다	to fall down, to tumble down
넣다	to put in
네(가)	you (plain word)
네거리	intersection
넥타이	necktie
노랗다	to be yellow
노래를 부르다	to sing a song
노력하다	to make an effort
노어	Russian language
녹음기	a tape recorder
녹음실	recording room
녹음하다	to record
놀다	to play
놀라다	to be surprised
농담하다	to joke
높다	to be high
누가	who, somebody
누구	who
누구의	whose
누님	older sister (man's)
누르다	to press
누이동생	younger sister (man's)
눈	eyes, snow
눕다	to lie down
느리다	to be slow
늘	always
늦게	late
늦게까지	until late

(ㄷ)

다	all, everything
다녀오다	to go around to see, and then return
다니다	to go about, to attend
다르다	to be different, to be unlike
다른	another, other
다리	leg, bridge
다물다	to close (mouth)
다방	tea room
다시	again
다음 날	next day
다음 해	next year
다치다	to get hurt
다행	good luck
다행히	fortunately
닦다	to clean, to polish
단	only, single
단어	word, vocabulary
닫다	to close (door)
달다	to be sweet
담배	cigarettes
답답하다	to be stifled, to be stuffy
답장하다	to answer a letter
닷새	five days
당신	you
대개	generally, mostly
대단히	very (much)
대답하다	to answer
대만	Taiwan, Republic of China
대학교	university
대학생	college student
대학원	graduate school
대포	whiskey, a drink
대포집	bar, tavern

더	more
더듬더듬 읽다	to falter over (a passage)
더럽다	to be dirty
더운 물	hot water
덕택에	thanks for your help
덜	less
덥다	to be hot
덮다	to cover, to close (book)
데리고 가다	to take (someone somewhere)
도와주다	to help
도저히	not (at all)
도착하다	to arrive at
독감	bad cold
독일	Germany
독일말	German language
돈	money
돌다	to turn
돌다리	stone bridge
돌아가다	to return, to turn and go
돌아오다	to come back
돕다	to help
동네	village
-동안	during, for
동창생	classmate
될 수 있으면	if possible
두껍다	to be thick (paper)
둘러가다	to go around
뒤	behind, in back of
뒷	behind, in back of
드디어	finally
드리다	to give
듣다	to hear
들다	to cost, to catch a cold, to be needed, to eat, to drink
들르다	to drop in
들리다	to be heard
들어가다	to go in
등산하다	to climb a mountain
따뜻하다	to be warm
따라 읽다	to read after
따라 하다	to repeat after
딱지를 떼다	to give a ticket
딸	daughter
때때로	sometimes
떠나다	to leave
떠들다	to make noise
또	again
똑바로	in a straight line, straight
뚱뚱하다	to be fat
뛰어가다	to run, to rush
뜨다	to open (eyes), to rise (sun)
뜻	meaning

(ㅁ)

-마다	every
마당	garden
마르다	to be dry
마시다	to drink
마음대로	as one wishes
마차	carriage, coach
마찬가지	the same
마침	fortunately, at the right moment
막	carelessly, at random
막내	the last born
만나다	to meet
만년필	fountain pen
만들다	to make
만지다	to finger, to touch
많다	to be many, to be much

많이	a lot, many
말리다	to make dry
말씀하다	to say, to speak
말을 잘 하다	to speak well
말하다	to speak
맛	taste
맛없다	to be not tasty
맛을 보다	to taste
맛있다	to be delicious
망년회	year-end party
맞다	to be correct, to be right
맞은	the opposite
맞은편	the other side, the opposite side
맞춤법	rules of spelling
매다	to tie
맥주	beer
맵다	to be hot (food)
머리	the head
머리가 나쁘다	to be slow (in study)
머리가 좋다	to have a clear head, to be intelligent
먹다	to eat
먼저	first, ahead
멀다	to be far
멎다	to stop
며칠	what date, a few days
면도하다	to shave
몇분	how many persons, how many minutes
몇 살	how old
몇 시	what time
몇 시간	how many hours
모두	all, together
모르다	to not know
모임	gathering, party
목	throat
목사님	minister
목요일	Thursday
목욕하다	to take a bath
몰다	to drive
몸	one's body
몸조심하다	to take care of oneself
몹시	exceedingly, awfully
무겁다	to be heavy
무덥다	to be humid,
무섭다	to be fearful, to be frightful
무슨	some kind of, what kind of
무슨 요일	what day of the week
무엇	what
무엇보다도	above all
무조건	unconditionally
무척	exceedingly
문제없다	no problem
문형	pattern
묻다	to ask
물건	things, goods
물론	of course
뭍	all sorts of
미국	America
미국사람	American
미안하다	to be sorry
미리	in advance
믿다	to believe
밑	under, underneath

(ㅂ)

바꾸다	to change, to barter
바람	wind
바로	just, exactly
바쁘다	to be busy
박사학위	doctor's degree
밖	the outside

반	half
반갑다	to be glad
받아쓰기	dictation
받아쓰다	to write down, to take dictation
발음	pronunciation
밝다	to be bright
밤	night, chestnut
밥	boiled rice
방	room
방금	just now, a moment ago
방문하다	to visit
방학	vacation (from school)
방해하다	to disturb, to interfere with
배	boat, pear, stomach
배가 고프다	to be hungry
배우다	to learn
백화점	department store
버스	bus
번개	(a bolt of) lightning
벌다	to make (money)
벌리다	to open (one's mouth)
벌써	already
벗다	to take off
변명하다	to defend oneself
변하다	to change
별로	in particular, especially
별안간	suddenly
병에 걸리다	to get sick
병원	hospital
병이 나다	to get sick
보다	to see
보이다	to show, to be seen, to be visible
보통	usually, ordinarily
복숭아	peach
복습하다	to review
복잡하다	to be complicated
볼일	business
볼일을 보다	to do one's business
봄	spring
뵙다	to see
봉사하다	to serve
부근에	in the vicinity of
부르다	to call
부모님	parents
부산	Pusan
부엌	kitchen
부인	wife
부잣집	richman's house
부탁하다	to ask a favor
-부터	from
분필	chalk
불	a light, fire
불고기	pulgogi
불다	to blow
불란서	France
불어	French language
불친절하다	to be unkind
불편하다	to be inconvenient
불행하다	to be unhappy
붓다	to pour
붙잡다	to seize, to grasp
비	rain, broom
비다	to be empty
비를 맞다	to be exposed to the rain
비싸다	to be expensive
비키다	to step aside, to get out of the way
비행기	airplane
빌리다	to borrow
빗다	to comb

빠르다 to be fast
빨갛다 to be red
빨리 fast, quickly
빼앗다 to snatch (a thing from)

(ㅅ)

사과 apple
사과하다 to apologize
사냥가다 to go hunting
사다 to buy
사랑하다 to love
사무실 office
사양하다 to refuse respectfully
사이 between
산보하다 to take a walk
산소 grave
산책하다 to take a walk
-살 age, years old
살다 to live
삶다 to boil (solid object)
삼남 the third son
삼남이녀 three sons and two daughters
상관없다 (it) doesn't matter
상당히 considerably
새 new
새벽 dawn
생각하다 to think
생기다 to happen, to take place
생일 birthday
생활비 living expenses
서다 to stand up
서당 village schoolhouse
서두르다 to be in a hurry, to make haste with
서로 each other
서반아어 Spanish language
선교사 missionary
선물 gift
선생(님) teacher
선선하다 to be cool
설명하다 to explain
설탕 sugar
섭섭하다 to be sad, to miss
성 castle
성탄절 Christmas
-세 age of years
세계 the world
세상 the world
세수하다 to wash one's face
세탁소 laundry
세우다 to stop (a car), to park
셋이서 three of us
소개하다 to introduce
소나기 shower
소년 boy
소련 the Soviet Union
소리 voice, sound
소식 news
소용이 없다 to be useless
소풍가다 to go on a picnic
소화 digestion
소화가 잘되다 to digest well
속 inside
속눈썹 the eyelashes
속상하다 to be worrisome
손 hand
손수건 handkerchief
송별회 farewell party
수건 towel
수고하다 to work hard, to take great pains
수녀(님) Sister

수박 watermelon
수사(님) Brother
수술하다 to operate
수업 a lesson, a class
수업료 school fees
수영하다 to swim
수요일 Wednesday
수입하다 to import
수출하다 to export
숙녀 lady
숙제하다 to do one's homework
쉬다 to rest
쉽다 to be easy
술값 drinking money
술집 bar, tavern
숨을 쉬다 to breathe
슬프다 to be sad
시간이 되다 time is up
시계 a watch
시끄럽다 to be noisy
시내 downtown
시다 to be sour
시시하다 to be worthless, dull, boring
시원하다 to be refreshing, to be cool
시월 October
시작하다 to begin
시장 market
시집가다 to get married (female)
시청 City Hall
시키다 to order (food), to force (a person to do)
시험 examination
시험을 치다 to take an exam
식당 dining-room
식사 meal
식성 taste, likes and dislikes
식욕 appetite
신경을 쓰다 to worry about, to strain one's nerves
신년회 New Year's Party
신부(님) Father
신자 believer
싣다 to load
실례하다 to commit a rudeness
싫다 to dislike, to hate
심하다 to be serious
싱겁다 to be insipid
싸다 to be cheap, to wrap
싸우다 to fight
싸움터 battle field
쓰다 to write, to use, to be bitter, to put on (a hat)
씹다 to chew
씻다 to wash

(ㅇ)

아까 sometime ago, a little ago
아들 son
아래 below, underneath
아름답다 to be beautiful
아마 probably
아무 anybody, anyone
아무것도 없다 to have nothing
아무리 no matter how
아버지 father
아이 child
아이구! Oh My!
아이들 children
아주 very
아직 still
아침 morning, breakfast,
아프다 to be painful, to be sick

안 inside
안기다 to be held in one's arms
안내양 bus girl
안녕하다 to be peaceful
안녕히 in peace
안다 to hold in one's arms
앉다 to sit down
안됐다 to be very sorry, to be too bad
안부 one's state of health, one's best regards
안부를 전하다 to give one's best regards
알고 보니 finally he (found out that)
알다 to know
알려 주다 to inform
알아 듣다 to understand, to comprehend
암기하다 to memorize
앞에 in front of, before
앞으로 in the future
앞일 things to come, the future
야단치다 to scold
약 medicine, about
약방 drugstore
약속하다 to promise
약혼자 engaged person, a fiancé(e)
약혼하다 to get engaged
얇다 to be thin (paper)
얕다 to be shallow
애기 baby
어기다 to break, to violate
어느 which
어둡다 to be dark
어디 where
어떤 a certain, what kind of
어떤 때는 sometimes
어떻게 how
어떻습니까? How is he (or it)?
어렵다 to be difficult
어리다 to be infant
어린애 child, infant
어머니 mother
어서 without hesitation, please
어제 yesterday
어젯밤에 last night
어지럽다 to be dizzy
어쨌든 anyway, anyhow
어쩌면 perhaps, possibly
억양 intonation
언니 older sister (woman's)
언제 when
언제나 always
언제라도 anytime
얼굴 face
얼마 how much
얼마나 about what distance, about how far
엄마 mom, mommy
없다 to not have, to not be
없어지다 to disappear
엉망 mess, bad shape, ruin
-에 대해서 about
-에서 at, in, on, from
여간 some or a little
여기 here
여동생 younger sister
여러 가지 all kinds of
여러분 all of you, ladies and gentlemen
여름 summer

여자	woman, female
여쭈다	to ask, to inform
여학생	girl student
여행하다	to travel
연말	the end of the year
연습하다	to practice
연탄	briquette
연필	pencil
연하장	New-Year's card
열다	to open (a door)
열리다	to be opened
열심히	ardently, eagerly
염려하다	to worry about
영국	England
영어	English
영화	movie
옆	beside, side
예	yes
예쁘다	to be beautiful
예습하다	to prepare one's lesson
예정	schedule, plan
옛	ancient
옛날(에)	ancient times, old days
오늘	today
오다	to come
오래간만에	after a long time
오른	right
오른 쪽으로	to the right
오빠	older brother(woman's)
오전	the forenoon, the morning
오후	afternoon
온	all, whole
온갖	all sorts of
올라가다	to go up
올라오다	to come up
올해	this year
옳다	to be right
옷	clothes
왜	why
왜냐하면	because
외국	foreign country
외국사람	foreigner
외다	to memorize
외딴	isolated, out-of-the-way
외출하다	to go out
왼	left
왼 쪽으로	to the left
요금	fare
요즈음	these days, nowadays, recently
용서하다	to forgive, to pardon
우리	we
우산	umbrella
우연히	by accident
우유	milk
운동장	playground
운동하다	to exercise
운전기사	driver
운전하다	to drive, to operate
울다	to cry
웃다	to laugh, to smile
원래	originally
월말	the end of a month
월요일	Monday
위	above, on
위반하다	to violate
위험하다	to be dangerous
윗	the upper, the above
유명하다	to be famous
유치원	kindergarten
유학가다	to go abroad for study

유행하다 to be prevalent, to prevail
육교 overpass
6·25 동란 Korean War
-으로 by, with, to
음식 food
의사 medical doctor
의자 chair
이 tooth
이것 this thing
이기다 to win
이런 데서 in a place like this
이렇다 to be like this
이를 닦다 to brush one's teeth
이름 name
이리 here
이상하게 strangely
이상하다 to be strange
이야기하다 to talk, to speak
이웃동네 neighboring village
이제 now
이층집 two-storey house
이치 reason, principle
이해하다 to understand
인도 sidewalk
인도어 Hindustani
인사하다 to make a bow, to greet, to say good-bye
-인분 portions
인형 doll
일본 Japan
일본말 (일어) Japanese language
일어나다 to get up
일요일 Sunday
일주일 a (one) week
일찍 early
일하다 to work
일학기 the first term
읽다 to read
잃다 to lose
입 mouth
입다 to put on (clothes)
입원하다 to be hospitalized
잇다 to unite, to connect
있다 to be, to exist
잊다 to forget

(ㅈ)

자! Come on!
자가용차 private car
자기 oneself, one's (own)
자꾸 repeatedly, continuously
자다 to sleep
자동차 automobile
자랑하다 to boast of, to be proud of
자매 sisters
자신 self-confidence
자전거 bicycle
자주 often, frequently
작다 to be small
작문 composition
작정하다 to intend (to do)
잔돈 small change, loose money
잘 well
잘못 fault
잘못 걸다 to get the wrong number
잘못하다 to do wrong
잠 a sleep
잠그다 to lock
잠이 들다 to fall asleep
잠깐 a little, a minute, for a while
잡수시다 to eat (honorific verb)

-장	a piece of (paper)
장난으로	for fun
장남	the eldest son
장녀	the eldest daughter
장마	the rainy season
재미	interest, pleasure
재미없다	to be uninteresting
재미있다	to be interesting
재수	luck
재작년	the year before last
재주	talent
저(는)	I
저것	that thing over there
저기	that place over there
저녁	supper, evening
저렇다	to be like that
저리	there, over there
저분	that person (over there)
저쪽으로	in that direction over there
적다	to be of little quantity, to be of small number
적당히	reasonably
적어도	at least
전공하다	to major in
전사하다	to be killed in action
전에	ago
전하다	to convey, to give
전화	telephone
젊다	to be young
점심	lunch
점원	salesman, salesgirl
점잖다	to be gentle
점점	gradually
젓다	to stir, to row (a boat)
정말	the truth, really
정신	mind, spirit
정신없이	absent-mindedly
정신이 없다	to be distracted, to can not think straight
정중하게	with courtesy, politely
젖다	to get wet
제(가)	I
제법	quite
제시간에	on time
제일	the first, number one
조금	a little
조금 있다가	a little later
조금 후에	a little later
조심하다	to be careful
조퇴하다	to leave school early
조용하다	to be quiet
조용히	quietly, silently
조용히 하다	to keep quiet
졸다	to doze
졸업하다	to graduate (from)
좀	some, a little
좀 더	a little more
좁다	to be narrow
종일	all day long
종점	the last stop, the terminal
좋다	to be good
좋아하다	to like
죄송하다	to be sorry
주다	to give
주로	mainly
주말	a weekend
주무시다	to sleep (honorific)
주유소	gasoline station
주의하다	to be careful
주인	the owner, the master
주차장	parking lot
준비하다	to prepare

줍다	to pick up
중공	People's Republic of China
중국말	Chinese language
중순	the middle third of a month
중어	Chinese language
-중에서	among, between
중요하다	to be important
중학교	middle school
쥐약	rat poison
즐겁다	to be delightful, to be joyful
지각하다	to come to school late
지갑	purse, wallet
지금	now
지나가다	to pass by
지나다	to pass by, to pass through
지난	last
지내다	to spend time
지다	to lose (a game),
지우개	eraser
지우다	to wipe out, to erase
지키다	to keep
지하도	underpass
지하철	subway
질문	question
집	house
짜다	to be salty
-짜리	worth, value
짧다	to be short
쭉	throughout, all during
-쯤	about

(ㅊ)

차남	the second son
차녀	the second daughter
차도	traffic lane
차례	turn, order
찬물	cold water
찬바람	cold wind
참	very
참다	to bear, to endure
참말	the truth, really
참외	melon
창피하다	to be ashamed
찾다	to look for
찾아가다	to go and visit
찾아오다	to come and visit
책	book
책방	bookstore
책상	desk
-처럼	as (like)
처음	first time
처음에	at the first time
천만에요.	You're welcome.
천천히	slowly
첫	the first
청소기	vacuum cleaner
청소차	garbage wagon
청소하다	to clean
쳐다보다	to look at, to look up
초대를 받다	to receive an invitation
초대하다	to invite
초순	the beginning of a month
초인종	a (call) bell
축하하다	to congratulate
춥다	to be cold
충분히	sufficiently, fully
취하다	to get drunk
치다	to flash, to hit
치약	toothpaste
친구	friend
친절하다	to be kind

친하다 to be intimate, to be close
칠판 blackboard
칭찬하다 to praise

(ㅋ)

켜다 to turn on
코 nose
코피 coffee
크게 loudly
크다 to be big
큰 애 the oldest child
큰 일 serious matter

(ㅌ)

타다 to get on, to ride
태우다 to give a ride
태풍 typhoon
택시 taxi
텔레비존 television
토요일 Saturday
통행금지 curfew (hour)
통화 중이다 the line is busy
튼튼하다 to be strong
틀다 to turn on (the radio or water)
틀리다 to be wrong

(ㅍ)

파랗다 to be blue, green
팔다 to sell
퍽 very
펴다 to open (a book)
편리하다 to be convenient
편지 letter
편히 comfortably
폐를 끼치다 to cause (a person) trouble
포도 grape
표 ticket
푹 deeply, completely
품 the bosom, the breast
피곤하다 to be tired
피로하다 to be tired
피우다 to smoke
필요하다 to be necessary

(ㅎ)

-하고 같이 together with
하다 to do
하루 a day
하루에 in a day
하마터면 by a close shave
하순 the last third of a month
하얗다 to be white
학교 school
학기말 the end of a school term
-학년 a grade
학생 student
한가하다 to have spare time
한국말 Korean language
한국사람 Korean
한국일보사 the Hankuk Daily News Building
한문 Chinese Characters
한번 once
한복판에 in the middle of
한식 Korean food
한식점 Korean restaurant
한잔 내다 to treat to a drink
한잔 하다 to have a drink
한턱 내다 to treat someone
한해 one year
할머니 grandmother
할수없이 reluctantly, helplessly
할아버지 grandfather
해 the sun
해방 liberation

행복하다	to be happy
헌	old, worn-out
헛	vain, fruitless
헤어지다	to separate
혀	tongue
형님	older brother
형제	brothers
혼나다	to have a hard time
혼내주다	to give (someone) a hard time
혼자(서)	alone
홀쭉하다	to be thin, to be slim
홍차	black tea
화가 나다	to get angry
화를 내다	to get angry
화식	Japanese food
화요일	Tuesday
화장실	toilet
확실히	for certain
환영회	welcoming party
환자	patient
회사	company
회의	meeting
휴가	vacation, furlough
휴게실	recreation-room
흐르다	to flow
흐리다	to be cloudy
흔히	frequently
흙	soil, mud, clay
힘들다	to be laborious, to be difficult

INDEX

INDEX TO STRUCTURE NOTES

(References are to pages.)

about ……………………130, 333
accompaniment ……………113, 155
act[illegible]s ……………62
adjectives ……………………156
adverbs ………………………138
and ………………114, 155, 233, 254
answers to negative questions ……128
-아(-어, -여) 놓다……………373
-아(-어, -여)도 ……………243, 335
-아(-어, -여)도 괜찮다………244
아무도+V.S.+-지 않다………267
-아(-어, -여) 버리다…………412
-아(-어, -여) 보다……………266
-아(-어, -여) 보이다…………422
-아(-어, -여)서 ……………254, 264
-아(-어, -여)서 죽겠다………315
-아(-어, -여)야 ………………454
-아(-어, -여)야 되다…………434
-아(-어, -여)야 하다…………245
-아(-어, -여) 있다……………374
-아(-어, -여) 주다……………172
-아(-어, -여) 지다……………392
아직도…………………………364
안- ……………………………106
-았(-었, -였)…………………97
-았(-었, -였)으면 좋겠다……225
-에 ………………76, 85, 90, 115
-에 대해서……………………333
-에서……………………………69
여간+V.S.+Negative ………275
-와 ……………………………155
-와 같이………………………155
-으니까 ……………………274, 296
-으러 …………………………196
-으려고 ………………………306
-으려고 하다…………………305
-으로 ………………………76, 120
-으면 …………………………188
-으면서 ………………………383
-으면 안 되다 ………………246
-으시……………………………70
-은 ……………………99, 156, 217
-은가요? ………………………382
-은 것 같다 …………………208
-은 다음에……………………247
-은데 …………………………295
-은데요 ………………………121
-은 일이 있다 ………………342
-은지+Time Word+되다 ……287
-은 후에………………………334
-을 ………………………69, 218
-을 거에요……………………108
-을 것 같다 …………………218
-을까요? ………………………98
-을께요 ………………………180
-을 때…………………………234
-을 때까지……………………235
-을 때마다……………………235
-을 때부터……………………235
-을래요 ………………………225
-을 뻔했다……………………402
-을 수 있다 …………………179
-을 예정이다…………………455
-을 일이 있다 ………………305
-을 줄 알다 …………………413
-음 ……………………………197
-읍시다…………………………81
-의 ……………………………179
-이………………………………68
-이나 …………………………324

-이다 ······ 68
-이든지 ······ 344
-이라도 ······ 334, 433
이젠 ······ 364
있다 ······ 63
because
-기 때문에 ······ 198
-(으)니까 ······ 274
-아(-어, -여)서 ······ 264
-느라고 ······ 424
but
-지만 ······ 199
-ㄴ(-은, -는)데 ······ 295
-ㅂ시다 ······ 75
-보다 ······ 207
-부터 ······ 91
cardinal numbers ······ 83
Chinese numbers ······ 77
classifiers (counters) ······ 84, 285
comparisons ······ 207
compound vowels ······ 14
concessive ending ······ 243
conditional ······ 188, 444
consonant chart ······ 30
consonants ······ 14, 30-47
contrastive ······ 199
coordinative ······ 233
-처럼 ······ 288
declarative ······ 75, 353
denial of obligation ······ 246
denial of permission ······ 245
description verbs ······ 62
double consonants ······ 14
-다(가) ······ 256
-다가는 ······ 444
-더- ······ 442
-더니 ······ 423
-도 ······ 137
-도…-도 ······ 325
-도록 ······ 412, 443
-든지 ······ 344
-들 ······ 276
exalted (status) words ······ 144
exclamatory endings
-(는)군요 ······ 114
-ㄴ(-은, -는)데요 ······ 121
existence verb ······ 63
family terms ······ 144
favors ······ 172
final contours ······ 48
formal-polite style ······ 75
declarative ······ 75
imperative ······ 75
interrogative ······ 75
propositive ······ 75
future tense infix ······ 108
gender ······ 148
Hangŭl ······ 13
honorific infix ······ 70
honorific suffix ······ 52
honorific verbs ······ 86
how to form syllables ······ 17
how to write Hangŭl ······ 15
humble verbs ······ 171
-하고 ······ 114
-하고 같이 ······ 113
-한테 ······ 147
-한테서 ······ 147
identification (verb) ······ 68
imperative ······ 75, 354
indefinite pronoun ······ 96
independent nouns and dependent nouns ······ 136
indirect discourse ······ 392
indirect question ending ······ 403
informal-polite question ending ······ 382

informal-polite style ····················61
irregular verbs
-ㄷ ·······································333
-ㄹ ·······································187
-르 ·······································414
-ㅂ ·······································373
-ㅅ ·······································365
-으 ·······································443
-ㅎ ·······································343
intentionals
-겠-·······································108
-ㄹ(을)께요 ····························180
-ㄹ(을)래요 ····························225
-ㄹ(을)예정이다 ·······················455
-(으)려고 하다··························305
interrogative ·······················75, 352
interrogative+A.V.S.+든지 ·········344
interrogative+A.V.S.+아도 ·········335
interrogative+-(이)든지 ··············344
interrogative+-(이)라도 ··············334
intonation ·····································48
introductory non-final ending·········295
제일···209
-짜리 ·······································164
-쯤 ···130
-줄 알다/모르다 ·························432
-지 ···403
-지만 ·······································199
-지 말고·····································316
-지 말다·····································164
-지 않고·····································316
-지 않으면 안 되다························246
-지요 ·······································120
Korean alphabet ······························13
Korean numbers ······························83
Korean sound system ························18
Korean verbs··································62
-가 ································68, 403
가장···209
-까지··91
-게 되다·····································453
-겠-···108
-께 ···266
-께서 ·······································266
-고 ···233
-고 말고요·································121
-고 싶다·····································187
-고 있다·····································314
-고 하다·····································392
-과 ···155
-과 같이·····································155
-군요 ·······································114
그만- ·······································165
-기 ···196
-기 때문에·································198
-기로 하다·································297
-기 전에·····································257
-ㄹ ···217
-ㄹ 거에요·································108
-ㄹ 것 같다 ·······························218
-ㄹ까요? ····································98
-ㄹ께요 ·····································180
-ㄹ 때·······································234
-ㄹ 때까지·································235
-ㄹ 때마다·································235
-ㄹ 때부터·································235
-ㄹ래요 ·····································225
-ㄹ 뻔했다·································402
-ㄹ 수 있다 ·······························179
-ㄹ 예정이다·······························455
-ㄹ 일이 있다 ·····························305
-ㄹ 줄 알다 ·······························413
-라도 ·······························334, 433
-러 ···196
-려고 ·······································306
-려고 하다·································305

-로 ……76, 120
-를……69
modifier suffix+줄 알다 ……432
multiples ……186
-ㅁ ……196
-마다 ……218
-만 ……136
-만에 ……363
-만큼 ……209
-면 ……188
-면서 ……383
못……129
negatives
negative constructions of verbs…106
그만……165
못……129
안- ……106
-지 말고……316
-지 말다……164
-지 않고……316
neutral (status) words……144
noun modifiers ……156
-ㄴ(은) ……217
-는 ……217
-ㄹ(을) ……218
noun+밖에+없다 ……163
numbers
Chinese numbers ……77
Korean numbers ……83
multiples ……186
ordinal numbers ……226
-ㄴ ……156, 217
-ㄴ가요? ……382
-ㄴ 것 같다 ……208
-ㄴ데 ……295
-ㄴ데요 ……121
-ㄴ 다음에……247
-ㄴ 일이 있다 ……342
-ㄴ지+Time Word+되다 ……287
-ㄴ 후에……334
-나 ……324
누가 ……72
누구 ……72
-느라고 ……424
-는 ……99, 217
-는가요? ……382
-는 것……395
-는군요 ……114
-는데 ……295
-는데요 ……121
-는 일이 있다 ……345
-니까 ……274, 295
obligations
-아(-어, -여)야 되다……434
-아(-어, -여)야 하다……245
-지 않으면 안 되다……246
ordinal numbers ……226
particles
-가……68
-까지……91
-께 ……266
-께서 ……266
-과 ……155
-과 같이……155
-나 ……324
-는……99
-도 ……137
-도…-도……325
-라도 ……334, 433
-로 ……76, 120
-를……69
-마다 ……218
-만 ……136
-만큼 ……209
-부터……91
-에 ……76, 85, 90, 115

-에서 ······ 69
-와 ······ 155
-와 같이 ······ 155
-으로 ······ 76, 120
-은 ······ 99
-을 ······ 69
-의 ······ 179
-이 ······ 68
-이나 ······ 324
-이라도 ······ 433
-처럼 ······ 288
-하고 ······ 114
-하고 같이 ······ 113
-한테 ······ 147
-한테서 ······ 147
particles used in verb phrases ······ 147
past tense infix ······ 97
permission ······ 244
phonology ······ 18
plain style ······ 352
pluralizing suffix ······ 276
potential ······ 179
progressive ······ 314
propositive ······ 75, 353
provisional ······ 454
pure vowels ······ 14
벌써 ······ 364
request ······ 172
resemblance ······ 208
retrospectives
-더- ······ 442
-더니 ······ 423
rhythm ······ 47
Shall we (I)…? ······ 98
styles of speech ······ 60
suffixes
-님 ······ 52
-씩 ······ 218
-짜리 ······ 164
-쯤 ······ 130
superlative marker ······ 209
syllables ······ 16
-시- ······ 70
time patterns
-기 전에 ······ 257
-ㄴ(은) 다음에 ······ 247
-ㄴ(은) 지 ······ 287
-ㄴ(은) 후에 ······ 334
-다가 ······ 256
-ㄹ(을) 때 ······ 234
-ㄹ(을) 때까지 ······ 235
-ㄹ(을) 때마다 ······ 235
-ㄹ(을) 때부터 ······ 235
-만에 ······ 363
-아(-어, -여)서 ······ 254
-(으)니까 ······ 296
-(으)면서 ······ 383
transcription ······ 13
transferentive ······ 256
-도록 ······ 412, 443
verbal noun formation ······ 196
-기 ······ 196
-ㅁ/-음 ······ 196
vowel chart ······ 19
vowels ······ 20-29
want (to do) ······ 187
who ······ 72
whom ······ 72